MODERN GROUP BOOK VI

Group Treatment of Mental Illness

BOOKS BY DRS. KAPLAN AND SADOCK

Comprehensive Textbook of Psychiatry
Alfred M. Freedman and Harold I. Kaplan, Editors

Studies in Human Behavior
Alfred M. Freedman and Harold I. Kaplan, General Editors

Modern Synopsis of Comprehensive Textbook of Psychiatry
Harold I. Kaplan, Benjamin J. Sadock, and Alfred M. Freedman

Comprehensive Group Psychotherapy
Harold I. Kaplan and Benjamin J. Sadock, Editors

Modern Group Books
Harold I. Kaplan and Benjamin J. Sadock, Editors

HAROLD I. KAPLAN

Harold I. Kaplan received an undergraduate degree from Columbia University and an M.D. from the New York Medical College. He trained in psychiatry at the Kingsbridge Veterans Hospital and Mount Sinai Hospital in New York and became a Diplomate of the American Board of Psychiatry and Neurology in 1957; presently he is an Associate Examiner of the American Board. He began the practice and teaching of psychiatry and was certified in psychoanalytic medicine at the New York Medical College in 1954 where he became Professor of Psychiatry and Director of Psychiatric Training and Education in 1961. He is Attending Psychiatrist at Metropolitan Hospital Center, Flower and Fifth Avenue Hospitals and Bird S. Coler Hospital. He is the Principal Investigator of ten National Institute of Mental Health training programs, specializing in the areas of undergraduate and graduate psychiatric education as well as the training of women in medicine. He is the author of over seventy scientific papers and co-author and co-editor of the books listed on this page.

BENJAMIN J. SADOCK

Benjamin J. Sadock received his A.B. from Union College and his M.D. from New York Medical College. He trained at Bellevue Psychiatric Hospital. During his military service as an Air Force psychiatrist he was also on the faculty of Southwestern Medical School. Dr. Sadock became a Diplomate of the American Board of Psychiatry and Neurology in 1966 and is an Assistant Examiner for the American Board. Currently Associate Professor of Psychiatry and Director of the Division of Group Process at New York Medical College, Dr. Sadock directs the training program for group therapists and is Chief of Continuing Education in Psychiatry, Chief Psychiatric Consultant to the student health service and co-director of the Sexual Therapy Center. He is on staff of Flower and Fifth Avenue Hospitals, Metropolitan Hospital, and the New York State Psychiatric Institute. Dr. Sadock is active in numerous psychiatric organizations, an officer of the New York County District Branch of the American Psychiatric Association, a Fellow of the New York Academy of Medicine, and has written and lectured extensively in general psychiatry and group psychotherapy. He is co-editor with Dr. Harold I. Kaplan of *Comprehensive Group Psychotherapy* (1971) and co-author with Drs. Alfred M. Freedman and Harold I. Kaplan of *Modern Synopsis of Comprehensive Textbook of Psychiatry* (1972).

Group Treatment of Mental Illness

Edited by

HAROLD I. KAPLAN, M.D.

Professor of Psychiatry and Director of Psychiatric Education,
New York Medical College, New York, New York

and

BENJAMIN J. SADOCK, M.D.

Associate Professor of Psychiatry and Director,
Division of Group Process, New York Medical College,
New York, New York

Jason Aronson, Inc.
New York, New York

Library of Congress Catalog Card Number: 72-97012
Standard Book Number: 0-87668-082-1

The editors express their appreciation to the following persons, publishers and publications for permission to reprint portions of the works cited.

Aldine-Atherton, Inc. for "The Marathon Group," by G. R. Bach, reprinted from Hendrik M. Ruitenbeek, editor, *Group Therapy Today* (New York: Atherton Press, 1969); copyright © 1969 by Atherton Press. Reprinted by permission of the author and Aldine-Atherton, Inc.

Bruner/Mazel, Inc. for "The Use of Videotape in the Integrated Treatment of Individuals, Couples, Families, and Groups in Private Practice," by Milton M. Berger, M.D., reprinted from *Videotape Techniques in Psychiatric Training and Treatment*, Milton M. Berger, M.D., editor. Bruner/Mazel, Inc., New York, 1970.

Dr. Herbert Holt for the unpublished essay, "Existential Group Therapy: A Phenomenological Methodology for Psychiatry."

International Journal of Group Psychotherapy for "Sexual Acting Out in Groups," by the members of the Workshop in Group Psychoanalysis of New York: A. Wolf, R. Bross, S. Flowerman, J. Greene, A. Kadis, H. Leopold, N. Locke, I. Milburg, H. Mullan, S. Obers, and H. Rosenbaum. *International Journal of Group Psychotherapy*, Vol. 4, pp. 369-380, 1954.

for "Accelerated Interaction: A Time Limited Approach on the Brief Intensive Approach," by Frederick H. Stoller. *International Journal of Group Psychotherapy*, Vol. 18, pp. 220-235, 1968.

for "Group Therapy and the Small Group Field: An Encounter," by Morris Parloff. *International Journal of Group Psychotherapy*, Vol. 20, pp. 267-304, 1970.

International Universities Press for "Group Therapy with Alcoholics," by A. Stein, M.D. and Eugene Friedman, Ph.D., Chapter III of *Fields of Group Psychotherapy*, S. R. Slavson, editor. International Universities Press, 1956.

American Psychiatric Association for "Phoenix House: Therapeutic Communities for Drug Addicts," by M. S. Rosenthal and D. V. Biase, *Hospital and Community Psychiatry*, Vol. 20, p. 27, 1969.

W. W. Norton & Co., Inc., and the Hogarth Press Ltd. for an excerpt from *An Outline of Psycho-Analysis*, Volume XXIII of Standard Edition of Sigmund Freud, revised and edited by James Strachey. Copyright 1949 by W. W. Norton & Co., Inc., and copyright © 1969 by the Institute of Psychoanalysis and Alix Strachey.

The Williams & Wilkins Co. for an excerpt from "Group Therapy in Married Couples," by Helen Papanek, M.D., reprinted from *Comprehensive Group Psychotherapy*, Harold I. Kaplan and Benjamin J. Sadock, editors. Copyright © 1971 by The Williams & Wilkins Co.

for an excerpt from "Videotape Feedback in Group Setting," by F. Stoller. *Journal of Nervous and Mental Disorders*, Vol. 148, No. 4, pp. 457-466.

Seymour Lawrence/Delacorte Press for an excerpt from *Cat's Cradle* by Kurt Vonnegut, Jr. Copyright © 1963 by Kurt Vonnegut, Jr. A Seymour Lawrence Book/Delacorte Press. Reprinted by permission of the publisher.

Contents

Preface

The emergence of group psychotherapy within the past two decades constitutes one of the most significant and extraordinary developments in the field of psychiatry. Gradually during this period, but particularly within the past five years, group therapy has come to be chosen for the treatment of a widening range of patients with highly diverse problems. Concurrently, professionals and laymen alike see a growing interest in the relationship of group therapy to sociocultural and educational concepts, processes, and systems. Predictably, these theoretical developments are accompanied by the development of myriad therapeutic approaches which vary with respect not only to their underlying philosophy but also to the planning and conduct of treatment.

Psychotherapy is an art as well as a science. What is taught via the lecture hall or seminar room constitutes just one aspect of the teaching curriculum. Training in psychotherapy must also include clinical exercises performed under the supervision of an experienced clinician who acts as a model for the student. The editors' commitment to this project, and its concomitant goals, evolved from their extensive experience as both educators and clinicians. The editors' special interest in group psychotherapy as a treatment technique, and an awareness of the need for more intensive training in this discipline to ensure its continued growth and development, led to the establishment, at the New York Medical College, of the first medical-school-affiliated postgraduate certification program in group psychotherapy. In addition, they have participated in the organization of training programs in group therapy for workers in other mental health disciplines —psychology, psychiatric social work, and psychiatric nursing.

The stated goal of this series—to provide a survey of current theoretical and therapeutic trends in this field—carries with it the obligation to pursue an eclectic orientation and to present as comprehensive an account of events at every level of its development as is possible. The organization and orientation of this series attempts to provide a comprehensive survey of the theories, hypotheses, and therapeutic techniques which dominate contemporary group practice. There are no final answers, as yet, to the problems and issues which currently face group psychotherapy. But we may help to identify these problems and issues and place them in proper perspective.

This book is one of a series of paperback volumes based on *Comprehensive Group Psychotherapy*, which we previously edited. New articles have been written for each of these volumes and certain subjects have been updated or eliminated in an effort to reach a wider audience. Invitations to participate were extended to those workers who have made major and original contributions to the field of group psychotherapy and who are acknowledged experts in a particular area of theory and/or practice. Thus the preparation of this series afforded the editors a unique opportunity to engage in a stimulating interchange of ideas and to form many rewarding personal relationships. As a result, what would appear to have been an ardous undertaking has in fact been a most gratifying experience.

The editors have received dedicated and valuable help from many people to whom they wish to express their appreciation. For their secretarial and editorial help, we would like to thank Robert Gelfand, Sylvia Houzell, Mercedes Paul, Paulene Demarco, Louise Marshall, and in particular Lois Baken, who coordinated these efforts. Special thanks are extended to our publishers, E. P. Dutton, and to our outstanding editor, Robert Zenowich.

Finally, the editors wish to express their appreciation to Virginia Sadock, M.D., who acted in the capacity of assistant to the editors and assumed the multitudinous tasks of that office with grace and charm.

HAROLD I. KAPLAN, M.D.

BENJAMIN J. SADOCK, M.D.

Introduction

The current literature is filled with accounts of successful group treatment of a widening range of patients with diverse problems. This book is limited to those numbers of the patient population whose problems have traditionally been treated in this setting, as well as those whose special problems require variations of group treatment techniques.

Homogeneous vs. Heterogeneous Groups

The treatment of patients in special diagnostic situations presents certain methodological problems. These center on group organization, particularly on the question of whether treatment success rests on their placement in homogeneous or heterogeneous groups. This issue of homogeneity vs. heterogeneity has long been a source of disagreement among workers in the field. Furthermore it raises a question: Can any group, in fact, be considered truly homogeneous?

Depressive Patients

The group whose membership is purportedly restricted to depressive patients is a case in point. Insofar as all the patients manifest the signs and symptoms that are typical of but not restricted to depressive illness (even in varying degrees), such a group appears to be homogeneous. But examination of the information elicited from individual members in the course of their initial diagnostic interviews usually discloses that they differ in certain crucial respects. In one case, the patient's depressions may have been precipitated by an object loss, such as the death of a parent; in another case, the depression may stem from the patient's fear of an object loss, generated by a spouse's threats of divorce; in a third instance, the patient's depression can be ascribed to a fantasied object loss, such as his obsession about the death of a loved one. The situation is further complicated by the fact that, although object loss frequently plays a major role in depression, other causative factors may also be involved, such as injury or the fear of injury. In short, such a group is heterogeneous with respect to the genesis and dynamics of the depressive syndrome they share in common. Consideration of these factors in each individual case must, of course, play a crucial role in treatment selection.

Because of these crucial differences, and for other reasons, an increasing number of therapists are advocating the heterogeneous group because it provides greater opportunity for group interaction and ensures more effective treatment. Yet there are exceptions. The chapters included in this book deal with some of those patients who, experienced group therapists believe, can best be treated in homogeneous groups.

Special Problems

Interesting empirical observations have been reported by therapists who work with a variety of patients in groups. Although male and female homosexuals share inversion and many of the problems this creates, they may not get along well together. This does not mean that they should not be included in the same group; they have much to learn from each other. But the therapist who attempts the combined treatment of male and female homosexuals must be aware of the strong possibility of group disharmony and consequent disruption of the therapeutic process; and he must be prepared to take measures to counteract such crises.

Although male and female homosexuals can be included in a group of heterosexual patients, Bieber delineates some of the problems that may arise in this setting and provides clinical evidence in support of her view that homosexuals can be treated most effectively in homogeneous groups. In addition, the editors have included in this volume a most interesting case report on the group treatment of a homosexual woman. The report demonstrates the effective resolution of a difficult clinical situation and together with Bieber's chapter enables the reader to grasp the dimensions of the homosexual experience.

Peer Groups

Despite the fact that they are eminently suited to these techniques, some patients in certain categories have not had sufficient exposure to group treatment. At present, most group therapists treat young adults and middle-aged patients; few have been trained for or are willing to undertake the group treatment of children, adolescents, or geriatric patients.

The crucial importance of peer relationships for character formation during the latency period has been well-documented by the proponents of the psychoanalytic theory of behavior. Admittedly, the child's character has already been molded by the nature of his early object relationships and identifications with parental figures. But when he reaches latency, the child begins to emancipate himself from his family and to establish extrafamilial relationships. At this point, other persons become important as objects for identification. In the treatment setting, the therapist and the child's peers become meaningful objects and contribute thereby to multiple significant identifications important for his eventual character development. This child's rebelliousness against parental ties gathers momentum, so that in adolescence he is mainly oriented toward his peer group, the gang. Gang formation is a normal phenomenon at this stage of development, and membership in such a group contributes to the achievement of the essential goals of adolescence—relative emancipation from the parents and a greater measure of autonomy and independent function. In fact, Harry Stack Sullivan saw the isolated adolescent as the potential schizophrenic. It follows, then, that for many children in latency and adolescence, the group can provide a significant corrective emotional experience, one capable of undoing or at least minimizing the damage inflicted by early traumatic experiences.

In recent years, the helping professions have been criticized for their neglect of the elderly, and this criticism applies to group therapists. The geriatric patient can derive great benefit from a peer experience, and clinicians who have worked with the aged report that this experience has been a source of great personal gratification. Yet, on the whole, they are reluctant to accept such patients for treatment. Perhaps some of the themes dealt with in the group, such as death and dying, are more anxiety-provoking for the therapist than they are for the patients. Since these topics can be expected to evoke anxiety in young adults and middle-aged patients, it is often difficult to include an elderly patient in a heterogeneous group. Consequently, most efforts have been directed toward working with the elderly in homogeneous groups.

Clinical Diagnosis

The editors' decision to include a chapter on clinical diagnosis was based on their belief that a delineation of the patient's history, his past way of functioning, his mental status, and his way of coping in the present, are essential to the efficacy of group psychotherapy. Moreover, it has become evident in the light of recent therapeutic developments that diagnosis is essential if casualties resulting from group experience are to be averted.

Regardless of the group therapist's orientation—whether he emphasizes the here and now or the historical antecedents of behavior, whatever his goals—careful evaluation and diagnosis help him determine whether the patient is suited to group treatment and, if so, what type. In addition, the psychiatric interview, the major tool of diagnosis, may in itself serve an important function; it underscores the nature of the therapist's attitude toward and his preception of the patient, which plays a crucial role in treatment.

The editors have included a brief description of the American Psychiatric Association's *Diagnostic and Statistical Manual of Mental Disorders,* which provides a common nosological and descriptive basis for mental health professionals in this country and around the world. It distinguishes the varieties of emotional disorders that exist despite varying causes.

Neurotics and Psychotics

The chapter by Semrad and Day on the differences between group therapy with neurotics and psychotics is significant for many reasons: Although it may be as distressing and incapacitating from the patient's point of view, neurosis is considered to be a less severe type of mental illness. The neurotic's prognosis is generally more favorable than that of the psychotic's, even though the latter may, in many instances, be restored to a full, active, and satisfying life. Both may benefit by group treatment, but differences in technique and therapeutic orientation are necessary if effective personality change is to occur. For example, where the neurotic is able to assimilate in-depth interpretation of unconscious material, the psychotic may be unable to do so as effectively. The psychotic is generally more sensitive to rejection and usually comes from a background fraught with emotional upheaval. Additionally, if casualties from the group experience are to be avoided, differential diagnosis between psychosis and neurosis become very significant.

Groups can produce strong emotions, and the psychotic more than the neurotic is vulnerable to the harmful effects of strong affective states. These differences are clarified in this chapter, which provides many clinical examples.

Psychosomatically Ill Candidates

Psychosomatic illness is one of the most important areas of medicine. The intimate relationship between psyche and soma was first recognized by Hippocrates; as medical knowledge increased to its present level of sophistication this interaction proved to be even more valid; the mind can influence physical functioning, and vice versa. Mental stress and its relationship to ulcers is well-known. Less well-known is the relationship of many infections, neoplasms, and metabolic disorders, such as diabetes, to stress. In addition, a specific physical disease may have its first manifestation in the psyche. Thus, a brain tumor may be heralded by a depressive state of mild mental confusion rather than by a headache, as is more commonly assumed.

Today many conditions are designated as psychosomatic, and Stein, in his chapter on "Group Psychotherapy with Psychosomatically Ill Patients" outlines the variety of diseases so designated, as well as the use of the group as a preventive, ameliorative, and curative vehicle in their management.

Marriage and the Family

The sections in this book which direct themselves to the family and marriage are most timely. Family strife at this time is widespread and the divorce rate in the United States is rising. The effects of this trend on the individuals involved, as well as on society generally, are evident. It stands to reason that group therapists direct their attention to these issues. In the chapters by Anthony and Bowen, it is not the individual member of the family that is labeled as pathological; it is the family unit and its interactions. Similarly, married couples are viewed as a unit in the chapter by Papanek dealing with group treatment of married couples. One member of the unit is not considered "sick"; the interaction between the two is the subject of study. Both approaches—the treatment of the family and of the marital pair—have been eminently successful, and these treatment methods are growing in popularity with both therapists and patients. Whether group treatment will be able to reverse the trend toward dissolution of the nuclear family remains to be seen. Both availability of treatment and its effects need further evaluation, but present results are promising.

Group Treatment of Mental Illness

1

Clinical Diagnosis in Group Psychotherapy

Harold I. Kaplan, M.D. and Benjamin J. Sadock, M.D.

INTRODUCTION

To be of help, the group therapist must have detailed knowledge of each individual patient's intrapsychic and interpersonal disturbances, and he must be aware of the patient's psychological strengths and assets. In addition, the therapist must understand how and why the patient's problems developed—which means that he must study the patient's developmental history. Finally, the therapist must try to identify the various causes of the patient's illness—the stresses, adverse social and cultural influences, and somatic factors. With all this information in hand, the therapist can then proceed with his formal diagnosis and begin treatment.

In one-to-one therapy, diagnostic evaluation and the first steps in treatment may sometimes be conducted at the same time. But not in group therapy. For one thing, the therapist is not able to concentrate on any one patient long enough to collect the extensive data he needs for accurate diagnosis. For another thing, the therapist may jeopardize the treatment of the group as a whole and the treatment of the individual if he is not aware of the patient's diagnostic classification beforehand. The presence of just one unsuitable patient in the group may reinforce the pathology of his co-patients and create intolerable tension.

Clearly, then, the therapist must see each prospective candidate for group psychotherapy individually before he is admitted to the group. One or more psychiatric interviews will give the therapist an opportunity to make his diagnostic evaluation. Of course, the therapist may later modify his initial assessment of the patient. Indeed, he must be alert to changes in intrapsychic and interpersonal functioning and in somatic structure and function. But he cannot start group treatment with any degree of confidence until he establishes the patient's diagnostic classification.

Diagnostic competence begins with an understanding of the psychodynamics of behavior—both how the patient acts and how his conscious and unconscious mind works.

PSYCHOANALYTIC THEORY OF BEHAVIOR

The Theory of the Instincts

The term instinct refers to the influence of body needs on mental activity and behavior. Mediated through the central nervous system, such influences are experienced psychologically in the form of various sensations and various perceptions of the environment associated with the satisfaction or frustration of body needs. In the course of a person's development, psychological representations of these experiences become established in his mind and are referred to as drives or instinctual drives.

Certain behavior and psychic activity aim at contact, union, or closeness with objects in the environment. Other behavior and psychic activity aim at the destruction of objects. This difference suggests the presence

3

of two instincts—sexual instincts and aggressive instincts.

Libido. As defined by Freud, libido is that force by which the sexual instinct is represented in the mind. Sexual instinct undergoes a complex process of development and has many manifestations other than genital union. And sexuality is not limited to those sensations and activities typically considered sexual or to those parts of the body usually associated with erogenous zones.

Phases of Psychosexual Development. The earliest manifestations of sexuality involve bodily functions that are basically nonsexual. In the oral phase, which extends into the second year of life, erotic activity centers on the infant's mouth and lips and is manifested by sucking and biting. Between the ages of two and four, the child is increasingly preoccupied with bowel function and control, and his dominant erotic activity shifts from his mouth to his anal region. Usually by the fourth year, the child is increasingly aware of pleasurable feeling from his genitals. The penis and clitoris become the new erotic zones, and masturbatory activity is manifested.

Development of Object Relationships. In earliest infancy, the child depends on certain elements or objects in the environment and is driven to behave in ways that will assure the supply of these objects. Such behavior occurs without the infant's being aware of the external world or of the objects he seeks. In fact, he becomes aware of the objects partly because of some degree of frustration. Awareness of food evolves out of repetitive experiences of being hungry and then being fed. Awareness of his mother evolves out of separation and reunion with her.

At this point the mother starts to be recognized as the source of nourishment and as the source of the pleasure the infant derives from sucking. She becomes the first love object. Later sexual development and psychosocial development reflect the child's attachment to the crucial people in his environment and his feelings of love or hate or both toward them.

During the oral phase, the infant is essentially passive. His mother must gratify or frustrate his demands. But during the anal period his mother demands that he use the toilet, thereby giving up some of his freedom. And so the battle is joined as he attempts to continue enjoying the pleasurable sensation of excretion. Later on, he may derive even more pleasure by retaining the fecal mass, stimulating his anal mucosa. During this period, the child wields power over his mother by giving up or refusing to give up his feces. Expelling and retaining feces are endowed with erotic and aggressive meanings, symbolizing submission and defiance, love and hate, conflict and ambivalence.

During the oral and anal phases of development, the child makes some progress toward finding a love object, but most of his libidinal activity is autoerotic: He directs his sexual impulses toward his own body and discharges them by masturbating. The task of finding a love object belongs to the phallic phase of development. At that time the child discovers the anatomical differences between the sexes, and the pattern is set for later object choices—and for later psychoneuroses. The Oedipus complex—the intense love relationships, rivalries, hostilities, and identifications formed during this period—represents the climax of infantile sexuality. These oedipal strivings must be replaced by adult sexuality if the person is to develop normally. If he clings to oedipal tendencies, he will develop neuroses.

Aggression. At first, Freud equated aggression with sadism. Later, he thought of aggression as self-preservative impulse. But when he saw self-destructive tendencies in depressed patients, self-inflicted injuries among masochistic patients, and wanton destructiveness by small children, he concluded that aggression was often not self-preservative. So Freud gave aggression a separate status as an instinct, noting that the source of the instinct is largely in the skeletal muscles and that its aim is destruction.

The Psychic Apparatus

The Mind. Mental activity takes place on three levels: the unconscious, the preconscious, and the conscious. In the unconscious, personality forces strive for discharge, but strong counterforces block them from conscious awareness.

The preconscious, which develops in childhood, is accessible to both the unconscious and the conscious. Elements in the unconscious reach the conscious only by first reaching the preconscious. One of the functions of the preconscious is to repress or censor certain wishes and desires.

The conscious is the sense organ of the mind. Words, thoughts, impulses, and feelings may be brought to consciousness only with effort and attention, or they may intrude into consciousness unbidden. Keeping some things from becoming conscious and letting other things become conscious involves ego functions. Except for feelings, the things that come into consciousness are associated with symbols or words. The capacity to organize conscious experience in a logical, coherent, reality-oriented way marks the difference between primitive and mature mental functioning.

Structure of the Psychic Apparatus. The psychic apparatus is divided into three provinces: id, ego, and superego. The id, the locus of the instinctual drives, operates in accordance with the pleasure principle, with no regard for reality. The ego, on the other hand, is a coherent organization that controls contact with reality and avoids pain by inhibiting or regulating the discharge of instinctual drives to conform with the demands of the external world. The ego makes use of such defense mechanisms as repression, displacement, reaction formation, isolation, undoing, rationalization, intellectualization, denial, projection, regression, counterphobic mechanisms, withdrawal, and sublimation to oppose the id impulses. The superego, which contains the internalized moral values of parental images also regulates the discharge of id impulses. The aim of the human being is satisfaction of the basic biological influences and adequate adjustment within the environment.

DIAGNOSTIC PROCEDURES

The Psychiatric Interview

The clinical interview, as described by Ripley, whose work forms much of the basis for the discussion that follows, is the psychiatrist's principal diagnostic tool—one that may be supplemented by medical and neurological examinations and by psychological tests. During the interview, the psychiatrist tries to evaluate the patient's developmental history, his present life situation, and his current emotional status and mental capacity.

The psychiatrist begins with signs and symptoms. He listens to the patient's story, subjects him to various types of examinations, and then tries to diagnose his illness. Within this broad framework, the organization of the interview and the techniques employed vary from patient to patient and from one interview to another with the same patient. The therapist's personality, response to the patient, and clinical experience also modify the structure of the interview. Whatever his technique, however, the psychiatrist must focus his attention on the patient, not simply on the manifestations of disease. The psychiatrist must try to understand the disease in terms of the patient's life.

Goals. Before the therapist can make a diagnosis, he must get a description of the patient's symptoms. His symptoms are the focus of the patient's immediate concern, and the therapist must be tolerant of the patient's preoccupation with his symptoms and receptive to his efforts to describe them even if they are not evidence of psychiatric disease. Moreover, the therapist should become aware not only of the symptoms the patient describes but also of those symptoms he minimizes or conceals. The therapist must also understand what the patient says, have some insight into what he is trying to say but is reluctant to put into words, and realize when he is denying the presence of symptoms.

The psychiatrist's second task is to get information about every aspect of the patient's biological, psychological, and social history past and present. With this information, the therapist should be able to identify those factors that helped cause the illness. In addition, he will have a preliminary picture of the patient's personality—his attitudes, character traits, and intrapsychic conflicts and the psychological devices he uses to deal with these conflicts. And the therapist may have some insight into the causes of the patient's symptoms.

At the end of the interview, the therapist may try to make a tentative diagnosis and prognosis. He should also make a preliminary decision about the disposition of the patient. But if the therapist needs more information before he can make even a tentative conclusion about the patient's illness, he may schedule additional diagnostic interviews or recommend other diagnostic procedures—psychological tests and medical or neurological examinations. Once the diagnosis has been made, the therapist may accept the patient for treatment, refer him to another therapist, or recommend some other form of treatment.

The therapist must help the patient understand his illness. The patient who is symptom-free must be made aware of his illness. And the patient with subjective symptoms must learn to accept the fact that he has to change his underlying emotional attitudes.

The interview may be therapeutic as well as diagnostic.

The therapist must try to relieve the patient's immediate suffering by offering reassurance, understanding, and sympathy. Above all, he must empathize with the patient.

The Psychiatrist-Patient Relationship. Whether the psychiatrist achieves his goals depends on how he conducts the diagnostic interview and on the quality of his relationship with the patient.

A satisfactory psychiatrist-patient relationship depends on the psychiatrist's ability to achieve rapport with the patient—to create a feeling of harmonious responsiveness, to make the patient feel that the psychiatrist understands him, accepts him despite his liabilities, and recognizes his assets and that the psychiatrist is someone he can talk to.

Achieving rapport in a clinical setting is contingent on the psychiatrist's ability to understand the patient's symptoms, personality, and behavior on an intellectual level. More important, it is contingent on the therapist's capacity for empathy—his ability to put himself in the patient's place—and for self-examination—his constant awareness of his responses and attitudes toward the patient, and of the psychodynamic factors underlying those responses and attitudes.

The Patient's Attitude toward the Psychiatrist. The patient's reactions to his illness and to the interview as well as his usual ways of dealing with other people will influence the attitude toward the psychiatrist.

The patient's reactions to his illness depend on personal, social, and cultural factors. His personal experiences affect the manifestations of his illness and his affective responses to pathological changes in his personality and behavior. The defenses he mobilizes to deal with these unpleasant feelings reflect his usual way of dealing with such feelings. Social and cultural factors may determine what symptoms he describes to the therapist and what symptoms he conceals, since different cultures have different standards of what is acceptable and what is shameful. Social and cultural factors may also determine when, how, and where the patient goes for help.

Almost all patients approach the first psychiatric interview with some anxiety. The perception of psychiatric symptoms invariably gives rise to fears, realistic and unrealistic, that are as diverse and complex as the forms of psychiatric illness. The patient may express his fears and anxieties verbally or only in his nonverbal behavior. He may deliberately withhold information, give evasive answers, or, in extreme cases, simply refuse to communicate. He may try to charm or endear himself to the psychiatrist, or even behave seductively in an effort to divert him from the real issues. Or, he may use such defense mechanisms as denial and projection.

Some patients place the psychiatrist on a pedestal and endow him with magical powers. The inevitable disillusionment may strengthen their resistance to treatment. They may at times feel that, once they have consulted a psychiatrist, they don't have to do anything else. At other times they may see the seeking of psychiatric help as an act of surrender, an admission of weakness.

The patient often sees the psychiatrist as an authority figure who has the power to control every aspect of his life. This reaction grows out of anxieties and guilt feelings surrounding his illness and also out of his unresolved dependency needs, which may be reactivated during periods of psychological or physical stress and redirected toward an idealized parental figure, such as the psychiatrist.

Finally, the patient's attitude toward the psychiatrist reflects his usual way of relating to other people—aggressive and domineering or dependent and submissive, detached and disinterested or manipulative and seductive.

The Psychiatrist's Attitude toward the Patient. At some time, the patient is negative or ambivalent toward the psychiatrist. The effect of these attitudes on the psychiatrist-patient relationship is minimal if the psychiatrist understands their origins and deals with them appropriately. But if the psychiatrist's attitudes toward the patient are inappropriate, the effects on the psychiatrist-patient relationship, the diagnostic process, and the course and outcome of treatment can be disastrous. So the psychiatrist must be aware of his feelings toward the patient, understand the origins of his countertransference, and work through his inappropriate attitudes. Self-understanding is the key, which is why a personal analysis is considered an essential part of psychiatric training.

The psychiatrist's initial reactions to the patient are based on his first impressions. He may like the patient immediately and feel attracted, or he may automatically dislike him and be repelled by his appearance or behavior. These initial reactions often form part of the basis for a tentative diagnosis.

If the patient is hostile or aggressive, the psychiatrist may perceive such behavior as a personal attack and try to fight back, calling forth more hostility from the patient. Their relationship quickly reaches a stalemate in such a situation. Ideally, of course, the psychiatrist does not overreact. Instead, he evaluates and deals with the patient's attitudes objectively. To do so, he must understand the psychodynamics of the patient's behavior and the psychogenesis of his own response to such behavior.

If the patient's symptoms evoke anxiety, the psychiatrist may ignore them or side-step the patient's efforts to discuss them. Or if the patient's behavior is unorthodox and unexplained by current theories of personality, the psychiatrist may condemn him out of hand. When he reacts with shock or fear, the psychiatrist may try to defend against his feelings. He may adopt a grave, magisterial facial expression that gives the patient the impression that he is being judged or that his condition is worse that it actually is. Or the psychiatrist may put on a cold, expressionless facade that freezes the patient or a pedantic expression that makes him feel like a small child. Whatever form they take, these defensive patterns convey a message of rejection.

A positive reaction that exceeds the proper limits of the therapist-patient relationship can be just as destructive as a negative reaction. If the psychiatrist overempathizes with the patient, he may want to solve his problems and make his decisions for him. Efforts to protect the patient from life can sabotage the psychiatrist's diagnostic and treatment efforts.

The psychiatrist's positive reactions to the patient may also be based on envy, awe of the patient's social or economic status, or admiration of his intellect. If the psychiatrist feels inferior to the patient, he needs to examine the roots of his own feelings. And, he must be alert to any effort by the patient to intimidate or manipulate him.

A written record of the psychiatrist's impressions of attitudes toward, and emotional responses to, the patient can facilitate systematic self-evaluation. A check-list of the variables that may shape the psychiatrist's reactions to the patient is particularly useful.

Number and Duration of Diagnostic Sessions. If, at the end of the initial psychiatric interview, the psychiatrist needs more diagnostic data, he will schedule at least one more diagnostic session. The need for more interviews depends on the skill with which the therapist conducts the initial interview and on factors he cannot control—the nature and severity of the patient's symptoms, the setting in which he is seen, and the time available. How the therapist conducts the initial interview and the quality of the patient-therapist relationship affect the patient's willingness to follow through and cooperate.

As a general rule, the psychiatric interview should last no more than an hour, but it may be extended to an hour and a half, if the patient is particularly alert and receptive. Whatever the length of the interview, the patient should not have the feeling that he is being rushed to produce the kind of information he thinks the therapist wants. Some patients need time to warm up and relax before they can discuss their symptoms. If the patient's anxiety is too great to continue the interview he should be allowed to leave if he wants. Trying to persuade him to stay serves no useful purpose. But the therapist should assure the patient that he is interested and concerned, and that his services are available whenever the patient is ready to discuss his problems.

The Physical Setting. The therapist's office is ideal for the interview, providing privacy, quiet, and seclusion. Such interruptions as telephone calls and the transmission of messages should be kept to a minimum. Sometimes an interruption serves a useful purpose—the patient has a chance to pull himself together and gather the courage to confide some shameful detail—but more often he uses the interval to mobilize his defenses and resistance. Moreover, the therapist has no assurance that the interruption will not occur at a strategic point. And the patient may interpret interruptions as a sign that the therapist is not interested or is hostile toward him.

When the therapist greets the patient he should introduce himself, invite the patient to be seated in a comfortable chair, and try to make him feel at ease. Explaining the purpose of the diagnostic interview is helpful. The therapist might tell a naive patient that he needs to know more about his difficulties if he is to help him. A more sophisticated patient may require a more elaborate explanation and a brief description of the treatment process. Questions about the therapist's professional qualifications should be answered frankly to reassure the patient.

Note-Taking. Notes should be made as unobtrusively as possible so that the patient will not be inhibited. If the patient objects, the therapist may reassure him that the notes are confidential and help to ensure diagnostic accuracy—and proper treatment. If the patient persists in his objections, the therapist should stop taking notes. By contrast, some patients object when the psychiatrist does not take notes. They look on note-taking as a sign of the therapist's interest and recognition of the importance of what the patient is saying.

If the therapist does not take notes during the interview, he can record the relevant data immediately after the patient leaves. But his own reactions may contaminate the patient's record. Sound recordings are a better alternative to note-taking. They are more complete than notes and do not interfere with spontaneous communication.

Observations of the Patient. Observation of specific details of the patient's appearance and behavior begins when the therapist hears the patient's voice on the telephone for the first time or sees him in his waiting room, and it continues throughout the interview. Agitated movements, disturbances in speech, changes in the patient's appearance, or changes in his respiration may give the therapist important clues about the patient's unconscious feelings and attitudes. Such observations may indicate inconsistencies between the emotional reactions the patient reports and those that exist on an unconscious level. In addition, the patient's attire, posture, behavior, and voice may indicate the nature and severity of his illness. Indeed, the therapist's observation of these nonverbal phenomena may be his only diagnostic tool when the patient talks too little, too much about irrelevant matters, or not at all because of his need to avoid discussion of his emotional conflicts.

The therapist should record his observations systematically, under such headings as patient's preinterview behavior, initial response to therapist, attire, body characteristics, facial expression and features, voice and speech, gait and posture, patterns of motor activity.

The patient's behavior in the waiting room, before he is summoned into the private office, gives the therapist his first clues about his mental and emotional status. The patient's behavior when he meets the therapist is an index of his response to his illness and his attitude toward the therapist and may provide insights into the quality of his object relationships.

Excessive fastidiousness in dress may suggest an obsessive-compulsive disorder. Extreme slovenliness may be an early sign of depression or schizophrenia. Seductive dress may indicate a hysterical neurosis. Exhibitionistic attire is worn by certain male homosexuals. Somber, drab clothing may indicate depression, or an effort to discourage sexual interest. Childish patterns of dress may express a regressive clinging to childhood. But the therapist should be aware of dress standards in different cultures—including the teen-age culture. Attire that looks eccentric to the therapist may be acceptable to or even required by the patient's peers.

The patient's physical characteristics may indicate distortions in his body image. He may be excessively preoccupied with particular body parts, feel inferior or proud because of his appearance, or be troubled by problems of sexual identity.

The patient's voice and speech, gait and posture, and pattern of motor activity are clues to his affective state. Increased motor activity—loud speech, chronic restlessness, excessive smoking, irritability—may be part of the anxiety and depression syndrome. Decreased motor activity, abnormal posture and gait, halting speech may express the underlying affects of helplessness and hopelessness found in simple depression.

Some aspects of the patient's behavior and appearance may be only transient phenomena. His increased or decreased motor activity, somber attire, angry or sad facial expression may not be components of his illness but simply his response to his illness and the interview situation.

Interviewing Techniques. The success of the initial interview depends on the therapist's knowledge of what he must find out from the patient and of how he can find it out. The good interviewer, like the good conversationalist, has verbal facility, intuitive tact, and, above all, the ability to listen. In addition, the therapist must have empathy, genuine interest in other people, and tolerance of human frailties.

Opening the Interview. The physical setting and the therapist's observance of the basic social amenities are particularly important at this point. He can use superficial techniques to convey his interest in and acceptance of the patient and his illness and to set the tone for the interview. Then the therapist proceeds to focus on the patient's chief complaint by asking a general question, such as, "What brings you here?" or "What seems to be your trouble?" This approach defines the purpose of the interview and shapes its direction.

Guiding the Interview. Listening is one of the therapist's major tools. By keeping his directive role to a minimum, he can encourage the patient to expand on his thoughts, bring up relevant topics, and lower his resistance.

The therapist's quiet attentiveness can generally lessen the patient's anxiety, blocking, and silences. But at times, he may have to play a more active, directive role. Traumatic, emotionally charged, or painful subjects may cause the patient to fall silent or become angry, tearful, or fidgety; or he may try to change the subject or terminate the interview. These reactions—forms of resistance or blocking—can be attributed to the emergence of a painful emotion, such as anxiety, conflict, shame, embarrassment, or guilt. The therapist can help the patient to overcome or lessen the intensity of these reactions.

If the patient suddenly falls silent, the therapist may ask him one or two direct questions or simply look at him questioningly and nod his head encouragingly. The patient often interprets such activity as a sign of the therapist's interest, which is a potent weapon against resistance.

If the patient remains silent, the therapist may return to the source of the patient's resistance ("You were saying. . ."). If the patient's pain is clearly apparent, the therapist may find it helpful to put into words what the patient is feeling as a sign that he understands him ("You seem to be feeling depressed [or angry, resentful, anxious, ashamed]"). Or the therapist may interpret the patient's reaction ("You suddenly became upset when you were talking about . . ."). Often the therapist tries to allay the patient's anxiety by expressing empathy and sympathy ("That must have been an upsetting experience.").

If the patient summarily drops a subject, the therapist may defer to his wishes and hope that he will resume the discussion at a later date. Or he may openly confront the patient about his reluctance to discuss the subject.

Blocking and emotional reactions are brought on not only by sensitive subjects but also by the patient's reactions to his illness and to the diagnostic situation. If the illness evokes feelings of guilt or shame, the therapist should try to bolster the patient's self-esteem by emphasizing his achievements and positive qualities and the facts that psychiatric illness is not a sign of weakness and that others also have the illness. And if the patient has fears and doubts about the diagnostic situation, the therapist's professional competence, confidentiality, and the treatment process, the therapist can best deal with them by bringing them out into the open.

The therapist must allow the patient to tell the story of his illness in his own words. Only if he is permitted to talk about himself frankly and to express his thoughts and feelings freely, without interruption, can the patient find out about himself. Early in the interview is no time to elicit all the details and the complete factual history. Gaps in the patient's account can be filled in later. Nor should the therapist at this time challenge the patient's statements or correct his misrepresentation or misperception of the facts. These areas can be explored later, when rapport is established.

Questions, however, can be helpful if injected at strategic points in the patient's monologue. When the patient provides appropriate leads, perceptive questions can help the patient develop an understanding of himself. Tactful questioning is indicated when the therapist is not sure what some piece of information means to the patient. And, by discreet questioning, the therapist can get information about intimate topics that the patient may be reluctant to discuss. Topics such as sex can be introduced by asking the patient questions about physical development, for example.

The questions should be open-ended, somewhat ambiguous, leaving room for explanations and elaborations by the patient. Restrictive questions answered by a "yes" or "no" cannot help the therapist understand the patient or help the patient develop an understanding of himself.

The therapist should avoid leading questions. For example, in asking the patient about his current emotional status, the therapist should not ask him whether he has a bad temper. "How is your temper?" is a more appropriate question.

Excessive questioning should also be avoided. It may overwhelm the patient, interrupt his train of thought, or block his effort to express an emotional reaction. The therapist must overcome any tendency to use precipitate questioning as a way to cope with his own anxiety.

The therapist's questions should be relevant to what the patient is talking about. Questions from out of left field may confuse or inhibit the patient. If the therapist feels that he is belaboring a topic—a sign of resistance—he can change the subject by saying, "There are other important things to cover." As the patient gives his account of his problems, the therapist may ask him whether he had similar problems in the past. This question will bring forth information about the patient's past history, which will give the therapist an insight into the origins of the patient's illness.

Finally, the therapist's vocabulary and the content of his questions and comments should be influenced by the patient's intelligence, level of sophistication, and symptoms. Whenever possible, the therapist should use the patient's own words and phraseology. Doing so assures the patient that the therapist understands him. And the therapist, in turn, minimizes the possibility that the patient will distort what he says.

Concluding the Interview. At this point, the therapist must play a more active and directive role. He must make decisions about the patient's future management, and try to make sure these decisions are carried out.

No matter how little he feels he has accomplished, no matter how frustrated or discouraged he feels, the therapist must give the patient a feeling of optimism and convince him that the diagnostic interview has been useful. But the therapist cannot guarantee a cure or even a favorable response to treatment. Nor can he estimate how much treatment the patient will require.

If no further diagnostic interviews are needed, the therapist may recommend a plan of treatment. If additional interviews are needed, he may tell the patient that there is a need for further discussion, express his continued interest, and suggest that he think about the material covered so far and about the topics he would like to discuss in the next interview. The success of later interviews depends largely on how much the patient cooperates with the therapist.

If the patient cannot face the prospect of treatment or additional interviews, he may convince himself that such procedures are unnecessary, that he only needs to change some aspect of his current life situation—get a new job, earn more money, get divorced or married, take a vacation. The therapist must persuade him that such solutions are rarely effective—and only when the patient's illness is a transient situational disturbance.

During the final phase of the interview, the therapist must tell the patient what he needs to know about his illness. Giving the patient too much information or presenting it improperly may exacerbate the patient's symptoms or create new ones. But obviously withholding information may increase his anxiety by convincing him that the therapist is keeping something from him and that his illness is more serious than he had been led to believe. As a result, the patient's confidence and trust in the therapist are undermined. Generally, it is wise to give the patient whatever information is necessary to enlist his cooperation.

As a rule, the therapist's appraisal is reassuring to the patient. For one thing, it indicates the therapist's recognition and understanding of the patient's illness. Second, when the illness is brought out into the open, it no longer lurks in the realm of the mysterious and frightening unknown.

Later Interviews. The techniques used in subsequent interviews are much the same as those used in the initial interview. The patient is encouraged to continue telling his story and to express his thoughts and feelings freely. And the therapist asks appropriate

questions, expresses empathy and understanding, and occasionally interprets the patient's remarks in an effort to help him overcome his reluctance to discuss the emotional conflicts evidenced by blocking and prolonged silences.

One difference is that the therapist usually plays a more directive role in later interviews. Since he scheduled further meetings with the patient to get additional information, the therapist may ask the patient to expand on topics introduced during the first interview, or he may ask about areas that were not discussed at all.

Whatever new information is disclosed, the therapist must maintain his nonjudgmental, understanding attitude, neither condoning nor condemning the patient's behavior and values. His questions may evoke emotional reaction, anxiety, shame, guilt, withdrawal. The therapist must counteract these responses or at least lessen their intensity by reassuring and supporting the patient and by indicating his awareness of the patient's strengths as well as his weaknesses.

Specialized Interviewing Techniques. Interviewing techniques vary according to the patient's personality reactions. The therapist's usual nondirective approach may at times make the patient feel abandoned and anxious. At such times, the therapist must modify, or temporarily abandon, his basic diagnostic technique in favor of guidance and more explicit reassurance.

At other times, the therapist must try to stimulate anxiety so that an apathetic patient experiences enough discomfort to talk about his conflicts. Or the therapist may probe, challenge, and confront the indifferent patient to arouse feelings that will make him participate actively in the diagnostic process.

Interviewing techniques may also vary according to the patient's illness. A depressed patient, for example, generally has a short attention span and should have a relatively brief interview. Moreover, the therapist may have to interrupt because the patient tends to reiterate in a destructive, self-deprecatory way. Often, such a patient does not mention his depression. Instead, he may complain of insomnia, loss of appetite, diurnal changes in feelings, irritability, or difficulty in concentration. The depression is clearly evident, however, in the expressions of futility, hopelessness, self-depreciation, shame, and thinly veiled hostility.

During the interview the therapist should investigate the depressed patient's suicidal tendencies by asking about his interest in life, whether life seems to be worth living, and whether he has thoughts about dying or taking his own life. If the patient has already tried to commit suicide, he should be asked how others reacted and how they would react to his death. If he admits to contemplating suicide, he should be asked what method he would use.

With a delusional patient, the psychiatrist should demonstrate his interest, understanding, and acceptance and should try to convince the patient that he realizes he is expressing thoughts and feelings with a significant meaning, although the meaning may not be clear at the time. But he must not give the impression that he subscribes to the patient's delusions. He should neither agree with nor contradict the patient. A skeptical attitude may help to raise doubts in the patient's mind and make him more receptive to the psychiatrist's efforts to find out more about the delusional thoughts and who he feels is responsible for them.

A withdrawn patient may be so absorbed with his inner world of fantasy that he is unable to talk spontaneously about his feelings, and so the psychiatrist must ask him questions. But the therapist should change the subject when he sees that he has touched on an area of conflict. Shifting to less disturbing subjects helps the patient accept the psychiatrist. If the patient does not respond to any questions, the psychiatrist may express an interest in talking to him again later, emphasize that he is always available, and plan frequent, brief visits.

A manic patient may be so highly excited that the therapist cannot establish rapport with him. The psychiatrist should remain calm and receptive, paying particular attention to the content of what the patient says. Overtalkative, disturbed patients often reveal underlying conflicts that they conceal when they regain control.

Evaluation of Interviewing Techniques. The therapist's interviewing techniques can be considered effective if the patient reacts in certain ways during the interview: He becomes less tense and anxious, more relaxed. His speech becomes more spontaneous and natural, less inhibited and defensive. He shows increased interest in his feelings and in the origins of his symptoms and illness, and he accepts more responsibility for his condition. His feelings of guilt, self-blame, self-contempt, self-hate, and hostility decrease. His despair gives way to hopefulness. He expresses an interest in further diagnostic procedures or in treatment.

Improvement in the patient's symptoms between the initial interview and later interviews may indicate the effectiveness of the therapist's interviewing techniques, or it may be just still another manifestation of the patient's psychopathology. Contact with the therapist may have temporarily satisfied the patient's irrational dependency needs or given rise to unrealistic expectation about treatment. He may have been temporarily removed from external stress and relieved of responsibility, or he may feel relieved of the obligation to try to help himself. Or symptomatic improvement may be a natural evolution of the illness.

The Psychiatric Report

The patient does not usually present diagnostic information in a logical, orderly fashion. But if the therapist prepares a report—whether for his personal use or as a source of information for others—he is compelled to collate and organize the information so that he gets a picture of the patient and a sequential, logical account of the development of his illness. Properly evaluated, this information then enables him to arrive at a preliminary diagnosis, make a prognostic statement, and recommend an appropriate course of therapy.

There is no single correct form for recording the information gathered during the psychiatric interview. But the therapist should follow a prescribed outline, such as the one used below, to make sure important developmental areas are covered and to point up any contradictions in the material presented.

Identification. This section should include the patient's name, age, sex, ethnic and cultural background, marital status, occupation, source of referral, housing situation, and hospitalizations. Identify informants.

Therapist's Personal Impressions. The therapist should give a brief, nontechnical description of the patient's appearance and behavior.

Chief Complaint. If possible, the patient's own words should be used to describe the complaint. He should be encouraged to explain its duration and occurrence, possible causes, intensity, and effects on him.

History of Present Illness. This section should include a chronological account, in the patient's own words, of how his symptoms and signs developed, including a description of his premorbid personality, his life circumstances when his symptoms began, the precipitating stresses or events, and the effects on his behavior, health, attitudes, and personal relationships.

Previous Illnesses. These illnesses may be categorized as emotional or mental disturbances, physiological disorders that may be psychogenic, medical conditions, and neurological disorders.

Personal History. This section should include a separate description of each period in the patient's life—infancy, childhood, adolescence, and adulthood. Gaps may be filled in later, when additional facts emerge during treatment, or information may be gathered from other sources. Also, such gaps may indicate that the patient is repressing particularly stressful or conflictual developmental events.

The personal history gives the psychiatrist an understanding of the patient's development, the environment in which it occurred, the significance of certain people, and the patient's adaptive techniques. The history is also a current commentary. It includes a description of the patient's present environment, of its stresses and sources of pleasure, and of the persons who are significant and influential. For each period of the patient's life, the report should include information about his social, sexual, and vocational functioning, the inhibitions imposed by excessive or inappropriate fear or guilt, and his sources of pleasure.

Family History. This section should include a description of the patient's parents and siblings and anyone else who lived with the family, including their names, ages, occupations, economic and social status, marital records, and major physical and emotional illnesses. Of particular importance are depression, psychiatric hospitalization, suicide, alcoholism, drug addiction, mental retardation, convulsive disorders, and syphilis. This section should also indicate how the patient felt about each relative, what their relationship was like, and what it is like now. Finally, the therapist should include a description of the family's ethnic and religious traditions and the psychological atmosphere in the home.

Mental Status Examination. The mental status examination gives the psychiatrist a precise picture of the patient's emotional status and mental capacity and functioning at the time of the psychiatric interview. The report should be organized in a certain order and according to certain categories, but the examination itself need not be conducted in that order. The psychiatrist may decide to emphasize certain areas of the mental examination, depending on the patient's problem and history, cooperation, and sensorium.

The report's categories might include a general description of the patient's appearance, behavior, and attitude; his speech; his alertness and orientation; his affective state; his level of anxiety; his stream of thought—including verbatim quotations—and content of thought; his memory; his information and intelligence; his ability to count, calculate, and do abstract thinking; his judgment and insight; and his dreams, fantasies, and value systems.

Summary of Positive Findings. The psychiatric report should include the findings derived from medical and neurological examinations and from psychological tests. The report should also list any drugs the patient has been taking, including dosage and duration of intake, since most sedative and hypnotic agents reduce perceptual acuity and motor skills when taken in small amounts and produce somnolence and stupor when taken in large amounts.

Diagnosis. Any diagnosis made after the psychiatric interview must be tentative. Some crucially important information may not have emerged, the patient may have withheld data deliberately, or he may have a severe disorder that is in a state of temporary remission. However, even the psychiatrist's tentative diagnosis should adhere to the standard nomenclature of the American Psychiatric Association.

Prognosis. The report should include the psychiatrist's assessment of the future course and outcome of the patient's illness, taking into account such factors as the particular illness and its natural history; self-limited treatment goals; the patient's assets and liabilities, such as his age, duration of the illness, and his early traumatic experiences; motivations for treatment; accessibility for treatment; and current life situation.

Recommendations for Treatment. After his systematic study of the patient, the psychiatrist should recommend an appropriate course of therapy—or no psychiatric treatment—on the basis of his understanding of the patient's development and the vicissitudes of his life experiences.

Ancillary Diagnostic Procedures

The psychiatrist may need findings derived from medical and neurological examinations and psychological tests to determine whether the patients' symptoms are psychiatric, physiological, or neurological in origin or whether he is suffering from a severe psychoneurosis or a borderline psychosis.

Medical Examination. The central nervous system can react to emotional stress or to physical stress by producing similar symptoms, and these symptoms can be physiological or psychological or both. Diagnostic difficulties arise when a systemic disease produces emotional symptoms. Anxiety, depression, fatigue, headaches, irritability, dizziness, poor or excessive appetite, drowsiness, and insomnia are usually due to psychogenic factors, but they may also be produced by infectious, toxic, metabolic, degenerative, neoplastic, and nutritional disorders. Depression may be an early sign of hepatitis, cirrhosis of the liver, or carcinoma of the pancreas. And fatigue, frequently associated with depression or anxiety, may be caused by a chronic infectious disease.

Neurological Examination. Disorders of perception and apperception, such as depersonalization phenomena or hallucinations, are sometimes caused by lesions or electrical stimulation of the temporal lobe or by certain chemical agents. Similarly, disorders of intellectual function—such as defects in memory, retention, and recall—may be caused by metabolic deficiency or damage to certain brain structures.

Behavioral assessment is a necessary part of neurological evaluation. Psychological tests and clinical observation sample the same aspects of behavior—speed of response, level of comprehension, use of language—but the tests are more reliable and precise. Psychological tests currently used to assess brain damage are summarized in Table 1 (Freedman and Kaplan).

Psychological Tests. Psychological tests are generally used to facilitate assessment of particular aspects of personality function, the nature and extent of psychopathology, the patient's intellectual potential, and possible brain damage. Some commonly used tests—measuring devices, which provide scores and normative standards; behavior samples, which allow qualitative observations within given areas of psychological functioning; and projective techniques—are described in Table 2, which was prepared for Freedman and Kaplan's *Comprehensive Textbook of Psychiatry.*

Psychological tests of personality function are particularly helpful when the psychiatrist needs more information about sensitive areas and he does not want to question the patient directly, lest his probing arouse excessive anxiety. And psychological tests of intellectual function can help the psychiatrist determine whether the patient's impaired functioning is due to cerebral disease, a basic intellectual deficiency, sociocultural factors, or a psychiatric disorder.

Nomenclature

Psychiatric clinical syndromes are currently classified according to the official nosological system of the American Psychiatric Association as published in the *Diag-*

Table 1. *Tests for Assessing Brain Damage**

Category	Subcategories	Remarks
General scales	Wechsler Adult Intelligence Scale (WAIS) Stanford-Binet Wechsler Intelligence Scale for Children (WISC)	Given the availability of adequate normative standards in relation to the patient's educational and cultural background, a performance significantly below expectations should raise the question of cerebral damage. This generalization applies to both adults and children.
Reasoning and problem solving	Abstractions (Shipley) Progressive matrices (Raven) Proverbs (Gorham) Perceptual mazes (Elithorn) Object and color-sorting tests (Goldstein and Scheerer)	Performance level is closely related to educational background and premorbid intellectual level. In general, the clinical application of these tests is more useful in the case of educated patients. If specific language and perceptual defect can be ruled out as determinants of defective performance, failure suggests frontal lobe involvement or diffuse cerebral disease.
Memory and orientation	Immediate auditory memory—repetition of digits Immediate auditory memory—reversal of digits Immediate visual memory (Benton, Graham-Kendall) Recent auditory memory—words or stories Recent visual memory—words or pictures Temporal orientation (Benton, Van Allen, and Fogel)	For complete assessment, a number of memory tasks (auditory vs. visual, verbal vs. nonverbal, immediate vs. recent) should be given. Minor defects in temporal orientation may be elicited and suggest weakness in recent memory.
Visuoperceptive and visuoconstructive	Identification of hidden figures (Teuber-Weinstein-Rudel) Identification of fragmented figures (Street-Gestalt) Block design construction (Kohs, Goldstein-Scheerer, Wechsler) Stick arranging (Goldstein-Scheerer) Copying designs (L. Bender, Benton visual retention) Three-dimensional block construction (Benton-Fogel) Inkblot interpretation (Rorschach, Holtzman) Perceptual mazes (Elithorn) Responsiveness to double visual stimulation (M. B. Bender)	These types of task are relatively sensitive indicators of the presence of cerebral disease. Analysis of qualitative features of performance and comparison of performance level with the status of language and reasoning abilities often provide indications with regard to locus of the lesion.
Somatoperceptual	Tactile recognition (Parker, Ross) Finger recognition (Benton) Right-left orientation (Benton) Responsiveness to double tactile stimulation (M. B. Bender)	Frequently useful indicators of the presence and locus of cerebral disease.
Language	Token test (De Renzi-Vignolo) Abstractions (Shipley) Proverbs (Gorham) Word fluency (Benton-Spreen-Fogel) Illinois test of psycholinguistic abilities (Kirk-McCarthy)	Test performance is dependent on educational background, and it is essential that clinical interpretation allow for this and other possibly significant factors. In adult patients, defective performance (particularly in relation to other abilities) suggests dysfunction of the cerebral hemisphere that is dominant for language. In children, defective performance does not have this localizing significance but does raise the question of the presence of cerebral damage.
Attention, concentration, and motor abilities	Continuous performance test (Rosvold) Visual vigilance (McDonald-Burns) Reaction time (Blackburn-Benton-Joynt) Motor impersistence (Garfield) Imitations of actions (Bergès-Lézine)	Valuable behavioral indicators of the presence (and sometimes locus) of cerebral disease that deserve more extensive clinical application.

* Adapted from *Comprehensive Textbook of Psychiatry*, edited by A. M. Freedman and H. I. Kaplan, Williams & Wilkins, Baltimore, 1967. Chart by Arthur Benton, Ph.D.

Table 2.   Some Instruments Commonly Used by Clinical Psychologists*

Instrument	Description	Comments
Measuring Devices Benton Visual Retention Test	An individually administered test designed to measure visual memory, used for subjects 8 years of age and older.	This is one of a class of instruments used to investigate memory functions. It is most useful in differential diagnosis and in the evaluation of brain damage.
Cattell Infant Intelligence Scale	A downward extension of the Stanford-Binet test to cover ages 3 to 30 months.	This test has little predictive value for future intellectual level, particularly in the early ages. However, it does yield a good description of current functioning and is useful for the early diagnosis of mental retardation and brain damage.
Gesell Developmental Schedule	A scale based on behavioral observations, to measure development in different areas from the age of 4 weeks to 6 years.	Although the scale yields poor predictions for later developmental quotients, particularly during the early ages, it does yield a satisfactory picture of current functions. Clinically, it is most useful as a supplement to other data or when successive measurements are taken over a period of time.
Minnesota Multiphasic Personality Inventory	A questionnaire type of personality test for ages 16 years and over. May be administered individually or in groups. Yields 14 scores in scales representing diagnostic categories (such as hysteria, schizophrenia) and test-taking behavior (such as lying).	Besides the scales noted in the test manual, other scales, such as ego strength, have been reported in the literature. Although the administration and scoring of this test are quite simple, the interpretation of the score profiles may become rather complex and requires considerable experience.
Stanford-Binet Intelligence Scale, Form L-M, 1960	An individually administered age scale intelligence test designed to range from 2 years up. This is a revision based on the 1937 Forms L and M. It yields a mental age and a deviation I.Q.	This scale presents a wide variety of items and item difficulty. It is organized by item difficulty (i.e., age level). The choice between this scale and the WISC is often a matter of the preference of the individual clinician, with the Stanford-Binet usually being the most helpful at the lower age levels and at the extremes of intelligence.
Wechsler Adult Intelligence Scale (WAIS)	An individually administered intelligence test for ages 16 years and over. It yields scores for 11 subtests as well as verbal, performance, and full-scale I.Q.'s.	The items of this scale are organized according to the task presented, with a separate score for each type of task. Besides yielding information concerning the intellectual and cognitive functions, analysis of the pattern of subtest scores and qualitative examination of the protocol may yield information concerning the impact of psychopathology in these areas.
Wechsler Intelligence Scale for Children (WISC)	A downward extension of an earlier form of the WAIS to cover the ages below 16 years. Yields scores similar to the WAIS (one additional optional test) but with subtest scores based on chronological age; covers ages to 16 years.	As with the WAIS, the scale is often used for more than the determination of level of intelligence. The grouping of items by type of task involved makes it easier for the clinician in actual practice to use it as an instrument to investigate the impact of pathology in the intellectual and cognitive areas.

Table 2—Continued

Instrument	Description	Comments
Vineland Social Maturity Scale	An individual interview schedule aimed at determining rate of development. An age scale, it covers from birth to maturity. It yields a development quotient (D.Q.), which is the ratio of developmental age to chronological age.	This scale is simpler to administer and to score than is the Gesell scale, but it is based on reports rather than on direct observation. It does furnish a helpful picture of current developmental status, and it is strongest when used to supplement other data or to provide successive measures over time.
Behavior Samples Bender-Gestalt Test	An elicitation of visual-motor behavior by having the patient copy a set of geometric designs. Various modifications of administration may be introduced, such as having the designs redrawn from memory.	Although several scoring systems have been developed for this test, it is usually used qualitatively. Deficits in this area are often associated with brain damage, and the test is most used for differential diagnosis of brain damage. It may also be used to investigate developmental and intellectual levels in children and the characteristics of ego functions in adults. A number of clinicians use the instrument as a projective technique.
Examining for aphasia (Eisenson)	A systematic survey of the ability to receive and to express meaning through different modalities. It includes the aphasias, agnosias, and apraxias.	This instrument provides for behavior samples in various areas of language and symbolic function and at several levels within each area. As a quick survey, it is extremely useful where brain damage is suspected. However, further examination is usually necessary for treatment planning.
Goldstein-Scheerer Tests of Abstract and Concrete Thinking	A battery of five tests (cube test, color sorting, object sorting, color form sorting, stick test) to examine the ability to attain and to maintain the abstract attitude.	These tests afford opportunities to observe the patient attempting to solve problems that require abstraction and shifts in abstractions. Although other thought disorders, such as schizophrenic thinking, may be elicited, concrete thinking tends to be highlighted. The tests are most used for the diagnosis and the evaluation of brain damage.
Concept Formation Test (Kasanin and Hanfman)	A complex problem of grouping the Vigotsky Blocks is presented. Clues given and explanations of groupings are questioned.	The attempts to solve the complex problem provides opportunity to observe the patient's modes of thinking. The test is particularly useful in revealing patterns of schizophrenic thinking.
Projective Techniques Blacky Pictures	A series of 11 cartoons about a dog (Blacky) and his/her family. The patient makes up stories, answers more structured questions, and indicates like-dislike for the pictures.	The stimulus pictures depict different stages of psychosexual development. Its major use is with children, but it can be used with adults. Some writers suggest the following sequence: Blacky with younger children, CAT with older children and adolescents; TAT with adults. This, however, is very much at the discretion of the individual clinician.

Table 2—Continued

Instrument	Description	Comments
Draw a Person	The basic instruction is simply to draw a person, then to draw a person of the opposite sex. Many elaborations exist, including interviews about figures drawn.	This is one of a number of drawing projective techniques, including the drawing of a house, tree, person; of the family; of animals. The figure drawings, in general, may be interpreted as yielding data concerning self-concept, perception of significant figures, problem and conflict areas, mood, affect, and anxiety.
Rorschach	A series of 10 symmetrical inkblots. The patient tells what he sees in each. This is followed by an inquiry concerning the responses. Different sets of stimulus cards are available, but the original Rorschach plates are by far the most frequently used.	This is the most useful single instrument of the clinical psychologist. Through analysis of perception, cognition, and content, information concerning almost every aspect of psychological organization may be revealed.
Sentence Completion Test	Incomplete sentences are completed by patient (e.g., "My mother . . . ."). Sentences may be aimed at specific potential conflict areas. Standard forms, such as the one by Rotter, are available.	This technique may be used at different levels from the prediction of overt behavior to the uncovering of deep personality dynamics. It yields data concerning conflict areas and emotional attitudes. This technique has the advantage of flexibility, for the skilled clinician may devise incomplete sentences tailored for a specific patient.
Thematic Apperception Test (TAT)	Patient makes up stories about stimulus pictures. Some pictures are specially designed for girls, boys, women, or men. Other sets of stimulus cards for special groups are available, such as the Children's Apperception Test (CAT), which uses pictures of animals.	This test helps to furnish the content of the patient's inner life. It may be said with some truth that the Rorschach furnishes the skeleton on which to hang the flesh and blood of the TAT. It yields data concerning, among other things, needs, pressures, self-concept, motives, fantasies, attitudes, and feelings.

* Adapted from *Comprehensive Textbook of Psychiatry*, edited by A. M. Freedman and H. I. Kaplan, Williams & Wilkins, Baltimore, 1967. Chart by Herbert Fensterheim, Ph.D.

nostic and Statistical Manual of Mental Disorders (*DSM-II*) and as outlined in Table 3. This system of nosology is not entirely satisfactory, chiefly because the causes of many psychiatric disorders are not yet fully understood. The system is, therefore, based on superficial characteristics and must be considered artificial. But an artificial system is far better than none at all, and so it is generally used.

More than one category of disturbance may be seen in a patient, and so the first edition of the manual (*DSM-I*), published in 1952, supported the concept of multiple diagnoses, but certain combinations of diagnoses were not permitted. For example, Alcoholism could not be listed as a separate diagnosis when it was associated with an underlying disorder. In contrast *DSM-II* encourages clinicians to diagnose every disorder present, even if one is the symptomatic expression of another. Also, *DSM-II* makes greater use of qualifying phrases—acute and chronic, not psychotic, in remission, mild, moderate, and severe.

Table 3. *Classifications of Mental Disorders According to DSM-II**

I. Mental Retardation—subnormal intellectual functioning. Retardation begins during the developmental period and is associated with impairment in maturation or in learning and social adjustment or both.

> Borderline: I.Q. of 68 to 85
> Mild: I.Q. of 52 to 67
> Moderate: I.Q. of 36 to 51
> Severe: I.Q. of 20 to 35
> Profound: I.Q. under 20

Clinical Subcategories of Mental Retardation:

After Infection and Intoxication (congenital cytomegalic inclusion body disease, rubella, syphilis, toxoplasmosis; encephalopathy associated with other prenatal infections, due to postnatal cerebral infection, associated with maternal toxemia of pregnancy, bilirubin, and postimmunization).

After Trauma or Physical Agent (encephalopathy due to prenatal injury, mechanical injury at birth, asphyxia at birth, and postnatal injury).

Associated with Disorders of Metabolism, Growth, or Nutrition (cerebral lipoidosis, lipid histiocytosis, phenylketonuria, hepatolenticular degeneration, porphyria, galactosemia, glucogenosis, and hypoglycemosis).

Associated with Gross Brain Disease, postnatal (neurofibromatosis, trigeminal cerebral angiomatosis, tuberous sclerosis, encephalopathy associated with diffuse sclerosis of the brain).

Associated with Diseases and Conditions Due to Unknown Prenatal Influence (anencephaly, malformations of the gyri, congenital porencephaly, multiple congenital anomalies of the brain, craniostenosis, congenital hydrocephalus, hypertelorism, macrocephaly, primary microcephaly, and Laurence-Moon-Biedl syndrome).

Associated with Chromosomal Abnormality.

Associated with Prematurity.

After Major Psychiatric Disorder.

Associated with Psychosocial Factors (environmental deprivation).

II. Organic Brain Syndromes—disorders characterized by impairment of brain tissue function and resulting in impairment of orientation, memory, intellectual functions, and judgment and in shallow affects (the acute form is reversible; the chronic form is permanent).

A. Psychoses Associated with Organic Brain Syndromes:

Senile Dementia—occurs with senile brain disease in old people; manifested by self-centeredness, childish emotionality, difficulty in assimilating new experiences, and deterioration—sometimes to the point of vegetative existence.

Presenile Dementia—covers cortical brain diseases similar to senile dementia but occurring in younger people; examples include Alzheimer's and Pick's diseases.

Delirium Tremens—acute brain syndrome caused by alcohol poisoning and characterized by delirium, visual hallucinations, and coarse tremors.

Korsakov's Psychosis—(alcoholic) chronic brain syndrome caused by long-time alcohol poisoning and characterized by confabulation, memory impairment, disorientation, and peripheral neuropathy.

Other Alcoholic Hallucinosis—hallucinosis caused by alcohol but not categorized as delirium tremens, alcoholic deterioration, or Korsakov's psychosis. The patient may have threatening auditory hallucinations, while his sensorium is relatively clear.

Alcohol Paranoid State—paranoid state in chronic alcoholics characterized by excessive jealousy and delusions of the spouse's infidelity.

Acute Alcohol Intoxication—covers acute brain syndromes caused by alcohol and of psychotic proportion but not categorized as delirium tremens, acute hallucinosis, or pathological intoxication.

Alcoholic Deterioration—covers chronic brain syndromes caused by alcohol and of psychotic proportion but not categorized as Korsakov's psychosis.

Pathological Intoxication—acute brain syndrome of psychotic proportion after a small intake of alcohol.

Psychosis Associated with Intracranial Infection, General Paralysis—psychosis characterized by signs and symptoms of parenchymatous syphilis of the nervous system and usually by positive serology.

Table 3—Continued

Psychosis with Other Syphilis of Central Nervous System—covers all other psychoses caused by intracranial infection by *Spirochaeta pallida*.

Psychosis with Epidemic Encephalitis (von Economo's Encephalitis)—disorder caused by post-World War I viral epidemic encephalitis.

Psychosis with Other and Unspecified Encephalitis—includes disorders caused by encephalitic infections other than epidemic encephalitis and encephalitis not otherwise specified.

Psychosis with Other and Unspecified Intracranial Infection—covers acute and chronic conditions caused by nonsyphilitis and nonencephalitic infections, including meningitis and brain abscess.

Psychosis with Cerebral Arteriosclerosis—chronic disorder caused by cerebral arteriosclerosis; it may coexist with senile dementia or presenile dementia.

Psychosis with Other Cerebrovascular Circulatory Disturbance—disturbances such as cerebral thrombosis, cerebral embolism, arterial hypertension, cardiac disease, and cardiorenal disease.

Psychosis with Epilepsy—condition associated with idiopathic epilepsy; the patient's consciousness may be clouded or he may be dazed, confused, bewildered, and anxious; on occasion he may have an episode of excitement, hallucinations, fears, and violent outbreaks.

Psychosis with Intracranial Neoplasm—includes primary and metastatic neoplasms.

Psychosis with Degenerative Disease of the Central Nervous System.

Psychosis with Brain Trauma—covers posttraumatic chronic brain disorders and disorders that develop immediately after a severe head injury or brain surgery and that produce significant changes in sensorium and affect.

Psychosis with Endocrine Disorder—covers disorders caused by complications of diabetes and by disorders of the endocrine glands.

Psychosis with Metabolic or Nutritional Disorder—covers disorders caused by pellagra, avitaminosis, and metabolic disorders.

Psychosis with Systemic Infection—covers disorders caused by such severe general systemic infections as pneumonia, acute rheumatic fever, typhoid fever, and malaria.

Psychosis with Drug or Poison Intoxication (other than alcohol)—covers disorders caused by drugs such as psychedelic drugs and by hormones, gases, heavy metals, and other intoxicants except alcohol.

Psychosis with Childbirth—not used unless all other possible diagnoses have been eliminated.

Psychosis with Other and Undiagnosed Physical Condition—covers psychoses caused by physical conditions not already listed and brain syndromes caused by physical conditions not yet diagnosed.

B. Nonpsychotic Organic Brain Syndromes—children with mild brain damage often show hyperactivity, short attention span, easy distractibility, and impulsiveness; they are sometimes withdrawn, listless, perseverative, and unresponsive; a few have difficulty in initiating action. Subcategories include nonpsychotic organic brain syndromes with intracranial infection; with drug, poison, or systemic intoxication; with brain trauma; with circulatory disturbance; with epilepsy; with disturbance of metabolism, growth, or nutrition; with senile or presenile brain disease; with intracranial neoplasm; and with degenerative disease of central nervous system.

III. Psychoses Not Attributed to Physical Conditions Listed Previously:

A. Schizophrenia—covers disorders manifested by disturbances of thinking (alterations of concept formation that may lead to misinterpretation of reality and sometimes to delusions and hallucinations), mood (ambivalent, constricted, and inappropriate responsiveness and loss of empathy with others), and behavior (withdrawn, regressive, and bizarre).

Simple Type—schizophrenia characterized by slow reduction of external attachment and interests, by apathy and indifference, by impoverishment of interpersonal relations, by mental deterioration, and by a low level of functioning.

Hebephrenic Type—schizophrenia characterized by disorganized thinking, unpredictable giggling, shallow and inappropriate affect, silly and regressive behavior and mannerisms, frequent hypochrondriacal complaints, and, occasionally, transient and unorganized delusions and hallucinations.

Catatonic Type—the excited subtype is characterized by excessive and sometimes violent motor activity; the withdrawn subtype is characterized by generalized inhibition—stupor, mutism, negativism, waxy flexibility, or, in some cases, a vegetative state.

Paranoid Type—schizophrenia characterized by persecutory or grandiose delusions and sometimes by hallucinations or excessive religiosity; the patient is often hostile and aggressive.

Table 3—Continued

Acute Schizophrenic Episode—condition characterized by acute onset of schizophrenic symptoms and confusion, emotional turmoil, perplexity, ideas of reference, dreamlike dissociation, excitement, depression, or fear.

Latent Type—schizophrenia characterized by clear symptoms but no history of a psychotic schizophrenic episode; sometimes called incipient, prepsychotic, pseudoneurotic, pseudopsychopathic, or borderline schizophrenia.

Residual Type—covers patients with signs of schizophrenia after a psychotic schizophrenic episode but who are no longer psychotic.

Schizo-affective Type—covers patients with a mixture of schizophrenic symptoms and pronounced elation (excited subtype) or depression (depression subtypes).

Childhood Type—schizophrenia that appears before puberty. It is characterized by autistic, atypical, and withdrawn behavior; failure to develop identity separate from the mother's; and general unevenness, gross immaturity, and inadequacy in development.

Chronic Undifferentiated Type—schizophrenia with mixed symptoms or with definite schizophrenic thought, affect, and behavior not categorized elsewhere.

Other and Unspecified Types—schizophrenia not previously described.

B. Major Affective Disorders—psychoses characterized by a single disorder of mood—extreme depression or elation—that dominates the patient's mental life and is responsible for loss of contact with his environment but that is not precipitated by any life experience.

Involutional Melancholia—psychosis occurring during the involutional period and characterized by anxiety, agitation, worry, and severe insomnia and frequently by somatic preoccupations and feelings of guilt.

Manic-Depressive Illnesses—psychoses marked by severe mood swings and by remission and recurrence.

Manic Type—manic-depressive illness that consists of manic episodes only—excessive elation, talkativeness, irritability, flights of ideas, and accelerated motor activity and speech.

Depressive Type—manic-depressive illness that consists of depressive episodes only—severely depressed mood, mental and motor retardation, and sometimes apprehension, uneasiness, perplexity, agitation, illusions, hallucinations, and delusions of guilt.

Circular Type—manic-depressive illness characterized by at least one attack of a depressive episode and of a manic episode.

Other Major Affective Disorder—psychosis with no more specific diagnosis or mixed manic-depressive illness, in which manic and depressive symptoms appear almost simultaneously.

C. Paranoid States—psychotic disorders in which a persecutory or grandiose delusion is the essential abnormality.

Paranoia—a rare condition characterized by gradual development of an elaborate paranoid system based on an actual event; the patient often considers himself unique and superior; the chronic condition rarely interferes with his thinking and personality.

Involutional Paranoid State—paranoid psychosis characterized by delusional formation in the involutional period.

Other Paranoid State—covers paranoid psychotic reactions not previously classified.

D. Psychotic Depressive Reaction—psychosis characterized by a depressive mood caused by a real experience but with no history of repeated depressions or mood swings.

IV. Neuroses—disorders characterized by anxiety but not by gross personality disorganization or gross distortion or misinterpretation of external reality.

Anxiety Neurosis—neurosis characterized by anxious overconcern to the point of panic; often associated with somatic symptoms.

Hysterical Neurosis—neurosis characterized by involuntary psychogenic loss or functional disorder; symptoms begin and end suddenly in emotionally charged situations symbolic of underlying conflict.

Conversion Type—hysterical neurosis in which the special senses or voluntary nervous system is affected, causing blindness, deafness, anosmia, anesthesias, paresthesias, paralyses, ataxias, akinesias, or dyskinesias; the patient often shows inappropriate lack of concern and may derive some benefits from his symptoms.

Dissociative Type—hysterical neuroses in which alterations in the patient's state of consciousness or his identity produce amnesia, somnambulism, fugue, or multiple personality.

Table 3—Continued

Phobic Neurosis—neurosis characterized by intense fear of an object or situation that the patient knows is no real danger to him but that causes faintness, palpitations, perspiration, nausea, fatigue, tremor, and panic?

Obsessive-Compulsive Neurosis—neurosis characterized by the involuntary and persistent intrusion of thought, urges, or actions and often accompanied by anxiety and distress.

Depressive Neurosis—neurosis marked by excessive depression caused by an internal conflict or an identifiable event or loss.

Neurasthenic Neurosis—neurosis characterized by complaints of chronic weakness, easy fatigability, and exhaustion, which distress the patient.

Depersonalization Neurosis—syndrome characterized by a feeling of unreality and estrangement from the body, self, or surroundings.

Hypochondriacal Neurosis—condition marked by preoccupation with the body and persistent fears of presumed disease.

Other Neurosis—covers psychoneurotic disorders not classified previously.

   V. Personality Disorders and Certain Other Nonpsychotic Mental Disorders:

   A. Personality Disorders—disorders characterized by deeply ingrained, generally life-long maladaptive patterns of behavior that are usually recognizable by adolescence or earlier.

Paranoid Personality—behavioral pattern characterized by unwarranted suspicion, hypersensitivity, jealousy, envy, rigidity, excessive self-importance, and a tendency to blame and ascribe evil motives to others—symptoms that often interfere with ability to maintain satisfactory interpersonal relations.

Cyclothymic Personality—behavior pattern characterized by recurring and alternating periods of elation (marked by optimism, ambition, high energy, warmth, and enthusiasm) and depression (marked by pessimism, low energy, worry, and a sense of futility)—moods that are not attributable to external circumstances.

Schizoid Personality—behavior pattern characterized by shyness, oversensitivity, seclusiveness, avoidance of close or competitive relationships, and eccentricity and sometimes by autistic thinking without loss of capacity to recognize reality, by daydreaming, and by inability to express hostility and aggression.

Explosive Personality—behavior pattern characterized by sudden, gross outbursts of aggressiveness or rage that differ strikingly from the patient's usual behavior.

Obsessive-Compulsive Personality—behavior pattern characterized by excessive concern with conformity and standards of conscience; patient may be rigid, overconscientious, overdutiful, overinhibited, and unable to relax.

Hysterical Personality—behavior pattern characterized by emotional instability, excitability, overreactivity, vanity, immaturity, dependence, and self-dramatization that is attention-seeking and seductive.

Asthenic Personality—behavior pattern characterized by low energy, easy fatigability, lack of enthusiasm, inability to enjoy life, and oversensitivity to stress.

Antisocial Personality—covers unsocialized persons in conflict with society—persons who are incapable of loyalty, selfish, callous, irresponsible, impulsive, unable to feel guilt or learn from experience, with a low level of frustration tolerance and a tendency to blame others.

Passive-Aggressive Personality—behavior pattern characterized by both passivity and aggressiveness, which is often expressed passively in obstructionism, pouting, procrastination, inefficiency, and stubbornness.

Inadequate Personality—behavior pattern characterized by ineffectual responses to demands—by ineptness, poor judgment, social instability, inadapatbility, and lack of stamina.

Other Personality Disorders of Specified Types.

   B. Sexual Deviations—covers persons whose sexual interests are primarily directed toward objects other than people of the opposite sex, toward sexual acts not usually associated with coitus, or toward coitus performed under bizarre circumstances. Included are such deviations as homosexuality, fetishism, pedophilia, transvestitism, exhibitionism, voyeurism, sadism, and masochism.

   C. Alcoholism—covers patients whose alcohol intake damages their physical health or personal or social functioning and those to whom alcohol is essential.

Table 3—Continued

Episodic Excessive Drinking—condition when alcoholism is present and person becomes intoxicated at least four times a year.

Habitual Excessive Drinking—condition when alcoholic becomes intoxicated (impaired speech, co-ordination, or behavior) more than 12 times a year or is recognizably under the influence of alcohol more than once a week, though not intoxicated.

Alcohol Addiction—condition when patient is dependent on alcohol—suffers withdrawal symptoms.

D. Drug Dependence—covers patients addicted to or dependent on drugs other than alcohol, tobacco, and caffeine beverages. Patient may be dependent on opium, opium alkaloids, and their derivatives; synthetic analgesics with morphinelike effects; barbiturates; other hypnotics, sedatives, or tranquilizers; cocaine; *Cannabis sativa* (hashish and marijuana); other psychostimulants such as amphetamines; and hallucinogens.

VI. Psychophysiological Disorders—disorders characterized by physical symptoms caused by emotional factors and involving a single organ system, usually under autonomic nervous system control.

Psychophysiological Skin Disorder—covers reactions like neurodermatosis, pruritis, atopic dermatitis, and hyperhydrosis, caused by emotional factors.

Psychophysiological Musculoskeletal Disorder—covers disorders like backache, muscle cramps, myalgias, and tension headaches caused by emotional factors.

Psychophysiological Respiratory Disorder—covers disorders like bronchial asthma, hyperventilation syndromes, sighing, and hiccoughs, caused by emotional factors.

Psychophysiological Cardiovascular Disorder—covers disorders like hypertension, vascular spasms, paroxysmal tachycardia, and migraine caused by emotional factors.

Psychophysiological Hemic and Lymphatic Disorder—covers any hemic and lymphatic disturbances caused by emotional factors.

Psychophysiological Gastrointestinal Disorder—covers such disorders as peptic ulcer, constipation, chronic gastritis, ulcerative and mucous colitis, hyperacidity, pylorospasm, heartburn, and irritable colon caused by emotional factors.

Psychophysiological Genitourinary Disorder—covers such disorders as dyspareunia, impotence, and disturbances in menstruation and micturition that are caused by emotional factors.

Psychophysiological Endocrine Disorder—covers endocrine disorders caused by emotional factors.

Psychophysiological Disorder of Organ of Special Sense—covers any disturbance, except conversion reactions, in the organs of special sense that are caused by emotional factors.

VII. Special Symptoms Not Elsewhere Classified—covers psychopathologies manifested by a single specific symptom that is not the result of an organic or other mental disorder. Included are speech disturbance, specific learning disturbance, tic, other psychomotor disorder, sleep disorder, feeding disturbance, enuresis, encopresis, and cephalalgia.

VIII. Transient Situational Disturbances—temporary disorders of any severity that occur without any apparent underlying disorder and that are acute reactions to environmental stress. Disorders are classified as adjustment reaction of infancy, childhood, adolescence, adult life, or late life.

IX. Behavior Disorders of Childhood and Adolescence—disorders that are more stable, internalized, and resistant to treatment than transient situational disturbances but less so than psychoses, neuroses, and personality disorders. Characteristic symptoms include overactivity, inattentiveness, overaggressiveness, delinquency, shyness, feeling of rejection, and timidity.

Hyperkinetic Reaction of Childhood or Adolescence—disorder characterized by overactivity, restlessness, distractibility, and short attention span, especially in young children.

Withdrawing Reaction of Childhood or Adolescence—disorder characterized by shyness, timidity, seclusiveness, detachment, sensitivity, and inability to form close interpersonal relationships.

Overanxious Reaction of Childhood or Adolescence—disorder characterized by chronic anxiety, sleeplessness, nightmares, excessive and unrealistic fears, and exaggerated autonomic responses. The patient is usually immature, self-conscious, conforming, inhibited, dutiful, lacking in self-confidence, approval seeking, and apprehensive in new situations and places.

Runaway Reaction of Childhood or Adolescence—covers patients who characteristically run away from home for a day or more to escape threatening situations, who steal furtively, who are immature and timid, and who feel rejected at home, friendless, and inadequate.

Table 3—Continued

Unsocialized Aggressive Reaction of Childhood or Adolescence—disorder characterized by hostile disobedience, aggressiveness, quarrelsomeness, vengefulness, destructiveness, temper tantrums, solitary stealing, lying, and hostile teasing of other children. The patients usually have no consistent parental discipline or acceptance.

Group Delinquent Reaction of Childhood or Adolescence—covers patients, usually boys, who accept the values, behavior, and skills of their gang, with whom they steal, skip school, and stay out late at night.

Other Reaction of Childhood or Adolescence—covers children and adolescents with disorders not previously categorized.

X. Conditions without Manifest Psychiatric Disorder and Nonspecific Conditions:

A. Social Maladjustments without Manifest Psychiatric Disorder—covers persons who are psychiatrically normal but who have severe problems.

Marital Maladjustment—covers normal persons with significant conflicts in marriage.

Social Maladjustment—covers culture shocks and conflicts caused by loyalties to two cultures.

Occupational Maladjustment—covers normal persons who are grossly maladjusted in their work.

Dyssocial Behavior—covers persons who follow criminal pursuits but are not categorized as antisocial personalities.

B. Nonspecific Conditions—covers conditions not classified under any other category.

* This table is based on the American Psychiatric Association's *Diagnostic and Statistical Manual of Mental Disorders*, second edition (DSM-II).

REFERENCES

American Psychiatric Association. *Diagnostic and Statistical Manual of Mental Disorders*, ed. 2 (DSM-II). American Psychiatric Association, Washington, 1968.

Blum, R. H. *The Management of the Doctor-Patient Relationship.* McGraw-Hill, New York, 1960.

Deutsch, F., and Murphy, W. F. *The Clinical Interview*, vol. 1. International Universities Press, New York, 1955.

Finesinger, J. E. Psychiatric interviewing: principles and procedure in insight therapy. Amer. J. Psychiat., *105:* 187, 1948.

Freedman, A. M., and Kaplan, H. I., editors. *Comprehensive Textbook of Psychiatry.* Williams & Wilkins, Baltimore, 1967.

Freud, S. The dynamics of the transference. In *Collected Papers*, vol. 2, p. 312. Hogarth Press, London, 1946.

Freud, S. Fragment of an analysis of a case of hysteria. In *Collected Papers*, vol. 3, p. 13. Hogarth Press, London, 1946.

Gill, M., Newman, R., and Redlich, F. C. *The Initial Interview in Psychiatric Practice.* International Universities Press, New York, 1954.

Lewin, B. D. Counter-transference in the technique of medical practice. Psychosom. Med., *8:* 195, 1946.

Lewis, N. D. C. *Outlines for Psychiatric Examination*, ed. 3. State Hospitals Press, Utica, N. Y., 1943.

Menninger, K. *A Manual for Psychiatric Case Study.* Grune & Stratton, New York, 1952.

Ripley, H. Psychiatric interview. In *Comprehensive Textbook of Psychiatry*, p. 491, A. M. Freedman and H. I. Kaplan, editors. Williams & Wilkins, Baltimore, 1967.

Rogers, C. R. *Client-Centered Therapy.* Houghton Mifflin, Boston, 1951.

Sullivan, H. S. *The Psychiatric Interview.* W. W. Norton, New York, 1954.

Whitehorn, J. C. Guide to interviewing and clinical personality study. Arch. Neurol. Psychiat., *52:* 197, 1944.

2

Group Therapy with Homosexuals

Toby B. Bieber, Ph.D.

HISTORY

The first paper on the treatment of homosexuality was a report by Schrenck-Notzing (1892) who used hypnosis on 70 male patients. The hypnotic suggestion consisted of commanding the patient to suppress perverse practices and ideas, to think of perversion as repulsive, and to think of heterosexual objects as attractive. This mode of treatment, seemingly a forerunner of modern behavioral therapy, was reported to achieve 37.5 per cent cures and another 34 per cent improvement. The criterion of cure was the patient's ability to have heterosexual intercourse.

With the eclipse of hypnosis by psychoanalysis, optimistic reports of treatment of homosexuality all but disappeared for half a century. The psychoanalytic literature of that epoch turns up occasional papers on successful outcome, but the dominant note is pessimistic. In two statements Freud's message was bleak. He notes, in *A Case of Homosexuality in a Woman* (1920):

In general, to undertake to convert a fully developed homosexual into a heterosexual does not offer much more prospect of success than the reverse, except that for good practical reasons the latter is never attempted. The number of successes achieved by psychoanalytic treatment of the various forms of homosexuality, which incidentally are manifold, is indeed not very striking.

The patient, however, had not acted out her homosexuality. Freud, in fact, never treated an active lesbian.

The second statement by Freud (1951) appears in a letter to the mother of a homosexual written as late as 1935:

In a certain number of cases, we succeed in developing the blighted germs of heterosexual tendencies which are present in every homosexual. In the majority of cases it is no longer possible. What analysis can do for your son runs in a different line. If he is unhappy, neurotic, torn by conflicts, inhibited in his social life, analysis may bring him harmony, peace of mind, full efficiency whether he remains homosexual or gets changed.

A change in the rather dreary analytic view toward homosexuality was heralded by Bergler (1944) in a paper read in 1942 in which he stated:

It is worth noting . . . the general though misconceived therapeutic pessimism as to the curability of homosexuality. . . .

The real breakthrough, however, occurred in the 1950's with the publication of several volumes by him and papers by others dealing with the effectiveness of dynamic therapy in reversing homosexuality. In the preface of *1000 Homosexuals* (1959), Bergler declared:

I am reaffirming my conclusion based on actual clinical cases that homosexuality, if treated appropriately, has an excellent prognosis and *is* curable in the short period of eight months in psychiatric-psychoanalytic treatment.

Ellis (1956) also supported an optimistic prognosis and found, as had Bergler, that a favorable outcome was associated with motivation for change but that homosexuals who remained in treatment for an extended period of time were more likely to change, especially if they were young. Rubinstein (1958–1959), working in England, differentiated between two etiological constellations—psychopathology associated with the pre-oedipal stage and psychopathology associated with the oedipal phase. He found that homosexuals whose difficulties were rooted in the later oedipal era had a better prognosis. Starting in about 1955, Hadden (1958) organized the first homogeneous homosexual group. Of the three initial participants, two became increasingly oriented toward heterosexuality.

The 1960's saw a steep rise in clinical interest. Bieber et al. (1962) published the findings of a long-term clinical-statistical investigation of 106 male homosexuals compared with 100 male heterosexuals distributed in treatment among 77 analysts. The study highlighted etiological and psychodynamic features, and a survey of treatment results showed a successful shift to heterosexuality in one-third of the cases. The favorable prognostic indicators were: (1) the patient was bisexual at the beginning of treatment; (2) analysis was started before the age of 35; (3) the analysis was continued for at least 150 hours and preferably 350 hours or more; (4) there was motivation for change; (5) the patient's father was not detached and at least at times communicated positive feelings; (6) heterosexual genital intercourse had been attempted at some time in the patient's life; and (7) manifest dream content depicted erotic heterosexual activity.

Since this study, publications on homosexual patients in series have appeared, reporting as high as a 50 per cent rate of reversal, as in the investigation of lesbians by Kaye et al. (1967). Now that the successful treatment of homosexuality has been established and generally accepted, pessimistic therapeutic attitudes are rapidly on the wane, promoting optimism among homosexuals as well as among therapists.

A concatenation of circumstances has greatly increased the numbers of homosexuals seeking psychotherapy. Less than ten years ago, inversion could be discussed openly only in scientific publications, not in the mass media, where it was practically taboo. With the rapid development of a freer sociosexual climate, homosexuality can now be written about in lay publications, talked about over the radio, and seen and discussed on television and in movies; thus, there are various opportunities to disseminate the information that homosexuality has a 30 to 50 per cent chance of reversing with psychiatric treatment. More sophisticated understanding of the dynamics of homosexuality and the development of newer treatment techniques, notably group therapy, now offer realistic therapeutic possibilities.

THEORIES OF TREATMENT
Heterogeneous vs. Homogeneous Groups

The literature on homosexuals in group therapy is not yet extensive. A central question that has emerged concerns whether homosexuals should be treated in mixed or homogeneous groups. As long as therapy groups were conducted in institutional settings, the problem of group homogeneity vs. heterogeneity was not very pressing. In a sense, all patients in psychiatric hospitals formed, by virtue of their hospitalization, a homogeneous group. Therapists had a wide selection of patients within that general category to choose from, and they could mix or match patients by diagnosis, length of illness, age, sex, color, and so forth.

When group therapy came of age in private practice, it became difficult to put together groups to fulfill this or that criterion, since a large enough patient pool was seldom available. It became expedient to explore the effects of diversity on the group. Thus, when homosexuals began to be treated in groups, they were assigned to mixed groups. Some of the early reports were negative. Powdermaker and Frank (1953) found that the introduction of a homosexual patient seemed to create a degree of diversity the group could not tolerate or that the patient himself developed such guilt and anxiety about discussing his pathology with heterosexuals that he had to drop out.

Hadden, who has had the most extensive experience in treating homosexuals in groups, has opted for the homogeneous group. He found that in mixed groups the hostility directed by the heterosexuals toward the homosexuals caused too many of the latter to drop out.

He has reported (1966) that, of 32 homosexual patients he treated in homogeneous group therapy, 12 became exclusively heterosexual and others appeared to be moving in that direction. The groups were open-ended, met once weekly for one and a half hours, and ranged in size from four to eight members. In 1966, these groups had been meeting for several years, one group for ten years.

The therapy is dynamically oriented. Emphasis is placed on dream analysis and on the feelings and fantasies associated with current sexual behavior, which, in turn, is related to early life experience. Prior to joining the group, patients are seen individually a number of times, detailed histories are obtained, and the patient is oriented about his inversion. He is told that homosexuality is a product of adverse life experiences and that the barriers to his heterosexuality are to be found in the experiences and fantasies of childhood. Although a shift in sexual adaptation is not promised, it is made an explicit goal of therapy. Hadden emphasizes the value of the group in breaking down rationalizations about the normalcy and desirability of homosexuality and in extinguishing effeminate attitudes and behavior. He notes the tonic effect on an entire group when a single member makes progress and the support that member is given by the group for his progress.

Slavson (1964) also takes exception to treating homosexuals in mixed groups, although his reasons are somewhat different. In his view the homosexual patient provokes too much anxiety in the heterosexual members and is, on the whole, disruptive to the group process.

Some therapists, however, not only find that the heterogeneous group is a valid therapeutic technique, but they may even prefer the challenge of diversity over homogeneity. Kadis et al. (1963), Litman (1961), and Stone et al. (1966) report positive results and find it advantageous to include homosexuals in their groups. Fried (1955) emphasizes that the mixed group encourages assertiveness among its homosexual members. Mintz (1966) finds that the mixed group helps eliminate ideas of homosexual superiority and normalcy, that it favors the development of stronger masculine identity, and that the precipitation of anxiety about heterosexuality offers the possibility for a corrective emotional experience.

Male and Female Therapists

A modification of homogeneous group technique has been described by Singer and Fischer (1967), who acted as co-therapists. Initially, the group had two male therapists. When a woman replaced one of them, the sparks began to fly. The members accused her of being controlling, attacking, condescending, devouring, and insatiable, yet verbally she participated very little. One can infer from the data that the group recovered from heterosexual shock after a few months. They then settled down to an attack on the male therapist in the classical design of rivalry. The members allied with the female therapist, tried to win her favor and competed with each other for her. Although male-female co-therapists are not novel in group or individual therapy, this is the first report of such treatment with homosexual patients.

Several other male-female teams are now treating homosexual groups. According to anecdotal descriptions, not only are oedipal responses more easily facilitated, but the patients respond favorably to the opportunity to move from one therapist to the other. Thus, if a member develops serious resistances toward the male therapist, this intensifies a relatedness with the female therapist, and the flow of the treatment process continues, particularly if occasional or regular individual sessions are scheduled.

Orientations

The treatment of homosexuals has been approached from three main orientations:

(1) Above and beyond the inversion, the patients' problems and difficulties are seen as human ones shared by other neurotic sufferers. Therefore, one treats the homosexual, not his homosexuality, which may reverse as his personality sheds neurotic disabilities. (2) The homosexual adaptation is the psychopathological nucleus, which serves to generate even more problems. Therefore, the inversion itself must serve as the central focus of treatment. (3) Homosexuality is not, simplistically, a symptom on the surface of personality organization comparable, say, to a writing block in a previously productive writer. The psychopathology of homosexuality broadly pervades the personality. And there is no demarcation between the individual and his problems. Each of these themes will become discernible as the chapter develops, since each has application relative to the on-going therapeutic context.

The goal of all reconstructive therapy is to resolve as much of the patient's psychopathology as possible, though therapeutic procedures may vary from psychoanalysis, psychoanalytically oriented psychotherapy, and psychotherapy in groups to a combination of group and individual therapy. The practice of the present writer has consisted of using combined therapy for those patients, homosexual or heterosexual, for whom a group experience holds promise.

Some homosexuals at the outset of treatment say they wish to change their sexual direction; others are convinced that heterosexuality is an achievement quite beyond their capacity for change; still others declare they prefer to remain as they are and wish to be helped only with symptoms of depression, work problems, and so forth. Few, if any, homosexuals are satisfied with their condition, whether or not this is consciously admitted. Those who cling to their homosexual orientation and avoid contemplating possibilities for change are, by and large, chronically depressed, although episodes of gloom and despair may be rationalized to other situations. Strident public declarations about happy homosexuality are evidence of denial mechanisms. The disruption of an affair may trigger the marked agitation

and depression that propels many into seeking psychotherapy. Previously denied bitterness and hopelessness about their situation surfaces at such times in their lives. As patients, however, they are fearful about shifting to heterosexuality for the reasons that steered them into a homosexual adaptation in the first place.

Those who begin therapy with the stated objective of maintaining a *status quo* tend especially to become quickly alerted and defensive against any analytic moves sensed as blocking homosexual prerogatives or as encouraging heterosexual behavior. Barring dangerous acting out, such as picking up potentially assaultive partners or risking arrest in public places, homosexual behavior as such must be pursued analytically only when the patient is ready to recognize the nature of its defensive usefulness and its irrationality as a psychosexual reparative attempt through psychopathological means. Homosexuals who are introduced into a group before developing sensitivity to their own psychodynamic processes and an understanding of the influences that have given rise to their difficulties run the risk of becoming therapeutic drop-outs. Groups do not respond to defensive cues and reparative maneuvers as do trained therapists. A group may disturb a patient whose denial mechanisms leave him unprepared to withstand the distress that may accompany the group's attack against his emotionally charged defenses.

CLINICAL PRACTICE

Heterogeneous Groups

Therapists whose groups are formed from their own patient roster in private practice, as pointed out earlier, are usually restricted in the selection of members for their groups. Most mix homosexual and heterosexual patients, male and female. Heterogeneous groups usually consist of about eight people. It is an advantage to increase the membership by one or two patients when homosexuals join a group.

In order to minimize their sense of difference, where possible, two homosexuals rather than one should be included in the mixed group, which tends to have stress points for the single homosexual member. When such a patient enters a mixed group, he is usually preoccupied with self-doubt and anxiety about acceptability as a homosexual. The recognition that heterosexual members, too, have difficulties does not diminish the initial concern and fear of rejection by the group. The presence of a familiar and trusted analyst is helpful, but the patient must still face the group as a homosexual, a condition he may wish to hide at first. When a group member reveals that he is homosexual, the others invariably accept this new information with equanimity. They almost always accept homosexuals as individuals but they tend not to accept the inversion itself.

Revealing Sexual Practices. In individual treatment, most homosexuals are reluctant to discuss the details of their sexual practices, but the resistances are pursued analytically. In a group, the withholding of details of homosexual practices is even more apparent. The other members, in turn, usually refrain from inquiring into these matters. In fact, on one occasion, when a young homosexual started to describe his experiences at an orgy, he was accused, not inaccurately, of being an exhibitionist. The one member who showed an avid interest was a woman whose obsessiveness about her sexuality was part of her symptomatology. By his attempted revelations the homosexual member stirred up fantasies, homosexual problems, and anxieties in several other members, thus setting the theme for their individual sessions in the weeks that followed.

Heterosexual group members also omit intimate details of their sexual practices, but they generally discuss at length their fears about sexual inadequacy and their relationships with the opposite sex. Homosexuals, in contrast, tend to be reticent even about their partners. After they have told of their inversion, for the most part, they refer to it thereafter in generalities.

Reconstructive psychotherapy enables patients to come to grips with their irrational belief systems. Much of this work is accomplished in individual sessions through analysis of dreams and free associations; similar goals may be facilitated through the interactive processes of the group. The flow of responses arising in a group setting offers patients the opportunity to observe neurotic reactions in themselves and others with a vividness that does not emerge as concretely through the analysis of transference nor through the reportage of the dyadic sessions.

Competition within the Group. The recognition of competitiveness felt by homosexuals toward other men cannot easily be resisted and rationalized in a group. During many a sequence when a female member has shown sexual or affectional interest in a male member, jealousy has been expressed not only by heterosexual members but by homosexuals as well. The heterosexuals, however, tend to regard man-to-man sexual rivalry as masculine, and as a rule they respond in constructive ways to a homosexual who is being heterosexually rivalrous. When a deviate member has a modal response—albeit neurotic, as in the example cited, which has its roots in unresolved oedipal and sibling conflicts—the other males readily accept it. The effect is that of strengthening masculine bonds, minimizing guilt, and promoting fraternal feelings. It also lowers the entire group's anxiety and inhibition about achieving individual heterosexual goals.

Such sequences enable the homosexual patient to see for himself that revealed competition for a female does not arouse murderous jealousy and retaliative aggression in heterosexual males, a core fear that helps preserve a homosexual adaptation. He also learns that, should some men become sexually competitive, it in no way constitutes a clear and present danger. When homosexuals start to make inroads into heterosexuality, group support and encouragement ease the anxiety about initial attempts. Since constructive intragroup sexual attitudes have highly positive effects, patients should be excluded whose difficulties tend to be expressed in obsessive and chronic self-absorption or in intractable hostility and competitiveness.

Reactions to Women. Homosexuals differ, as do all individuals. Some, like the bisexuals, may be potent with women; others avoid making heterosexual attempts, in part because of fears about being impotent. Some know full well that women find them attractive, but many, despite their good looks, feel themselves to be sexually unacceptable and undesirable.

Women in a group sometimes express wishes for sexual gratification and speak of their feelings of frustration accompanying sexual deprivation. This may come as a surprise to the homosexual patients, many of whom believe that women are sexually undesirous and disinterested. After a discussion by women members along these lines, one patient became encouraged enough to make sexual advances to a woman he knew. He had not been able to tolerate, hence risk, sexual rejection by a woman. This type of vulnerability is commonly observed and often appears to be more painfully felt than sexual rejection by other homosexuals.

The apprehension and dread of sexual rejection by women are, however, eclipsed by fears related to sexual *acceptance*. During a session one evening, a female patient revealed that she was sexually attracted to a homosexual member. He became very anxious and indicated confusion and embarrassment. When this type of sequence occurs in a seasoned group that is working well together, several other members will usually perceive the meaning of such anxiety responses and will point it out, while forming a phalanx of reassurance and support, as happened in this instance. If the therapist's style encourages humor, then laughter, wit, and banter will rise up on frequent occasions and will soften tension-laden situations.

Other Benefits of Group. Groups offer homosexuals a corrective emotional experience on nonverbal levels as well by virtue of the intimate intermember contact over time. Participation in a therapeutic, heterosexual milieu helps prepare homosexual patients who suffer from feelings of unacceptability, alienation, and guilt for more relaxed participation in other "straight" groups.

Further, the opportunity is provided for observing the analyst's impartial behavior in the group and for correcting distorted perceptions of partiality. This often brings to the surface the wish to be special and favored, a dynamic reminiscent of the overclose, inappropriately intimate mother-son bond so often in the background. Through the continuous feedback between the individual and the group sessions, the homosexual patient learns that, as one of a group and without an exclusive relationship, he can still be valued and respected and have access to the analyst's affectional feelings, thus highlighting the irrelevancy and irrationality of preference strivings.

Transference. The problem of transference is a central one. This subject has been given detailed attention in the literature. Several workers have pointed out that transference varies with the personality and sex of the therapist.

In the experience of this writer, homosexual patients form various types of transferences with a female therapist. Younger men usually develop a mother-son transference. Older homosexuals, however, sometimes relate as to a fantasied love object. Not infrequently, they reveal a feeling of pride that at least their therapist is a woman. Within the safety of the professional relationship, a heterosexual attachment is made that has importance as a role-playing experience and as an attitude-testing situation. One very important parameter concerns the analyst's sexual acceptance. In various ways, attempts are made to elicit positive answers to the nonverbal question, is my masculine sexuality acceptable to you?

Homosexuals who are deeply distrustful of women or who assiduously avoid heterosexual arousal invariably choose a male therapist. Others require actual interaction with a male therapist by virtue of unfulfilled needs for masculine identification and support. But when the therapist is a female—and many homosexuals who become patients seem to prefer a woman analyst, though most do not openly admit to it—the needed interaction with other men is acquired by participating in a group.

Homogeneous Groups

A sufficient number of homosexual male patients have presented themselves to the writer for psychoanalytic therapy to permit the organization of an open-ended, continuous group consisting entirely of male homosexuals. Many fewer lesbians have requested therapy. Only one was treated in a mixed group, but by the time she joined, after individual analysis, she was no longer homosexual. As mentioned earlier, patients are invited to join a group after a sufficient period of individual therapy, during which time at least the outlines of basic pathological constellations and major defensive systems are worked out. If the patient has had previous therapy, this may take a few sessions; if it is an initial analytic experience, it may take six months to a year or more.

Fewer than four members restrict active, variegated group development and interaction; more than eight members create overcrowding on the one hand and too diffuse an emotional atmosphere on the other. Compatibility in intellectual development favors group cohesion and communication, and patients should be chosen with this variable in mind. Limitations on age range are not as important as in heterosexual groups, seemingly because homosexuals resemble each other more closely than do other patients. Conformities in family relationships, psychodynamic trends, and, in many cases, a social accommodation to younger-older man homosexual pairings create a commonality of experience that tends to neutralize the dissonances one often observes in heterosexual groups when there are significantly disparate differences in age. As in heterosexual groups, the members do not socialize outside the therapeutic chamber, nor are alternate sessions held. Erotic response to a co-member is rare; homosexual acting out outside the group never occurs.

Advantages. In this writer's experience, a homogeneous group for homosexuals offers many therapeutic advantages. It is considered here to be the method of choice. Patients have been less resistive about joining a group composed of other homosexuals, where they are less guarded and where they open up more quickly. Since they are more comfortable in each other's presence, they seem able to concentrate on their problems and to verbalize them more effectively. In the

individual sessions, prolonged resistances and repression of heterosexual feelings have been noted while, in a heterogeneous group, women members may elicit sexual responses. The latter development is all to the good, but it nonetheless allows the homosexual patient to continue to repress sexual content concerning his female analyst. The homogeneous group heightens the potency of her feminine impact; it facilitates affectivity; it lowers resistances against expressions of heterosexual strivings, particularly as it concerns a mother figure, a transferential development that occurs quite commonly.

In the homosexual way of life, a woman may become a central figure within a group's social system, though she may be scathingly referred to as a "fag hag." She usually plays a mother role, and there is competition for her favors and her protection. A woman analyst may, therefore, have misgivings that such a situation will develop in an all-homosexual therapy group. Well-timed analysis of transference and caution about countertransference reactions preclude such developments.

Profound anxiety, guilt, and fears of retaliation about incestuous feelings have central importance in the homosexual adaptation. After witnessing expressions of oedipal responses, group members cannot easily avoid participating in the working through of nuclear psychodynamics.

THE HOMOSEXUAL SYNDROME

A summary review of the homosexual syndrome as detailed in the study by Bieber et al. (1962) will serve to highlight the regularities with which specific etiological and developmental features occur. Each patient in the study came from a family in which interparental and child-parent relationships were pathological in characteristic ways. In about 75 per cent of the cases, the mothers had had an inappropriately close, binding, and intimate bond with their sons. More than half of these mothers were described as seductive. They were possessive, dominating, overprotective, and demasculinizing. In families where there were other children, the mother had generally favored the patient, spent much time with him, and demanded a great deal of his attention. Usually she formed an alliance with the son against the father and openly preferred son to husband. The son was often her confidant with whom she shared intimacies; in some instances, intimate details of her sexual life. Yet, she also appeared to be puritanical and frigid. She did not encourage her son's masculine attitudes and behavior; in fact, she actively discouraged it.

Most such patients grew to manhood burdened with anxiety about expressing assertiveness; many felt very uneasy in the presence of aggressive, heterosexual men. Significantly more homosexuals than heterosexuals recalled that their mothers had been overly concerned with illness and physical injury during childhood. Most had been actively discouraged from participating in gangs and prevented from joining in the strenuous scrambling activities of boyhood. Parental, but usually maternal, social snobbery often played an important role in cutting off peer group participation. Most patients described a childhood and adolescence beclouded by interference and meddling with normal pursuits, particularly those suggestive of heterosexual interest. Girls, and later women, were depicted as dangerous exploiters, not to be trusted.

The modal response to the close-binding, intimate nurturance described was that of submissiveness and a marked tendency to worry about displeasing the mother or hurting her feelings. From childhood on, most homosexuals turned to the mother for protection and sided with her in family quarrels. The mothers were almost always inadequate as wives. They usually dominated the husband, minimized him, and were openly contemptuous. The son might feel anger, rage, and disappointment toward the mother or both parents, but profound fear responses were found to be related to the father. Fear of the mother as a figure of powerful destructiveness was rarely noted.

Significantly contrasted to heterosexual patients, not one father-son relationship in the entire homosexual sample could be described as reasonably satisfactory. Of the fathers, 75 per cent were judged to be unaffectionate and detached, about half were explicitly hostile, and none was warmly related during the son's growing-up years. They spent very little time with the son who became homosexual, though they might with their other children, whom they usually preferred.

A question not infrequently asked is why, in a family of several sons, one turns out to be a homosexual while the others go on to lead heterosexual lives. Study of the multisibling families who produced a homosexual invariably revealed identifiable interactional patterns that differentiated the relationships between parents and children. The pathological elements for the homosexual were specifically sexually linked and sexually established. The mother chose a son (usually a younger son) and not a daughter for an overclose, overintimate relationship. The father's sexual rivalry was either overt or covert, but the message was clearly expressed within the disharmonious father-son relationship. Neither parent in the study related to daughters or other sons as each had to the patient. Outstanding was that parameter of parental behavior that traumatized, restricted, distorted, and inhibited the patient's heterosexual, masculine identification and pursuits. He was selected as victim; his siblings carried out other role assignments—father surrogate, athlete, and so forth. Though other personality and developmental systems were attacked, damage to *sexual* development and behavior was most pernicious. A theme composed of sexual prohibition, restriction, punishment, and demasculinization flowed from one direction; from the other, there was a ubiquity of maternal sexual overstimulation in an overclose clasp. It was a double bind that occurred within a triangular interactional system of oedipal fear of the father, enhanced and given a basis in reality by paternal hostility and sexual competitiveness.

Case Histories

In the five case histories that follow, the reader will note the recurring themes of lack of identification with a hostile and/or detached father and strong attachment to a

close-binding, intimate mother who undermined paternal influence in a show of open
partiality to the patient. These patients were
initially invited to join the homogeneous
group. They were to meet once a week for an
hour and a half concomitant with their individual sessions, which would continue on the
regularly established basis. The members
ranged in age from 24 to 35. Each was in a
profession or skilled craft (as was each subsequent member); each had been exclusively
homosexual before undertaking treatment;
and each had verbalized a wish to become
heterosexual.

Milton. As a child, Milton had had fleeting interests in homosexuality but considered
himself to be heterosexual. While in college,
he had an intense affair with a girl, which
resulted in her becoming pregnant. The circumstances surrounding her subsequent
abortion were fraught with the usual indig-
nities and financial pressures the young are
heir to, but the procedure was otherwise
uneventful, and the patient behaved in a
responsible way throughout. The experience,
however, had a shattering effect. He became
extremely anxious and described feelings of
depersonalization that were displaced to his
genitals. "My penis felt like a 'thing' between
my legs. It was just sort of *there*. It wasn't
part of me." Soon after, he began to act out
homosexual impulses and, before long,
drifted into a homosexual way of life, an
adaptation he has retained.

Milton's family consisted of two younger
sisters, a younger brother, and highly exploitative parents. His mother was ambitious
for him, sexually repressive, and infantilizing. She was closely attached to him and
esteemed him as intellectually much above
his detached, hostile father, a chronic "loser"
who collected pornography. Yet the patient
had always thought the parents had an active sexual life and that his mother enjoyed
it, despite protestations to him about his
father's sexual crudities. From childhood
until he left for college, where he achieved a
fine record, the patient had been pressed
into service as a nursemaid for his younger
siblings. Any money gifts from family, as on
the occasion of his bar mitzvah, became
parental property. About seven years ago, he

abandoned work on a graduate thesis, left
his home town, came to New York, got a
menial job, and found his way into treatment.

In individual therapy, the patient made
marked progress in the work area and in a
much-improved self-image. Though compulsive cruising and extraordinary promiscuity abated (once in the men's room of a
movie house he made about 20 contacts), no
heterosexual attempts were made aside from
taking a girl to a party on a date. The few
women with whom he associated were lesbians, ex-lesbians, or platonic office friends.

While he was a member of a mixed group,
Milton took the role of agreeable listener
and adviser. He seldom referred to his inversion and tended to withhold private
thoughts and feelings. Nonetheless, the
group experience helped him insofar as he
became consciously more aware of a wish to
change and of his anxiety about doing so. He
took the opportunity, when it was offered,
to transfer to the homosexual group.

Ted. Ted, the most disturbed member,
had been brought for treatment while still in
his teens by his father, who had learned of
his son's homosexuality. The father—a successful, driving, controlling man—openly
preferred his older, married son and showed
open contempt for the patient. The mother,
a compensated schizophrenic, had been close-
binding, very seductive, and demasculinizing. She identified the patient with herself in
looks and personality and the brother with
the father. All his life the patient felt extremely threatened by the domineering
brother, whom he hated. He was jealous of
him yet admired him and sought affection,
which was not given.

After four years of individual treatment,
Ted joined the mixed group, where, on the
whole, he was unpopular. The other members
did not tolerate well his tendency toward
repetition, his obsessive preoccupation with
his father and brother, his occasional childlike behavior, his self-conscious flirtatious-
ness with women members, and his flamboy-
ant homosexuality. It was agreed all around
that he leave, and he seized the opportunity
to transfer. He looked forward to joining the
homosexual group, where he felt he could be

himself and relax. He felt uneasy in the presence of heterosexuals in and out of the group situation.

Herbert. Herbert had been in sporadic individual treatment for more than three years. During that time he made one heterosexual attempt with a woman he admired and who attracted him, but he was completely impotent. Only occasionally involved in homosexual affairs, he usually chose a partner he considered to be and who, in fact, was his inferior. Sometimes an affair would last for months, but mostly he would pick up a hustler in the Times Square area. He was robbed on more than one occasion but managed to avoid physically dangerous partners. Brilliant, articulate, and witty, he had always been consciously oriented to women. During the course of therapy he began to date regularly and indulge in light petting, although he avoided a real sexual encounter. He masturbated daily, always wrapping a handkerchief around his penis to avoid direct contact. By the time he joined the group, his sexual fantasies were mostly of women, although, after stress situations, homosexual fantasies would sometimes occur. He had not acted out a homosexual impulse for more than a year and he seemed to be strengthening his heterosexual orientation through his participation in the group when, alone and somewhat depressed in Europe, he had several homosexual encounters.

In those European encounters, Herbert had not, as on other occasions, short-circuited homosexual arousal by an unusual sensory technique he had discovered. In late adolescence, when homosexual acting out began, he found he could turn off an erotic response to a male by conjuring up a sense image of the smell of a man's buttocks and anus; however, the smell of a woman, including genital odor, was sexually exciting. *Portnoy's Complaint*, he reported, turned him on during passages that described the genital smells of one of the female characters. The work of I. Bieber (1959) and, later, of Kalogerakis (1963) on olfaction provide explanatory clues. These authors emphasize the role of olfaction in sexual development, and they offer suggestive evidence that odor

is the earliest psychobiological sexual link between child and cross-sex parent, ushering in and establishing a heterosexual orientation.

Herbert had grown up feeling utter contempt for his father, a passive man and meager provider who was dominated and humiliated by the mother. She would compare him, always unfavorably, with her rich, successful brother, head man in the extended family. The father, who died during the patient's early college years, preferred his daughter. The patient was extremely attached to his sister, with whom he shared a bedroom until her marriage, when she was 23 and he was 19. He continued to be haunted by the memory of hearing his sister masturbate during the night.

The parents were Jewish, had liberal ideas, and idealized Roosevelt, yet, as a boy and up through his teens, Herbert was a secret Nazi. He was anti-Semitic, greatly admired Hitler, whom he saw as a powerful leader, and esteemed only the Gentile neighborhood boys, whom he also feared, especially the tough gang who played rough games. He was afraid to go out to play when these boys were about. Given a choice, Herbert selected the homosexual group with great enthusiasm.

George. George grew up in a small, tight community with strong pressures toward group conformity. The parental profile was most like Ted's, and the two men felt a kinship, an identification that had a salutary effect on Ted, especially since he had evoked negative reactions in the previous group. George's father was successful, controlling, castrating. He was considerably older than the seductive, narcissistic mother, who made a confidant of the patient and preferred him quite openly to her older daughter, who, in turn, was preferred by the father. As a child, George consciously hated and feared his father. As he grew up, he continued to fear him but also admired and respected him for his capabilities and effectiveness.

George had become aware of his homosexuality when he was about ten years old. He had many experiences involving mutual masturbation with peers through early adolescence and developed more sophisticated homosexual behavior as he matured, though he never had a steady partner. At an out-of-town college, he "found" himself socially; his friends were heterosexual, and he was popular with "straight guys" for the first time in his life. As a boy, his mother had dressed him too elegantly; he was polite, conforming, miserable, and filled with self-hatred and shame. In his newly found world, he dated girls, sometimes petted lightly, but would never date a girl again if she showed any inclination to have intercourse. He continued to seek occasional, furtive homosexual encounters, which would flood him with guilt afterward.

After graduation, he returned to his home city to start a career. He became depressed as he once more was drawn into a romance with his mother, into an intolerable situation of submissive helplessness with his father—who frequently, loudly, and publicly humiliated him—and into entrapment as escort to his unhappy, inept sister. A distant cousin, now dead, whom the patient thought of as "Uncle," had always shown him the affection and respect the father had not, but his mentor was no longer there to offer the needed support and encouragement. It was extremely difficult for the patient to break away, but he marshaled enough strength to do so. He left for New York, where he found employment and established himself in his own apartment, to the utter chagrin of his guilt-provoking parents.

Although the patient had obtained a position with a promising future, his fear of authority interfered with optimal performance, a situation that deepened his depression. His dissatisfaction with homosexuality, coupled with his work problems, led him to seek help. Having read an account of Hadden's work in *Harper's* magazine, George found his way into treatment with the stated purpose of joining a homosexual therapy group. Highly motivated toward change, he thought of himself with deep shame as a homosexual.

Justin. Justin, a highly intelligent, self-taught designer and artist of considerable talent, had been exclusively homosexual until the age of 31, when he entered analysis. He had lived with an older man for many years, although from time to time, he had

other casual affairs. The arrangement was terminated when the patient became involved with a man younger than himself. He entered therapy severely depressed because the liaison was deteriorating. In his initial interview he expressed disillusionment with homosexuality and shyly expressed the hope to change but wondered whether this was possible. After some months he and his homosexual partner picked up a couple of girls and spent the night with them. The partner was also in treatment by this time and was trying to shift to heterosexuality. Justin had successful intercourse; his friend did not.

Except for a single homosexual experience during a period of stress almost three years ago, the patient has remained heterosexual. He has been living for more than a year with a young woman he loves and intends soon to marry. Justin joined the group shortly after the romance began. As a heterosexual initiate, he has played a pivotal role in the group.

Justin's parental profile, in the main, conforms to the others. He had a close-binding, intimate, sexually repressive mother, but his father, now dead, was affectionate until the patient was about four. At that time, the father became detached and hostile and began to show marked preference for his older son, who would tease and torment the patient. The brothers never see each other now. There are two older sisters who were affectionate, particularly one, who, in a power struggle with the mother, took a maternal role with the patient.

The Group Process

Although the analytic work proceeded as in any other group, many clinical parameters became especially apparent in this group. These parameters were strongly concerned with motivations to change, heterosexual yearnings, fears about it, resistances toward heterosexuality, the search for masculine identity, and sexual rivalry. Another important feature concerns the polarization of response, a development more discernible in a homogeneous than in a heterogeneous group; that is, ambivalence emerged in much clearer relief in this setting. As in figure and ground perception, constructive attitudes of the members toward each other on the one hand and jealous rivalry on the other kept changing in dominance in easily delineated forms. The following sequences are illustrative:

Justin had remained silent about his heterosexual shift for the first five group sessions. This silence occurred against a background of a hostile exchange between two members in the opening sessions. Ted had greeted Milton, his previous group co-member, as an old comrade-in-arms, a display of "in" behavior that was barely acknowledged by Milton. Then, when Ted interrupted at one point with a *non sequitur* rather typical of his previous behavior, Milton put him down with an abrupt, hostile criticism of his tendency to cut in with disruptive, inconsequential remarks. Milton had never shown this type of aggression in the mixed group, where his fear of showing hostility in the presence of the heterosexual men had inhibited him. Ted was shocked into a hurt, resentful silence. He felt betrayed and cast aside in a recapitulation of the father-brother relationship. Milton's antagonism was also traced to its true source and analyzed. It had to do with his feeling that the analyst had treated Ted in a special way; that is, Ted was felt to be the pet. In a rare exposure of feelings, Milton admitted to feeling resentful toward Ted as the youngest member, a position Milton wished for himself.

The display of aggression between Milton and Ted had a repressive effect on Justin, and in going around, when the members spoke of reactions to the others or described themselves, Justin said nothing about his love affair. Five sessions later, with the help provided by his individual sessions and concomitant with a growing trust of the group, he was able to break through the resistance created by his guilt about having a woman when the others did not and his fear of envy and retaliative aggression. He was now able to reveal his current sexual status. Comments such as "Congratulations," "Gee, that's wonderful," "Why didn't you tell us before?" "It should happen to me," and so forth led to a discussion of guilt and fear of jealous, hostile attack by other males should a sexual relationship with a women be achieved.

The members were much affected, since it was the first concrete evidence to which they could respond with a conviction that heterosexual fears based upon apprehensions about retaliation from other men were, in fact, irrational. Another positive feature was that Justin's shift to heterosexuality aided in establishing a spirit of optimism and achievement in the group. It served to reassure the members that a change in sexual direction was possible, a reversal denied by the homophile publications several members had read. Moreover, the group now had a male leader who could provide them with first-hand information such as: How soon was intercourse attempted—on the first date? the second? the third? Where did they meet? What was said? Did the girl's parents know? Did Justin's family know? Is it better than homosexual sex?

The last question was, of course, the salient one. Justin told them that sex with a woman could not even be compared to homosexual sex; heterosexual sex was so much better and more satisfying. Milton, who had renounced heterosexuality in early youth, did not contradict him.

The questions and discussion opened up important dynamic material. For example, Justin told the group that, when he informed his mother over the phone that he was about to become engaged, she gasped, "Oh, no!" As he described it, "She sounded as though I just got orders to go to Viet Nam."

The recounting of this incident directed the group's attention to the parental stake in a son's homosexuality and to the recall of instances of personally experienced sexual repressiveness and parental dissatisfaction about interest shown in girls. Further, it mobilized reactions against tolerating such injustices in the future.

In ensuing sessions, intermember envy and rivalry began to emerge with greater frankness. Some responses consisted of transferences to Justin as father or preferred brother; at the same time he stimulated projections of idealized, heterosexual self-images. These phenomena became manifest in dreams and in expressions of hostility displaced toward each other rather than to Justin himself, who was preserved as the figure of benevolent, masculine power, leadership, and sexuality.

It is a generally accepted psychoanalytic assumption, based on repeated observation, that favorable personality and sexual development depend in large part on identification with a same-sex parent or parent surrogate. The patterning and reinforcement of masculine traits and identification are linked to the ways in which they are encouraged by the father and/or other important male figures. The father, if he discourages filial attachment and affection through hostile competitiveness or detachment, blocks and dislocates masculine identification processes. When the group's need to identify with a masculine sexual figure was primary, a reparative configuration became evident, and they turned to Justin as to a good father. When rivalry or anxiety emerged, they turned their attention toward each other with hostile expressions and criticisms of the group as a whole or to one member in particular—but not to Justin. Or, something the therapist said would be challenged, revealing transparent resistances or a paranoid displacement of hostility. Justin's dignified and somewhat unrevealing personality lent itself to such developments, which then provided rich, dynamic material for the on-going combined analysis of the members.

Early in the life of the group, when status maneuvers were still prominent, one member expressed homosexual interest in another. George had arrived looking particularly well-turned-out; Ted made a surreptitious play for him. George noticed it and brought it out into the open. On probe, it was revealed that Ted felt jealous of him. Projecting his feelings, he then distortedly perceived that the therapist was favoring George and admiring him sexually. Ted's automatic defense was to eroticize the threatening masculine figure and attempt to separate him from the therapist in a homosexual ploy. This acting-out maneuver served to emphasize certain of the destructive, competitive dynamics of homosexuality.

It is of interest, too, that the group sessions usually stop on a positive note. The need for mutually constructive ties seems to over-ride hostilities. If hurt feelings are sensed, the members tend to jolly each other on the way out.

Results

George. George became involved in an affair with a girl, and intercourse was attempted on several occasions, but each time vaginismus precluded full penetration. He broke up with her and began to date other girls. Before long, he was involved in a serious love relationship with an attractive, effective young woman, whom he married after a year and a half. During the early part of their courtship, the patient was impotent on occasion, although first intercourse had presented no difficulties. The group had provided continuing support as he approached a heterosexual confrontation, and they received the news of his successful experience in a mood of congratulatory enthusiasm, jocularity, and open envy but without destructive hostility. *Esprit de corps* was much in evidence at the time of the marriage, when the group chipped in for a wedding gift.

George has established a stable heterosexual adaptation. When under stress, he has reported an occasional episode of impotence, but he himself no longer considers it to be significant. Homosexual behavior had ceased shortly after he began treatment, and there have been no manifestations of homosexual arousal for more than two years. Recently, by mutual decision and group approval, George left to join a mixed group.

Ted. Ted had had heterosexual intercourse at an orgy when he was still a member of his previous group; he attempted it unsuccessfully on two later occasions under less bizarre circumstances. Each time he developed severe anxiety and quickly reverted to intensified homosexual activity.

When the business interests of his family required him to leave the city, he suspended therapy for a year. He returned to individual treatment recently, having suffered pronounced psychiatric deterioration. His work inhibitions are more severe than ever; he has begun to experiment with drugs other than marijuana, such as LSD and mescaline; he lives entirely in the gay world but no longer tries to fool his disbelieving father and brother with elaborate, although transparent, heterosexual pretenses. The patient's psychiatric prognosis and the likelihood that he will orient himself to heterosexuality are very poor.

Herbert. Herbert has not been able to resolve his fears sufficiently to go beyond petting, but his general improvement is considerable. He has become successful and creative in his work, has many friends, leads a pleasant social life, and has acquired a handsome appearance since he lost weight through exercise and diet. The possibility that he may not be able to change his inversion deeply depresses him. He is convinced that, if only he could overcome his impotence with women (he is sometimes impotent in homosexual situations as well), he would be able to shift permanently to heterosexuality. He has been referred to a behavioral therapist, and psychotherapy has been suspended.

Milton. Of the original group, Milton and Justin are the only two remaining members. Milton has made no heterosexual attempts and is weakly motivated toward change, but he no longer lives a mean, restricted existence. He now works in an executive capacity, lives in a comfortable apartment, travels occasionally, and has stopped making his earnings available to his family. Now and then he takes a mild fancy to a woman, but his heterosexual interests are soon expressed in homosexual acting out.

Justin. Justin is not yet ready to join a mixed group. He has made a stable heterosexual adaptation, has no homosexual symptoms or impotence, but intercourse is infrequent, and he experiences anxiety about his approaching marriage. His future wife is talented, intelligent, and pretty, but she suffers from a neurosis of long standing and is currently in analytic therapy.

Changes in the Group

Four other members have joined the group. The first to join is exclusively homosexual; the second is a previously treated pedophile who has not acted out for many years; the third is a previously treated, exclusive homosexual; and the fourth is a previously treated bisexual.

The first replacement, Tony, after six months of individual therapy and several weeks of combined therapy, attempted heterosexual intercourse. He was successful and has not reverted to homosexuality. His sexual partner, a devoted friend and colleague, knew of his sexual problems. She was herself in psychoanalysis and persuaded him to undertake treatment. What was a platonic relationship is now an on-going, passionate affair. The patient's recovery was spectacular in that he not only shifted quickly but has been able to maintain and add to his gains in all areas crucial to a favorable and happy adaptation—sexuality, work, and meaningful interpersonal relationships.

The personality mix of each group gives it its own distinctive cast, which alters and changes as members leave and new ones join. The air of *gemütlichkeit* that characterized the charter group is less apparent now. The members more openly and aggressively assess each other, and they tend to be more often critical of the direction the group may be taking if the theme appears to be unproductive. Shifts in member leadership have occurred. Justin is still a major figure, but George, before he left, and now Tony share the experience of heterosexual achievement. George is remembered as the one who made it fully and completely—from exclusive homosexuality to marriage and the extinction of homosexual symptoms. He serves as a model for the patients who had worked with him and for those who were told about him.

Summary of Results

In toto, nine homosexuals have participated in the group described. In a heterogeneous group, one exclusively homosexual member who entered therapy at the age of 30, after three years in individual treatment, shifted to exclusive heterosexuality. He then spent two more years in combined therapy and was discharged as recovered. First, he had had a stormy but sexually gratifying affair with an older, married woman. He then went on to form a stable relationship with a fellow artist, whom he married.

The rate of recovery among the homosexuals treated in these groups is 40 per cent. The results in this series compare favorably with the reports of treatment outcome by other therapists.

CONTRAINDICATIONS

As has been discussed, a group experience offers special advantages for many homosexual patients. For some such patients, however, group therapy is contraindicated. Those who cannot bring themselves to speak of their inversion to others, those whose contact disorders are such that they cannot tolerate forming the multiple relationships of a group but require instead the intensity of person-to-person communication, those who are in decompensatory states (as illustrated by Ted), and those whose distortions and anxieties would interfere with group process should be treated individually.

Sometimes the patient's style of relating to others dictates whether or not group therapy should be suggested. In one on-going case, the patient is being treated individually because of a continuing tendency to become readily distracted from himself. A script writer by profession, he becomes absorbed by the personalities and the adventures of others. When he picks up a "trick," he is as much interested in the life story he invariably elicits as in the homosexual activity. He introspects very well and presents little resistance against picking up the analytic line when reminded to do so. But a group would most probably be too diversionary, and such a patient should join a group only when he becomes able to relate to the other members as participant, not as audience.

SUMMARY

Homosexuals can be treated successfully in groups, as demonstrated in this chapter. Combined therapy with homogeneous groups

has been described as the treatment of choice. If there are no contraindications—and therapists must evaluate the clinical circumstances of each patient—the group experience is clearly a therapeutic method that facilitates the treatment of inversion.

REFERENCES

Bergler, E. Eight prerequisites for the psychoanalytic treatment of homosexuality. Psychoanal. Rev., *31:* 253, 1944.

Bergler, E. *1000 Homosexuals.* Pageant Books, Paterson, N. J., 1959.

Bieber, I. Olfaction in sexual development and adult sexual organization. Amer. J. Psychother., *13:* 851, 1959.

Bieber, I., Dain, H. J., Dince, P. R., Drellich, M. G., Grand, H. H., Gundlach, R. H., Kremer, M. W., Rifkin, A. H., Wilbur, C. B., and Bieber, T. B. *Homosexuality—A Psychoanalytic Study of Male Homosexuals.* Basic Books, New York, 1962.

Bieber, T. Acting-out in homosexuality. In *Acting-Out,* p. 142, L. E. Abt and S. L. Weissman, editors. Grune & Stratton, New York, 1965.

Ellis, A. The effectiveness of psychotherapy in individuals who had severe homosexual problems. J. Consult. Psychol., *20:* 191, 1956.

Freud, S. Letter to the mother of a homosexual. Amer. J. Psychiat., *107:* 786, 1951.

Freud, S. A case of homosexuality in a woman. In *Standard Edition of the Complete Psychological Works of Sigmund Freud,* vol. 18, p. 157. Hogarth Press, London, 1955.

Fried, E. Combined group and individual therapy with passive narcissistic patients. Int. J. Group Psychother., *5:* 194, 1955.

Hadden, S. B. Treatment of homosexuality by individual and group psychotherapy. Amer. J. Psychiat., *114:* 810, 1958.

Hadden, S. B. Treatment of male homosexuals in groups. Int. J. Group Psychother., *16:* 13, 1966.

Kadis, A., Krasner, J.D., Winick, C., and Foulkes, S. H. *A Practicum of Group Psychotherapy.* Harper and Row, New York, 1963.

Kalogerakis, M. G. The role of olfaction in sexual development. Psychosom. Med., *25:* 420, 1963.

Kaye, H. E., Berl, S., Clare, J., Eleston, M. R., Gershwin, B. S., Gershwin, P., Hogan, L. S., Torda, C., and Wilber, C. G. Homosexuality in women. Arch. Gen. Psychiat., *17:* 626, 1967.

Litman, R. E. Psychotherapy of a homosexual man in a heterosexual group. Int. J. Group Psychother., *11:* 440, 1961.

Mintz, E. E. Group and individual treatment. J. Consult. Psychol., *30:* 193, 1966.

Powdermaker, F. B., and Frank, J. D. *Group Psychotherapy.* Harvard University Press, Cambridge, 1953.

Rubinstein, L. H. Psychotherapeutic aspects of male homosexuality. Brit. J. Med. Psychol., *31–32:* 14, 1958–1959.

Schrenk-Notzing, A. Therapeutic suggestion. In *Psychopathia Sexualis,* p. 320. F. A. Davis, Philadelphia and London, 1895.

Singer, M., and Fischer, R. Group psychotherapy of male homosexuals by a male and female co-therapy team. Int. J. Group Psychother., *17:* 44, 1967.

Slavson, S. R. *Textbook in Analytic Group Psychotherapy,* p. 215. International Universities Press, New York, 1964.

Stone, W. N., Schengber, J., and Sengried, F. S. Treatment of a homosexual woman in a mixed group. Int. J. Group Psychother., *16:* 425, 1966.

3

The Treatment of a
Homosexual Woman in a Mixed Group

Walter N. Stone, M.D., John Schengber, M.D.,
F. Stanley Seifried, M.D.

INTRODUCTION

Perusal of the literature regarding group treatment for sexual deviants reveals a usual recommendation of treatment in homogeneous groups (Hadden, Foulkes, and Anthony; Powdermaker and Frank; Slavson). The reasons for such a recommendation are not always explicitly stated, but they seem to fall into three main categories: (1) For the therapist the degree of difficulty increases as composition changes from homogeneous to heterogeneous groups (Furst), and it is implied that by choosing patients with diverse problems, as with the introduction of a homosexual patient, this difficulty is further accentuated; (2) there is concern over the effect on the group itself, that is, that patients will react in a ''negative'' manner to the revelation of the homosexuality either by rejecting the patient or becoming anxious and fleeing the group; and (3) a concern that the homosexual patient will be unable to reveal this secret problem to the group and will be blocked in making significant progress. It would seem that the sum total of these three anticipated reactions has led to a tradition against the placement of homosexual patients in mixed groups.

There are only infrequent references reporting the treatment of homosexual pa-

tients in mixed groups. Beacher, Fried, and Litman describe treatment of homosexual men in outpatient heterogeneous groups. They conclude that there were characterological changes as a result of the therapy. Stern reports the treatment of homosexual women but does not specify the composition of his groups. He indicates that treatment in mixed groups is advantageous.

The authors accepted for treatment a 21-year-old woman—a college student and an active homosexual—and placed her in an ongoing group of heterosexual young adults who were heterogeneous both to dynamic and diagnostic categories. We shall describe some of the dynamic forces which resulted from this patient's participation in the group. Our focus will be on the group and individual—including the therapists'—reactions, gradual understanding, and resulting changes during the inital eight months of therapy.

GROUP PRESENTATION

The group, selected from a clinic population, was open-ended and consisted of four men, three women, two therapists, and a silent (physician) recorder. The patients were 19 to 25 years old; four members attended college; one was a housewife, the only married patient; and two were regularly employed. The major problem areas as formulated in diagnostic interviews revolved around "identity" and dependence-independence axes. No patients with psychotic diagnoses were included. The meetings were held at weekly intervals and lasted for 90 minutes. None of the group members were in concomitant individual therapy. Several had had individual therapy of brief duration prior to recommendation for the group. (Individual sessions could be arranged with the therapists for those who might need some additional support, especially at the time of entry into the group.) The group had been meeting for 16 months before the homosexual patient entered. The orientation of the therapists was emphasis on group processes with the individuals contributing to and attempting solution of a group focal conflict, as outlined by Whitman and Stock.

PATIENT DESCRIPTION

Nan, a 21-year-old college student who had had multiple homosexual contacts, was referred to the group by her individual therapist with whom she had been in therapy on a once-weekly schedule for approximately one year. She was to continue her individual therapy. She had initiated the request to join a group because she felt markedly restricted in her interpersonal contacts. She presented, in an intellectual way, her homosexual problems as inhibiting her from relating easily to "normal" people. This she sensed as a deterrent to her career plans, which involved extensive interpersonal relations. The referring therapist understood her homosexuality as a defense against hostile competitive and close relationships with men. It also seemed that her homosexuality was a manner by which she maintained social contacts, though she recognized this as unsatis-

factory. Her homosexual affairs had been intense, short-lived, and stormy, with feelings of isolation and depression at times of separation from her partners. Her only reported heterosexual relationship was in response to an argument with a homosexual partner in which she had attempted to make her partner "jealous." She described this heterosexual relationship as unsatisfactory.

GROUP PROCESS

Nan, Bill, and George entered the group at the same time following a three-week recess during which a search had been made for new patients to bring the census to a level the therapists felt was optimal. Their entrance created an atmosphere similar to the beginning of a new group. Tentative techniques of relating were observed, with Nan rapidly taking the lead in demanding of others that they reveal their problems, but clearly not revealing anything of herself. She would berate the rest of the group and the doctors for not talking about anything significant, for being superficial, and disparagingly compare the lack of frankness within the group to the openness of her individual sessions. The early meetings rapidly took on a repetitious pattern as Nan, under mounting anxiety, became more vehement in her exhortations and criticisms of the group, thereby preventing meaningful interaction. She succeeded in becoming an irritant to the other patients, but she also fulfilled a wish for them by expressing hostile-aggressive comments to the therapists. This wish had been in part determined by the introduction of new members, a plan the older members secretly hoped would fail. Nan seemed to be proving to herself and to the others that she could not fit in. Collaboration with the individual therapist corroborated an impression of Nan's intense anxiety about "acceptance-rejection" fantasies in the group vis-a-vis her homosexuality.

Conflict between Therapists

In private post-meeting discussion between the two group therapists, one of them revealed his reluctance to treat Nan in the group. From the beginning he had suppressed his opinion that she would be disruptive to the group because of her homosexual problem. There had existed a subtle battle between the two therapists, each taking a different view of the patient's acceptability in the group. One therapist had passively participated in the group's defensive maneuvering by relinquishing his leadership position and identifying with a portion of the patients' wishes to reject Nan. As these differences were aired and dynamic significance in the group conflict clarified, the two therapists were able to resume a collaborative active leadership. This led the group to understand Nan's defensive maneuvers, and the rest of the patients' ambivalent but silent reinforcement of her impulse to flee from the anxiety of the group setting.

Confession of Homosexuality

At a meeting about three and one-half months after she entered the group, Nan was able to reveal her homosexuality directly. She chose to do this at a meeting when Bill was absent, since she saw Bill in a role which personified the group's rejecting her. Bill was arbitrarily judgmental and volatile in his anger, and, as was predictable, the group was unable to mention Nan's homosexuality in his presence (Bill, an irregular attender, very soon dropped out of the group). The group response to the confession was at first guarded. Although intellectually accepting Nan's homosexuality, there were suggestions of moral condemnation and disgust. However, Nan seemed to retain a certain leadership with this revelation, and as clarification to the fantasied rejection and/or retaliation progressed, others were able to reveal "secret" portions of their personal lives, which led to a closer shared experience and laid the groundwork for further therapeutic gains.

At one session in the course of a go-round, Nan was defining her reaction to the others in the group: Joan threatened her because she was married and seemed a successful mother; George threatened her because he was of similar religious background and he might be a person she could marry. As Nan continued, the group observed and understood her intense anxiety about closeness, her fear of rejection, and her ambivalence over accepting the role of a mature woman. She seemed almost childlike and pleading in her wish to be accepted. Some of these needs the group was able to gratify.

Soon Nan began to report fleeting contacts with George at school, as if she were reaching out to him socially. She would tell of alteration in her adolescent, self-effacing social behavior at school as an attempt to please George, and then would follow by relating tales of homosexual contacts. George responded by denouncing Nan's immaturity, and through his protest, clearly indicating his underlying interest.

Two Patients Drop Out

In the midst of this phase, two patients dropped out of the group. Ann (a borderline personality), who had been in a highly competitive battle with Nan for attention from the therapists, quit several weeks after Nan revealed her homosexual problem. Ann's past history of intense sibling rivalry for dependency gratification which had led to her flight from home seemed to be repeated in the group. The competitiveness of Ann and Nan had been heightened by the coincidence of their having similar first names, a fact which led at times to confusion as to who was being discussed. In addition, Ann's homosexual impulses had clearly been stimulated and were threatening to her. The second drop-out, Bill, a narcissistic character with depression, had never been able to relate to the group which he had entered with grave misgivings. Although he was frequently the focus of discussion because of his hostile withdrawal, arbitrariness, and potential explosiveness, he had never become committed to the group.

Fear of Group Dissolution

Along with these two drop-outs, scheduled alternating vacations by the therapists occurred. Within the group the focus shifted to concern and fantasies over disintegration of the group. The "reality" existed for the patients because of the previously mentioned three-week recess. One evening, in the absence of one of the therapists, Nan arrived in the company of a girl friend known to the group as a homosexual, and asked to bring her into the meeting. There was reluctance to deal with this request in the hope that the therapist who was present would intervene. Finally, Joan, the married patient, very softly said she did not like the idea. George, with a sigh of relief, blurted out that if one person was against it, that was enough. In the course of the meeting, the group began to understand this as an attempt in part by Nan to hold the group together.

Adding to this fear of group dissolution was the increasing anxiety in the group as a scheduled change in therapists approached. George arranged to take an out-of-town summer job, and it became clear that he was handling his concern over separation from the therapists with this reality planning. The group focused on the problem of separation as seen through the interaction of George and Nan. During the meeting which preceded George's departure, Nan commented she had come at the risk of failing a final examination the following morning, having mistakenly thought that this was George's last meeting. At several moments she reached the point of seeming ready to tell George directly of her warm feelings, but she was only able to say that she would probably go out afterwards and tell her homosexual partner the feelings she was experiencing, although wishing instead to tell George. She seemed to be pleading for interest and limits. The group responded, with Joan offering to take Nan home to help her control these impulses. Nan, although not accepting, responded to the offer as a concrete example of the group's wish to be supportive. The following week she appeared for the first time in a

dress, bleached bouffant hairdo, high heels, and reported no homosexual contact. (She had previously dressed in leotards.) The group hailed this as a positive step, except for George, who felt she was overdoing it. He had responded to Nan's tentative and imperfect first steps of seeing herself as a more mature woman with anxiety over the closeness this implied.

DISCUSSION

Group Conflict

Several effects of Nan's participation could be distinguished in the development of an effective working group. (The emphasis, for purposes of this discussion, is placed on the patient's contributions and dynamics.) Initially, Nan's conflict over the revelation of her homosexuality and fantasied rejection was solved by her characterological defense of attack first; isolating herself and provoking rejection was preferable to the shame of nonacceptance because of being "abnormal." This defense dovetailed with the group's verbally unexpressed conflict over wanting to maintain the status quo and not share the therapists' attention with anyone new, versus the fear of disapproval and feelings of shame. Their silent encouragement of Nan's own isolating techniques served to focus group anger on her as the one preventing successful progress in the group. A crucial factor in the process of group acceptance of Nan was a preconscious but nonverbalized conflict between the two therapists. The stereotyped negative attitude about treatment of homosexuals in a "straight" group had led one of the therapists to ally himself with the patient group and reinforce the rejection of Nan. This resulted in a conflict between the therapists which went unrecognized for several weeks. When this conflict was brought into the open and clarified, the patient group no longer needed to be used as the arena in which the therapists' differences were played out. It seems clear that the countertransference attitudes mobilized by the addition of a homosexual patient were very potent in adding to the initial difficulty experienced by Nan.

The gradual clarification of the group conflicts allowed Nan to reveal her homosexuality and her fear of rejection, with the result that others were able to share the experience, focus on their own anxiety, and in the process reveal some of their own secret, shameful experiences. In this manner, Nan discovered that the revelation of what she perceived as her greatest vulnerability was a meaningful entrée into group participation. The drop-out of another patient, Ann, that occurred at this time could be partially attributed to an increased anxiety over homosexual impulses. This must be viewed as a negative result directly related to Nan's beginning integration into the group.

Situations arose in the group in which there was marked stimulation of homosexual feelings. In several instances positive and helpful responses were elicited, rather than excessive anxiety, resulting in nontherapeutic response. Clearly, Joan's offer to take Nan home after a meeting in which Nan had expressed the thought of talking after-what she perceived as her greatest vulnercated erotic wishes. The stimulation of these wishes had not been paralyzing, as Joan was able to respond to the more overt request for controls. Joan seemed to be an object of other homosexual feelings in her response to Nan's request to bring a known homosexual woman into the group, because it was Joan who said no. The erotic impulses during that meeting were secondary to the group focal conflict revolving around fear of dissolution of the group.

Group Understanding of Homosexuality

The extent to which homosexuality became understood as a symptom by the group was demonstrated during the phase prior to the change of therapists. The patients, in attempting to work through their feelings of loss at departing members

(George and both therapists), cognitively and affectively understood Nan's turning to a homosexual partner and were able to mobilize support for Joan in her effort to lend Nan controls. This afforded the group an experience of mutual support in the face of a crucial period in therapy. In contrast, previous patterns in the face of separation anxiety had led to increased demands for individual attention or to flight, as shown by George.

Positive Theraputic Results

For Nan the group experience provided several positive therapeutic results. It diminished her excessive shame over homosexual feelings. In the protected setting, she was able to evaluate her concerns over her own hostility and her fear of rejection, and the experience enabled her to attempt a tentative heterosexual relationship. Nan brought certain strengths into the group which were pertinent to her success in integrating into the group; her intellectualized but strong desire to relate to peers and to test her acceptability were positive attributes.

Although the authors have not stressed the progress of therapy in individual sessions, we had the general impression that the concurrent individual treatment was of special value for Nan. Her intense initial anxiety would probably have proved intolerable to her without the supportive individual relationship. We hesitate to speculate on what may have been a positive advantage of having an individual therapist distinct from the group therapists; this problem remains open for further evaluation.

SUMMARY

The authors have described an experience with the treatment of a homosexual 21-year-old woman in a heterogeneous group of young adults, none of the other patients having overt problems with homosexuality. The patient requested referral for group treatment from her individual therapist, indicating a desire to have meaningful relationships in addition to her homosexual contacts.

A primary factor in her delayed integration into the group was a preconscious conflict between the co-therapists arising from a stereotyped attitude toward treating homosexuals in a mixed group. This delay was further enhanced by the patient's own initial intense anxiety over acceptance-rejection fantasies. The patient derived a good deal of support in her group contact from her ongoing individual sessions.

The patient learned that revelation of her homosexual feelings would not lead to her being rejected and that underlying needs which had led to her choice of homosexuality could be explored in the group. She made her first tentative steps toward heterosexual contact during the eight-month period after beginning group treatment. The group experienced an intense relationship with a person they felt was unacceptable because of her defensive patterns, and through the process, were able to share more of their shameful and anxiety-laden feelings than they had previously felt capable of revealing.

We conclude that homosexual patients can be treated in mixed groups in selected situations and that a highly beneficial therapeutic experience can be achieved.

REFERENCES

Beacher, A. Psychoanalytic treatment of a sociopath in a group situation. Amer. J. Psychother., *16:* 278, 1962.

Foulkes, S. H., and Anthony, E. J. *Group Psychotherapy.* Penguin Books, London, 1957.

Fried, E. Combined group and individual therapy with passive narcissistic patients. Int. J. Psychother., *5:* 194, 1955.

Furst, W. Homogeneous versus heterogeneous groups. Topic Probl. Psychother., *2:* 170, 1960. Basel, New York: Kargia.

Hadden, S. B. Treatment of male homosexuals in groups. Int. J. Group Psychother., *16:* 13, 1965.

Litman, R. E. Psychotherapy of a homosexual man in a heterosexual group. Int. J. Psychother., *II:* 440, 1961.

Powdermaker, F. B., and Frank, J. D. *Group Psychotherapy.* Harvard University Press, Cambridge, 1953.

Slavson, S. R. *A Textbook in Analytic Group Psychotherapy.* International Universities Press, New York, 1964.

Stern, E. M. Group psychoanalysis with individuals manifesting sexually deviate patterns. Acta Psychother., 7 Suppl.: 365, 1959.

Whitman, R. M., and Stock, D. The group focal conflict. Psychiatry, *21:* 269, 1958.

4

Child and Adolescent Group Therapy

Irvin A. Kraft, M.D.

INTRODUCTION

Group psychotherapy, although begun in the early twentieth century, today reflects the spasms and convulsions inherent in the evolution of treatment techniques in psychiatry and related fields. Certainly the recent outbreak and upsurge of interest in encounter groups indicates that the turbulence for growth increases rather than diminishes as plateaus of accepted techniques and procedures fail to appear. Perhaps thicker and stabler strata exist beneath the surface turmoil, and in them rest the major therapeutic routine gains within group psychotherapy.

Less experimentation and way-out technical feats characterize group psychotherapy with children. Psychotherapy techniques for children remain primarily within a classical psychoanalytic framework. New methods that vary from the classical technique encounter inertia initially. In a survey of group psychotherapy for children, this investigator found that only a few therapists describe techniques that might be termed strictly psychoanalytic. Anthony, one of the major pathfinders in group psychotherapy, suggests this pattern for work with children, as seen in Gratton's work in Canada and Fisher's therapy in the Children's Center at Tulsa.

History

Most writers base their work on derivatives of the Slavson theory. A towering originator in the field, Slavson innovated a unique approach to therapy for late-latency youths when he originated group psychotherapy for children in 1934, working with latency-age children in what he called activity group psychotherapy. Activity group therapy differed from groups of children in common activities, such as scouting or group work, by adhering to a specific theory of personality development and its corollaries.

Witmer, who established a psychoeducational clinic for emotionally disturbed children at the University of Pennsylvania in 1896, preceded activity groups and set the stage for specific interest and facilities for treating children with emotional disturbances rather than waiting for them to outgrow their illnesses.

A therapeutic classroom, although it helps the child achieve ego growth and integration, differs from group psychotherapy by its goal of education of the intellect. The teacher primarily concentrates on bolstering the child's ego by exploring conscious manifestations of his unconscious patterns rather than on using the classroom group in a directed way to promote emotional health. Therapeutic use of peer group phenomena undoubtedly occurs, but this use would not meet the criteria for group psychotherapy. This thread in education and the team concept of the child guidance centers, which evolved in the 1920's and 1930's, both helped enrich the soil in which Slavson planted his work.

Activity group therapy served as a base for further developments in group psychotherapy with children and adolescents. In 1937, Bender reported using groups in the treatment of children on a hospital ward. Glatzer and Durkin applied relationship therapy in small groups of children in 1944. They developed the use of play materials but emphasized the verbalization of feelings with direct interpretation. The child-therapist relationship served as the nucleus, with the impact of the group as an added advantage. Other investigators in the 1940's devised different methods to suit the usual age groupings of children, especially latency and adolescence. Techniques were tried for different settings, such as correctional institutions, public schools, hospitals, residential treatment facilities, and pediatric specialty clinics.

THEORIES OF TREATMENT

Foulkes and Anthony, Slavson, Corsini, and other investigators stated theoretical positions for all group psychotherapy. Client-centered psychotherapy, Adlerian concepts, and classical psychoanalytic principles dominated the practice of group psychotherapy for children. Despite the particular theoretical background of the therapists, certain assumptions pervaded their work, such as the unconscious topological mental constructs (like ego), psychic determinism, infantile sexuality, and the oedipal conflict.

Behavior of Child

A child or adolescent's activity—such as play, gestures, and interactions—is based on his inner fantasies that seek expression and resolution in development, family transactions, and other phases of growth-promoting adaptation. Motor activity may be considered the dominant phase of total action by a child to express himself in the language of action. To alter disordered or deviant behavior in children, more than in middle-to-late adolescents, one attends to action-talk and behavioral meaning. Group psychother-

apy offers unique opportunities to study, translate, and affect these communications as they occur.

Group psychotherapy of children sets up a goal of education and control of the emotions to be accomplished in various ways that simply and effectively state the acceptance of feelings and specific types of behavior. The therapist, in his role as leader of the group, furnishes situations that encourage behavior containing messages, the emotional content of which lends itself to interaction and intellectual translation. For example, a situation in a psychotherapy group provokes a child into an outburst of rage, which is verbalized by the therapist into further acceptance and understanding: "Sometimes it is really difficult to control anger." The child feels better and gains insight at several levels of brain organization.

Experiential insight arises from the verbalization of such a violent feeling and from realizing that retribution need not necessarily follow the expression of a true, albeit misplaced, feeling. Additional ways for this insight to occur come through interactions with other group members, which utilize such defense mechanisms as identification, rationalization, denial, catharsis, and identification with the aggressor in an atmosphere of impunity and safety.

As the child proceeds in treatment, his response can be measured in terms of his verbal as well as his nonverbal behavior, his activity level, and his inter-relationship with other group members and the leader. These responses correlate roughly with alterations in his behavior at home and in school. Group learning experiences translate into the less contrived, more natural occurrences in the outside world.

Since the child's mind differs in its synthetic capacities and ability to control both emergency and welfare emotions, methods and techniques commonly used in adult group psychotherapy cannot be applied to children without significant alterations. In a treatment situation the child requires freedom to emote and to speak what crosses his mind—but all within limits set by the leader consistent with his view of himself and the setting. Generally, the therapist allows motoric expressions by small children, less so with adolescents in a group, knowing he can and must intervene at times.

Flexibility of Treatment

When to do what and how with theoretical formulation beleaguers beginning therapists, who often want a settled, directed statement of theory to guide them. The therapist should be exposed to several theories from which he can evolve both a pragmatic self-fit for work and a vocabulary to describe what transpires. From the theories and from his supervised experiences, he produces an individualized therapeutic style that enables him to work well and comfortably with his patients. Danger lurks beneath such flexibility, for at times a therapist may choose patterns that coincide with antiestablishment trends for that sake rather than for intrinsic values carefully thought through and circumspectly tried.

Certain assumptions, often tacit, pervade group psychotherapy with children. Parental rejection, for example, is interpreted one way by adult-aged therapists, a different way by a child. A great variety of descriptions of parents by their children complicates group psychotherapy of children and adolescents. Descriptions by children of parental behavior are summarized by Goldin.

Phenomena can also be perceived from a social psychological perspective. Sherif and Cantril propose a sophisticated theory based on a dynamic conception of the individual in relation to society. Sherif based his work on extensions of Cooley, who postulated that social process and control were basic to all group dynamics and rested on face-to-face interactions in the primary group. This primary group demonstrated a psychological structure characterized by close identification and intimacy. Hyman and Sherif focused on how this group process and structure instilled its attitudes and values into the individual.

Foulkes points out that, although human living always has been group living, modern times emphasize the individual, his property, and competition, as if the person always saw the world outside of himself. Yet group configurations dominate the individual's actions in action with groups or by reaction to them.

He feels and responds to the group in a total or Gestalt fashion. The community of origin and present relationships penetrate the treatment process.

Age of Child

Since group formation occurs as a natural phenomenon in human development, the age and developmental stage of the child influence the growth of group psychotherapy techniques more than any other factors. Therapists invariably group children by age, usually in conjunction with the nature of the presenting difficulties (Kraft, 1968; Soble and Geller). Children are grouped in six age categories: (1) preschool and early school age —ages 4 through 8; (2) late latency—ages 9 through 11; (3) puberty—ages 12 through 13; (4) early adolescence—ages 13 through 14; (5) middle adolescence—ages 15 through 16; and (6) late adolescence—ages 17 and above.

Gratton describes an entire psychotherapeutic approach, a psychoanalytic one, modified for each age division but basically utilizing interpretations throughout. Another interesting experience with the consequences of age emerges in Quinn's work. When some of the older girls in the latency-age group moved into puberty, they needed a separate group to manage their different modes of behavior. Early adolescents require techniques somewhat different from those suitable for late latency (Duffy and Kraft), as in the activity patterns of the therapist.

Setting of Treatment

Just as developmental patterns lead to age divisions of group members, so the setting in which therapists operate greatly influence their procedures and work patterns. Group psychotherapy of children, including adolescents, occurs wherever they are treated or confined. The outpatient clinic or child guidance center, except with delinquents, tends to be the arena most described in the literature.

Private Practice. With the great increase of child psychiatrists and other professionals in private practice, more information in this area should be published. As yet, comparatively little information exists to describe differences of technique and other considerations, such as the length of time a particular group should exist.

The supply of patients differs at various times, so it may be difficult to maintain enough children of a given age range. In some instances the diagnostician has referred the child to a colleague who had a group suitable for the patient and referred the parents to another colleague or treated them himself. Splitting the family does not impair therapeutic effectiveness as long as the therapists communicate effectively.

The private practice world operates with rules that differ from those in a clinic or community mental health center. For example, the therapist in one community is known for her ability to treat adolescent girls, especially girls who act out. This therapist always has enough of a patient population to maintain a group of adolescent girls. In effect, she is a community resource for the care of girls whose families can afford private care since other therapists do not have the patient flow to sustain such a group. With community facilities strained by changing personnel and major service demands, such a private sector of care becomes extremely valuable.

Clinics. The physical environment for group psychotherapy of children influences the type of care immediately. For a teaching clinic to set aside the space required for a large activity group psychotherapy program means a significant financial commitment. At one time, staff members of one clinic were interested in doing this, but they failed to garner the space and equipment necessary. The administration acknowledged the need but could not find the space, especially if it could not be used effectively for other responsibilities at other times. Imagine the cost to a private practice of the square footage and equipment for doing activity therapy twice a week, for example. In one case these realistic limitations led to the development of interview group psychotherapy with latency and early-to-late adolescents (Duffy and Kraft; Hart et al.).

The geography of an urban setting sets up pragmatic considerations that influence group therapy activity. If public transporta-tion is lacking or ineffective, children have to be brought by their parents, usually mothers. In a clinic the mothers can be in their own group at the same time.

Both private patients and those from a catchment area for a mental health center usually attend the same schools. Confidentiality becomes a problem to a degree, as do outside social therapy and play involvements. Little information on this vector's effect on group process exists in the literature.

With mixed-gender adolescent groups, dating, parties, and other activities can strongly influence the group at its weekly meeting. One such incident proved productive for the group when 17-year-old Mary and 16-year-old Jim began to see themselves and be seen by the group as steadies. While holding hands in the group, Mary showed uneasiness, often looking questioningly at the therapist. In time, oedipal-type dynamics emerged and were shared verbally by all group members. The group and Mary somehow believed that the leader, a man, would find her relationship with Jim a threat.

During the past decade or so, group psychotherapy of children, independently or concomitantly with treatment of the parents, has been used in most orthodox child guidance centers (Boulanger; Geller; Novick; Slavson [1964]; Smolen). These units and in many cases the current community mental health centers found their traditional divisions of labor, notwithstanding the cross-over propensities of group therapy, so that social workers, as well as psychiatrists and psychologists, began seeing themselves as therapists. Somehow there is a quality about group therapy that attracts all the disciplines to participate. People with little background of therapeutic experience feel little constraint in entering the lists of encounter groups, mostly with adults except in family therapy. In the literature, little if any information exists on "wild" therapy of children.

Outpatient Departments. Several therapists have described the diagnostic use of groups in outpatient settings. Field described two activity groups as providing an exploring, role-taking and testing medium whose main contribution may be the accumulation of behavioral data for the psychiatric social worker who guides the therapeutic effort at home and at school.

In such a setting, an unusual use was made of a mixed adolescent and adult group in an evaluation process. A content analysis revealed that most of their transactions fell into the areas of authority, dependency, and identity conflict (Knorr et al.). Smolen demonstrated diagnostic as well as therapeutic group work with severely disturbed young children preparatory to their total hospitalization. In these circumstances, several of the children improved, and the clinical diagnosis altered.

Hospitals. In a hospital setting for chronic diseases of children, Ghory worked with the parents of the children by group methods, primarily groups with both mothers and fathers. The children presumably did not receive much psychotherapy. In contrast, Andre and his coworkers dealt with difficulties in the social functioning of the children, including

the separation from an accustomed environment, confrontation of his illness in relation to himself, the illness of others, sleeping in a strange and sometimes fearful place. . . .

They brought children together in beds, in wheelchairs, and on foot, and they sought verbalization of concerns. One worry was a sense of difference from their nonhospitalized peers.

Konopka and Wallinga described a residential treatment program for severe character disorders with delinquent, prepsychotic symptoms, including aggressive, destructive, acting-out behavior. They used group approaches to avoid creating extra anxiety so that stress-immunized, indifferent children could eventually be reached. Hostility from these children seemed rampant in group situations. In time the first phase strengthened their healthy components with a lessening of immunity and an increase in the ability to feel discomfort. Individual therapy could then be instituted with a later increase of their group therapy involvement.

Anderson described his treatment of four boys, ages ten through 13, in a state hospital. They demonstrated brain damage and retardation with severe behavior problems and I.Q. levels ranging from 61 to 75. They showed poor peer relationships, inadequate self-control, faulty judgment, fire-setting habits, disobedience, hyperactivity, and impulsivity. The therapist took a passive role, using the group as a catalytic agent. He used gestures and facial expressions to stimulate or control the group. No props—such as coats, toys, and magazines—were permitted. Short-term group therapy proved valuable for the patients, judging by their hospital behavior and home-visit patterns.

Other reports (Shellow et al.; Straight and Werkman) describe the pattern of group therapy in mental institutions as tailor-made to the problems constantly besetting adolescent patients. Struggle against authority, often enhanced and intensified by the setting, requires the construction of rules for sensible limits to provide the children with another opportunity to work and to live through their conflicts with the therapist, the representative of the institutional authority. Therapists in these circumstances face the question of control each time the group meets: regulation of the motor apparatus, restraint of destructiveness, restriction of fighting and bodily harm, and distribution of pleasurable variations, such as parties, outside the group meetings.

Schools. Another place in which the children can undergo group psychotherapy is within their schools, where they often have their first and most sustained extrafamilial social contacts (Davidson). Exploratory usage of group therapy naturally raises the ancient question of how to use schools as sites for early detection of emotional problems and how to manage these problems. Ample opportunity for subject population exists, since most surveys, dating back to Wickman's in 1928, demonstrate a 10 per cent incidence of emotional problems. Any attempt to find and to treat patients involves many basic problems, a major one being selection of patients. Teachers identify as problem children anyone who interrupts educational procedural flow and interferes with classroom management at whatever level the teacher personally finds comfortable. The quietly schizoid or the compulsively achieving child may escape the designation of being troubled.

Davidson suggests that his technique of using the small activity group serves as an adjunctive measure to the school counselors and programs for the emotionally disturbed child. In these groups, which are held on the school campus, the additional adult attention and permissiveness especially aid the withdrawn, aloof, shy, or fearful child. Presumably, the positive results encourage further involvement by teachers and enhance interest in the nondisruptive child. As long as the school principal, who sets the tone of receptivity to mental health concepts, accepts this work, the less perceptive and less involved teachers become involved also.

Some school systems provide a continuous spectrum of care for their emotionally disturbed children. Services range from the enlightened approach of an individual teacher in a regular classroom through activities of the school counselor or social worker to referral for day hospital or other forms of intensive care. Group therapeutic work occurs at several points along the continuum.

Self-contained classrooms on the school campus offer unique therapeutic challenges to their teachers and associated caretakers. Integration of emotionally disturbed children with the other pupils at assemblies and in play after school presents realistic and often stringent problems. Chigier used a unique twist to group psychotherapy of the children in such a setting where nine boys and girls, ages 11 through 13, with severe educational difficulties made up a class. Five of them had failed in individual therapy. The nine children met once a week for an hour as a social circle for a lesson on matters of topical interest. Chigier emphasized the natural atmosphere, habitat, and theme that fitted the group process well into the on-going flow of educational activities. He found, however, that the children underwent differentiation from their schoolmates until he began to rotate healthy children from other classes as auxiliary therapists. Interestingly, the free, permissive give-and-take tone of the group entranced some of the visiting chil-

dren, who then wanted to remain beyond their turns.

One could study this technique, used in psychodrama, for its usefulness in all forms of group psychotherapy for children and their families. Spontaneous visitation occurred in outpatient adolescent group psychotherapy when a patient brought a friend, usually of the same gender, to the group. Visitation brought out new facets: the curiosity of the friend, who had his own brand of problems, the interest and acceptance by his nonpatient peers of the patient's participation in such a group, the presentation of a girlfriend to the group for her better understanding of his situation, and the wish to gain status and greater involvement with the group members by sharing a friend with them. Visits by nonpatient peers might augment the therapeutic progress of the group, especially if the healthy child serves as auxiliary therapist without damage to himself and with helpful reflections to the group of a normal, contrasting response to the topics preoccupying the children, often with their explosive responses and helter-skelter involvements.

Another method for use in the public school setting originated with the work of Berman and his colleagues in the Boston area. The author replicated this work in a large junior high school and found it successful and valuable on an impressionistic basis. However, when the teacher's attitudes toward pupils were measured by a set of standardized tests, no significant shift was detected, once again raising the spector of how appropriately to quantify attitudinal shifts detected by the clinician qualitatively. In essence, this psychoanalytic group seminar approach offers teachers in a small group of less than 20 an opportunity to explore their own attitudes and reactions to the children, to the principal, and to their fellow faculty members. A surprising degree of candor develops, as long as the leader skillfully guides the interaction to prevent indepth baring of personal information that does not move the group properly along to its purpose. A program of this type adroitly and successfully helps the troubled student by offering him a classroom situation better able to answer his affective needs. Invariably the teachers report using modifications of their seminar experiences in their classrooms, so that in an attenuated manner the children undergo a group psychotherapeutic experience.

Warkentin describes a similar approach with grade school teachers, emphasizing an appreciation of their role in the affective learning of the students.

His very position before a class makes the teacher a recapitulation of other parental figures, whose attitudes are inadvertently learned by students; yet the social responsibility for such affective learning may not always be consciously acknowledged by the teacher.

In the two-year experiment, feelings, attitudes, and motivation were consciously emphasized by the teacher in a directly therapeutic approach. Warkentin stressed his role in preventing the excessive development of anxiety.

A borderline area of working within school settings, described by Garai, uses classroom discussion to promote personality growth. He emphasizes interweaving themes that reflect a national concern, such as divorce, and their reflections in the lives of the students. Group interactional discussion, guided closely by the teacher, constitutes the method. One may question how properly this fits the concept of group psychotherapy, but Garai (and presumably Moreno, since he included it in his *Handbook*) believes he achieves significant therapeutic effects:

I was able to refer 13 students to competent psychotherapists for individual treatment within a single year.

A provocative book by Shiffer describes play group treatment, a form of therapy utilizing activity group therapy for experiential undoing of family traumata. He suggests that the therapeutic play group has four evolutionary phases: (1) preparatory—the introduction to the play group and the children's initial reactions to permissiveness; (2) therapeutic—the phase of longest duration, it covers the development of transference on multiple levels; (3) re-educational—integrative and maturational; (4) termination. His play groups are homogeneous as to age and sex with six children as the maximal number.

Day Hospitals. Another setting, which resembles the school, is the day hospital or day-care center devoted to a psychoeducational goal. Specifically, psychoeducation represents a combination of psychiatric and educational sources that are used in special settings to remedy learning deficiencies and emotional disturbances. Two working models have evolved. The first, a clinical model encompasses traditional diagnostic and, treatment patterns for deviant personalities. The second is a competence model emphasizing the development of various social, physical, and cognitive skills. This approach helps to modify and prevent developmental problems in children at various age levels (Blom).

The author is most familiar with a psychoeducational unit that is part of a pediatric general hospital and linked with a large public school system. The boys and girls of elementary school age range widely in activity levels, symptoms, and family psychopathology. The day hospital creates an environment that influences a disturbed child positively while concomitantly altering the child's family milieu. Since cihldren spend 25 hours or more each week in the day hospital, the psychoeducation program should have high impact value. Where does group psychotherapy fit in with these therapeutic conditions? Is it best utilized for parents? What modifications, if any, would be most appropriate?

The patient population totaled 12 to 14, often with two age groupings called the upper and lower school groups. The staff first held group meetings using an educational format to promote interaction. The group leader met with the children in a classroom. Teachers were available in the back for rescue operations and possible interaction with the children and the leader. The ostensible content of the brief session was a neuropsychological description of the human brain and its functions. This discussion led to questions by the children and sometimes the teachers. These questions could be deflected to incidents and dynamics of daily life in the day hospital. Thus, in discussing midbrain functions, the author readily focused on some of the many outbursts of fears and rages illustrative of emergency emotions out of control and ill-used.

The children and teachers began to use this new vocabulary in the classrooms and on the playground, providing a frequent connection and common vocabulary with the group meeting. This use also linked the leader, who was the medical director and ultimate authority figure of the day hospital, with daily therapeutic activities, diminishing his administrative distance and bringing into focus some of the tranference phenomena. Themes that emerged in the group could be reiterated by the teachers, by the individual therapists, and in dance therapy, so that psychodynamics expressed by the group reverberated for the children in all circumstances of their therapy.

Although unable to measure the effect of the sessions directly or with any precision, the staff believed impressionistically that clinical gains occurred from these brief (15 to 30 minutes), thrice-weekly group meetings. With other staff members present in the sessions, mutually necessary confrontations took place. A teacher could point out to a child how he had aggravated her to the point of anger with his trap-setting behavior determined by his emotional brain taking over and controlling his learning, abstractive brain. Other children and staff members joined in the interaction with honest depth of feeling displayed. The brain lecture group sessions extended to almost any therapeutic activity. The staff began to think of it as reverberational, total group therapy, discovering the value of a group experience, shared by patients and staff, that served as a common focus of explanation for whatever mislearned, neurotic behavior occurred.

Even the various parent group meetings reflected the effects. The children spoke in brain-terms at home, often sharply and deftly pin-pointing a parent's emotional brain takeover and trap-setting. The author mentioned these concepts in the parents' couples group in the belief that the more commonalities of communication the better, and he found some gains from it.

The author tried a small, interview-type, directly interactional group with boys and girls of the upper school division. These children, ages 11 through 13, were patients in the day hospital program for more than a year. They had established communication and behavioral patterns with each other and the staff that presented major therapeutic obstacles. The author hypothesized that their group patterns would be the object of attack, the purpose being to break apart their fortress-like nature, and he believed that he could promote enough noise in the system by a group therapy approach to the six children. He failed, for the group therapy situation enhanced emotional contagion and untoward rule-breaking behavior. What they had, they flaunted, leaving the staff bothered and daunted. They were uncontrollable in behavior, and their verbalizations rarely touched areas suitable for therapeutic endeavor. This conventional technique failed these children, who had spent hours in their educational contacts perfecting their disruptive skills. The group effort demanded abandonment after about two months of weekly meetings.

Other types of group sessions, on crisis occasions, prove worthwhile in a day hospital setting. For example, one seven-year-old boy's schizophrenic parents became simultaneously so disturbed that immediate hospitalization for both was necessary. Jimmy had no relatives nearby, so staff members took him in for several nights until an aggreeable relative several hundred miles away accepted him. This sudden departure and the concomitant rise in concern of the other children led to a group therapy session to explore their reactions and fantasies about parental disappearance. A great deal of catharsis occurred, questions emerged, and much distortion diminished.

Group therapeutic endeavors demand flexibility and ingenuity to match the exigencies of the different settings and patients. Often the format relates to the treatment theory of the director, especially in small, residential treatment units. In larger ones, manpower considerations often make the increased use of group methods necessary.

Sex of Child

Many vectors influence the kind of group psychotherapy performed. Certainly the sex of the children and adolescents becomes a significant variable, partially influencing the considerations for therapist selection. Guidance centers usually have a three-to-one boy-girl ratio, making it hard to form groups with girls. Some attention has been given the question at various age and developmental levels, but the literature emphasizes separate sex groups.

Gratton's groups were composed of girls, apparently because of the lack of boys. In the latency period and in adolescence mixed-sex interview groups work satisfactorily, the author found. Girls leavened the often boisterous actions and productions of the boys, and their presence gave a more realistic life aspect to the therapy for the boys. Some therapists. however, especially in treatment of adolescents, believe that mixed-sex groups present hazards. This opinion dominated the literature of the 1940's and first half of the 1950's (Axelrod et al.; Gabriel; McCormick; Parrish; Patterson; Spotnitz). In 1955, Ackerman stated vividly the potential for growth and discomforting action in such mixed groups, running counter to the earlier general desire to have a calm atmosphere. As the Commission on Group Psychotherapy of the World Federation for Mental Health (1952) concluded, mixed groups have

resulted in more intense emotional reactions, more acting out, and marked tendencies to develop physical illnesses, such as the grippe and cold.

One concern has always been the possibility of acting out sexually, yet in the author's experience with more than 25 adolescent and younger age groups, no such acting out has occurred in outpatient settings. Similar findings were reported in 1959 by Schulman, who, along with others, has cautioned that sexual acting out might be possible but was less likely if the patients included various personality types, such as those with exaggerated superego development, and if there were co-therapists (Becker et al.; Fried; Godenne [1964 and 1965]).

Psychotherapists of groups made up of one sex usually believe the choice is self-evident, as in an institution or in a situation of delinquency. Barnwell reports a successful program of group treatment with older boys (15 to 17 years old) in a family agency. A clear statement of preference for one-sex groups emerges in Teicher's discussion of his hospital-centered out patient work in which mixed groups tend to be too stimulating, probably as a result of his population's usual history of early sexual experience.

Diagnosis of Child

Should diagnosis, as inadequate as the nomenclature is for children, be a major consideration in patient selections? Should the therapist think of emotional age as more pertinent than chronological age? Should he mix retarded or cerebral palsied or blind children with physiologically sound, emotionally disturbed youngsters? Suppose a preadolescent girl of 12 has had sexual intercourse and oral-genital activities with her older brother or father. Should she be placed in a mixed-sex group of other preadolescents? Anticipate the effects of including in a mixed-sex, midadolescent group a 14-year-old boy who has blithely stolen cars, cannibalized parked autos, and peddled drugs. How does the therapist manage the early adolescents and the other teenagers who often get stoned on marijuana and drop acid on weekends? Suppose in the course of the vicissitudes of group interaction they introduce others to the ways and means of psychedelic drug vistas. How does the therapist evaluate this likelihood as he decides on his patient selection?

Patient composition of a children's group is determined to a significant extent more easily than the theoretical conceptions of the therapist may indicate. The setting, the availability of patients, and the therapeutic bent of the therapist over-ride a particular theoretical position. Some investigators in state hospital settings find that, even with a large number of children available, the group membership follows the criterion of accessibility to insight and to group interaction. Psychotic children tend to be treated in like-membership groups, although Coffey and Wiener used nonpsychotic children as catalyzers to influence autistic children by promoting communication and interaction. They termed this behavioral contagion.

Homogeneity vs. heterogeneity with reference to sex, diagnostic category, age, and other criteria still besets the therapist, unless he has made up his mind firmly. The composition of the group, however, can be almost any kind if the therapist is flexible enough in his outlook. Generally speaking, the degree of ego strength is a major factor in patient selection, especially when combined with an estimate of the degree of hyperactivity and the possible disruptions created by impulse-ridden youngsters. Hyperkinesis—which may be thought of as a function of ego strength, since it is often more relative to the situation than to aberrant brain impulses—could exclude some children who were too disruptive to the group. This holds true particularly for late-latency children being treated primarily for school performance problems.

Boenheim reported:

It took considerable time to select the membership of a pilot group of boys and girls. We therefore determined not to overburden our difficult task by accepting cases of widely different intelligence, social status, and upbringing. I did not include psychotics or delinquents, but concentrated on boys and girls who had difficulties in mixing with members of their own and the opposite sex, who were shy, introverted, self-conscious.

Ackerman included all categories of personality and types of adolescent emotional disturbance excepting frank psychoses. In Schulman's work with adolescents, he excluded schizophrenics, for he found the group proved too stimulating to their fantasies and too threatening to their defenses. Psychopathic adolescents and intensely manipulative, aggressive adolescents fail to tolerate the interacting, goal-directed experience, and they can cause disintegration of the group. Other therapists, such as Parrish, sought in the patients the commonalities of problems of individual identity, background of traumatic and neurotic family relationships, and ego strength without regard to specific diagnostic categories.

The author (1961) found that his groups worked better if he excluded homosexuals, hallucinating delusional psychotics, and severely antisocial patients while mixing the silent and loquacious, the bright and the low intellectual level, and varied socioeconomic levels. It was provocative to read Godenne's

(1964 and 1965) description of her evolution of selection criteria. In her initial group the prevalence of behavior disorders required much more attention than just the group process itself; in her second group the diagnostic categories varied and included one chronic schizophrenic boy with severe learning problems. The same range of patient types occurred in Teicher's group.

The therapist and the over-all structure of the group constitute the over-riding considerations of patient selection, for if the group, especially a latency-age one, already contains several withdrawn and taciturn members, it behooves the leader not to include another similar child at that time. Patient choice, although hopefully not too limited by availability factors, can also be based on intuitive ideas and a spirit of experimentation. Personal contact between a prospective group member and the therapist before entry into the group makes it easier for all. Only one meeting proves sufficient to establish the patient-therapist relationship so that the child can enter the group.

Latency-age groups tolerate rather severe behavioral disturbances, especially if the child has had previous individual therapy. Ginott's criteria for patient selection in play therapy groups prove useful in a therapist's initial selection process. The author agrees with Ginott on excluding the incorrigible psychopathic child, the homicidal child, and the overt, sexually perverse child. The author finds that the group helps children with a not-too-fixed symptom of stealing, those possessing intense sibling rivalries, and those showing accelerated sexual drives. A severely threatened, ritualistic, socially bizarre and peculiar child may not establish effective communication at any useful level and, therefore, not enter the group. But children possessing physical deformities, tics, protruding teeth, and lower intellectual levels find the group experience helpful. They do not, as predicted initially and dourfully expected, lapse into hurt withdrawal from the often vehement interactions and taunts about the deformity, for the group perceives the victim's feelings and tends to support him.

In the author's preadolescent groups, the

diagnoses of most of the patients were behavioral problems with symptoms of immaturity, poor school and home adjustment, tantrums, and enuresis. A smaller number manifested neurotic patterns, such as anxiety attacks, tics, extreme shyness, and withdrawal. Psychotic and severly delinquent young adolescents were excluded. An interesting phenomenon occasionally appeared when a young adolescent adamantly rebuffed the idea of group therapy. The therapist insisted forcefully that a trial period was in order and, almost invariably, despite being made to attend, the youth remained in the group as a productive member.

Other clinicians who have described their selection decisions do not differ significantly from the foregoing. One survey (Peck and Stewart) of 280 child treatment institutions, including inpatient and outpatient facilities, showed 24 per cent use group play therapy. Nearly all regarded age and sex criteria as indispensable. Race was a relevant factor when state laws so dictated. Most respondents regarded intelligence, race, religion, and socioeconomic status as mixable elements in patient selection. Most frequently (79 per cent), group heterogeneity was deliberately sought. Children with extreme pathology, who were very aggressive, who acted out, who disrupted. and who possessed severe physical handicaps were excluded.

Size of Group

In group play therapy of preschool children, a group includes four to perhaps six children. Activity group therapy uses a larger number of children, not exceeding eight. Latency and preadolescent groups, mixed-sex or not, accommodate up to eight children well. When groups of early, middle, or late adolescents are being formed, however, getting enough group members is sometimes difficult. The adolescents, although 12 to 15 may be immediately available on a waiting list, develop obstacles, such as participation in important school events, jobs, or transportation difficulties. The therapist must screen 20 or 30 adolescents to wind up with a group of 15. Absenteeism resolves the group to about six or eight regular members, a secondary ring of three or four, and three who may be absent more than they appear. The larger size of groups reflects wider ranges of patient types and diagnoses with a mixture of the taciturn, the loquacious, the dull, and the bright.

Schedule of Meetings

Once the therapist forms his group, he confronts the questions of where, how often, and when the group should meet. Usually the circumstances of time, as a scheduled matter, determine how long the group meets. The range goes from 45 to 90 minutes, rarely longer. Once again, as with so many aspects of group psychotherapy of children, age levels create the variations of time. An hour with a latency-age group just about covers their attention span and tension accumulation. With longer periods they become restless, interruptive, and too tangential. Adolescents, especially in the middle and late strata, tolerate 90 minutes well and sometimes extend the period spontaeonusly to two hours, either with the therapist present or by other devices, such as gathering in the waiting room 15 to 30 minutes early. This phenomenon, or its counterpart of extending the session by gathering at a nearby drugstore or snack bar after the group meeting, creates administrative problems for the therapist, especially if he works at a busy clinic. His colleagues begin to report complaints by adult patients about that unruly group of kids who monopolize the waiting room.

The day of the week assumes importance and relevance, especially in private practice, for today's children are often so scheduled with lessons and appointments that fitting in the group's time becomes difficult. And a therapist needs to study carefully a situation in which a previously withdrawn 16-year-old youth now goes out for basketball. Should the therapist insist that he join the group or consider the ramification of the sport as possibly being of equal therapeutic value? Friday afternoon usually provides many more events competitive to the group than does Monday. The therapist also keeps in mind his own schedule for, if he is active in professional societies, his absences for meetings occur more often during the latter days of the week.

The time of the day for the group to meet confronts the therapist, parents, and school authorities with the basic questions of group values vs. school and social ones. Should the latency-age child attend his group during or after school hours? Generally speaking, for all ages it is preferable that the patient not miss school for the group. Leaving early every week on the same day and with the same patients sets him apart and acts negatively as a deterrent to progress. In urban areas with safe, adequate public transportation, adolescents find their way to the group without difficulty, but, if the group terminates too late in the day, traveling home, especially for the girls, may have unfavorable consequences.

The time of the year also presents problems. The summer school recess produces conflicts with camp, family trips, and, for adolescents, work hours. The author has found significant difficulties in outpatient work in keeping almost any age children's group going over the summer. Therefore, especially in a training setting, the author plans for such groups to form during late summer and begin in September. This schedule yields a run of nine to ten months of most productive meetings, possibly recessing for one to two months during the summer.

Attendance

Attendance at the group meetings presents certain unique problems. Usually the therapist believes regular involvement helps the child more than irregularities. This feature carries certain basic implications in outpatient settings of parental cooperation in situations where often the adolescent's symptoms complexly signal pathological family turmoil. When the adolescent starts to become healthier, the family patterns cannot stand the strain, the parents withdraw the youth prematurely or find excessive barriers to transporting him to the group meetings.

Another consideration about attendance confronts the therapist. If the child misses several sessions in sequence, does the thera-

pist drop him? When is absenteeism too much for the group's own integration and when does it go too far for the child's own good? Should a rule be set down at the start of the group that so many absences mean leaving the group? In general the author finds that absences reflect resistance at some level, usually in more than the child alone, and a family conference confronts the parents and the child with this resistance for resolution. Otherwise, rigid rules for attendance simply challenge the family, especially the adolescent, to violations and angry encounters.

Parents express another type of resistance by conning the child into telling them what happened in his group session and then using this information against the patient and others. Parents too severely disturbed for participation in concomitant parent groups may so use the child as their communication channel for their own extreme needs that they place an intolerable burden on the group and the patient, since the child cannot use his positive group experience at home without creating havoc. Family tensions and strife, when one parent insists on treatment and the other opposes it, catch the child in between, as his parents quarrel and dispute his attendance in the group.

Control of Group

Control means that group processes flow uninterruptedly but with some guidance by the leader when they threaten to engulf a member or become destructive. For example, in a midadolescent, mixed-sex group of the interview activity type, it is not unusual for the group to find a scapegoat, usually one of the boys who offers himself to be butted about. This phenomenon presents some merits, but sometimes the contagion grips the group so that they accelerate the teasing and the physical approaches beyond a point of value. One group had the victim volunteer to stand against the wall as they threw clay pellets at him. Then the therapist interceded quietly with a comment,

That's enough now. The group's feelings can hurt John and yourselves.

He rapidly asked each member what he or

she was feeling right then. As each responded, awareness grew of how the group movement had over-ridden individual compunctions to enlist strong, angry feelings against John. One girl shuddered and said,

I knew I was enjoying it, but it scared me, just like when my father loses control and yells at me.

Some children are too vulnerable at any age to be a group victim or even the leader of a group enterprise of average and uncontrolled emotions. The author witnessed one mixed group of early adolescents who had been permissively allowed to act out physically and to exhibit high degrees of generalized motor activity for four months. Some of the boys raced out of the room at times and chased each other through the corridors. The therapist permitted them to slap him on the back and address him by crude nicknames. Each session grew wilder and wilder until the author stepped in, replaced the leader, and changed the format. The next ten meetings remained disorderly and disorganized. The members milled about the room, making wisecracks or directing hostile remarks to each other. Any attempt by the new therapist, also a man, elicited rejection. Frequently the group members Indian-wrestled or played spin the bottle with a Coke bottle. Little verbal response met the therapist's attempts to focus on why they attended the group.

At times, the therapist directly asked a group member to refrain from aggressive or provocative behavior. This usually resulted in a temporary abatement. Gradually, total participation in group discussion, as compared with pairs or split-off small groups, increased. During the fifth meeting, the therapist was spontaneously offered the sole swivel chair in the room, symbolizing his acceptance as group leader.

A woman observer joined the group during the 15th meeting. She attempted to take notes, but this activity drew so much attention and criticism from the group that she soon abandoned her note-taking and participated in the group as a co-therapist. Her presence made the group leader more comfortable and also diminished the restlessness of the hyperactive girls in the group. Additionally, the withdrawn, anxious girls became less anxious and participated more in group

activity. The boys respond at first with a mixture of exhibitionistic and seductive behavior; after six or seven meetings, however, this behavior diminished. The loss of the first co-therapist and the subsequent addition of new co-therapists did not evoke intense responses from the group, and the group rapidly accommodated.

Group meetings showed periodic disorganization and disorderliness until two weeks before Christmas, at the 22nd meeting, when the group spontaneously planned a Christmas party. One boy, previously one of the most disruptive group members, was elected chairman of the planning committee. He enthusiastically organized the proceedings and produced a successful party, to which members brought refreshments, which they served, and where they exchanged gifts and played games. A minimum of hostile, acting-out behavior occurred.

This occasion appeared to mark a turning point in the evolution of the group. After the party, activity on a physical level declined considerably. Much less hostile, provocative behavior occurred. The group itself began increasingly to control disruptive or distracting behavior by focusing group attention on the instigators. The therapists now rarely needed to ask a group member directly to refrain.

Gradually, the adolescents ventilated and shared feelings on a verbal level. Typical adolescent problems—such as conflicts with authority, sibling rivalries, and fears of growing up—were discussed. The group and the therapists began to sense benefits from the therapy.

At the 40th meeting, one of the girls brought up the subject of leaving the group. Two meetings later she left the group. A report from her parents indicated general improvement in behavior at home and in school and amelioration of her presenting symptoms.

During the next nine or ten meetings, the group changed considerably, with only three or four of the original members remaining. In general, throughout the first year a core group of three to five patients remained relatively constant, and a fringe group of members showed less involvement, lower attendance, and a higher drop-out rate. Despite the introduction of new members, the group remained at the level of development it had achieved.

Group interaction and cohesiveness continued to grow. Feelings became verbalized instead of being acted out. Controlling disruptive behavior presented no serious problem as group authority became increasingly effective. Consequently, the therapists took a less active role in the group. Occasionally they gave support and offered a generalization by summarizing the discussion. The leaders evolved into guides and translators of behavior rather than distant authority figures.

Selection of Therapist

The above example of establishing control and direction of a group raises the question of therapist selection, a point alluded to indirectly in various discussions of the training of therapists. Berger indicates that a therapist who feels an obligation to cure his patients may hide a neurotic need to be omnipotent, and this need can block therapeutic progress by patients who feel coerced into getting better. A failure

to be aware of himself as an active participant as well as observer in the group therapeutic process and interaction and of his own transference and countertransference reactions

creates not-too-well-hidden anxiety, which the group in time senses. Stein describes an extensive set of training experiences with psychologists and social workers in a social agency, with beginning psychiatric residents, and with a third group made up of graduate psychiatrists in the psychiatric outpatient department of a general hospital—all in New York City. He found each group of trainees undergoing discernible degrees of anxiety. In each of the three groups, anxiety emerged from different causes—inexperience with any psychotherapy for the first group and the conflicts of the third group in shifting from years of practicing intensive, individual psychotherapy to doing group therapy. A summarizing statement of his experiences says,

The group psychotherapist needs to know something of mental and emotional illness and its treatment, especially the type of treatment that utilizes a group and a group method to facilitate communication in the groups, both verbal and nonverbal, through the establishment of relationships and interaction to the therapist and between the patients.

After training similar categories of trainees and others—including pediatricians, nurses, teachers, occupational therapists, and medical students—the author has concluded that the above ideals of training are excellent, but a basic consideration needs to be kept uppermost in the mind: the qualities of the person performing the act of therapy. Some psychiatrists with extensive experience and training in individual therapy cannot do well in group psychotherapy. Flexibility, sensitivity, responsivity, and personal, empathic warmth should underlie the successful group therapist's personality.

Do these qualities automatically exist in professionals—the psychiatrists, psychologists, and social workers who are traditionally the major contributors to group psychotherapy? If present in others, such as paraprofessionals, shouldn't provisions be made for adequate development and training?

Innovators encounter the credentials barrier and the basic problems of proper patient care. They know that people other than the traditional triad will enter the field. The growing concern for mental health manpower, especially in caring for children and their families, makes necessary some working notions of therapist selection, training, and supervision. Group psychotherapy will be a prominent feature of such work in community mental health centers, in well-baby clinics, and in so-called peripheral village or neighborhood health centers. Without enough superbly trained manpower available, the emphasis will shift to degrees of proficiency and skill in various designated levels of group psychotherapy. Senior professionals will prescribe the kinds of groups and their degrees of personality exploration according to the needs of the families, determining those needs by standardized tests and such family intake procedures as modified multiple impact therapy. Then, new group therapists—ministers, pediatricians, housewives, and others—will perform group therapy under a highly technical, electronic-based system of supervision, extensively using videotapes and other communication means. Throughout the growth and extension of good group therapy, the central theme will remain appropriate, planned selection of therapists with therapeutic designs for health care that meet the needs of the families who often do not fit our more traditional expectations of the model patient and family. Toussieng comments on the adaptations of traditional thinking to the novel needs of a training school in this respect.

Additional facets of therapist selection were scrutinized by Spruiell, who describes the countertransference in a situation of crisis for an adolescent group wherein the therapist's adolescent yearnings supplemented the group's transference, leading in a riot. Generally, the literature on outpatient group psychotherapy of adolescents and younger children focuses on sex and number of therapists, as do Solomon and Axelrod, who strongly suggest that the leader be of the same sex as members of one-sex groups. Speaking from the psychoanalytic model of the basically triangular configurations of mother, father, and child, Boenheim believes that the use of male and female therapists works well by simulating a father figure and a mother figure. Some theorists might argue that one treats the group, and the group processes induce pairing as a main dynamic of the patient in the group with the leader, thus probably negating the need for a male-female leader duality (Bion). Whether this notion, based on group psychotherapy with adults, applies to children's work remains untested experimentally. Perry found that:

It is a definite advantage in group therapy with children to have therapists of the opposite sex for purposes of interpretation and discussion.

Adler and Berman and Westman et al. consider dual, mixed-sex leadership valuable. Corrothers indicates the value of a woman therapist for an all-girl group, especially for the adolescent ages, as a person with whom they can identify. In 1964 and 1965, Godenne discussed this point, coming to the conclusion that the identity of leadership proves valuable but that the male leader should assume the dominant role.

The author has used variations in work with all age groups of children. It is not an automatic advantage to have two therapists, for the main consideration is their ability to demonstrate effective communication between themselves, between each of them and the group members, and between both of them and the group members. Interestingly, opposite-sex observers or recorders known to the children evoke similar oedipal-type responses, even if the observer is behind a one-way mirror. One group insisted the observer come out from behind the screen and join them, silently and nonparticipating though she might structure her role. They wanted her in their midst, and she became the target of comments such as, "She and the doctor have something going between them."

Christmas described another vector in working with disadvantaged youths:

Trained nonprofessional mental health personnel can provide an added therapeutic dimension in group treatment. . . . Because the patient of lower socioeconomic status generally identifies more easily with the nonprofessional of his own social class than with the middle-class or upper-class professional, he can more readily use nonprofessionals as role models.

She points out the language barrier. In the Southwest many patients of Mexican descent speak and communicate primarily in a preliterate language that combines Spanish and English in unique ways that are difficult to understand. Christmas goes on to say:

Ease of communication in the language of the deprived community and knowledge of reality factors in the lives of the patients supplement identification. The use of indigenous aides, mainly from the patients' own socioeconomic groups (working class or lower socioeconomic class), in varied mental health roles, not only provides new types of mental health services, but also makes possible identification of the effect of these new roles on group interaction, patient progress, and on family, community, and professional attitudes.

CLINICAL ASPECTS

Jobless Adolescents

Jobless, aimless adolescents need more than vocational testing or aptitude delineation. Group psychotherapy has been effective in helping these youths find ego-syntonic pathways. MacLennan and Kline extensively used groups in their work of focusing on and learning occupational roles and associated behavioral patterns, and they found groups to be the technique that was the most useful, productive, and congruent with the demands of the system. Similarly, Gavales combined individual and group counseling and vocational training for an aggregation of 85 adolescents, the majority of whom were high school drop-outs. Using the Manson Evaluation Test and counselor ratings, he found 72 per cent improved after six months.

Unwed Mothers

Adolescents in another sociomedical difficulty showed significant responses to group therapy. Kaufmann and Deutsch worked with pregnant, unwed adolescents, ages 12 to 16, in a milieu approach using group psychotherapy as an integral part. The staff of the clinic and the parents of the patients were involved in a combination of group psychotherapy and counseling, orientation, and education. The therapist, a woman who was flexible, refrained from imposing her middle-class standards, and she fed the girls symbolically and emotionally.

Twenty unwed adolescent primiparas were assigned randomly to an experimental group of eight and to a control group of 12. A 12-month follow-up, after termination of the 18-month treatment period, showed that none of the eight girls in the treatment group repeated the pregnancy; in the control group, nine of the 12 girls had become pregnant for the second time.

Delinquents

Almost uniformly excluded from routine outpatient treatment groups, delinquents are treated in homogeneous groups. Little mention occurs in the literature of group psychotherapy with delinquent, latency-age boys and girls; the focus rests on the adolescents. Sex considerations in patient selection become finalized at once, for no one discusses mixing the sexes in groups of delinquents.

Work with delinquents concerns their sociopathic behavioral patterns and related themes, such as reading disabilities and deprivations. Most therapists work with adolescents in institutional settings, rather than in clinics. The therapists encounter conflicts of institutional rules with their traditional impartiality, passivity, and authority roles. Perl describes the delinquent's view of reality, pointing out that authority is the one theme really grappled with in the institution.

What the delinquent feels to be the reality of life is so rejected by him, the bleak hopelessness of that reality is so fully ascribed to others, that the mere prospect of talking about it evokes in him an amount of hostility which militates against any real involvement in the psychotherapeutic process. It is the fear of having to face reality, not the often repeated platitude of "resistance to authority," which forms the most reasonable and therefore the hardest to overcome source of resistance in the delinquent. In fact, authority is exactly that part of reality which many can handle with the most ease, as the incarcerated delinquent, often with the most severe sociopathic traits, who soon succeeds in coming to terms with the authority of the administration, is buddy-buddy with the toughest guard or administrative supervisor, only to continue delinquency after release.

Emotional deprivation accompanies authority problems, and, this, in turn, places such pressures on the therapist that Kassoff comments:

The tremendous emotional demands of such deprived boys are really too great for the therapist.

Shellow and his colleagues describe an emphasis on limits, in contradistinction to Thorpe and Smith, who suggest that the therapist's role is characterized by warmth, understanding, and permissive disidentification from institutional authority. This same concern influenced Head in his estimation that one of the striking characteristics of many delinquent youths is their lack of motivation for change. This resistance to change implies rejection of community values as reflected by the adults in the adolescent's environment.

Change, the goal of most therapeutic endeavors, presents problems of measurement, especially in the role prescriptions of the staff, who have their own assumptions of what the youth bring with them and how delinquents should behave to demonstrate improvement. Since anxiety purportedly underlies behavioral deviance, it would be affected by treatment techniques producing change. Schulman (1957) described the antisocial adolescent as being

grossly intolerant of anxiety, or for that matter of any ego-dystonic feelings. The "solution" he has developed to keep tension at a minimum is to react impulsively, usually with motor aggressiveness and a disregard for the values and feelings of others.

Modifications of group psychotherapy techniques occur for adolescents in general and specifically for subgroups. Redl discusses the psychology of gang formation and how to relate it to the treatment of delinquents. Schulman (1957) suggests that the key to therapy of the delinquent adolescent is to re-establish an authority-dependency relationship leading to an outcome different from that which the adolescent previously experienced. Perl uses fantasy for a breakthrough with hard-to-reach delinquent boys. He selects desires for occupational achievement as expressed in hero fantasies and does this in a psychodramatic way. Stranahan and his colleagues report on activity group therapy with delinquent boys in an outpatient setting, which Epstein used successfully in residential treatment, as did Phelan. Studies of the use of a modified form of analytic group psychotherapy (Epstein and Slavson; Schwartz; Slavson, 1960) describe favorable results as based on clinical impressions.

Adler and Berman report on their use of multiple leadership in groups of delinquent adolescents.

We believe that dual leadership, which combines authoritive and nonauthoritative representatives, is the key factor in our project. By dividing the adult figure into two representatives—one representing the authoritative and denying aspect of the adult, the other representing an effort to understand and to make interpersonal contact—the problem of ambivalence is temporarily by-passed.

Kassoff suggests that there are advantages to multiple therapists for severely acting-out adolescent boys.

In work with delinquent adolescent boys, the therapists are usually men. This sex proclivity fails to hold true in reports about group psychotherapy with institutionalized delinquent girls; both men and women therapists are used (Hersko; Patterson). Gadpaille discusses the sequence of resistance in groups of institutionalized delinquent adolescent girls, pointing out that their resistance is first directed against dangers seen as emanating from the environment and later against internalized dangers. Head reports on sociodrama and group discussions with both boys and girls in which he finds the delinquent adolescent revealing

his perceptions of himself through choice of roles, identifications, projections, and through the content of his portrayals of each role situation.

In both clinic and inpatient settings the goals of ego organization and integration remain paramount, but the treatment styles differ with the kind of institution. Peck and Bellsmith report extensive use of group approaches to the treatment of delinquent adolescents in an extramural setting, including intake and parent counseling.

In a classical psychoanalytic mode, Gratton and colleagues believe

it is possible to have a consistent, fundamentally similar approach in the treatment of children throughout the age spectrum of adolescence, latency, and childhood. Group psychoanalytic therapy seems to be possible in all three stages, the theoretical framework and the material worked on being the same, only the mode of communication differing.*

Their patients seem to be neurotic, and acting-out behavior is part of that syndrome. Whether intense character disorders of the

---

* From the *Canadian Psychiatric Association Journal*, volume 11, pages 430–440, 1966.

degree described above by Hulse, Gadpaille, Head, and Peck would be treated likewise remains unstated. If interest can be judged by a count of topics, the literature on adolescent group therapy shows a major emphasis on the delinquent and on the neurotically disturbed adolescent.

Generic to all therapy is the problem of treatment techniques suitable to the uniqueness of the adolescent, who in our culture has always occupied a neither-hither-nor-yon position. The adolescent is neither adult nor child. As Slavson (1964) describes him, he no longer speaks primarily in a language of action but does not yet use primarily verbal communication, the content of which

consists of ideas and open communication of feelings and stress.

Most authors—except Gratton, Boulanger, and perhaps Anthony—suggest that adolescent group therapy differs from treatment of younger children.

In a recent paper, Quinn et al. poignantly described their technical dilemma in a three-year period of activity group therapy of latency-age girls as they developed the behavioral and biological traits of early adolescence. Since the therapists did not believe their patients were ready for adolescent discussion groups, they provided a setting in which their leadership moved from the neutral permissive parent mode to a more active directive role. This enhancement of therapist activity seemed inherent in working with adolescents.

The author has emphasized a union of the interview or discussion form with the activity type. Activity, as he uses the term, is not oriented to specific tasks but is allowed in a general way to permit the adolescent to manage the anxieties engendered by the therapy (Kraft, 1961). As in the work of Ackerman, Gratton, and most other authors, the object is to help the process of re-integration of ego structure, to give insight into peer relationships by means of knowledge and identification, and to smooth the paths of authority relationships.

The author suggests that the therapeutic role of the leader calls for more than interpretive passivity with these youths. Dependency on parents and adult authority figures is strong; yet there is a great deal of ambivalence toward the dependency itself. The ultimate maturation of the adolescent is in danger when he cannot express the need for both dependence and independence and gain gratification in each. The adolescent needs protection while he takes the opportunity to experiment and look about. He cannot, as Josselyn points out, be protected from all frustrations and dangers. He must try his strength. There is a need for delimitation of freedom in the adolescent. If adolescents give full vent to their impulses, they tend to become upset and anxious. Limits are very important in helping the adolescent see how he can guide his path to maturity.

Group therapy significantly meets the needs of the adolescent for peer acceptance and also meets the increasing peer orientation of latency-age children. Naturalistic observations of children in our culture indicate such a trend (Boulanger; Coolidge and Grunebaum). From a psychoanalytic viewpoint, Buxbaum belives that two peak periods of group formation occur in the lives of children. The first crisis occurs in the five- to seven-year-old age period and the second in adolescence. The child seeks and finds satisfaction for certain needs in the group more than in any other social setting or organization. Buxbaum suggests that the childhood period of group formation occurs during the phallic phase, when the child is forced to give up his physical dependence on his mother. As the child's close relationship with his mother undergoes gradual severance, he achieves independence in motility, expression, and body care. He no longer needs his mother for survival, and his relationship to her changes from an anaclitic to an object-libidinal character. Rejection of his sexual wishes for her leaves him frustrated and drives him into transferring his feelings for her to other people. The young child finds support for his new-found physical independence from mother and a welcome shelter in the group experiences. Fears connected with separating from mother and home diminish as the child transfers allegiance to the group leader. Elements of transference are an essential factor in childhood and adolescent group formation and serve as a major motivating force in group formation and a co-hesive force among group members.

Because of the legal technicalities and paucity of facilities, most reports refer to adolescent groups. Usually these are in societal settings geared specifically to this grouping and not accessible to admixtures of widely varying other diagnostic categories. The usual procedures for group psychotherapy of disturbed adolescents require modification to account for the contingencies of the character disorders of delinquents. These adolescents differ in their dyssocial patterns from those who, in the adjustment reaction of adolescence or a transitional neurotic acting-out incident, violate the legal, moral, and social values of the community. The adolescent with a delinquent character disorder persistently steals, is truant, runs away, or engages in other activities that usually mean removal to an institution.

Group psychotherapy for these adolescents has many difficulties, and the therapeutic form is complex. In the delinquent, characterological pressures for dissent and chronic uncooperativeness enhance their order of magnitude more than do the passive aggressive and other neurotic personality deviations. Yet Gersten's study in 1951 of group psychotherapy with male delinquents in an institution reported improved intellectual and school functions and enhancement of emotional maturity on psychological tests. Thorpe and Smith reported a repeating sequence of events, the first being episodes of testing and the second, a series of acceptance operations.

Since the delinquent adolescent often operates in a gang formation to some degree, studies of this phenomenon help make clear the efficacy of group psychotherapy with them (Redl). Group case work with street gangs and other studies have shown that adolescents are reachable on their home territory. Group therapy in an institution complicates the group process by the omnipresent demands of the administration, which create design and procedural difficulties.

Schulman (1956) emphasized a three-fold reason to integrate group psychotherapy into the total care and rehabilitation of these patients: (1) Intellectual insight and reality-testing occur in the group milieu. (2) Alloplastic symptoms and superego development can be observed. (3) The group situation readily tests the development stage of new attitudes, since each patient continues to perform and to exist in a homogeneous group of delinquents. In this framework the author assumes that delinquent youths use aggression predominantly to reduce internalized anxiety in the uniform presence of a weak ego structure and a defective superego.

Schulman suggested that the delinquent's inherent difficulty with society and its authority symbol could serve as the nidus for a therapeutic relationship if the therapist could manage this outlook. Modifications of the traditional therapist-patient relationship were built into the institutional situation. At the start, the adolescent group member knew without doubt that his getting out depended on the therapist, thus automatically endowing him with omnipotence. Then, as the therapist continued to model early life experiences—without their inconsistencies of feelings, exploitations, and dishonesties—he became somewhat of an ego-ideal for an embryonic superego.

In institutions for delinquent girls, the adolescents feverishly preoccupy themselves with sex, carrying it over to their group therapy, introducing a theme which they perseverate if not detoured by the therapist. Patterson describes "crushing," a term with a distinctive meaning among the girls and personnel of the school. This refers

to the intense and sexually charged friendships which develop between the girls at the school, particularly between the girl of one cottage and that of another.

These relationships, rather than out-and-out homosexual affairs, substitute for the previous heterosexual ones experienced by most of the girls.

As "crushing" is a forbidden activity, it becomes immediately desirable. . . .

and serves as defiance of authority. The group therapist must tussle with this phenomenon in the therapy sessions. Should he take the side of the institution or work it out? How?

Gadpaille observed this resistance and

others in what he termed a sequence of resistances. Apparently, the therapist's personality, as well as his choice of techniques, prevails in this circumstance. A well-constituted leader does not go overboard against the patient's maneuvers or with their often justified complaints about the paucity of understanding by institutional personnel of their needs and of their reactions to need frustration. And Head notes:

The loss of freedom, restrictions on communication, morale destroying dependency fostered by overly rigid controls, monotony, and lack of acceptance and respect accorded to adolescents by institutional staffs often create strong resentment, which constitutes a serious barrier to the therapeutic efforts.

Parrish describes ego strengths of the girls. Their emphasis on sex consciousness probably is one facet of establishing independence. Parrish suggests that the most compliant girls, who were in the least trouble in their communities, had the least ego strength, but those having the most difficulty showed considerably more ego strength in their attempts to solve their problems by seeking compatriots among others with similar problems. In group therapy these girls gained a sense of self-worth

through having their dress, speech, and actions sanctioned by the group members.

Retardates

The intellectual level of a child often signifies his functioning in a therapy group, depending on the age and I.Q. level of the other children in the group. Generally, therapists believe that children with average or above-average intelligence function adequately in a group. Major problems occur with children who have I.Q. levels below 85 and, oddly enough, often with children who are extemely brilliant. Difficulties arise for the less intelligent children when they do not understand what is going on and are the butt of jokes injected by the brighter group members. It proves unrealistic in most cases to expect a group of bright neurotic children to accommodate to the slow pace and often grossly immature development of a retard-

ate, despite the frequency of emotional immaturity in disturbed children.

Most investigators prefer to place retardates in groups that are homogeneous without reference to intellectual ability. Some therapists, assuming a type of intellectual insight as the *sine qua non* of successful group therapy, disparage retardates as group members. Sternlicht opposes this notion in his strong support of group therapy for retardates. The group process tends to be egosupportive, often focusing on social reinforcement as a major goal (Neham). Cowen stresses group play techniques in working with the exceptional child. Even children with limited imagination find outlets and strength in the group.

In the adolescent age range of retardates, one biosocial concern overwhelmingly concerns parents, institutional personnel, and therapists: how to protect the adolescent retardate from exploitation physically and socially? Girls present the serious problem of possible pregnancy, despite the pill. Group psychotherapy can address these issues. Consequently, the age range of retardates in the group may extend into the twenties (Fisher and Wolfson; Kaldeck; Miezio). Generally, the range of retardation covers the mild to moderate, with I.Q. levels of 50 to 70.

Astrachan contends that mental conflicts in mental retardates do not differ substantially from those of the normal child. Since the number of individuals in this range who are institutionalized is decreasing, she suggests that the basic problem rests in a social and personality defect. The group offered an outlet for the release of situational anxieties in an institutional setting while continuing as a constant source of support. Outpatient groups, as well as institutionalized groups, offer opportunities to form adequate interpersonal relationships. Fine focused on the here-and-now of daily living in groups in various settings while emphasizing for these girls their future role in the community. Treatment methods centered about confrontation and anecdotal examples in a supportive and educative manner. The present world received maximal attention in an extensive project by Stubblebine and Roadruck, in which they used interview and activity groups as integral parts of an over-all treatment plan. They found that the groups positively aided their total-push plan.

Underachievers

Underachievement occurs in any age bracket. Some parents look for it in pre-school nurseries. In its broadest definition, the term applies to any failure to achieve expected biopsychological, age-adequate performance. Thus, most disturbed children show development as a major criterion for improvement. How often does the child psychiatrist listen dolefully to a parent suggesting the termination of treatment, since the patient's grades have picked up to the point of over-all palatability. In his excellent survey of the subject, Gurman discusses in detail this question of definition, how to detect valid manifestations of the condition, and how to measure achievement discrepancy.

Underachievement by gifted students probably represents a different psychological phenomenon than that of less able, poorly performing students. In the student, what is situational and what is chronic? Each term carries different implications. Some investigators suggest there is no specific behavior syndrome which can differentiate its occurrence from that of other personality problems. Gurman concludes that

most concerned parties now accept under-achievement as a psychological and social reality and therefore have attempted to deal with its occurrence and to a lesser extent its prevention.

After examining the literature on the effectiveness of group counseling and the multiplicity of methodological problems, Gurman finds a lack of work using behavioral modification techniques. Leader-structured groups seem to be the most effective group method and, consequently, insight,

as it is defined by psychoanalytically oriented counselors and therapists, is not essential to the successful treatment of underachievers.

The author's work with children along the entire range of age and the varieties of under-achievement indicates that grades and scores do not equal success, but they surely help everyone if they soar in the course of therapy. More meaningful, however, are the trends indicated by the annual achievement test scores, which, unfortunately, often rest unattended in the child's office records and unknown to his parents. The children in the author's groups use grades the way their parents use them, as clues to competing but often with the trust of acceptability in the group regardless of the grade obtained. In such circumstances, the therapy group works through the envy, the rebellion, and the frustrations of the bright and the average over their failures to achieve.

Various ways of taking examinations, techniques of studying, the emotional investment of parents and other significant people in grades, the role of pleasure in school work, and the inevitable intense involvement in hindering, binding fantasy—all emerge for scrutiny and comparison. Usually, unless the family psychopathology devastates the gains the parents seek, report cards and teacher comments substantiate gains by the children. Underachievement, although often the presenting problem or a major component, becomes one of several areas of difficulty examined in the group. As this topic occurs, especially in the pre- and mid-adolescent groups, the therapist gives more information and solves more problems.

One technique the author has used successfully is the academic and didactic approach by using charts, diagrams, and brief lectures on the neuroanatomy of the nervous system. Emotional thinking and abstract thought become rationally organized for the patients as the ideas are presented in Rado's framework of reference. Often the children mock the therapist and each other in this new terminology:

Say, Doc, we got to your emotional brain on that one.

Oh, shut up, John, you know what the Doc said. You just muddle around in the deep and won't let your thinking brain take over—ever. What would your old lady do if you really hit the books? They'd cut you up some other way.

Having a scientific baseline affords these disturbed children a significant springboard for further self-confidence.

Drug Users

Linked to underachievement in ever-increasing frequency among mid- and pre-adolescents is the use of mind-altering drugs, marijuana, methedrine, LSD, mescaline, and other drugs. The majority of the adolescents we see in private practice consultation use these drugs to varying degrees. And, as the availability increases, younger children, such as those in late latency, begin to speak of grass as a precursor to new adventures.

There is no single, practical, acceptable approach to use with these patients to end drug usage, assuming that this goal holds merit. With major figures of governmental agencies testifying to the lack of hard data on any ill effects of marijuana and with the children cognizant of this, a therapist chooses his path carefully. If he forthrightly and baldly states he believes marijuana to be inimical to their interests, he sets up special paths of resistance to therapy. The author suggests to these patients that no one can stop them from turning on and that the group therapy is for emotional disturbances and family problems. In the course of the group's life they may make decisions about a number of items of life, including marijuana. As hackneyed as this may seem to the experienced therapist, it purveys novelty and unusualness to the teenager, so used to having rules, boundaries, and decisions made for him. Experience with this phenomenon is still time-limited, and the therapist has no way yet to evaluate a long view of this approach. Since marijuana may well become as much a part of life as alcohol, it behooves therapists to work carefully with these youths, preferably laying a framework with marijuana accepted as a fact of life to be integrated like others into a self-concept.

More difficult to work out, however, are the roles that harder drugs play for these patients. Rarely do we encounter a user of speed or acid who hasn't been turning on with grass. This does not imply, however, that marijuana usage leads to heroin.

Little in the literature on group psychotherapy deals with adolescents and hard drugs; no article discusses preadolescents and younger children. Eliasoph worked with drug addicts, some of whom apparently were adolescents, and said that psychodrama techniques proved helpful

in eliciting feelings about treatment and in bringing the patients into fuller participation in the therapy sessions.

He found these patients ineffectual in coping with interpersonal relationships. For example, a patient in role-playing would enact his inability to say "No" to a user of drugs for fear that the other person would be antagonized and no longer friendly to him.

Galbis, who became interested in the hippie population of Georgetown in the District of Columbia, founded the Washington Free Clinic, which rapidly grew into a busy psychiatric service utilizing crisis intervention and individual and group therapies. Narcotics usage among his adolescent patients increased, but LSD intake seemed to decline. These alienated youths, living in a drug-controlled world, worked in his groups, but some of his patients required methadone treatment after intensive individual and group psychotherapy failed.

In the author's recent experiences with drug-knowledgeable adolescents, the group confronted immediately in the first session what the ground rules would be for alcohol, cigarettes, destructiveness, and marijuana. No one disputed a prohibition against coming drunk or high on alcohol to the group or bringing liquor to the meetings. They did assert the right to be turned on before the sessions, meanwhile readily accepting a prohibition of the smoking of pot during the meetings.

After all Doc, you can't run the risk of a raid. What would the hospital here think of you?

No one brought up other drugged states such as LSD or mescaline, perhaps because the group meeting time was late Monday afternoon and the start of a new week. The important item, it seemed to the author, was the immediate defense of marijuana as all right for those who chose to turn on with it before the group meeting, despite the historical data we had on the group that all but one or two actually performed their dissipations with alcohol, not marijuana. Weed, a term in some ways also aptly descriptive of their hair styles, was a symbol of their group and their generation around which they could readily rally, though perhaps not consort with.

The group tended to perseverate on the multivariegated experiences known from these drugs. One could compare his "travels" with another's and lose the themes being pursued by the therapist and the group. Another problem was the junior narc, the adolescent nondrug-user who works with the local police to catch users. He is looked down on by most of his peers, and, when he becomes a group member, scapegoating presents serious obstacles for a while. The members, including the junior narc, assume the confidentiality of the group without much discussion and freely discuss their illegal activities connected with the procurement and distribution of drugs.

Children with Physical Problems

In 1948 Cruikshank and Cowen described their group work with physically handicapped children. Several years later, Dubo reported a study of 25 hospitalized tuberculous children treated in both individual interviews and groups. They preoccupied themselves with thoughts of death and other morbid content, as they were menaced by an introjected malignancy and needed to flee. Their motoric patterns reflected these fantasies, despite the medical injunctions against activity that would aggravate their illness. In the group work identification was established easily, as children who found the verbal expression of anxiety quite difficult in individual sessions empathized with fellow patients. They could then verbalize their feelings. Dubo commented wryly that the group discussions proved far more effective than the traditional explanatory movies commonly shown to tuberculosis patients.

Extrapolations of these experiences included classes for diabetic, allergic, and other afflicted children. Contrasting functions of the group emerged, Dubo noted, since

in tuberculosis or rheumatic heart disease the focus must be to probe the effect of anxiety on the course of illness, in the allergies psychogenic factors as precipitating causes must be uncovered. Because of this different emphasis, homogeneity in grouping is vital.

Patient identification and empathy with the verbal group member served to release emotions from restrictive intellectualized bonds.

Parental involvement in a pediatric setting also plays a significant role, as Ghory indicated in working with asthmatic children. The Convalescent Hospital in Cincinnati de-emphasized psychotherapy for the children and concentrated on the parents. Their program had separate groups for the mothers and fathers.

In addition to the prime value of educating the parents to the disease itself, these group sessions have allowed the parents to ventilate their feelings of anxiety, apprehension, and concern over their children and, where it exists, their own frustrated feelings of anger and hostility.

Wohl, who worked directly with the groups at the Convalescent Hospital, believed that the child in such a milieu was a responsible and participating member of the treatment community, and he was urged to react, identify, and rebel rather than be covertly instructed to be dependent and to regress. The mothers' groups clarified family processes, especially those affecting the sick child, and enabled them to accept hospital programs for their children in their fullest implications.

Foster Children

These children number more than 300,000 in a given year. The difficulties they encounter in their frequent shifts from one foster setting to another are notorious, and almost any treatment procedure that diminishes the trauma and alienates the distress is valuable. Watson and Boverman used group discussions to explore and to resolve the foster child's particular problems. They chose children in the late-latency age range, ages eight to 12, who were of the same sex and without symptoms of emotional illness. The children, strangers to one another at the start, met once a week for 90 minutes for five to seven sessions. Self-worth, dependency, and identity themes continually recurred in the substrates of such questions as: What will I grow up to be? Why aren't my parents raising me? Who will care for me tomorrow?

The processes of each group, report Watson and Boverman, showed common traits:

At first, the children denied there were any problems. Once the group was underway, however, the children shared problems and feelings about being foster children. The talk flowed freely, but as the children continued to talk, they became anxious about what they were sharing and the questions the leaders posed. As a result, they were reluctant to get the meetings started on time, their stories became longer and less relevant, their attention spans shorter, and their conversations more diffuse. The increased anxiety led to changes within the groups. The natural leader was no longer the child who could best put his problems as a foster child into words but rather the child who could either keep the discussion away from the subject producing anxiety or who could throw oil on the increasingly turbulent waters. Another step in the group process came at about the midway point. This was the gradual exclusion of the psychiatrist consultant as a leader. The children realized that the anxiety aroused at the group meetings was not going to be handled within the group but rather within their relationship with the agency. Since the consultant was not a full-time employee of the agency, the children turned to the agency's worker for leadership and the reassurance implicit in his presence that the agency would continue to help them once the group meetings were over.

The authors commented in an understated way how difficult it was to get their agency's social workers to accept this novel way of working with the children as a routine part of their programs.

Psychotic Children

Psychiatry has been challenged for decades by both the diagnosis and the treatment of psychotic children. With etiologies unknown in either the area of psychogenicity or organicity, we have adduced relationships that, according to psychoanalytic or other theories, produce the deep psychopathology observed in these children. Individual psychotherapy to instill correct object relations, sensory deprivation to reduce input to a minimum (Schechter et al.), LSD treatment, behavioral modification, and group psychotherapy—these and other procedures have been used in attempts to heal these aggrieved children. Eisenberg states that

it is evident that no over-all statement about outcome is justified.

Another opinion, by LaVietes, says that psychotic children tend to collect in special study centers and that

therapeutic techniques of varying types became established in these separate centers, which have, by and large, continued to refine their methods. As a result of this and the generally poor progress, there is no systematized psychotherapy of childhood schizophrenia, and varying methods are found from one center to another.

During the past ten years, psychotherapy has been used in a few units. Since psychosis in children does not occur so frequently that a private practitioner could have enough patients to treat, most group therapy studies have been in treatment centers at universities or in agencies. Speers and Lansing placed four psychotic children in a group treatment plan; later they added another preschool psychotic and traveled a treatment path for more than four years and 828 hours. Their consultant, E. James Anthony, originally predicted that therapeutic developments would be slow and sparse in providing satisfaction to the therapists and that the patients would not be kept in the place for long by their parents. Both surmises were wrong, and Anthony concluded:

I was left with the feeling that a major contributing factor lay in the metamorphosis that led gradually and most invertibly to the emergence of a communicative, conscious, cooperative self and of something impersonal and anonymous.

Were the changes in the children primarily from their own growth, with the group experience of little note, or from the technique involved? Anthony concluded that the group techniques were deeply involved in the children's improvement. The investigator's theoretical position was based on the development of group ego, which then sustained the defective egos of the individuals in the group. This theory seemed especially applicable to symbiotic psychotic children, offering them a therapeutic symbiosis. Results included enhanced or achieved communicative speech, some degree of self-identity, and movement upward in the developmental scale.

In contrast, Coffey and Wiener reported on 12 years of the East Bay Activity Center, which began almost spontaneously in response to the needs of several disturbed children, a number of whom were psychotic and excluded from social, recreational, and educational activities. The founders of the center believe it was necessary

for the child to have a place where he could be with other children and have an opportunity to express, at whatever rudimentary level, his social interest.

When their program faced the question of how to be therapeutic, one response was to turn to group therapy on an empirical basis. Later they found group psychotherapy bridged the gap between psychotic and nonpsychotic children in the same center.

Since some investigators believe that social hunger must be present and that the group provides a permissive environment where ego defenses are reduced, how would these two basic principles be realized in a group of autistic children without any speech and already unable to manifest ego defenses of even minimal strength? Not knowing the deck was so stacked, the staff of the East Bay Activity Center plunged into group therapy with zeal and enthusiasm, beginning with a small number of children and adding others later. They included catalyst children who had greater ego strength than the autistic and who had communicative speech and the capacity to distinguish between reality and fantasy. Reality-testing was a goal far more than catharsis, for the latter proved too destructive to the weak egos of the autistic children. Few interpretations were made and those were made individually to the catalytic children. The leaders attempted clarification of reality on a group basis, for example, explaining that certain behavior could lead to accidents or that so-and-so had not tried to hurt someone. The investigators believe that group experience helped the children. Certainly, if one is working with four or more psychotic children and the physical requirements of space and personnel are available,

group psychotherapy should be part of the total treatment regimen.

Jensen and his colleagues used various modalities with their schizophrenic patients, but their group efforts were aimed mainly toward the parents. Their paper fails to describe in detail their decision not to use group psychotherapy for the children.

Straight and Werkman described the intense control problems inherent in treating aggressive adolescent boys in a hospital. Their diagnostic labels included catatonic schizophrenic reaction, behavioral reactions with mental retardation, antisocial reaction in a sociopathic personality, emotionally unstable personality, and chronic brain syndrome. Their symptoms focused on fighting, stealing, homosexual activity, and homicidal acts. Such impulse-ridden patients from different parts of the hospital met twice a week as a group whose treatment goal was to modify impulse to enable them to fit into their wards and eventually the outside world. The therapists established a strict sameness of time, place, and therapists, the presence of relatively indestructible furniture, individualization of limits, active intervention in fights and in withdrawals from the group, and a pleasurable variation of activities, parties, and games outside of the regular group sessions. Controls included directly gratifying needs rather than denying degrees of freedom.

The Family

Implicit in this discussion is the group's relationship to the child's family of origin, for that biosocial structure remains a powerful influence on his performance and production within a group. Peer orientation overcomes the immediate, directly discernible family background, especially in the older age groupings, and it dominates the interactions when the group member must confront his fellow family members in full view. Few studies describe the results of this therapy in children, although the multiple-impact therapists report favorable results in 75 per cent after 18 months (MacGregor).

In family therapy more than two people are involved, and the interaction to that extent is not confidential, in contrast to the usual patient-therapist dyad. Nonverbal interaction assumes a primary importance along with the verbal. And family therapy is often briefer than individual therapy, although length of treatment is enormously variable. The aims are changes in the family system of interaction, not changes in the behavior of individuals. Beels and Ferber note:

> Family group treatment is a consulting sociological or socio-psychological technique and as such is unlike psychological treatment methods that aim for the welfare of an individual.

The family should function better as a family: That is the goal of family therapy.

The author tested this goal by assuming that children's signs and symptoms would change for the better if the major figures in the family system, the father and the mother, clarified their marital system of communication patterns by group psychotherapy. One patient, who originally was an encopretic, became free of soiling, but his next younger sibling began to soil. As the tides of parental relationship rose and receded, so did the symptoms of the children, who by design did not undergo concomitant psychotherapy or other treatments. This preliminary work indicated to us how necessary to therapeutic efforts with children was parallel counseling, family therapy, or other care for the parents.

The author considers family therapy that involves the children in group interaction—whether it be regularly, such as weekly, or intermittently—as a form of group psychotherapy for children. He has experimented with various modalities, now concluding that a therapist should be experienced in a variety of procedures and techniques. From his experience and self-knowledge, the therapist can decide which technique to use for a particular family system. Obviously at this stage of knowledge, not any one program works well for all.

The author has found multiple-impact therapy an excellent therapeutic device for opening a family. He has used the original format described by MacGregor and also a number of modifications, depending on the circumstances. Using a full-scale multiple-impact therapy proved very valuable for

teaching family dynamics and children-parent interactions to first-year psychiatry residents and to other professionals (Kraft, 1966). But owing to time and space limitations in the Child-Family Clinic of the Texas Children's Hospital, where multiple-impact therapy was emphasized for teaching family psychodynamics to pediatric residents, the staff contracted the customary format from 48 hours to four hours. Further alterations met the different needs in the psychoeducational day hospital program, where the therapy was found very useful as a means to acquaint the entire staff with the total family of the child patient.

Certain trends appeared over the years of usage. The individual interviews could be done by various staff members, such as a teacher, who would emerge with a greater appreciation of the family member, be he parent or sibling of the patient. The teachers, who had in their regular school experiences conducted parent conferences, found the multiple-impact therapy interviews of a different caliber, for these involved emotions and feelings behind the usual facade previously encountered.

Team-family sessions lasted 90 minutes and first occurred at the beginning of the two days of four or more hours each day with the family. These sessions revealed facets of the parents and the children in their self-presentations that often stood in sharp contrast to their views the next day in the last meeting of the family and team. For example:

> John, a severely disturbed six-year-old, had already by the end of his first year of regular school been designated as completely unsuited to the routine educational process. Multiple-impact therapy brought out the sadistic pattern the father used in his relationships with John, his mother, and his younger brother. John's mother's needs to be the object had not revealed this trend to the staff in the preliminary intake procedures, but therapeutic interaction uncovered the pattern. As one team member interviewed the father and the four-year-old brother simultaneously, the little boy's separation anxiety over his mother being elsewhere came through by his whining and complaining behavior. The father, when questioned how he

felt at that time, turned to the boy and told him to be quiet or he would take him downstairs and leave him in the car.

The multiple-impact therapy format has proved quite alterable and still productive. The team interactions among themselves receive less emphasis, especially since the number of student observers has increased via closed-circuit television and one-way mirrors. The basic intent of opening the family to itself and to the staff is accomplished in varying degrees in each of the variations employed.

The incorporation of another interactional device, dance therapy, into multiple-impact therapy has had highly promising results. Communication through body movements (Kraft and Delaney), generically termed dance therapy, offers an exciting approach to a family study, for parents and children reveal actions not usually available for study in the interviewing techniques ordinarily used. The room used by the author is 20 feet by 15 feet and is carpeted and bare of furnishings except for a conference table at one end. Two one-way mirrors open the room to observers and cameras. The dance therapist, sometimes aided by one of the family therapy team, introduces the parents and children to basic rhythmic patterns, relaxation exercises, and then dramatizations by nonverbal expressions of key human interactions, such as an episode of anger or sadness. The ways in which the participants interact often reveal nonverbalized power positions. For example, in one family the father's power veneer began to crack as his wife became freer with her body movements; he asserted direction over the choice of records and what to do next. She humbly resubmitted but covertly encouraged Phil, their nine-year-old disturbed son, to carry out her rebelliousness.

RESULTS

The author has impressionistic opinions about the results of dance therapy and other techniques. These modifications of dance therapy, termed discovery therapy, have become a form of group therapy for children in the day hospital setting, especially for those who have the worst problems of communication. Children who utilized mutism, hyperkinesis, logorrhea, schizoid withdrawal, and pugnacious behavior could be worked with in groups as well as individually. Using fantasy, creative mini-dramas, and other techniques, the dance therapist involves the children in group interaction, which is then integrated with other psychoeducational therapeutic tactics in the total treatment program.

Jody, a girl who was extremely tall for her age, came to the day hospital for completely uncontrollable rage episodes that disabled her academically and behaviorally everywhere. One subarena of involvement that reached her deeply was discovery therapy in a small group of three or four children. Later, as she improved in her behavior, she turned to the dance therapist for individual sessions of more academic, pureform dance exercises. Jody had learned additionally in this form of group therapy to relate herself to others in ways formerly too dangerous for her.

Other dance therapists have worked with autistic children in a group manner that differs from our usual conception of the group method. These pioneering efforts deserve support and further investigation. They differ from the flowering encounter group movement, and they do offer new means for children to communicate through body movements messages and information not readily communicable by other means.

The results of these various enterprises in group psychotherapy of children are difficult to assess and to evaluate. Some studies used control groups, but evaluating the results of these and other studies proves as difficult as assessing individual psychotherapy of children. Novick attempted a comparison between short-term group and individual psychotherapy to effect behavioral changes in eight- to ten-year-old boys. He found that children who are classified as having good ego strength respond to psychotherapy, independent of whether it is group or individual psychotherapy, provided that a minimum period of psychotherapy occurs, e.g., 20 sessions.

Group therapy does not supplant or replace individual therapy. It is an effective tool that needs to be learned and used under supervision. Group therapy offers continued promise for use in community mental health clinics, in private practice, and in other circumstances attempting to meet the growing therapeutic needs of our youth.

REFERENCES

Ackerman, N. W. Group psychotherapy with a mixed group of adolescents. Int. J. Group Psychother., *5:* 249, 1955.

Adler, J., Berman, I. R., and Slavson, S. R. Residential treatment of delinquent adolescents. V. Multiple leadership in group treatment of delinquent adolescents. Int. J. Group Psychother., *10:* 213, 1960.

Anderson, J. E. Group therapy with brain-damaged children. Hosp. Community Psychiat., *19:* 175, 1968.

Andre, R., Heligman, A., Higgins, R., Karatz, J., and Kottler, A. Short-term social group work in the hospital. Ment. Hyg., *50:* 226, 1966.

Anthony, E. J. Age and syndrome in group psychotherapy. In *Topical Problems of Psychotherapy*, vol. 5, p. 75, A. L. Kadis and C. K. Winick, editors. New York, 1965.

Asperoff, B. J., and Simon, D. Problems and approaches in child group psychotherapy in a public school milieu. Group Psychother., *16:* 39, 1963.

Astrachan, U. Group psychotherapy with mentally retarded female adolescents and adults. Amer. J. Ment. Defic., *60:* 152, 1955.

Axelrod, P. L., Cameron, M. S., and Solomon, J. C. An experiment in group therapy with shy adolescent girls. Amer. J. Orthopsychiat., *14:* 616, 1944.

Barnwell, J. E. Group treatment of older adolescent boys in a family agency. Soc. Casework, *41:* 247, 1960.

Becker, B. J., Gusrae, R., and MacNicol, E. A clinical study of a group psychotherapy program for adolescents. Psychiat. Quart., *37:* 685, 1963.

Beels, C. C., and Ferber, A. Family therapy; a review. Family Process, *8:* 280, 1969.

Bender, L., and Woltman, A. S. Use of puppet shows as a psychotherapeutic method for behavior problems in children. Amer. J. Orthopsychiat., *6:* 341, 1936.

Berger, M. Problems of anxiety in group psychotherapy trainees. In *Group Psychotherapy and Group Function*, p. 555, M. Rosenbaum and M. Berger, editors. Basic Books, New York, 1963.

Berman, L. Mental hygiene for educators; report on an experiment using a combined seminar and group psychotherapy approach. Psychoanal. Rev., *40:* 319, 1953.

Bion, W. R. *Experiences in Groups and Other Papers*. Basic Books, New York, 1961.

Block, S. L. Multi-leadership as a teaching and therapeutic tool in group psychotherapy. Compr. Psychiat., *2:* 211, 1961.

Blom, G. E. The psychoeducational approach to emotionally disturbed children. Med. Rec. Ann., *61:* 348, 1968.

Boenheim, C. Group psychotherapy with adolescents. Int. J. Group Psychother., *7:* 398, 1957.

Boulanger, J. B. Group psychoanalytic therapy in child psychiatry. Canad. Psychiat. Assoc. J., *6:* 272, 1961.

Buxbaum, E. Transference and group formation in children and adolescents. Psychoanal. Stud. Child, *1:* 351, 1945.

Chigier, E. Group therapy in a school by the school physician, in Israel. J. Sch. Health, *33:* 471, 1963.

Christmas, J. J. Group therapy with the disadvantaged. In *Current Psychiatric Therapies*, vol. 6, p. 167, J. Masserman, editor. Grune & Stratton, New York, 1966.

Coffey, H. S., and Wiener, L. L. *Group Treatment of Autistic Children*. Prentice-Hall, Englewood Cliffs, N. J., 1967.

Commission on Group Psychotherapy Report, World Federation for Mental Health. Int. J. Group Psychother., *2:* 172, 1952.

Cooley, C. *Social Process*. Charles Scribner, New York, 1918.

Coolidge, J. C., and Grunebaum, M. G. Individual and group therapy of a latency age child. Int. J. Group Psychother., *14:* 84, 1964.

Corsini, R. J. *Role Playing in Psychotherapy*. Aldine Publishing, Chicago, 1966.

Cowen, E. L., and Matthew, J. T. Psychotherapy and play technique with the exceptional child and youth. In *Psychology of Exceptional Children and Youth*, p. 526, W. M. Cruickshank, editor. Prentice-Hall, Englewood Cliffs, N. J., 1963.

Cruickshank, W. M., and Cowen, E. L. Group therapy with physically handicapped children. J. Educ. Psychol., *39:* 193, 1948.

Davidson, P. W. Comment on the small activity group project of the Montebello Unified School District. J. Sch. Health, *35:* 423, 1965.

Dubo, S. Opportunities for group therapy in pediatric service. Int. J. Group Psychother., *1:* 235, 1951.

Duffy, J. H., and Kraft, I. A. Beginning and middle phase characteristics of group psychotherapy of early adolescent boys and girls. J. Psychoanal. Group. *2:* 23, 1966–67.

Eisenberg, L. Psychotic disorders. I. Clinical features. In *Comprehensive Textbook of Psychiatry*, pp. 1433–1438, A. M. Freedman and H. I. Kaplan, editors. Williams & Wilkins, Baltimore, 1967.

Eliasoph, E. A group therapy and psychodrama approach with adolescent drug addicts. Group Psychother., *8:* 161, 1955.

Feder, B. Limited goals in short-term group psychotherapy with institutionalized delinquent adolescent boys. Int. J. Group Psychother., *12:* 503, 1962.

Field, L. W. An ego-programmed group treatment approach with emotionally disturbed boys. Psychol. Rep. *18:* 47, 1966.

Fine, R. H., and Dawson, J. C. A therapy program for the mildly retarded adolescent. Amer. J. Ment. Defic. *69:* 23, 1964.

Fisher, H., Sternberg, S., and Wetherill, B. A. Analytic group psychotherapy with pre-school-aged children and their mothers. Presented at annual meeting of American Group Psychotherapy Association, New York, 1967.

Fisher, L., and Wolfson, I. Group therapy of mental defectives. Amer. J. Ment. Defic. *57:* 463, 1953.

Foulkes, S. H. Some basic concepts in group psychotherapy. In *International Handbook of Group Psychotherapy*, p. 166, J. L. Moreno, editor. Philosophical Library, New York, 1966.

Foulkes, S. H., and Anthony, E. J. *Group Psychotherapy. The Psycho-Analytic Approach.* Penguin Books, Baltimore, 1957.

Fried, E. Ego emancipation of adolescents through group psychotherapy. Int. J. Group Psychother., *6:* 358, 1956.

Gabriel, B. Group treatment of six adolescent girls. Newslet. Amer. Assoc. Psychiat. Soc. Workers, *13:* 65, 1943.

Gadpaille, W. J. Observations on the sequence of resistance in groups of adolescent delinquents. Int. J. Group Psychother., *9:* 275, 1959.

Galbis, R., quoted in Med. Tribune, *11:* 5, January 5, 1970.

Ganter, G., Yeakel, M., and Polansky, N.A. Intermediacy group treatment of inaccessible children. Amer. J. Orthopsychiat., *35:* 739, 1965.

Garai, J. E. The use of classroom discussion as a special technique for the promotion of personality growth of students. In *International Handbook of Group Psychotherapy*, p. 629, J. L. Moreno, editor. Philosophical Library, New York, 1963.

Gavales, D. Effects of combined counseling and vocational training on personal adjustment. *J. Appl. Psychol.*, *5:* 18, 1966

Geller, J. J. Group psychotherapy in child guidance clinics. In *Current Psychiatric Therapies*, vol. 3, p. 219, J. Masserman, editor. Grune & Stratton, New York, 1963.

Gersten, C. An experimental evaluation of group therapy with juvenile delinquents. Int. J. Psychother., *1:* 311, 1951.

Gersten, C. Group therapy with institutionalized delinquents. J. Genet. Psychol., *80:* 35, 1952.

Ghory, J. E. The short-term patient in a convalescent hospital asthma program. J. Asthma Res. *3:* 243, 1965.

Ginott, H. *Group Psychotherapy with Children.* McGraw-Hill, New York, 1961.

Godenne, G. D. Outpatient adolescent group psychotherapy. I. Review of the literature of use of co-therapist, psychodrama, and parent group therapy. Amer. J. Psychother., *18:* 584, 1964.

Godenne, G. D. Outpatient adolescent group psychotherapy. II. Use of co-therapists, psychodrama, and parent group therapy Amer. J. Psychother., *19:* 40, 1965.

Goldin, P. C. A review of children's reports of parent behaviors. Psychol. Bull. *71:* 222, 1969.

Gratton, L., Lafontaine, C., and Guibeautt, J. Group psychoanalytic work with children. Canad. Psychiat. Assoc. J., *11:* 430, 1966.

Gurman, A. S. Group counseling with underachievers: a review and evaluation of methodology. Int. J. Group Psychother., *19:* 463, 1969.

Hart, J. T., Kraft, I. A., Williams, S. G., and Blair M. A preliminary study of interview group psychotherapy of boys and girls of latency age. J. Psychoanal. Group., *2:* 9, 1968.

Head, W. A. Sociodrama and group discussion with institutionalized delinquent adolescents. Ment. Hyg. *46:* 127, 1962.

Hersko, M. Group therapy with delinquent girls. Amer. J. Orthopsychiat., *32:* 1969, 1962.

Hulse, W. Psychiatric aspects of group counseling of adolescents. Psychiat. Quart., *34:* 307, 1960.

Hyman, H. The psychology of status. Arch. Psychol. *269:* 94, 1942.

Hyman, H. The psychology of subjective status. Psychol. Bull., *39:* 473, 1942.

Jensen, S. E., Boden, F. K., and Multari, G. Treatment of severely disturbed children in a community. Canad. Psychiat. Assoc. J., *10:* 325, 1965.

Josselyn, I. M. *The Adolescent and His World.* Family Service Association of America, New York, 1952.

Kaldeck, R. Group therapy with mentally defective adolescents and adults. Int. J. Group Psychother., *8:* 185, 1958.

Kassoff, A. L. Advantage of multiple therapists in a group of severely acting-out adolescent boys. Int. J. Group Psychother., *8:* 70, 1958.

Kaufmann, P. N., and Deutsch, A. L. Group therapy for pregnant unwed adolescents in the prenatal clinic of a general hospital. Int. J. Group Psychother., *17:* 309, 1967.

Knorr, N. J., Clower, C. G., and Schmidt, C. W., Jr. Mixed adult and adolescent group therapy. Amer. J. Psychother., *20:* 323, 1966.

Konopka, G., and Wallinga, J. V. Stress as a social problem. Amer. J. Orthopsychiat., *34:* 536, 1964.

Kraft, I. A. The nature of sociodynamics and psychodynamics in a therapy group of adolescents. Int. J. Group Psychother., *10:* 313, 1960.

Kraft, I. A. Some special considerations in adolescent group psychotherapy. Int. J. Group Psychother., *11:* 196, 1961.

Kraft, I. A. Multiple-impact therapy as a teaching device. Amer. Psychiat. Assoc. Res. Rep. *20:* 218, 1966.

Kraft, I. A. An overview of group therapy with adolescents. Int. J. Group Psychother., *18:* 461, 1968.

Kraft, I. A., and Delaney, W. Movement communication with children in a psychoeducational program at a day hospital. J. Amer. Dance Ther. Assoc., *1:* 6, 1968.

LaVietes, R. Psychotic disorders. II. Treatment. In *Comprehensive Textbook of Psychiatry*, pp. 1438–1444, A. M. Freedman and H. I. Kaplan, editors. Williams & Wilkins, Baltimore, 1967.

Lebovici, S. Psychodrama as applied to adolescents. J. Child Psychol. Psychiat. *1:* 298, 1961.

MacGregor, R., Ritchie, A. M., Serrano, A. C., and Schuster, F. P. *Multiple Impact Therapy with Families.* Grune & Stratton, New York, 1964.

MacLennan, B. W., and Kline, W. L. Utilization of groups in job training with the socially deprived. Int. J. Group Psychother., *15:* 424, 1965.

McCormick, C. G. Objective evaluation of the process and effect of analytic group psychotherapy with adolescent girl. Int. J. Group Psychother., *3:* 181, 1953.

Miezio, S. Group therapy with mentally retarded adolescents in institutional settings. Int. J. Group Psychother., *17:* 321, 1967.

Miller, S. M. Breaking the credentials barrier. Presented at meeting of American Orthopsychiatric Association, Washington, D. C., March 23, 1967. Reprinted by the Ford Foundation.

Neham, S. Psychotherapy in relation to mental deficiency. Amer. J. Ment. Defic., *55:* 557, 1951.

Novick, J. I. Comparison between short-term group and individual psychotherapy in effecting change in nondesirable behavior in children. Int. J. Group Psychother., *15:* 366, 1965.

Parrish, M. M. Group techniques with teenage emotionally disturbed girls. Group Psychother., *14:* 20, 1961.

Patterson, R. M. Psychiatric treatment of institutionalized delinquent adolescent girls. Dis. Nerv. Syst., *11:* 227, 1950.

Peck, H. B., and Bellsmith, V. *Treatment of the Delinquent Adolescent.* Family Service Association of America, New York, 1954.

Peck, M. L. and Stewart, R. H. Current practices in selection criteria for group play-therapy. J. Clin. Psychol., *20:* 146, 1964.

Perl, W. R. Use of fantasy for a breakthrough in psychotherapy groups of hard-to-reach delinquent boys. Int. J. Group Psychother., *13:* 27, 1963.

Perry, E. The treatment of aggressive juvenile delinquents in "family group therapy." Int. J. Group Psychother., *5:* 131, 1955.

Quinn, C., Robison, O. L., and Egan, M. H. A longitudinal experience with preadolescent girls in "transitional" group therapy. Presented at annual meeting of American Orthopsychiatric Association, New York, March 30–April 2. Amer. J. Orthopsychiat. *39:* 263, 1969.

Rado, S. *Psychoanalysis of Behavior.* Grune & Stratton, New York, 1962.

Redl, F. The psychology of gang formation and the treatment of juvenile delinquents. In *The Psychoanalytic Study of the Child*, vol. 1, p. 367. International Universities Press, New York, 1945.

Rosenbaum, M., and Kraft, I. A. Group psychotherapy for children. *In Manual of Child Psychopathology*, B. B. Wolman, editor. McGraw-Hill, New York, in press.

Schechter, M. D., Shurley, J. T. Sexauer, J., and Toussieng, P. W. Perceptual isolation therapy: a new experimental approach in the treatment of children using infantile autistic defenses. J. Amer. Acad. Child Psychiat., *8:* 97, 1969.

Schulman, I. Delinquents. In *Fields of Group Psychotherapy.* p. 196, S. R. Slavson, editor. International Universities Press, New York, 1956.

Schulman, I. Modifications in group psychotherapy with antisocial adolescents. Int. J. Group Psychother., *7:* 310, 1957.

Schulman, I. Transference, resistance and communication problems in adolescent psychotherapy groups. Int. J. Group Psychother., *9:* 496, 1959.

Shellow, R. S., Ward, J. L., and Rubenfeld, S. Group therapy and the institutionalized delinquent. Int. J. Group Psychother., *8:* 265, 1958.

Sherif, M., and Cantril, H. *The Psychology of Ego-Involvements.* John Wiley, New York, 1947.

Sherif, M., Harvey, O. J., White, B. J, Hood, W. R., and Sherif, C. W. *Intergroup Conflict and Cooperation: The Robbers Cave Experiment.* Institute of Group Relations, Norman, Okla., 1961.

Shiffer, M. *Therapeutic Play Group.* Grune & Stratton, New York, 1969.

Slavson, S. R. *Analytic Group Psychotherapy with Children, Adolescents, and Adults.* Columbia University Press, New York, 1950.

Slavson, S. R. The scope and aims of the evaluation study. Int. J. Group Psychother., *10:* 176, 1960.

Slavson, S. R. Para-analytic group psychotherapy: a treatment of choice for adolescents. Pathways Child Guidance, *6:* 1, 1964.

Slavson, S. R. *A Text Book in Analytic Group Psychotherapy.* International Universities Press, New York, 1964.

Smolen, E. M., and Lifton, N. A special treatment program for schizophrenic children in a child guidance clinic. Amer. J. Orthopsychiat., *36:* 736, 1966.

Soble, D., and Geller, J. J. A type of group psychotherapy in the children's unit of a mental hospital. Psychiat. Quart., *38:* 262, 1964.

Solomon, J. C., and Axelrod, P. Group psychotherapy for withdrawn adolescents. Amer. J. Dis. Child., *68:* 86, 1944.

Speers, R. W., and Lansing, C. *Group Therapy in*

Childhood Psychosis. University of North Carolina Press, Chapel Hill, 1965.

Spotnitz, H. Observations of emotional currents in interview group psychotherapy with adolescent girls. J. Nerv. Ment. Dis., *106:* 565, 1947.

Spruiell, V. Countertransference and an adolescent group crisis. Int. J. Group Psychother., *17:* 298, 1967.

Stein, A. The training of the group psychotherapist. In *Group Psychotherapy and Group Function*, p. 558, M. Rosenbaum and M. Berger, editors. Basic Books, New York, 1963.

Sternlicht, M. K. Psychotherapeutic techniques useful with the mentally retarded: a review and critique. Psychiat. Quart., *39:* 84, 1965.

Stevenson, H. W., and Knights, R. M. Social reinforcement with normal and retarded children as a function of pretraining. Amer. J. Ment. Defic. *66:* 866, 1962.

Straight, B., and Werkman, S. L. Control problems in group therapy with aggressive adolescent boys in a mental hospital. Amer. J. Psychiat., *114:* 998, 1958.

Stranahan, M., Schwartzman, C., and Atkins, E. Group treatment for emotionally disturbed and potentially delinquent boys and girls. Amer. J. Orthopsychiat., *27:* 518, 1957.

Stubblebine, J. M., and Roadruck, R. D. Treatment program for mentally deficient adolescents. Amer. J. Ment. Defic. *60:* 552, 1956.

Teicher, J. D. Group psychotherapy with adolescents. Calif. Med., *105:* 18, 1966.

Thorpe, J. J., and Smith, B. Operational sequences in group psychotherapy with young offenders. Int. J. Group Psychother., *2:* 24, 1952.

Toussieng, P. W. The child psychiatrist in a state industrial school. Ment. Hyg., *48:* 273, 1964.

Warkentin, J. An experience in teaching psychotherapy by means of group therapy. In *Group Psychotherapy and Group Function*, p. 577, M. Rosenbaum and M. Berger, editors. Basic Books, New York, 1963.

Watson, K. W., and Boverman, H. Preadolescent foster children in group discussions. Children, *15:* 65, 1968.

Westman, J. C., Kansky, E. W., Erikson, M. E., Arthur, B., and Vroom, A. L. Parallel group psychotherapy with the parents of emotionally disturbed children. Int. J. Group Psychother., *13:* 52, 1963.

Wickman, E. K. *Children's Behavior and Teachers' Attitudes*. Commonwealth Fund, New York, 1928.

Wohl, T. H. The group approach to the asthmatic child and family. J. Asthma Res. *4:* 237, 1967

5

Group Therapy with Neurotics and Psychotics

Max Day, M.D. and Elvin Semrad, M.D.

INTRODUCTION

The use of group psychotherapy with neurotics and psychotics has grown steadily during the past 40 years. Despite growing interest in special categories of patients, such as couples and families, and despite current attempts to effect changes by intense, short-term, or goal-directed approaches, the use of psychoanalytic group therapy with neurotics and psychotics has continued apace.

In 1921, Freud described the unconscious dynamics of groups when he speculated on the phylogenetic origins of the psychic structures and developed a study of the ego and the superego. Since then, a broad school of psychoanalytically based approaches to group therapy has arisen, ranging from those, like Wolf and Schwartz, who practice individual psychoanalysis in a group setting to those, like Bach and Foulkes, who see analytic group therapy as psychotherapy with a psychoanalytic orientation. In between are those, like Slavson, who concentrate on individual dynamics in the group setting, those like Kadis, who rely more on group approaches, and those, like Bion, who work with the group on the basis of the Kleinian theories of projective identification and the interplay between the paranoid-schizoid and the depressive positions.

Whatever the particular technique, the general goal of analytic group therapy is improvement in the neurotic or psychotic patient's personal functioning. The group helps the patient express and diminish his infantile sources of behavior by studying first his conscious motivations and then, gradually, his unconscious motivations. The study of spontaneous interaction leads to the intrapsychic and genetic sources of behavior.

The leader is present as an organizing force. Because of their contact with him, the group members engage in a series of interactions that show varying degrees of cooperation, competition, and conformity to the leader's objectives. Threats of trauma, frustration, jealousy, affection, anger, and loss constantly realign the members. They become increasingly dependent on the leader and, at the same time, struggle against him, so that anxiety grows. Their anxiety continues until they accept their dependency as natural in the situation. Group life thus poses certain problems for patients. Along with their usual need to deal with inner pain caused by instinct anxiety, ego anxiety, and superego anxiety, they have to cope with heightened object anxiety.

Group behavior is, in part, a reflection of the patients' mechanisms of defense, which vary according to their different levels of personality development. The relatively mature patient—the normal or neurotic—is preoccupied with problems of gratification and responsibility. He can deal with these problems at a price—he becomes neurotic. The borderline patient requires certain

78

qualities from his objects in order to maintain his equilibrium. He is more interested in equilibrium and in obtaining support for his inner equilibrium than he is in gratification. He may or may not carry out productive work, but he does so not for the sake of pleasure or self-expression but rather to ensure support. The least mature patient— the psychotic—is preoccupied with survival. With inordinate effort he wipes out manifestations of inner feelings, such as need, jealousy, yearning, pain, loss, anxiety, frustration, and self-expression.

The psychotic is concerned with dependence and tolerance. When he is not immediately gratified, he may become petulant or walk out of a group meeting, stay away from meetings, deny that he is getting anything out of the group, or complain of feeling rejected or unloved. In dealing with object anxiety, he may escape into fantasy or denial. The borderline patient may resort to surrender—putting his trust in the leader as a way of denying the necessity for personal effort. The neurotic struggles with problems of aggressive mastery and power-seeking; some of this behavior may be counterdependent, but some may show a trend toward assuming responsibility. Neurotics and borderline patients may use denial to deal with object anxiety and inner anxieties. They may also identify with the aggressor in an attempt to deal with their helplessness and to adapt to the group and its work.

By supplying ego functions missing in the members, the leader provides support and gratification so that they can contain their anxiety and proceed with the analytic work of the group. At times he must balance benefits to the group and benefits to the individual patients. As a scapegoat, he is an important neutralizing factor in the group and a productive substitute for the discharge of aggressive energy. Gradually, by identification with him, the members become increasingly independent of him.

The group offers its members a here-and-now replica of society, with possibilities for socialization, the testing of reality perception, and modulation of intense affects and behavior. It stresses the positive values of honesty, interpersonal relatedness, work,

perspective, knowledge, and the bearing of healthy tension. Ultimately, the members become aware of each other as separate persons with assets and liabilities, and they develop feelings of respect and warmth but not necessarily love.

THEORETICAL ASPECTS

Aims of Therapy

Sometimes the group therapist contents himself with helping a patient abreact— undo a regression by releasing repressed feelings related to a recent trauma and coming to terms with its ultimate meanings for the patient's life. Such work can most easily be done with patients who are reacting to some loss or related threat. More often, the patient has slid into a regression, neurotic or psychotic; the most recent insult is but the last of many in a downhill course. Such a patient requires long-term work in which the most recent traumata and many earlier ones have to be dealt with. What is required is a systematic review of all the determinants of the patient's personality structure.

The therapist and the group help him become acquainted with and master the unconscious motivations that led to the decompensation.

Type of Therapy

Analytic Group Therapy. The approach is psychoanalytic in that it is based on an understanding of the unconscious, the development and analysis of a transference neurosis, and the analysis of resistances as they become manifest in group interaction. The process is not the same as in individual analysis, but many of the same results can be achieved, including the establishment of a therapeutic alliance and a transference neurosis, the working out of the transference neurosis in relation to the leader and other members and figures in the patient's past, and a resolution of the transference. The leader extrapolates extensively about the patients on the basis of his psychoanalytic understanding of each group member.

The fact that about nine persons are present in the group, interacting and reacting to a single issue, prevents associations from being free—for external, interpersonal reasons as well as for the usual internal defensive reasons. The group members react in an apparently spontaneous way to common issues, yet it is really an externally forced or controlled way. As a result of this compromise way in which work is done in the group, more is required of each patient. He must often work out issues in derivative ways—in silence while someone else in the group is working on another aspect of an issue, on his own outside the group, and sometimes in additional sessions with the therapist. In individual analysis, there is the least possible amount of derivative expression and greater emphasis on the expression of details of nuclear fantasies. The group therapist sees derivatives of many of these fantasies being expressed in the group, but he is not always sure that the patient is aware of their significance; perhaps he need not be. What is impressive is the amount of relief, the coming to terms with the past, and the personality restructuring that takes place in response to group therapy.

Combined Therapy. With high-level neurotics—such as hysterics, phobics, and obsessives—group therapy can be limited to the work done in the group itself. But with the large group of borderline and psychotic patients, a point comes when the patient suffers so much pain that the group therapist must see him alone.

If the fact that a patient had an individual interview is brought up for group discussion and analysis, it becomes part of the group business. With a little encouragement, most patients bring into the group what they learned in the individual situation. The material worked on privately is useful to the patient and the other members only to the extent that the patient summarizes the individual transaction for the group. The therapist leaves the responsibility for revealing this information to the patient, who always needs the feeling that he is in control of what he reveals, when he reveals it, at what rate he reveals it, and for what purpose. The revelation of personal information implies readiness for closeness; at the same time, it can imply for most people

a loss of individuality, unless the patient barters away the information piecemeal and purposefully for specific therapeutic reasons.

Patients

Range. The range of patients treated in group therapy depends on the particular interests of the therapist and on the patients available. This second point is important because patients who are referred for group therapy are usually the problem patients from past therapies. Neurotics can be—and are—comfortably treated in group therapy. But they are, in style of object relations, closer than psychotics to most therapists, and so they are usually treated individually. Even so, most groups include higher-level neurotics and a good sprinkling of borderline and psychotic patients—homosexuals, alcoholics, and sadomasochistic, narcissistic, and depressive characters.

A mixture of character types increases the potential for interaction and for mutual exploration and self-exploration. Outpatient groups usually include a psychotic or borderline patient or two in groups of neurotics. With more than three psychotics in a group, their needs for special attention and for working on issues at a primitive level become so great that the neurotic members often refuse to tolerate the situation, and so they leave. But group members are generally tolerant of one psychotic if he tries to live up to the performance level of the group. If the psychotic is withdrawn, he may not take up much time—but his withdrawal has to be analyzed. He may be useful in the group because he is the kind of person who is very intuitive or a gadfly to the others. On the other hand, the extra attention the psychotic or borderline patient gets from the leader may make him feel guilty, since he may fancy that his early greed is being satisfied. Unless this situation is openly analyzed, it may lead to the psychotic's self-isolation from other members.

Groups with psychotic members only are seen most often in institutions on an inpatient or outpatient basis. Since such patients regress into psychosis when they consider crucial parts of their past, hospitalization must be available to ensure continuity of therapy. Hospitalization should be an adjunct to therapy, not an interruption.

Drugs should be used not so much to tranquilize the psychotic and make him allegedly available to therapy but rather to help him manage unbearable pain. The patient should be encouraged to assume responsibility for the use of medication—to use it as the need arises and to discontinue it when he is able to carry on without it. The patient should be encouraged to bear as much anxiety and depression as possible, since only through increased tolerance of both can there be growth.

Size of Group. With the authors, groups of eight patients are usual. But each therapist probably decides on what is an optimal number for him and then gives scientific rationalizations for the significance of that number. By making informal sociometric studies of groups and by asking members about the meaningfulness of other patients in their groups, the authors found that the average patient feels that five other members are important to him in a positive or negative way; he usually feels relatively neutral to the other patients in the group. Schizoid patients often attach themselves to only one other member.

Forming strong ties to four or five other people and sharing an important experience with some others—people they will never love and never hate, although they may take a respectful interest in them—is a valuable learning experience for many patients. They see in a balanced way what they can legitimately expect from people in general. With eight people in the group there are enough, even with occasional absences because of sickness and vacations, to ensure a rich mixture of interaction and a feeling of group continuity. But ultimately, the essential transferences to the leader and his abiding interest in the members keep them coming to the group meetings and working at their problems.

Evaluation of Patients. The therapist must make an evaluation, not merely a formal diagnosis, of each patient to be introduced into a therapy group. He must look for the short-term and long-term reasons the patient is coming for help, categorize his personality and its usual mode of operations, and determine his over-all life situation, including its strengths and the special problems it poses for the patient.

The patient's motivations in coming for help have little to do with his consciously expressed willingness to seek help. His motivations usually stem from a recent decompensation that causes him great discomfort or from a long-term style of life that has grown less and less gratifying. Most often, a loss precipitates an acute neurotic, borderline, or psychotic decompensation. But sometimes a gain or state of increasing closeness—such as an impending marriage, childbirth, or promotion—may lead to an emotional catastrophe.

The therapist has to know what the patient thinks are the causes of his difficulties. Many a therapy begins with only vaguely held notions of the reasons for the patient's coming for help. With the greatest of good will, the therapy then drifts into a state of general dissatisfaction with both patient and therapist floundering, since the goals are not clear. The therapy is often well-done but not well-directed.

The therapist must also point the patient in the general direction he regards as important. The conviction of the therapist and the general truth of his diagnosis help give the patient confidence that he can get help from this therapist, and they spur him to look for new information to confirm or deny the evaluation.

More important is the long-term evaluation the therapist makes to himself about the patient. This evaluation is not done in the formal terms of neurotic and psychotic but rather in terms of the type of object relations the patient is capable of at his best. The normal person comes close to his object for the sake of pleasure—mutual pleasure. The neurotic comes close to his object for pleasure at a price; he pays for his pleasure by a neurotic compromise—hysterical, phobic, or obsessive. The borderline patient may talk about pleasure but, in fact, comes close to his object for a required property, attitude, or ego function, which he needs to maintain his inner equilibrium. He may, for example, need object disapproval to hold in check his anger and legitimate independent strivings; he may need particular sexual qualities in his object to hold in abeyance his dread of dissolution when he gets close to a heterosexual object; he may need an object to minister to serious physical disabilities in certain psychosomatic conditions; he may need pain and disappointment to keep flogging him to perform. Finally, the psychotic needs his object for survival. His relationship to his object is especially close, binding, and primitive.

The diagnosis tells the therapist what kind of relations the patient will establish with him and the other members in the group, the kind of decompensation that may occur, the kinds of acting out to expect, and the kinds of crises to foresee. Forewarned, the therapist can then supply extra support, individual sessions, hospitalization, drug therapy to reduce unbearable pain, or collateral consultations and therapy. Any meaningful therapy brings surprises, but some of the grosser ones may be foreseen.

During the evaluation period, which may last for one to five meetings, the therapist also reviews the major traumata sustained by the patient as known to him by recollection or hearsay and finds out how the patient coped with them. It may be even more important to find out how he dealt with the normal developmental stages in his life. A study of these areas indicates the kinds of transferences and resistance the patient will develop in the course of therapy. Sometimes transference reactions become marked in the very first group meeting, so all foreknowledge is welcome.

CLINICAL ASPECTS

The New Member

The new member is prepared during the evaluation period for how the group operates generally, but the details are revealed by the group itself. Similarly, the patient reveals details about himself and his life at his own pace.

It usually takes several months for a member to work his way comfortably into the group. This period may be extended by testing-out behavior or shortened by a show of spunkiness. An initiation is inevitable, but its form is determined by the problems the new member is working on. Sheer misery, presented by a homosexual man who had been divorced by his wife, and seductive charm, shown by a hysterical woman, protect the new patient during his initiation.

An exhibitionistic artist flaunted his bestiality, perverse fantasies, and promiscuity to shock each newcomer. After he learned of his intense rivalry with an older sister and realized the dimensions of his guilt for having bested her, he became gentler to newcomers.

A phobic woman, who was at the height of working on her oedipal yearnings toward her father, shocked each newcomer with her masturbation fantasies, as she would have liked to shock her parents.

The tendency to initiate the newcomer is general, but the main thrust of an initiation is carried by one member, either because of the intensity of what that member is working on or because of the special meaning of the relationship between the member and the newcomer.

When a homosexual woman entered a group, an alcoholic woman seemed to have the tables turned on her during the initiation. The alcoholic woman had reacted to many painful situations in the group by running away. Again, she said that she was better and ready to leave. The group laughed, since they had heard this threat many times before and had an idea of how much she had yet to do. The newcomer said with a straight face that she hoped the alcoholic woman would leave, since she was better and since everyone should feel free to leave when he was better. The two women pretended to a superficial liking for each other for a while. For the alcoholic woman, the threat to leave was not only a fleeing from pain but also an attempt to make the leader suffer by losing her, as she had wanted to make her mother suffer for preferring her older brother. The newcomer was angry at her individual therapist for not continuing to see her, and she wanted to see the alcoholic woman go through the same suffering.

The process of initiation is influenced by the newcomer's defenses, with which the group can identify, so the process often ends in a stalemate.

A passive man, who had explosions of anger at work and could not detach himself from his family, entered a group after two years of unsuccessful individual therapy. In his anxiety, he denied all feelings about this disappointment and about the new situation. The group countered with a denial of all feelings about him. A wilderness of emptiness hung over the group. Finally, the group members could bear the atmosphere no longer, and they analyzed the reasons for their growing boredom. Only then did they let out the rage that they, like the newcomer, had been suppressing. The members then relaxed.

Testing Out

When a new member is introduced into a group, the interaction of the group and the newcomer during the initiation period leads to testing out by both new and old members. A patient's style of testing out stems from unresolved childhood conflicts. For example, the passive man mentioned above mobilized the sullen passivity he had known at home. The nature of the testing out is decided by the patient's character make-up at that time and is calculated to see if the group is safe for the newcomer and if he will be accepted and respected despite the extreme nature of his behavior. Some therapists regard testing as a necessary evil. In fact, it is the opening gambit in the patient's negotiation of closeness. Studied carefully, it reveals the patient's transferences and his significant past and helps explain his present attitudes and the difficulties he has created for himself.

Neurotics are closer than psychotics to most therapists in temperament and life style. Therefore, the therapist may submit to the testing behavior of neurotics or even pretend it is minimal or nonexistent. But a neurotic's testing behavior is just as important as that of a psychotic, whose behavior cannot be missed.

A phobic woman, whose mother had had a successful recovery in a psychiatric hospital run by the group method, came for group therapy. The therapist evaluated her situation and told her that she could certainly benefit from group therapy but that she was well-suited for psychoanalysis and would benefit greatly from it. She blew up at this suggestion and fled to a clinic for group therapy. There she was evaluated by one of the therapist's former students, who told her that the therapist was a teacher of group therapy and encouraged her to return to him. With qualms, she did so and reluctantly entered a group. She quickly attached herself to the therapist, as she had earlier attached herself to her mother. For a long time she regarded the least comment or nod by the therapist as highly significant and she constantly watched him for pearls. This behavior stemmed from her oedipal worship of her father.

Her early negative testing of the therapist was mildly surprising when it occurred, and it led at once to the positive side of the testing. If taken at face value, her later testing of the therapist was most flattering. To have yielded to such blandishments would have been dangerous to the patient, the therapist, and the therapy. An analysis of the patient's attitude led to a revival of old transference attitudes—the chief reason for studying testing behavior.

With borderline patients, testing becomes more complicated and startling, and it tries the mettle of the therapist and the group.

A man found himself in an impasse in his marriage, which was dissolving. In pain, he turned to group therapy and battled intensely with the therapist for individual attention and recognition, in part as a substitute for what he missed in his marriage and in part out of fear of letting himself become attached to the group. After eight months of strenuous battling in the group and of outside consultations, he relaxed. Only some 18 months later when he began planning to move to another part of the country did he let himself realize how much attached he had become to the whole group. By then he was also becoming aware of how much lay unresolved in his feelings toward his cold but physically seductive mother, against whom his passive father had offered little protection. In the group these recollections about his parents had emerged and the dangers of attachment had been highlighted and repeated when he bickered with one man and, painfully and slowly, allowed his warm feelings to show toward one safe woman. The stormy testing behavior was ultimately connected with his transferred fears of dependency in relation to his parents.

Testing out by psychotic patients is more intense and requires more patience on the part of the therapist. He must be ready to offer extra hours, drug therapy, family consultations, and transitory hospitalization as the need arises. Psychotics can bear even less anxiety and depression than borderline patients, they act out more, and, as they get close to the therapist, some may decompensate into psychosis. Such a development is a sign that involvement in the treatment and the group is deepening, and this impression has to be conveyed to the patient and the group, so they will not panic. The extreme degree of testing out shown by psychotics indicates the life-and-death nature of the anxiety they have to face and master.

Regardless of diagnosis, testing out is an important area of study, one that leads in a direct line from the work of the evaluation period to the study of the patient's transferences.

Transferences

Neurotic transferences may be strong, but they deal mostly with erotic feelings. These transferences can be dealt with easily enough in the group, and such patients rarely need additional help.

Borderline patients may suffer much more pain as they develop their transference feelings. Such patients may need individual sessions to support them during their great pain. The patient should be believed, since he is often the best judge of what he has to face internally.

Psychotic patients develop even stormier transference feelings and have to be seen individually as well as in the group. Behind the psychotic's storm of feelings lies much sadness. When this sadness can be reached, the patient can grow, relax in the group, and benefit from it.

An alcoholic woman constantly needed individual sessions until she came to terms with the sadness at the root of her disturbance. One and a half years of such combined therapy ended with a dramatic confrontation after a suicide attempt. She then gave up drinking on her own and discovered that behind the drinking lay many tears and much sadness.

Sometimes a piece of history picked up during the evaluation period highlights the transference attitudes that are acted out in the first group meeting.

A man came for help during a paranoid episode. He had left the employ of a man with whom he had become overinvolved in a way that he could not explain to himself. He had wanted to show his artistic ability to his boss. Instead, he felt misunderstood and controlled. Finally, he left the job.

This kind of situation had occurred three times in his life. In the most dramatic example, he had been one of three apprentices to an artist, but he felt used and subjugated by his teacher. After a sexual escapade with a woman, he got himself fired by his teacher. These patterns of behavior were related to his having felt that he could engage in only impotent fighting with his alcoholic father; he could never explain his views to his father or have his way with him.

Half an hour after he entered a therapy group, this mild, soft-spoken man had three men, who had long been in the group, sitting silently and respectfully listening to his detailed disclosure of what had brought him to the group. This behavior was unnatural for the group members, who usually interacted more freely. The therapist saw that the patient had at once begun to act out a piece of transference and was enjoying being the father or master artist to these men, who listened intently, He was bringing a piece of his past into the group, like a calling card. Instead of commenting on the general mood of the group, which would have been appropriate enough, the therapist pointed out, in terms of transference, that the patient had introduced this air of the powerful father controlling the men and that the three men were encouraging him to do so. The mood changed at once and the members resumed interacting more freely.

Transference reactions can be displaced and stimulated as in the following case.

A phobic woman seemed to attach her major transferences to the leader and two members. She did not ignore the other six members—she interacted with them and commented freely on their behavior—but the mainstream of her transferences was directed to certain people only.

She originally saw the therapist as untrustworthy until she learned that he was a respected teacher in the field of group therapy. Then she idealized him and sought his approval at every step. After this attitude was analyzed, she renounced men and began investigating the origins of her oedipal conflict in a series of dreams.

She also became attached to an older hysterical woman who had dared to have an incestuous affair, to marry and have three children, and to develop a life of her own. The younger woman, who felt that she was eternally trapped in sadomasochistic relationships with men and could never marry or enjoy tenderness and love, envied this married woman, who seemed to be able to take such steps in stride. In her transference worship the younger woman denied the many important problems that the older woman obviously had. The married woman served as the idealized part of her womanly self.

The phobic woman saw one man who was borderline in his object relations as a male counterpart of herself. She volunteered that, if they had not been in the group together, she would have liked to date him. She came from a Jewish home where the family worshipped intellect, and it was clear that she worshipped him for his intellect, for his ability to think about his feelings in detail. The rest of the group found his obsessive, tortuous ramblings at times confounding. She mistakenly saw herself as defective in intellect, a mere woman, and so she envied his hypertrophied intellect.

As this phobic woman finished reviewing and reliving, in the group and outside of it, her intense childhood love for her father, which an identification with the sadomasochistic side of her mother had kept concealed, she found a boyfriend after a year and a half of having no male friends. Furthermore, she set reasonable limits on him and herself, which he accepted after an initial shock reaction, and both ended up feeling respected and loved.

The therapist relies on the patient for clues about the accuracy of his interpretations and for signs that the transference has been worked out successfully. A shift from working intensely on issues in the group to deepening attachments to life outside the group is a good sign that the transference has been worked through successfully. But with psychotic and even borderline patients, the transference is often stormy. A stormy transference may require more work by the therapist, but it is preferable to a covert transference that is insidiously acted out, often in clique formation. Its existence can be guessed from the existence of the clique, but the therapist has to rely too much on extrapolations that are not very solid.

A middle-aged woman with strong paranoid trends came for help for totally unclear reasons. She was confused and confusing. Eleven years earlier she had had a postpartum paranoid episode after the birth of her third child. Now she was worried about her oncoming menopause, about her teen-age children's growing away from her, and about her sexual incompatibility with her husband. She often threatened to leave therapy, but she made many gains—in part because of the opportunity to get things off her chest, in part because she gained some understanding of

her dissatisfactions and emptiness as a child at the hands of a callous mother and a brutal father.

In the group was an alcoholic single woman in her early thirties who apparently came for help because she could not relate to men. It soon became clear that she came to mourn a cold, cruel mother and to come to terms with a mean, alcoholic father. She had opened up a bit as the group was forming. When the group grew in size and the paranoid woman joined it, the younger woman began to lean on her, seeing her as a fine, warm, understanding mother, despite the fact that the middle-aged woman readily confessed her problems and faults as a parent. After about two years of therapy, the middle-aged woman left the group because her husband's business took him to another part of the country, and they moved there. At this juncture, her main support gone, the younger woman also left. She steadfastly refused to return, even for an individual interview.

A year later, when she found herself in great distress, decompensating into a paranoid state, she called the therapist and asked for a referral for individual therapy. She still refused to see him personally, fearing he would force her to return to group therapy. She gratefully accepted his telephoned recommendation and entered into serious individual therapy.

In the group she had seen herself as being constantly let down by the leader. She became silent in relation to him and pinned her positive yearnings on the paranoid woman, whom she saw as an idealized mother. When this positive transference figure left the group, the younger woman so feared her negative transference feelings toward the therapist that she, too, had to leave the group. Her strong but lopsided transference to the older woman had made the younger woman comfortable in the group but had insulated her from effective therapy. In retrospect, the therapist realized that he should have seen the young woman individually when other patients joined the group and she became distressed at losing him.

Patients with strong needs for acting out closeness to overcome great pain need extra attention at certain junctures in their group therapy, as they would if they were in individual therapy. When a preliminary evaluation of the nature of the patient's object relations is possible, the therapist can be alerted as to the strength of infantile needs that will have to be coped with, and he can be prepared to provide for them.

A 40-year-old man was ridden with many fears about not being able to perform, especially at public speaking, which was becoming a growing necessity in the course of his duties. He was married and had three children. He had had years of individual and free-wheeling group therapy during the preceding 20 years. His reasons for coming to group therapy were not clear. The therapist did not know if the man was coming to therapy as a way of life or coming to finish off some unfinished business that had been stirred up in previous therapy. During the first year and a half, the patient made many demands and openly cried for immediate gratification and help. The therapist saw this behavior as a testing out of his firmness and ability to withstand the patient's intense demands. Just before the therapist's vacation, the patient began to mourn his first teen-age sweetheart. He had been demanding individual hours, but the therapist had felt, for purist reasons, that combining therapies would undercut the group therapy. He felt that the patient would see himself as justified in his old demands of love from his parents and all-powerful in now obtaining satisfaction and that he would be afraid of his dreaded powers. But now that the patient was suffering from a double loss—the recalled loss of his sweetheart and the current vacation loss of the therapist and the group—it seemed reasonable to provide the patient with a covering therapist, who saw the patient individually during the vacation period. The patient insisted that the substitute therapist help him persuade the group therapist to see him individually. The substitute refused, and the patient declared he was worthless. When the group therapist returned, the patient left and joined a group led by another therapist.

A year and a half later, the patient approached his former group therapist for help while his current therapist was out of the country. The former therapist agree to see him on condition that he go back to his current therapist as soon as he returned to work.

What emerged in the sessions was a loathing hatred for this first therapist—a negative transference stemming from the patient's blaming his father for the marital rift between the parents. The patient recalled sleeping in the same bed with his father. His mother slept alone in the next bedroom. In her anxiety and depression, she cried for help every night for years. The father rarely helped or comforted his wife. The patient hated his father for abandoning the mother and for leaving her potentially available to him. Feeling terribly let down by this silent, ungiving father, the patient had begun to re-experience this hatred during the group therapy with the first group therapist. If the therapist had not been engaged in so purist an approach, individual

sessions as well as group sessions might have tided the patient over during the emergence of this strong negative transference.

During four months of individual weekly therapy, the patient began to see a meaningful consistency in the silent, understanding, probing approach of the therapist, whom he had formerly seen as stone-faced and cruelly ungiving. Feelings other than hatred, disappointment, and emptiness began to emerge in relation to his father and mother.

Countertransference

Countertransference involves the totality of the therapist's reactions in the group, not merely his mistakes. But even his mistakes give him golden opportunities to work further with the patients.

An alcoholic woman often complained that she did not belong in the group, since she was older than the other patients. This age difference concerned no one but her. The therapist recognized the complaint as part of her resistance to involvement in therapy and as a way to push the other members away, so that she could feel left out.

After many threats to leave the group on this account, she called the therapist when he was asleep and feeling low and again asked to be allowed to leave the group because of the age difference. Feeling pushed to the end of his tolerance, he agreed on the phone to transfer her to another group with members closer to her age.

The next day he realized that his apparent capitulation was really an angry retaliation. He then met with the patient and reviewed the situation with her. He said he enjoyed treating her but would forgo this pleasure rather than accede to her request to be transferred to a group of age mates. The new group might have a turnover of patients, and she would again be the oldest, so there was no satisfying her demand. He reminded her that she could pressure all people, including the therapist, and should restrain this technique from self-destructive ends. Relieved that he had gone back to his usual stand, she returned to the group and began to turn somewhat more to the other members and to bring in her warm feelings, which she had avoided. In this case the therapist's mistake was used to show the patient her strength, which she had to master.

Pathological Use of Fees

Problems connected with fees are compounded in group therapy because of the presence of other patients, with whom feelings about the fee are shared and analyzed. Differences in fees arouse intense jealousy and sibling rivalry; fee differences also recall earlier feelings about worth and inferiority.

A young man paid a smaller fee than the other patients in a group because he earned only a marginal income and relied on his mother for support. He rationalized that he had to live this way, since he had to devote himself to his artistic work, in relation to which he had a block. It gradually emerged that this block was a neat device for not advancing personally, for staying dependent on his mother, for justifying his hatred of her, and for using her and all other women. Shortly after he began working in the group, he began to come five or ten minutes late to every meeting. Analysis of this behavior made it clear that he felt guilty toward the leader for paying less than the others and that he felt he deserved less time. Paying less reminded him that he got more things at home as a child, while his sister was comparatively deprived. His behavior was interpreted, but only after his fee was raised to the same level as the others did he begin to come on time.

The patient had appealed to the therapist's wish to help a struggling artist, and so the therapist had complied with the young man's need to be dependent on, guilty toward and angry at him, just as he was in relation to his mother. Analysis of this pattern was not enough to relieve the patient. The therapist had to change behavior before the patient could distinguish past from present and start to change.

A middle-aged woman came into a group just as the therapist had begun to increase his fees. For a while she was the only patient to pay at the higher rate. When another patient entered the group and also paid at this new rate, the first woman began to talk resentfully about paying more than the others, even though insurance was covering half her fees. As still another patient came into the group at the new fee level, the woman's resentment at paying more than the others grew, but she insisted on paying at the higher level. It was clear that she enjoyed the state of feeling picked out to be deprived.

At the same time she developed a pattern of talking mostly to the leader, devaluing the others and feeling unwanted by them. Above all, the middle-aged woman complained of being the oldest in the group and of being out of touch with the others because of the age gap. None of the other members felt this attitude was valid.

After she had been in the group for a year and a half, the fee was raised to the new level for all the other members, to their great relief. But this change aroused the greatest bitterness in the woman, since she could no longer feel that she was the least favored by the therapist. She was now considered equal to the others, and she did not wish to feel equal. The change to apparent equality went against her deepest transference yearnings to feel least favored by her mother. She had enjoyed this feeling for a year and a half, even though the basis for it was unrealistic. She hated to give up this feeling because it meant giving up an old relationship to her mother and changing her behavior in the group and toward her husband and family.

Anxiety and Depression

Anxiety can sweep in waves through a group. Members come late, leave early, drop out, fight, entertain others with sex talk, tell jokes, or generally stimulate one another to activity to avoid the anxiety-provoking issues. The therapist must rely on his own feelings, associations, and inner defensive struggle as well as on his knowledge of the interactions of the group to identify the source of the group's anxiety or sadness. As he tells them of the source of their anxiety, they relax and begin to give group associations to the issue.

Depression is often a more painful affect for the group to tolerate. It is very hard for a group of patients to sit and watch someone weep or suffer despair. Seeing him forces them silently or openly to review their own despair. As the crisis passes and others begin to contribute and participate, they reveal selected aspects of their own related sadness. Repeated successful sustaining of such affects and the working out of the meaning and use of such affects in various members increases the group's tolerance of them. Members can then turn more into themselves to look at the sources of their own inner despair.

With psychotic members, reactions to anxiety and depression are more severe than with neurotics. The manifestations are more overt and concrete—pacing about, leaving, shouting, fighting, psychotic decompensation. Building up the ability to tolerate such affects takes more time. But as the painful feelings are identified, the depth of their pain appreciated, and the source of anxiety or depression laid bare, psychotics as well as neurotics can relax and begin to tolerate the feelings—first by example and then by the experience of seeing that they themselves have successfully borne these affects.

As the patients identify the sources of their anxiety and depression and learn to bear these painful feelings, they grow stronger in searching out the sources of their neurotic and psychotic malformations and in dealing more reasonably with their present everyday life.

Dreams

Dreams, a personal expression of a patients' deepest yearnings and conflicts, become molded in the group by constant contact with the other members. This social pressure molds the content of the dreams, their meaning, and the use that the patient makes of them.

A woman had been working for months on her oedipal idealization of her father by renouncing men, by visiting her father, and by a long series of oedipal dreams, including various versions of infantile attachment to her father. In the midst of this, a new member—a quiet, passive man—entered the group. Her next dream seemed to belong to the same series of oedipal dreams, but it included elements that were cruder and more repulsive. The group reacted with amazement, but the therapist pointed out its shock value in initiating and scaring the newcomer. The woman's dreams then went back to working out her oedipal issues without such shock elements.

Sometimes a member incorporates pieces of another member's life or dreams into his own as an expression of closeness—to welcome someone back after a vacation or to show an identification of conflicts or aims. Other members are quick to pick up such a concurrence of elements.

The therapist cannot work out the detailed meaning of dreams in the group as he can in individual therapy, but he can focus on specific elements for the dreamer while listening to the other members sharpen their intuition and interpretive skills and work on related pieces of their own conflicts.

Absences

All absences are investigated in relation to the absent member's resistance to treatment and the way the other members deal with anxiety and yearning. As the members begin to see their importance to one another and the importance of the leader to them, absences are greatly reduced. When they do occur, they stand out in such bold relief that most members look to the group to understand the meaning of the behavior.

A patient was absent, and the other group members were afraid that he had committed suicide, since he had made such threats in the recent past. At the meeting, they were able to talk only of the empty chair. The therapist commented that they were afraid he had killed himself. They relaxed enough to face the issue of their concern for the missing member. The leader then reminded one member of his fight with the missing man. This member began talking about his guilt, and then relaxed.

Sometimes a vacation turns out to be a useful acting out, and its analysis leads to deeper involvement in therapy.

A married man with 15 years of experience in therapy went overseas for three weeks. It was his first vacation alone in his life, and he went six weeks before the group's vacation. He expected to be applauded for this apparently independent step. When he returned, he brought a memento that he knew had a particular meaning for the therapist. The group interpreted this gesture as a way of paying the therapist in advance for the coming vacation. This interpretation was probably true, but it was beside the point. The patient felt further outraged when the gift was not accepted; instead, its meaning was analyzed and he was held financially responsible for his time away from the group. The gift and all his apparent independence were bribes that he hoped would keep the therapist from expecting further analysis. This piece of acting out proved to be an invaluable source of material for group work. The other members also saw how they, too, offered pseudoprogress to avoid major efforts at self-understanding and change.

Termination of Therapy

When a member gets ready to leave a group, he transmits unconscious warnings about this prospect to the group, often in the form of increasing reality attachments outside the group, major changes in the member's outer life, and a gradual lessening of the member's regard for the importance of the group.

Table 1. *Differences between Neurotics and Psychotics in Group Psychotherapy*

Aspect	Neurotics	Psychotics
Indications	All psychoneurotic diagnostic categories can be included; special care is needed with depressive neurosis and suicidal ideation.	Borderline and latent schizophrenia are most amenable to treatment, but all schizophrenias can be included; results are limited with psychotic depressions, mania, and paranoia.
Composition	Patients are generally treated in groups that are homogeneous for psychoneurotic traits, although one or two psychoses can be included.	Patients are in groups homogeneous for psychotic states or are intermixed with patients with other diagnosis.
Reality-Testing	Reality-testing by group-as-a-whole is excellent; irrational attitudes are not prominent and are easily corrected when they do appear.	Reality-testing by group-as-a-whole may be poor; delusions and hallucinations may appear.
Leadership	Less leader activity is necessary for effective group functioning; generally less hostility to the leader is expressed.	Leader is generally more active in providing support and direction; potential and actual hostility to leader is greater because of schizophrenic ambivalence.
Standards	Group standards, such as confidentiality, are easily adhered to.	Group standards require repeated confirmation by the leader; they are not adhered to consistently because of prolonged testing out.
Socialization	Group is little or no substitute for social experience; there is less direct gratification of emotional needs; extragroup social contact between members is discouraged.	Group may provide the only real social experience for the majority of patients; there is more direct gratification of emotional needs; extragroup social contact with outsiders is encouraged.
Dependency	Group members show less exclusive dependency on the leader and more peer transactions; group shows greater tendency toward autonomous functioning although transferences among members represent displacement of transference to leader.	Members show more direct dependence on the leader; peer transactions need to be encouraged; autonomous functioning by the group as a whole is difficult to achieve.
Cohesiveness	Cohesiveness is generally high; members value the group and are libidinally tied to one another.	Cohesiveness is difficult to achieve; members may resent participation and may devalue the group; ties are of a hostile and dependent rather than a libidinal nature.
Communication	Communication level is high, with members sharing experiences; mutual identifications among four or five members are easily made; patients do not tend to feel alone.	Communication is inhibited, with little sharing of experiences; mutual identifications are with the therapist and often with one other patient; patients tend to feel alone.

Table 1—Continued

Aspect	Neurotics	Psychotics
Associations	Associations of members may center on a single theme or group event.	Therapist must work hard to clarify unifying themes related to survival and closeness, as revealed by acting out and in autistic expressions.
Acting Out	Group members are more prone to sexual acting out than to aggressive acting out; expression of affect needs to be encouraged.	Group members are more prone to aggressive acting out than to sexual acting out; affectual expression may have to be relieved by interpreting sources of anxiety and sadness.
Interpretation	Interpretations are made of unconscious conflicts in daily life and of dreams in libidinal and oedipal terms.	Interpretations are made of unconscious conflicts in daily life and of dreams in areas of anxiety, sadness, intolerance of affects, and aggression.
Insight	Patients are able to accept and examine group behavior as a manifestation of intrapsychic conflict; they are able to see the connection to original family group.	Patients examine intrapsychic conflicts in terms of fundamental problems of pain, sadness, and survival. As these problems are worked through, patients may also look at neurotic problems.
Problem Patients	Group monopolist is rare and is easily managed by patients; suicidal ideation is not prevalent; group tends to deal with crises effectively.	Monopolist is commonly exploited by members, and this behavior must be analyzed; suicidal ideation is common; members withdraw in crises, and then leader must show understanding support and direction.
Goals	Goal is to achieve complete reconstruction of the dynamics of personality organization for the majority of patients.	Goal is to relieve specific psychiatric symptoms and to improve functioning in one or several areas for the majority of patients.

After two and a half years of therapy, a woman in her mid-thirties had come to terms with her alcoholic and vain mother, whom she had formerly rejected and whom she now saw as having some strengths as a person, despite her failings as a mother. In addition, the woman now saw her father, who had been forced out of the family when she was four, no longer as the glamorized figure her mother had deprived her of but as a gambler and drinker who could not show care and concern for his family.

After a holiday weekend, the woman took off an extra day to stay out of town with her husband and thereby missed a group meeting. The group interpreted her absence as resistance to therapy, but the therapist sided with her need to be with her family, despite the group's needs. The members thought he was displaying favoritism.

The patient then decided to have her teeth extracted and to have dentures made. Again, the members, particularly a dental student, thought this a shameful and desperate move. The dental student insisted this was poor dentistry, and the woman countered that the teeth were too far gone to save. The therapist was undecided, and his vacillation was noted. The woman had her way and returned in a few days with new temporary dentures, proud of her smile.

Despite many doubts, she began planning to buy a house with her husband. This step implied a consolidation of her marriage, which had been shaky for many years.

This stream of changes—her taking vacations with her husband, taking steps to repair her body, consolidating her marriage, and seeing her mother in a more balanced light—showed that she had come to better grips with past disappointments and had taken hold of her current reality. She would soon be ready to leave the group. But it was getting clearer that the group's usually good intuition was murky. Their poor intuition toward and rebellion at each signal that showed she was getting ready to leave the group was unconsciously appreciated by the group, and they fought each bit of progress. In the end, the patient decided to leave. Although many issues were still not worked out, it seemed appropriate that she leave.

For months afterward, the group worked out the meaning of her leaving. At first, people missed her, were angry at her for having gone away, and hoped she would return. When the leader made it clear that she had made a reasonable decision in going away, that put an end to the wishful thinking. A silence settled over the issue. When a new member came into the group, she was seen as taking the former member's place—a sign that more bonds were being untied. When the newcomer found her own niche in the group, the others had to come to terms with the fact that the old member had indeed gone. Only then was the new member accepted as a new person to be recognized and understood separately and not as merely a replacement for the lost member.

CONCLUSION

Most patients, particularly neurotics and borderline patients, end their treatment satisfactorily. They enjoy relief from their symptoms and can reorganize their lives to gain satisfaction. Some patients interrupt treatment when they no longer feel any symptoms because of external factors in their lives or because they do not want to invest the effort needed for a major overhaul of their approach to life. Such limitations exist particularly in the treatment of borderline and psychotic patients. One homosexual man, for example, used the group to mourn the loss of his family and then decided to continue with his barren way of life. In this case, group therapy did not help the patient reorganize his life style, but it did give the man relief from his depression.

The therapist has to respect the patient's self-understanding and hold his own therapeutic zeal in check. But he must follow up his work in terms of treatment approach, relief of symptoms, reorganization, and the nature of the patient's object relations during decompensation and at the conclusion of treatment. Then he can judge how much

work has been accomplished and what problems future traumata may pose for the patient.

In general, the difference between neurotics and psychotics is one of degree (see Table 1). In dealing with psychotics, the therapist faces more work in dealing with problems of anxiety, depression, and sadness and with the dangers of closeness and extremely primitive superego demands. In dealing with neurotics, the therapist faces less work with these problems and perhaps more work in libidinal areas. Superficially, these may seem to be differences of kind and not of degree. But, as the therapist looks for the common underlying theme that interests psychotic and neurotic alike, he will be able to treat both categories of patients in the same group.

REFERENCES

Arsenian, J., Semrad, E. V., and Shapiro, D. An analysis of integral functions in small groups. Int. J. Group Psychother., *12:* 421, 1962.

Bach, G. R. *Intensive Group Psychotherapy.* Ronald Press, New York, 1954.

Bion, W. R. *Experiences in Groups.* Basic Books, New York, 1961.

Day, M. The natural history of training groups. Int. J. Group Psychother., *17:* 436, 1967.

Foulkes, S. H. *Therapeutic Group Analysis.* International Universities Press, New York, 1964.

Freud, S. Group psychology and the analysis of the ego. In *Standard Edition of the Complete Psychological Works of Sigmund Freud,* vol. 18, p. 65, J. Strachey, editor. Hogarth Press, London 1955.

Kadis, A. L., Krasner, J. D., Wenner, C., and Foulkes, S. H. *A Practicum of Group Psychotherapy.* Harper and Row, New York, 1964.

Kernberg, O. Borderline personality organization. J. Amer. Psychoanal. Assoc., *15:* 641, 1967.

Schniewind, H. E., Day, J., and Semrad, E. V. Group psychotherapy of schizophrenics. In *The Schizophrenic Syndrome,* p. 594, L. Bellak and L. Loeb, editors. Grune & Stratton, New York, 1969.

Semrad, E. V., and Day, M. Group psychotherapy. J. Amer. Psychoanal. Assoc., *14:* 591, 1966.

Semrad, E. V., Kanter, S., Shapiro, D., and Arsenian, J. The field of group psychotherapy. Int. J. Group Psychother., *13:* 453, 1963.

Slavson, S. R. *A Textbook of Analytic Group Psychotherapy.* International Universities Press, New York, 1964.

Wolf, A., and Schwartz, E. K. *Psychoanalysis in Groups.* Grune & Stratton, New York, 1962.

6

Group Therapy with
Psychoneurotically Ill Patients

Aaron Stein, M.D.

INTRODUCTION

The first reported use of group psycho-therapy, by Pratt in 1906, was designed to help patients deal with their physical and emotional—their psychosomatic—reactions to tuberculosis. Thus, from the very beginning, group psychotherapy has been used in the treatment of psychosomatic disorders, and specific features of group psychotherapy make it the treatment of choice for most patients with psychosomatic illness.

Many conditions, notes Stein (1956), are usually designated as psychosomatic:

Duodenal ulcer, certain types of ileitis and colitis, especially mucous colitis and ulcerative colitis, are commonly considered psychosomatic syndromes of the gastrointestinal system. In the cardiovascular system, the anginal syndrome, essential hypertension, coronary thrombosis or myocardial infarction, and certain cases of cerebral hemorrhage are considered to be psycho-somatic. Other syndromes designated as psycho-somatic are rheumatoid arthritis, hyperthy-roidism, diabetes mellitus, obesity, myxedema, migraine, certain cases of anemia, many skin conditions, especially alopecia areata, pleuritis, urticaria, and neurodermatitis, certain cases of conjunctivitis and blepharitis, certain types of rhinitis, some cases of bronchitis, and most cases of bronchial asthma.

Engel and Schmale indicate that most infections, many neoplasms, and many metabolic disorders should be included in the category of psychosomatic illness:

This list, which includes all sorts of conditions affecting every system of the body, could be extended, but these are the disorders in which it is generally recognized at the present time that the psychic reaction of the individual, including the factors noted above, play a major etiological role.

The dynamics of group psychotherapy in relation to the type of psychopathology manifested by patients with psychosomatic illness is discussed in two articles in the literature. Fortin and Abse, in reporting on their treatment of a group of university students with peptic ulcer, found that the group therapy at first heightened the pa-tients' dependent needs and the anger which stemmed from their unreal expectations from the therapist. Later, they worked out these feelings in the group interaction, and all the patients improved. Clapham and Sclare found that identification with other members helped a group of asthmatic pa-tients to overcome their initial guardedness and non-understanding and to move on to the production of affect-laden material with resultant improvement.

There are several reports of the use of group psychotherapy in the treatment of bronchial asthma, with most workers re-porting that patients received some benefit. Wohl, Reed, and Stokvis are among those who report these findings. Abramson and Peshkin found that group therapy with the parents of children with intractable asthma was useful in helping the patients become aware of some of the emotional factors involved. Groen and Pelser, reporting on eight years of group psychotherapy with asthmatics, found that it took several years for the patients to accept the idea of psychogenic factors and that most of the patients felt their illness entitled them to special care.

Group psychotherapy has been employed with deaf patients, using sign language and lip reading. Sarlin and Altshuler found such therapy useful with deaf adolescents in a school setting. Rainer et al. conducted group therapy with deaf psychiatric patients in sign language and considered it helpful to a considerable degree. Locke reports successful use of group psychotherapy in lessening deaf patients' feelings of isolation, inferiority, and suspicion. Landau states that group psychotherapy showed promise when used with deaf retardates.

Three papers (Adsett and Bruhn, Goldner and Kyle, and Mone) describe the use of group psychotherapy with patients who had cardiac illness, including some who had had a myocardial infarction. Adsett and Bruhn also included the patients and spouses. All the investigators found that the group therapy was most useful in helping patients overcome the resistance to talking about their illness; it also helped them verbalize their anxiety and depression, with considerable improvement in these symptoms. Titchener et al. found, however, that group therapy with hospitalized hypertensive patients tended to raise blood pressure more than individual therapy did.

The use of group psychotherapy in the treatment of skin conditions is reported in two papers. Milberg found that patients with neurodermatitis had different types of psychopathology; despite this, group psychotherapy gave positive results. Shoemaker et al. found that patients with atopic eczema were helped greatly by a treatment regime that included physical care and analytic group psychotherapy.

Frizzell found group therapy useful in helping diabetic psychiatric patients adjust to their diet. Hefferman used group therapy with the parents of diabetic children and found it helped them improve their understanding and management of the children.

In the treatment of patients with epilepsy,

Yaeger et al., Kamin et al., and Scarborough found that group psychotherapy, by permitting ventilation of emotional tensions and conflicts, helped to lessen the number of seizures.

Several authors report that group psychotherapy conducted on the wards of a general hospital with medical and surgical patients, including those with psychosomatic conditions, helped to allay anxiety and improved the ward atmosphere, enabling the patients to participate better in their treatment. Berry and Cunningham, Monteiro and Snyder, Graham, and Brody are the workers who found group psychotherapy useful with these patients.

The use of group psychotherapy in the treatment of obesity has continued to attract attention. Glomset, Freyberger, Mees and Kenter, and Wright et al. found it to be very helpful. Wolf, Dorfman et al., and Holt and Winick also found group psychotherapy very useful with obese patients, but they indicate that it has limitations and that not all obese patients are suitable for this form of treatment. Penick et al. used both behavior modification techniques in a group and conventional group therapy with obese patients and found both methods helpful, but they achieved better results with the behavior therapy. Kosofsky and Slawson report that group therapy did not help obese patients lose weight, although it did help to improve their emotional stability.

Group therapy in patients with central nervous system disease has been found to be very helpful. Edwards reports its use with brain-damaged patients; Kurasik and Priskor and Paleos used group therapy with hemiplegic patients; Whally and Strehl treated multiple sclerosis patients this way; and Lubin and Slominski used this treatment with adult cerebral-palsied patients. All found group therapy helpful in enabling patients to express their anxiety and depression, with resultant improvement in their mood and attitude toward their illness. Hirsch, Boles, and Bardach found group therapy very helpful in allaying the guilt and anxiety and in increasing the understanding of the relatives of patients with central nervous system disease. Cooper and

Katz felt that group psychotherapy was useful in treating patients with migraine.

Reports by Pion and Caldwell and by Reeder and Deck indicate that the use of group therapy in prenatal care helped reduce anxiety and benefited such psychosomatic symptoms as dizziness.

Group psychotherapy was found useful in helping orthopedic patients to deal with anxiety and to participate more effectively in their treatment, report Murray and Teitelbaum and Suinn.

There are several reports and reviews on the use of group psychotherapy in various settings with patients who have psychosomatic conditions: Berry and Cunningham, Suchanek-Frolich, Igersheimer, Sternlieb, Wittkower, Deutsch and Lippman, and Enke. In general, the authors found group psychotherapy useful.

In describing the use of group psychotherapy in the treatment of stuttering, Schneer and Hewlett found that the treatment enabled patients to express hostile aggression more freely, with a resultant improvement in their stuttering. Sadoff and Siegel also found that group therapy helped stutterers express themselves more freely, so they used stuttering less as a defense. Improvement in stuttering with the use of group psychotherapy is also reported by Laeder and Francis, Sadoff and Collins, Sommers et al., and Barbara et al.

PSYCHOSOMATIC ILLNESS

Modern Concepts

Neither group psychotherapy nor the concept of psychosomatic illness was given much recognition prior to 1940. Stein (1956) wrote:

Although Hippocrates had sensed the unity of psyche and soma, the subsequent mechanistic approach of medicine to disease (which reached its peak in the nineteenth century) separated the patient into a body and its psyche. Similarly, in psychotherapy, although some of the dynamic factors involved in group psychotherapy were long known, the approach to mental illness and the treatment of psychosomatic disorders that occupied the attention of psychotherapists was

the individual one. Beginning with the 1920's and then gathering momentum in the 1930's, unifying concepts appeared which led to the acceptance in the 1940's of the psychosomatic and group psychotherapeutic concepts.

According to Lipowski,

psychosomatic medicine is the discipline whose avowed purposes are to study and to formulate explanatory hypotheses about the relationships between biological, psychological, and social phenomena as they pertain to persons.

The subject matter of psychosomatics as a science is the psychosomatosocial relationships. Part of its activity has been in psychophysiological research—the study of the inter-relationship between physiological and psychological aspects of behavior, particularly in human beings—and possible cross connections are one of the fields of study to determine an observable connection between a psychological and a physiological event. Psychosomatic clinical research focuses on the interplay of psychological, biological, and social factors that help to precipitate, maintain, and counteract those states of the human organism that are called diseases. This type of research has gone beyond the study of psychogenicity and moved on to the study of such phenomena as delirium, in which somatic and psychic disturbances occur together—the somatopsychic reaction. A new and promising field is the study of neurophysiological and neuroendocrine processes, which enable transactions to occur between the cerebrum and the rest of the body. Also, work is being done with epidemiological and ecological research in psychosomatic conditions as part of the study and understanding of processes whereby man, adapting to his external environment, may develop reactions that are related to psychosomatic illness.

There has been an increasing awareness of disruptions of important personal relationships and the ensuing difficulties in replacing the loss as the antecedents of any illness—somatic or psychiatric. Psychophysiologic human development is being studied and may help in the understanding of typical patterns and attitudes that people develop.

The concept of psychogenicity, Lipowski

points out, developed from psychoanalysis, and excessive emphasis on psychogenicity has been misleading and has narrowed the field of investigation of psychosomatic disorders. He does not feel that the concept of psychogenesis should be abandoned, but it should be studied as only one of the factors in the production of psychosomatic disorders, and the concept of psychogenicity should include the study of cognition and perception as well as the effects of emotional disturbances.

Similarly, "psychosomatic disorder" is an unsatisfactory term that, despite its attempt to conceptualize the unitary response of the organism, actually perpetuates the split into psyche and soma. The concept of psychosomatic disorder should be a broad one, emphasizing the multiple factors involved, says Lipowski:

What matters is to determine in each individual patient how the interplay of psychological and other ideological factors influences the onset, course, and outcome of his illness, and by what psychophysiological mechanisms these processes are brought about, and what practical conclusions for prevention and management of the illness can be drawn from this knowledge.

Lipowski goes on to question the concept of specificity in psychosomatic disorders. He feels that the original concept of specificity has changed and cites a statement made by Grinker that psychosomatic diseases do not have any specific emotional ideology but are characterized by response specificity. Lipowski feels that the concept of specificity has some usefulness if it can be considered as one of the factors that may contribute to or facilitate the development of any illness and indicate what psychological intervention is possible.

Psychological stress is a new concept in the consideration of psychosomatic disorders. Lipowski summarizes the theoretical issues as follows:

Stimuli qualifying as psychologically stressful, whether originating from within or without must be perceived by the person; such stimuli have to be evaluated by the perceiving individual as dangerous or threatening to him; the results of such evaluation, as well as the process itself, may be partly or totally outside the person's awareness. The response to a psychologically stressful situation may include one or more dysphoric effects as well as one or more coping processes or activities.

All these processes are experienced, communicated, and described in psychological terms.

The onset of depression, object loss, severe environmental changes—all are factors involved in the production of psychological stress. Included in such concepts are the ideas of life crises and the failure of adaptive patterns. Also included are the person's characteristic response to such stresses, designated as attitude, and the nature of the perceptual reactance of the person, which will augment or lessen the effects of any of the psychological stress factors.

Lipowski points out that the concept of psychological stress is in the foreground of psychosomatic theory today. Such affects as anxiety, anger, and depression, which have somatic components, are being studied, as are neuroendocrine mechanisms by which affects are transmitted to the body structure. The concepts of the body image and its boundaries appear to be of value for the study of various aspects of psychosomatic relationships, Lipowski notes:

They reflect both cognitive and affective attributes and processes of persons that seem to show some correlation of physiologic reactivity. They may help predict what type of somatic symptom and physiologic dysfunction a person will develop in response to psychological stress.

As regards somatization, Lipowski cites the extensive literature, particularly the analytic literature, that has arisen concerning this concept and the difficulties in differentiating it from conversion. He is somewhat critical of the analytic definitions of somatization and feels that, like the term "vegetative neuroses" suggested by Alexander many years ago, they are not particularly clear concepts. However, he does feel that somatization as a

generic term designating the tendency to experience, conceptualize and/or communicate psychological states or contents as bodily sensations, functional changes, or somatic metaphors

is a useful concept, and he feels that there is a continuum of somatization reactions, which may be listed as follows:

subjectively perceived psychological concomitants of affects; somatic changes symbolically expressing ideational content, that is, conversion phenomena; secondary symbolic elaborations of perceived body changes regardless of their origin; excessive preoccupation with body sensations or functions, normal or abnormal, that is, hypochondriacal symptoms; nosophobia; somatic delusions and, finally, communication of psychological distress in bodily metaphors.

Lipowski concludes his extensive review by defining psychosomatic medicine as a method of approach, using the following key postulates:

(1) Human health and disease are viewed as states without a sharp dividing line between them; they are determined by multiple factors: biological, psychological, social; (2) any event at any level of organization of the human organism—from the symbolic to the molecular—may have repercussions at all other levels; (3) medical diagnosis should focus not only on an identification of a particular disease but should consider the total situation of the patient and developmental contributions of all determinants to the presenting clinical picture; (4) psychosocial factors must be considered in planning the preventive and therapeutic measures; (5) the relationship between the patient and those taking care of him influences the course of illness and efficacy of treatment; (6) psychotherapy may be of value whenever psychological factors are recognized as significantly contributing to the precipitation, maintenance, or exacerbation of any illness in a given person.

He feels that such postulates enables us to devise the most useful approach to the study and management of somatic reactions, which are the preferred mode of experience and of expressing or reporting psychological distress in certain individuals. This approach is based on the recognition that patients are persons and the psychosocial variables are relevant, albeit to a varying extent, in all illnesses.

This review of current theoretical concepts in psychosomatic medicine indicates the growing acceptance of the complex factors involved. Such acceptance represents a considerable advance over the original speculations of Freud, Ferenczi, and other analytic pioneers who examined what Deutsch and Ferenczi have called the mysterious leap from the mind to the body.

Many of the speculations that were current more than a quarter-century ago are still being considered, but new trends are constantly replacing the old in these speculations. For example, Alexander's concept of specificity is now replaced by what Lipowski calls the multifaceted concept of psychological stress, which he claims is the main unifying construct in current psychosomatic theory. Lipowski sums up the present state of affairs by stating:

Recognition of the complexity of the psycho-socio-biological processes determining health and disease has displaced earlier psychogenic hypotheses derived mainly from psychoanalytic theory.

However, the developmental experience of the patient and the unconscious, emotional activity characteristic of the patient—concepts originally derived from psychoanalytic theory—must still be considered as important factors in the complex processes involved.

Use of Psychotherapy

Ludwig, Kaufman, Karush, and many others have described the difficulties and limitations involved in the psychotherapeutic treatment of patients with psychosomatic illnesses.

Emotional Disturbances. Certain characteristic kinds of emotional disturbances tend to occur fairly constantly in patients with psychosomatic illness. Such disturbances are considered to be related largely to the developmental experiences of the person and to the unconscious emotional activity characteristic of him. Not all patients with psychosomatic illness show all these disturbances to an extreme degree, but the disturbances are usually present to some extent, even in the seemingly well-functioning integrated patient, such as the successful executive who develops an ulcer. Those in whom these factors are present to a very great degree are often quite ill from the psychiatric point of view.

Disturbed Early Relationships. Most of these patients show the persistence of an intense symbiotic relationship to the mother. For example, many ileostomy patients thought of mother all the time, of what she expected, of whether she would be critical. They tended to become moody if she was moody.

Separation Anxiety and Depression. Most patients with psychosomatic illness indicate persistent and often extremely severe—at times overwhelming—emotional reactions to object loss or to separation from any object. For example, they have colitis attacks, asthmatic attacks, or ulcer exacerbations when a significant person—mother, father, husband, wife—goes away; an attack can occur when the therapist goes on vacation or cancels an appointment.

Intense Emotional Needs and Conflicts. Intense oral cravings and oral aggressive tendencies are usually present at the unconscious level, and the same excessive intensity characterizes other unconscious drives. The needs or drives are almost always ambivalent, indicating a fixation at or a regression to early levels of development. Tensions of any kind, especially those relating to frustrations, are poorly tolerated and are at times overwhelming. As a result, primary destructive drives are frequently mobilized and necessitate specific defense reactions, often to an extreme degree. For example, when the therapist refuses a request for an early appointment, a colitis patient may have a severe attack of abdominal spasms and a very obese patient may faint.

Weak Ego. Ludwig notes that the ego is very weak,

precariously situated, and fragmented, crushed between overpowering primitive id forces and a punitive archaic superego.

The weakness of the ego in many of these patients is a major factor in their illness. It is one of the chief reasons why these patients continue to have intense, regressive types of emotional reactions. The weakness or regression of the ego leads to retention of primitive emotional reactions and inability to express or discharge these reactions in a more mature and effective fashion. Emotional reactions in these patients tend to be of the generalized, often explosive type, and affect is largely expressed through autonomic and somatic channels, with the patient often completely unaware of the presence of the affect.

Poorly Developed Object Relationships. Relationships are frequently of a primitive and narcissistic type, especially the passive-symbiotic type. Many of these patients are isolated or find extreme difficulty in developing and sustaining satisfactory relationships with others.

Punitive, Archaic Superego. This is probably the result of many factors, such as the regression or fixation at an early level of emotional development and the introjection of the phallic mother. As a result, these patients have excessive unconscious guilt, greatly increased by their ambivalence. Unconsciously, they greatly fear retaliation and punishment, so they often feel threatened and anxious in any close relationship.

Defective Body Image and Self-Image. This, obviously, is related to many of the factors already cited. It leads to the patients' not clearly knowing their own identity sexually and as a person and to their seeing themselves, especially in relation to others, in an incomplete or distorted fashion.

Rigid Character Social Role. As a defensive reaction, many of these patients develop such character traits as submissiveness, obedience, and pseudoself-sufficiency. Usually these characterological roles are excessively rigid and unrealistically maintained. They are brittle and quickly succumb to even small frustrations. The patients, as would be expected, are often completely unaware of the nature of these character traits or of their manifestations, particularly in their social roles or relationships.

Emotional Illiteracy. Many psychosomatic patients have extremely little knowledge, much less awareness, of the most usual type of emotional reaction. They are emotionally illiterate, to use Freedman and Sweet's term. The primitive defense mechanisms of isolation and denial are involved here. Often, even those who are highly educated and intelligent do not use the words that describe emotions. For example, a colitis patient with a Ph.D. in pharmacology who was in the midst of a bitter divorce experience said only that she was "a little upset," mostly because of an attack of colitis that occurred during this time.

Treatment. The underlying emotional disturbances in the patient with psychosomatic illness largely determine what kind of treatment is necessary and how effective it will be. The effective treatment of such complicated and profound disturbances, all agree, is extremely difficult. Ludwig, in discussing the psychotherapy for rheumatoid arthritis, makes the following point:

The psychotherapeutic methods and goals must vary with the stage of the disease. Since the most frequent precipitating event seems to be related to a separation trauma, by disruption of some vital relationship, the first task of therapy will be to attempt to restore a balance by establishing contact with the patient.

This is, of course, the greatest difficulty in treating these patients; they are often extremely reluctant—or unable—to establish contact in psychotherapy, especially in individual psychotherapy, as Karush et al. note. Karush et al. and Sperling point out that some patients have benefited from individual psychotherapy, including analysis, but the material frequently indicates that they were, often unwittingly, specially selected patients whose ego resources were more adequate than is the case with most of these patients.

One of the main reasons for the great difficulty in establishing effective therapeutic contact with these patients in individual treatment lies largely in the nature of the transference they develop to the therapist. These patients, because of the underlying emotional disturbances they have, tend to develop a primitive and regressive type of transference to the therapist, regardless of the kind of individual psychotherapy they receive.

Karush et al. give the results of psychotherapy in patients with chronic ulcerative colitis over a number of years. They found that the patients' emotional disturbances— weak ego, harsh superego, etc.—were responsible for the limitations of the psychotherapeutic treatment of this psychosomatic condition. Similar defects in the type of personality, type of object relationships, expression of affect, etc., were found in the group of ileostomy patients described later in this chapter; and it is of significance that group psychotherapy was found to be somewhat more successful than individual psychotherapy in the treatment of these patients.

GROUP PSYCHOTHERAPY AND PSYCHOSOMATIC ILLNESS

Theoretical Aspects

The factors that limit the effectiveness of individual psychotherapy in the treatment of psychosomatic illness are specific indications for the use of group psychotherapy. This is not meant to imply that only group psychotherapy should be used. Karush, among others, has reported good results with the use of individual psychotherapy in patients with psychosomatic illness when the defects were not extensive or severe. But, on both theoretical and clinical grounds, group psychotherapy is specifically useful in the treatment of patients with more severe defects.

In addition to the defects already noted in patients with psychosomatic illness—a tendency to have object relationships of the intense symbiotic type; very poor tolerance of separation, object loss, or any frustrating experience; an ego that is weak and buffeted by intense emotional reactions and the restrictions of a punitive, archaic superego; and affective responses that are excessive and intense and expressed through autonomic and somatic channels with blocking of outward expression—they have difficulties in establishing contact with the therapist. The primitive type of transference that does develop stems from the passive-symbiotic type of object relationships used by these patients.

Because of all these factors, group psychotherapy is useful in helping these patients enter into a psychotherapeutic relationship. In group psychotherapy, the relationships of the members to the therapist and among the members themselves are the important dynamic factors that facilitate the therapeutic interaction in the group and determine its nature. The interactions that result are related to two changes in the way the transference is manifested in group psychotherapy as contrasted with individual therapy: (1) Because of the presence of a number of members, the intensity of the transference is lessened. (2) The transference is split, since it is directed toward the other members of the group as well as toward the therapist. The diminution of the intensity of the transference to the leader and the fragmentation of the transference help these patients deal with their overly intense reactions stemming from their passive-symbiotic relationships and also provide opportunities to examine the nature of their relationships and to develop new types of relationships.

As a result of the inhibition and deflection of the transference, the intragroup tension among the members increases, and more frequent and more intense intermember transference reactions occur in the group. Patients use roles, based on unconscious fantasies, to interact with one another and to try to get the other patients to act out transference roles. The availability of multiple transference objects who are realistically present in the group and who actually respond to transference manifestations results in group-member interactions that constitute the therapeutic interaction in the group session. The initial, unconscious, uninterpreted response of one member to another's transference manifestations occurs in a very real fashion in the group session, and in this way it is readily available for therapeutic work in the group. Pathological character traits and attitudes become apparent quickly and clearly because of the intermember transference interaction and are readily available for therapeutic scrutiny. The rigid patient with psychosomatic illness, who is not usually aware of the nature and significance of his characteristic type of interaction, is helped to become aware of it and to understand its nature.

The emotional ties among the members of the group consist largely of a number of identifications, the most important of which is their sharing of a common object—the therapist. The basic nature of the relationship to the therapist in group psychotherapy differs from the one-to-one relationship in individual therapy, not only because it is lessened in intensity but also because the leader or therapist is shared by all members of the group. This is another reason why the transference to the therapist is much less intense and threatening and is felt on a much more realistic level, a process that is also aided by the patients using each other as transient multiple transference objects. As a result, the therapist becomes to each

member an idealized figure invested with the narcissistic libido. As this idealized figure, he is used during group psychotherapy as a substitute for the patients' own harsh superegos.

Because of several other factors, including the sharing of guilt and the use of various kinds of spokesmen, certain rigid superego attitudes are dealt with much more readily in the group than in individual psychotherapy. Again, these dynamic factors in group psychotherapy help the patient with psychosomatic illness stand and deal with the tensions resulting from the demands of his punitive, archaic superego.

The presence of a number of patients in the group—plus the fact that the patients themselves, through their identification with the therapist, assume the role of therapists in discussing each other's reactions—provides many stimuli for participation and helps the patients become aware quite rapidly and in a very real fashion of the emotional reactions and attitudes that are being discussed including characterological traits and social roles. Also, since projection and identification occur in a realistic fashion in the group and can be readily pointed out by the other members, patients are helped to understand these and other mental mechanisms much more readily—an insight of great value to emotionally illiterate patients with psychosomatic illness.

This increased awareness of emotional reactions, the knowledge that others also have intense "forbidden" feelings, and the understanding and accepting attitude of the therapist and other members toward the outward expression of these feelings—all help the patient with psychosomatic illness. They help patients express feelings through speaking, shouting, weeping, etc.—something they were previously unable to do.

The opportunity for increased interpersonal contact in the group and the group's realistic nature and atmosphere help to lessen isolation and strengthen contact with reality and lead to more effective ego functioning. The nature of the ties in the group, especially the identifications, helps the members supply each other with a great deal of emotional support, particularly in the areas of ego functioning and the strengthening of defenses—useful features for weak egos and the overpowering reactions of patients with psychosomatic illness.

Clinical Aspects

In a General Hospital. For the past 25 years, the writer and his colleagues in the adult group therapy division of Mount Sinai Hospital in New York have used group psychotherapy in the treatment of a number of psychosomatic disorders. The work has been done on the psychiatric ward and in the psychiatric and other outpatient clinics of a large general hospital. The first psychotherapy groups were set up for a number of chronic, psychosomatically ill patients when it was noticed that they spontaneously formed groups in the waiting room and that the relationships seemed to be useful and supportive for them. This, together with the fact that they had experienced difficulty or had ceased to make progress in individual treatment, led to the decision to form psychotherapy groups for the treatment of these patients.

The first group, consisting of 13 chronic menopausal patients, was set up in 1945. All the patients had multiple somatic complaints, rigid personalities, and marked guilt over their symptoms. Group therapy helped them overcome this sense of guilt and isolation and provided support so that they could verbalize many of their hostile feelings. All members of this group improved in varying degrees.

A year or so later, two groups of patients, all of whom had psychosomatic disorders and complaints, were treated with group psychotherapy. The first group consisted of five women and two men and included patients with ulcerative colitis, asthma, neurodermatitis, and peptic ulcer. Again, all these patients had rigid, constricted personalities with various neurotic traits, and all had negative attitudes toward individual psychotherapy. The group sessions helped them find support for their feelings and overcome their guilt in expressing some of these feelings, particularly their hostilities. Of the seven members, six improved: three slightly and three considerably. The second group consisted of six women and included patients

with ulcerative colitis, migraine, and neurodermatitis. These patients had infantile, dependent personalities and rigid characterological defenses. The group therapy helped them develop more positive relationships to the therapist and their psychotherapy, and all the patients in this group gradually improved.

In 1949 an experimental group was set up in the outpatient clinic to investigate the need for selection of patients. There were six men and six women in the group, and the psychosomatic conditions included asthma, ulcerative colitis, angina, retinitis, and various types of myalgia. All these patients had defective personalities, with severe underlying psychiatric disorders, as well as psychosomatic complaints. This group was treated for a period of a year, with the following results: One patient dropped out, three patients did not improve, and the other eight showed varying degrees of improvement. The group therapy provided support for these patients, particularly in expressing their feelings about their relationship to the doctor and the treatment of their illness. Negative and hostile attitudes were able to find expression quite freely, with definite benefit for the patients. However, the resistance of this group of patients to the uncovering of emotional factors was quite marked, and the results obtained with this group were not as good as with some of the others.

A group of peptic ulcer patients was organized in 1948, with the idea that group psychotherapy might be especially useful in a group of patients with similar psychosomatic illnesses. It was thought that peptic ulcer patients might have similar patterns of chronic emotional tension related to poorly tolerated oral or aggressive drives or both—drives that were largely unconscious and expressed through the psychophysiological disturbances characteristic of peptic ulcer. It was also thought that group psychotherapy might help such patients bring out and work through these tensions. In large part, this idea seemed to be borne out. Ten patients with peptic ulcers were treated with group psychotherapy over a period of 16 months. One patient did not improve, one improved only slightly, three improved moderately, and the remaining five improved and had no recurrence of ulcer symptoms during the two-year follow-up period.

The patients had rather rigid and constricted personalities, with severe underlying characterological and neurotic difficulties. Recognizing that they had the same illness and the same difficulties was particularly useful for them, and the nature of the relationships in the group, with a lessened intensity in the relationship to the therapist, helped them become less fearful and guilty of their dependent and aggressive drives. This fact, together with the support provided by the other patients, enabled them to reveal and work through their guilt over having these drives and symptoms. They then expressed resentment over not being cared for, finally acknowledging their strong, dependent needs. The group's attitudes were, at first, rigid and intolerant, but later they changed gradually and became more flexible and understanding. Here, again, the specific dynamics of group psychotherapy were especially useful for the type of psychological difficulty manifested by this group of psychosomatic patients.

Group psychotherapy has continued to be used in the hospital for the treatment of patients with psychosomatic conditions, but only a few groups have been organized to deal with specific psychosomatic conditions. Many groups have included patients without psychosomatic conditions as well as those with such illness. One group treated diabetic patients, another group treated geriatric patients, and still another group treated allergic patients. At the present time, most patients with psychosomatic conditions are included in regular psychotherapy groups, and, for the most part, experience has confirmed early impressions that group psychotherapy is a useful and generally effective form of treatment for patients with psychosomatic complaints and conditions.

In 1960, the need to help a nonpsychiatric physician handle problems related to orienting and educating medical and surgical patients in relation to their illness led to the use of group therapeutic techniques for such orientation groups, recalling the early experience of Pratt. The orientation groups—led by nonpsychiatric physicians or social workers or, occasionally, nurses—have been set up and are continuing to be used in the nutrition clinic, the allergy clinic, the medical clinic, and the obstetrical clinic.

Fried and Golob have reported that counseling or guidance groups led by social workers were set up in the 1960's to help chronically ill patients discuss and deal with their difficulties. The experience of such counseling groups has proved to be most useful, and a number continue to be used. Similar counseling groups are being set up to help addicts deal with methadone treatment and also to help orient and guide a group of hepatitis patients. Counseling and orientation discussion groups led by psychiatrists, nonpsychiatric physicians, or social workers have been and are continuing to be used with cardiac patients, the relatives of cardiac patients, and the relatives of kidney-transplant patients.

Patients with Ileostomies. The group of patients were members of the Ileostomy Club, an organization of patients with ileostomies. The club holds regular monthly meetings at which talks are given by physicians and others to instruct patients concerning the management of their ileostomies, demonstrate various techniques and appliances used in connection with the ileostomy, and help orient new patients who are to receive or have recently received ileostomies. These clubs also provide emotional support by means of reality-oriented group counseling, which was useful for most of the patients in the club. However, many patients continued to have physical and emotional difficulties, and it became apparent that they needed a more frequent and more definite form of psychiatric help.

Accordingly, it was decided to organize a small group of patients for group psychotherapy. It was announced at a meeting of the Ileostomy Club that group psychotherapy would be available and that those who wished to participate in it should give their names to the social worker who attended the club meetings. Because the group psychotherapy meetings were going to be held during the day, none of the men were able to attend. Finally, a group of women was set up.

The Patients. The pertinent facts concerning the patients who were in this group at one time or another are as follows:

Arlene developed her colitis shortly after her marriage, seven years before the group began. Because of the persistence of severe symptoms of ulcerative colitis, an ileostomy had to be performed about three years after her marriage.

Beverly also developed her colitis seven years before the group began. She had been married for 11 years, and the colitis began shortly after the birth of her first child. Because of persistent, severe symptoms of ulcerative colitis, she had the ileostomy performed three years later, after the birth of her second child. She came from a broken home.

Ernestine was a 39-year-old women who had been married for 17 years. She developed rectal symptoms shortly after the birth of her first child, about 12 years before the group began. Two years later, after the birth of her second child, the rectal symptoms turned into colitis. In another two years, after the birth of her third child, the symptoms of colitis became very severe. Because of this, she had had an ileostomy performed three years before joining the group.

Florence, a 22-year-old woman, began to have symptoms of colitis four years before, when she began to go steady with her boyfriend, whom she married a year later. Because of persistent, severe colitis symptoms, an ileostomy was performed $2\frac{1}{2}$ years prior to the group therapy.

Laura was 31 years old, married, and Catholic—the only non-Jew in the group. She had had her first attack of colitis when she became pregnant with her first child, four years previous to the group therapy. She developed severe ulcerative colitis a few days after the birth of her second child, two years before joining the group, and had an ileostomy performed six months prior to the beginning of the group therapy.

Judy was 21 years old and the only single woman in the group. Her father died when she was one year old. Her mother was a schizophrenic who had been sent to a hospital when Judy was ten and has been there ever since. A brother is a paranoid schizo-

phrenic and has also been hospitalized. Judy had severe ulcerative colitis from the age of eight to 15. She developed severe ulcers of the legs and at one time spent $2\frac{1}{2}$ years continuously in a hospital for treatment of her colitis and leg ulcers. Because of the persistence of severe ulcerative colitis symptoms, an ileostomy was performed two years prior to the group therapy.

Miriam was a 42-year-old woman who had been married 19 years and had two children. Four years before the group started, she became pregnant, had a miscarriage, and a few months later developed severe ulcerative colitis, which necessitated an ileostomy two years prior to the group therapy.

Of these patients, four had had abdominal-perineal resections of the rectum prior to the beginning of the group therapy. Two others had the abdominal-perineal resection performed after the group therapy was begun. Three of the women had had rectal-vaginal fistulas.

Procedures. The group psychotherapy sessions were held once a week in the outpatient clinic of the hospital and lasted for an hour and a half. There was no set procedure, and an informal atmosphere was maintained, with no special seating arrangement. The material of the session was the result of the spontaneous discussion between the patients, the therapist participating only to help maintain the spontaneous free-flowing discussion and to help the patients bring out and work through the emotional factors underlying the material. The group psychotherapy was psychoanalytically oriented.

The group began with four patients, one of whom dropped out after a few sessions. Shortly afterward, three other patients joined the group. The original group members had been informed that new people would be coming in. The six women who constituted the group as it was finally established attended the group sessions fairly regularly. The original four patients were seen for short, individual interviews just prior to the first group session, during which the nature of group psychotherapy was briefly explained to them. The other three patients came directly into the group. When it seemed necessary or was requested, the group therapist also saw the patients individually for short periods.

All the patients participated readily in the group discussions from the very first, and all took an active part in group discussions. This active participation was aided because they had known each other in the Ileostomy Club and because they all knew they had similar illnesses and operations, so they could readily identify with each other.

In the first few sessions, they tended to discuss problems in relation to the care of the ileostomy, in a fashion similar to the discussions in the Ileostomy Club. Slowly, they began to ask general questions about the relationship of emotional factors to ileitis, while insisting for the most part that they had no emotional problems of their own. The therapist did not directly oppose this denial but encouraged what were, at first, general intellectual questions concerning emotional tensions and then guided them toward a discussion of their specific emotional difficulties.

Although the talks centered on the problems of the care of the ileostomy, there was considerable giggling and embarrassment as they discussed certain details, giving the impression that they had invested the ileostomy stoma and its care with erotic significance. They spoke of how the opening had to be cleansed and the skin rubbed and of the various rituals they had developed in taking care of the opening. The impression was that gratification of a masturbatory and anal type was involved in the care of the ileostomy.

They then went on to discuss some of the fears connected with the ileostomy. An ever-present anxiety was whether the illness would recur and whether they might require further surgery. Some of these fears seemed realistic and justified, but some seemed more deep-seated and less realistic, and the therapist tried to help them become aware of this fact.

Once they began to discuss their emotional reactions, they all spontaneously brought up their relationships with their mothers. Their tremendous closeness to their mothers was a prominent factor with all of them. They thought of their mothers all the time. They tried to anticipate what the mother expected

and became very upset if the mother was critical or moody. They spoke of their dependent needs and the need for approval, indicating directly and indirectly strong feelings of guilt in connection with these needs. From there, they went on to discuss their feelings about the care they received from the hospital, doctors, and nurses. Underlying ambivalence toward doctors and nurses became apparent—at first in a very veiled fashion and then more clearly. Finally, quite hostile and resentful attitudes began to emerge, particularly in connection with their operations and their need for medical care.

They spoke a good bit about tensions in relation to their families and the problems of their daily lives. Only much later did they begin to talk about their sexual difficulties, although these difficulties had previously been hinted at. All the married women had marked sexual difficulty, and the unmarried woman was extremely fearful of sexual contact. With one exception, all the married women were completely frigid and the exception achieved sexual satisfaction only occasionally. They were all fearful of intercourse, believing it would harm them. This fear had some realistic basis for the three women with rectal-vaginal fistulas, but their fears were too intense and were obviously related, like those of the others, to unrealistic and fearful misconceptions of the sexual act as a violent assault that could be harmful.

Naturally, this material was not brought out as freely or in as orderly a fashion as this summary might indicate. There was much wandering back and forth. The strong sense of underlying guilt in all the patients diminished very gradually, and there continued to be a good deal of denial and resistance throughout the sessions.

Problems. All the women presented a fairly attractive appearance, and two were quite good-looking. On the surface, they were friendly and made a good impression, but it became clear that their friendliness was quite superficial. Underneath, they were quite tense and guarded. Two were borderline psychotics with vague and poorly sustained projective tendencies, and the others had definite infantile personalities, with characterological disturbances of the rigid-compulsive type.

They all showed poor object relationships of the narcissistic type. Their relationships to their mothers were quite similar, resembling what has been called a symbiotic type of relationship. They all showed intense, poorly tolerated conflicts involving dependent and aggressive needs, particularly in relation to their mothers, and the same type of disturbance tended to occur in their relationships with others. Deprivations and frustrations were reacted to with almost overwhelmingly intense reactions. Separation or the threat of separation stimulated the same type of intense emotional response. The failure of a woman's husband to compliment her on a new dress, a mother-in-law's criticism over some trivial matter—situations of this type could bring on the most intense, emotional reaction, with exacerbation of abdominal symptoms. The patients were all subject to periods of depression that were sometimes fairly severe. Often, these periods of depression were associated with episodes of diarrhea, when large quantities of watery stool would be passed through the ileostomy.

An outstanding feature that all of these patients had in common was their enormous sense of guilt. Obviously, from the psychoanalytic standpoint, they had all developed a harsh, punitive, archaic type of superego as a result of the introjection of the phallic mother.

Clearly related to their excessive sense of guilt were their feelings toward the ileostomy. They all felt that it made them different, that they were imperfect—like cripples. The ileostomy was an ugly thing that had to be kept secret; they could never let anyone see it. It was a fragile thing, easily hurt or damaged. It made them weak and frail and so they couldn't do things that other people did, lest they hurt themselves.

Some of these fears had some basis in reality, but their intensity and persistence clearly indicated a connection with underlying, unconscious misconceptions and fears. Some of their fears were obviously connected with their sexual difficulties and their feelings about sex as a type of dangerous, violent assault. In addition, they all showed confusion over their concept of themselves as women. Without exception, they had all been active and athletic as girls, enjoying and excelling in sports. They described themselves as restless people who had to be active. Poorly concealed hostility and rivalry toward men was evident. To such women, the ileostomies represented castration and a deformity to be borne as unmistakable evidence of their guilt, punishment, and inferiority.

Results. All the patients in this group were definitely helped by the group psychotherapy, some to a considerable extent and others only to a moderate extent. All the women became less tense and were less subject to periods of depression. Their attitudes toward their illness and their ileostomies became more realistic and less fearful, and two of the patients who needed to have the final stages of their operations performed— the abdominal-perineal resection of the rectum—were helped to deal with their fears and to go through the operations with relative calm. More flexible and freer attitudes in relationship to their families began to develop. Quite significantly, most of them reported an improvement in their sexual difficulties, with definitely less fearful and more open attitudes developing. One woman, who had not had sexual relations with her husband for four years, was able to consult her physician about this and, finally, to resume sexual relations.

Their improvement was confirmed when all the patients were seen a year after the termination of the group psychotherapy. They had all maintained their improvement in that they were much less tense, had far less frequent and severe episodes of depression, were much less fearful, were much better adjusted to the ileostomies, and had continued to improve their relationships with their families and even, to some extent, their sexual adjustments. Two of the women were seen again several years later, and they definitely indicated that they had continued to maintain and extend their improvement. The 21-year-old single girl continued group therapy with another group and improved to the point where she was able to marry and have two children. She has continued to maintain her improvement.

Surgically, all the patients have been seen

at frequent intervals, and all have continued to do well.

The successful outcome of group therapy with this group of patients is not necessarily typical for colitis patients, patients with ileostomies, and patients with other psychosomatic conditions. One of the original four patients in the group dropped out because of an inability to participate in the group psychotherapy. Some of the usual difficulties in group psychotherapy were lessened by the fact that the patients had all known each other and had participated together, to some extent, in the Ileostomy Club, so the usual hesitation and concerns about participating freely in discussions were considerably lessened. Being members of the Ileostomy Club enhanced one of the mechanisms in group therapy, the identification based on the realization that they all had the same kinds of difficulties, and it lessened their guilt and reluctance to discuss these difficulties. Finally, the fact that all the members voluntarily agreed to participate in the group after having known each other may have helped to bring about the positive results of the group psychotherapy.

Despite the readiness of the patients to participate, they all showed the usual characteristics of the patient with a psychosomatic condition—inability to become aware of underlying emotional tensions and reactions and a very marked tendency to deny the existence of such tensions and reactions. The women denied and avoided emotional topics in the initial stages of the group therapy. Even more important is the fact that, like all psychosomatic patients, these patients tended to somatize their emotional reactions—that is, to express them through physical and physiological manifestations and disturbances rather than through purely emotional responses. All these patients could become extremely upset over the slightest criticism or frustration, particularly in relation to their mothers. At such times, they would develop physical symptoms, usually an attack of cramps and increased bowel movements—a somatic expression, instead of an emotional one, of their rage and frustration.

All these patients were subject to frequent episodes of fairly severe depression. At such times, they tended to have attacks of severe cramps with an excessive amount of watery diarrhea, after which they became weak, sometimes faint, chilly, tremulous, and sleepy—another expression of intensely felt feeling through somatic channels. This tendency to somatize and channel emotional or affective disturbances through physiological and somatic outlets was characteristic of this group of patients, in common with other psychosomatic patients. One of the important manifestations of improvement in this group of patients was their ability to become aware of emotions psychologically and to express them by more purely affective means, such as anger, shouting, and weeping.

Patient with Bronchial Asthma. Janice was a 40-year-old woman who, at the time she entered treatment, was unmarried. She was an editor and a program co-ordinator. Her father had died when she was 13, the mother when she was in her twenties. She felt great guilt in connection with their deaths. Her asthma dated back to the age of 13, the time of her father's death, and had been moderately severe until her early twenties, when she left home to live abroad for a couple of years. On her return, the asthma became quite severe, necessitating the constant use of medication, aerosol ephedrine sprays, etc.; on a couple of occasions she had to be hospitalized because of the severity of the asthmatic symptoms.

Janice had always been a tense, easily upset person, who, despite being intelligent and articulate and very involved with organizations, led a minimal social life. She had girlfriends with whom she maintained a superficial relationship; she had very few boyfriends. She had a nice figure, but she dressed and carried herself in a way that emphasized her unattractive features. After her return to the United States, she began to have dates and to establish relationships with men to a greater extent than before. But the men were most unsuitable and she established sadomasochistic relationships, during which she was often taken advantage of and mistreated—often at her own provocation. In addition, she was frequently subject to the most intense periods of frustration, anger, and depression but often was unaware of her underlying feelings, since they manifested themselves in asthmatic attacks.

Janice began treatment in her early twenties after a depressive episode connected with one of her unsuccessful relationships with men. She was in analysis for several years and later in psychotherapy with the same therapist, with considerable improvement in her asthmatic symptoms and her emotional and social states. A couple of years after stopping treatment, she became depressed as a result of one of her unsatisfactory relationships with a man, made a suicidal attempt, was hospitalized, and started individual treatment with another therapist. Again, she showed some improvement, and, after a couple of years of treatment with the second therapist, she felt well enough to stop. About a year later she again became depressed as the result of another unsatisfactory relationship with a man, and she consulted a third therapist.

She was seen in individual therapy for about a year. During this time, she showed a recurrence of fairly frequent asthmatic symptoms, periods of agitation and depression, and inability to maintain any but the most superficial relationships with women and unsuitable relationships with men. She also felt dissatisfied and exploited in her work. With the individual treatment, she improved considerably.

Despite her intelligence and her previous experience with individual treatment, Janice found the therapy very difficult. She became quite tense and was either placatingly submissive or competitively aggressive during the individual sessions. She almost immediately spoke of the relationship between the therapist and herself as though he were her father, who expected her to go out with men, do well in her job, get married, etc.

Most important, she was frequently unable to speak freely in individual sessions, except when some crisis had arisen. She still showed denial of most strong feelings. When she did speak of these feelings, she usually spoke of them in an intellectual and analytic fashion, so that most of the emotion did not come through. At times, she gestured and assumed a look and expressed an attitude of helplessness at being unable to put into words some of her thoughts and feelings—

the most infantile kind of characteristic, which was most incongruous in such an articulate and intelligent woman. She was a deeply religious person, and her guilt and fear in connection with most impulses and strong feelings was extremely great. Emotional reactions of any strong nature were usually expressed by means of asthmatic attacks and, at times, when attempts were made to get her to express feelings in the individual session or to confront her with the idea that strong feelings were involved in some situations, she would become visibly agitated, take out her aerosol spray, and indicate that she had begun to wheeze.

Because of her limitations in understanding and expressing emotional reactions and because of the difficulties in the transference in the one-to-one relationship, the therapist decided to put her into a mixed group with three other women and four men. She was the only patient who had a fairly definite psychosomatic condition; a couple of the others had anxiety symptoms with somatic concomitants.

At first, Janice was quiet in the group and participated only with considerable difficulty. Gradually, the group began to point this out to her and to point out certain characteristic attitudes—her tendency to bring up important issues only in the last few minutes of the group session, her exaggerated inarticulateness when she had to speak, her denial of strong feelings in obviously emotion-laden situations, and her placating and submissive attitude toward the other patients in the group. On several occasions, she used the aerosal spray in the group, and with the help of the therapist the group was able to get her to speak about this habit and pointed out its relationship to emotional stress in the group. Finally, the members helped her to show some of her feelings and to express them openly toward the others in the group. At this point, about six or eight months after she had entered the group, she began to participate much more actively and to express a great deal more openly some of her difficulties and her feelings connected with them.

In the group, Janice's attitude toward the therapist was, at first, essentially playful and placating, the child-to-father attitude she had shown in individual therapy. When the group pointed this attitude out to her, she quickly abandoned it and began to express some of her angry and competitive feelings in relation to the therapist. After she began to speak freely in the group, she was helped to assume a relationship with a more suitable man and was able to talk about it freely in the group. The same masochistic pattern began to appear in the relationship, and the group with the help of the therapist was able to point out this recurring pattern. She was soon able to speak up more effectively on her job and get a promotion. After about a year and a half in group therapy, she was finally able to establish a good relationship with the man she had discussed in the group and, finally, became engaged and married him.

Shortly after the group pointed out the way in which she used the aerosol spray while in the group, she stopped using the spray. At the time she began to speak openly in the group, her asthmatic attacks, which had been mild and infrequent, subsided completely, although she occasionally wheezed.

This case illustrates the marked improvement of a woman with severe, chronic asthma, marked sexual difficulties, and difficulties in individual psychotherapy. Specific features of group psychotherapy were useful in helping this woman become aware of and deal with her psychosomatic and characterological difficulties. The change in her relationship to the therapist helped her to overcome a characteristic passive, submissive, masochistic attitude and enabled her to assume a more outgoing, outspoken, independent, and aggressive attitude in the group. Her characteristic denial, infantile characterological attitudes, and use of her asthma in dealing with emotions instead of expressing them were clearly demonstrated in the group; the group with the help of the therapist was able to point out these patterns, and the patient was able to see and accept them in a receptive fashion.

Her guilt—of the harsh, primitive, superego type and related to her orthodox, religious attitude—was discussed, and she was enabled, by a series of identifications with the therapist and the other members, to assume a more flexible, realistic, and tolerant attitude. As she began to express feelings about all this, she was able to bring out aggressive and competitive feelings, she asserted herself more effectively in social and work situations, and her somatic symptoms subsided and more or less disappeared. Even more important, she was able to move on to a much more suitable and realistic relationship with others, including men, so that ultimately she could get married. Finally, and most important of all, this articulate and intelligent woman, who had benefited to some extent from individual therapy but had not really been able to use it effectively, was now able to enter into relationships with the therapist and the other group patients in a fashion that enabled her to use the psychotherapy effectively. Here, specific features of the transference and the nature of the treatment were useful in the successful outcome of a case of severe chronic asthma.

Patient with Multiple Psychosomatic Symptoms. This patient, by contrast, showed only slight improvement when treated with group psychotherapy.

Cora was a woman in her late forties who had come for treatment of frequent episodes of depression associated with incapacitating attacks of constricting upper abdominal pains, dizziness, and generalized rashes and frequent pains in her arms and hands, so severe that she was unable to pick up a brush and paint—a major disability, since she was a professional artist of considerable ability. She was married and had two children, a girl of 16 and a boy of 14. One of the main reasons for her frequent episodes of depression was severe marital and sexual difficulty. She had a sadomasochistic relationship with her husband, who was only partially potent. She was submissive to his violent abuse and sadistic manipulations, including his sexual manipulations.

When Cora was about six, her mother had died of a gall bladder attack, which was significantly related to Cora's severe upper abdominal pains. Her father had remarried, and she, from the first, had difficulties with the stepmother and was often severely mistreated, she claimed. Her father was a seductive, manipulative figure with whom she had a sadomasochistic relationship. He would often berate her and accuse her of unworthy, immoral behavior, particularly after her adolescence. She left home in her late teens, worked as a commercial artist with some success, and had several affairs.

When she met her husband-to-be, she did not like him at first but, finally and at his urging, married him. Almost immediately after the marriage, a most unhappy relationship developed. After the birth of the first child, she became depressed and developed somatic symptoms. After the difficult birth of the second child, she again became depressed, had shock treatment, and then was in individual therapy for a few years. She stopped the therapy after some improvement. Three years prior to joining a group, her episodes of depression, severe abdominal pain, dizziness, and pains in her hands and arms began again and increased in severity, coinciding with exacerbations of difficulties in relationship to her son and husband. Because of the persistence and increase of these symptoms, she was referred for treatment.

Cora was an extremely intelligent and articulate person who showed strong denial when it came to most emotional reactions and whose attitude in individual treatment was a severely masochistic one. She would express feelings of hopelessness and despair, elaborate greatly on her physical symptoms, and constantly ask the therapist for help, saying, "I don't know what to do." In individual treatment, the nature of some of her masochistic and provocative attitudes and some of the emotional tensions that she expressed in somatic symptoms were indicated to her, and she improved to some degree. Because of her persistent, clinging, masochistic attitude in transference in individual sessions, it was decided to put her into a group because the amount of improvement she showed in individual treatment had stabilized.

She was put into a group with three other women and four men. One of the other women had a psychosomatic condition manifested by attacks of nausea and vomiting, associated with episodes of excessive overeating. The other patients manifested characterological and emotional disturbances but no psychosomatic symptoms. In the group, Cora participated very seldom in group discussions and spoke very little about herself at first. With the help of the group and guided by the therapist, her withdrawal and the long-suffering attitude that she portrayed nonverbally in the group were pointed out to her, and she began to speak of her difficulties. When she did so, she went into long, detailed, self-justifying accounts that monopolized a great deal of the group's time. She indicated such suffering and such a repetitive number of painful situations that the group was cowed into listening for long periods of time. Finally, with the help of the therapist, they were able to confront her with her behavior, and at this point— several months after she joined the group, she began very slowly to participate in the discussions of the others' problems.

At this time, a subgroup type of relationship developed between Cora and an insecure man who spoke disparagingly of women and who pontificated about what was wrong and what was right. She became extremely angry with him, and rather violent interchanges would occur, during which she was harshly critical and provocative toward him, indicating to him that he reminded her of her overbearing and unfair husband. These attitudes were pointed out to her, and with the help of the group she was able to see the excessive nature of her reaction and some of the provocative attitudes that she displayed. Her attitude toward the therapist, which had been submissive and complaining, slowly became freer in the group, and she was able to be critical and aggressive to some extent with him. After about 2½ years in group therapy, her psychosomatic symptoms had subsided to a degree, as had her periods of depression, and she had moved up to a more assertive attitude toward her husband and, finally, had separated from him. But for the most part she continued to see herself as a mistreated person whose only hope was to find someone who would take special care of her, pay special attention to her, and end the long, unjust suffering that she had had to endure since childhood. After a particularly angry interchange with the group, in which she denied some fairly obvious anger and competitiveness that she was showing, she felt she no longer wished to continue with the group, and she dropped out. She was then seen at infrequent intervals in individual treatment.

Although Cora showed some improvement in her psychosomatic symptoms, some lessening of her depressive attitude, and more realistic assertiveness in her unhappy marriage, her severe masochistic, characterological disturbance remained unimproved. The group helped her to become aware to some extent of her faulty characterological attitudes, but her denial of emotional reactions and her use of somatic symptoms to express these feelings, rather than expressing them directly, continued for the most part, although at a less intense level. She was able to overcome some of the harsh, superego guilt that she constantly felt, but group therapy, like individual therapy, was unable to help this severely ill woman overcome her difficulties. She was one of the patients that Freud described as victims of fate, and she used traumatic events that had occurred in her life to maintain her demanding, accusing, masochistic attitude rather than to deal with it effectively.

This patient, like the one previously described, showed many features that should have made the dynamic factors operative in group psychotherapy specifically useful in her treatment. But the nature of Cora's illness and the severity of the characterological and borderline disturbances involved were so great that they rendered the treatment relatively ineffective.

Results

A majority of the patients cited above improved to a considerable extent when treated with group psychotherapy. The results obtained with the various groups ranged as follows: menopausal group, all improved; first psychosomatic group, 50 per cent improved, 50 per cent improved slightly; second psychosomatic group, all improved; experimental psychosomatic group, 66 per cent improved, 33 per cent unimproved; ulcer group, 50 per cent improved, 40 per cent improved slightly, 10 per cent unimproved; ileostomy group, 50 per cent improved, 50 per cent improved slightly.

As noted above, several of the patients in the ulcer and ileostomy groups were seen some years after the termination of the group psychotherapy and were found to have maintained their improvement. No follow-up of the patients in the other groups was done.

Improvement or lack of it was estimated on the basis of psychiatric clinical examination; evaluation by means of psychological testing was not done.

The findings given are a little bit better than the usual estimate of improvement obtained with individual psychotherapy in the treatment of patients with psychosomatic illness. In the absence of specific evaluation data, this is only a clinical estimate. But, in terms of enabling these seriously ill patients to enter into and make use of psychotherapeutic treatment, group psychotherapy is more effective than individual psychotherapy. In group psychotherapy, the relationships that are established and the interaction that occurs help these patients overcome the pathological, regressive relationships and barriers to emotional expression that have led to the dysfunction resulting in their illness.

The diminution in intensity of the transference directed toward the therapist and its deflection onto the other members of the group enable these patients to overcome their regressive fixation at the passive-symbiotic level and to enter into a useful psychotherapeutic relationship. The idealized identification with the leader and the sharing of guilt help the patients deal with the excessive restrictions of their archaic superegos. The identifications with the other patients and the interactions that make transference manifestations and characterological traits quickly and realistically evident are readily available. The opportunity to become aware of and to express emotions in the accepting-peer atmosphere of the group enables these patients to experience and express feelings verbally and directly, instead of through somatic and autonomic nonverbal channels. The presence of the group members provides ego support and enables the patient not only to find new ways of expression but also to work out new types of relationships and new ways of dealing with emotional tensions.

In this way, group psychotherapy enables the patient with psychosomatic illness to deal with his psychopathology and thereby achieve a more useful realignment of intra-psychic forces so that the psychophysiological regression expressed through psychosomatic symptoms is no longer necessary. Accordingly, for most patients with psychosomatic illness, group psychotherapy is a specific and usually effective form of treatment, and for many it is the treatment of choice.

REFERENCES

Abramson, H., and Peshkin, M. Psychomatic group therapy with parents of children with intractable asthma. Ann. Allerg., *18:* 87, 1960.

Adsett, C. A., and Bruhn, J. G. Short-term group psychotherapy for post-myocardial infarction patients and their wives. Canad. Med. Assoc. J. *99:* 577, 1968.

Barbara, D., Goldart, N., and Oram, C. Group psychoanalysis with adult stutterers. Amer. J. Psychoanal., *21:* 40, 1961.

Bardach, J. L. Group sessions with the wives of aphasic patients. Int. J. Group Psychother., *19:* 361, 1969.

Barendregt, J. A psychological investigation of the effect of group psychotherapy on patients with bronchial asthma. J. Psychosom. Res., *2:* 115, 1957.

Berry, R., and Cunningham, E. Group therapy with medical patients. U. S. Armed Forces Med. J., *9:* 391, 1958.

Boles, C. Simultaneous group therapy with cerebral palsied children and their parents. Int. J. Group Psychother., *9:* 488, 1959.

Brody, S. Value of group psychotherapy in patients with polysurgery addiction. Psychiat. Quart., *33:* 261, 1959.

Clapham, H., and Sclare, A. Group psychotherapy with asthmatic patients. Int. J. Group Psychother., *8:* 44, 1958.

Cooper, M., and Katz, J. The treatment of migraine and tension headache with group psychotherapy. Int. J. Group Psychother., *6:* 266, 1956.

Deutsch, A. L., and Lippman, A. Group psychotherapy for patients with psychosomatic illness. Psychosomatics, *5:* 14, 1964.

Deutsch, F., editor. *The Psychosomatic Concept in Psychoanalysis.* International Universities Press, New York, 1953.

Dorfman, W., Slater, S., and Gottlieb, N. Drugs and placebos in the group treatment of obesity. Int. J. Group Psychother., *9:* 345, 1959.

Edwards, S. L. Group work with brain damaged patients. Hosp. Community Psychiat., *18:* 267, 1967.

Engel, G. L., and Schmale, A. H., Jr. Psychoanalytic theory of somatic disorders. J. Amer. Psychoanal. Assoc., *15:* 344, 1967.

Enke, H. Somatization and group psychotherapy. Psychiat. Neurol. Med. Psychol., *20:* 4, 1968.

Fortin, J., and Abse, D. Group psychotherapy with peptic ulcer: a preliminary report. Int. J. Group Psychother., *6:* 383, 1956.

Freedman, M. B., and Sweet, B. S. Some specific features of group psychotherapy and their implications for the selection of patients. Int. J. Group Psychother., *4:* 355, 1954.

Freyberger, H. Problem of group psychotherapy in primary organic diseases represented by constitutional adiposity. Acta Psychother., *6:* 327, 1958.

Fried, F. B., and Golob, M. A technique for the successful utilization of dual therapists in group psychotherapy with chronic psychiatric outpatients. Presented at 26th Annual Conference of American Group Psychotherapy Association, New York, February 1969.

Frizzell, M. K. Group therapy for diabetic mental patients. Hosp. Community Psychiat., *19:* 297, 1968.

Glomset, D. Group therapy for obesity. J. Iowa Med. Soc., *47:* 496, 1957.

Goldner, R., and Kyle, E. A group approach to the cardiac patient. Soc. Casework, *41:* 346, 1960.

Graham, E. Group psychotherapy in the rehabilitation of the physically disabled. Med. J. Aust., *47:* 537, 1960.

Groen, J., and Pelser, H. Experiences with and results of group psychotherapy in patients with bronchial asthma. J. Psychosom. Res., *4:* 191, 1960.

Heffernan, A. An experiment in group therapy with mothers of diabetic children. Acta Psychother., *7(Suppl.):* 155, 1959.

Hirsch, S. Group counseling with relatives of hospitalized patients. J. Jewish Community Serv., *37:* 236, 1960.

Holt, H., and Winick, C. Group psychotherapy with obese women. Arch. Gen. Psychiat., *5:* 156, 1961.

Igersheimer, W. Analytically oriented group psychotherapy for patients with psychosomatic illness. Int. J. Group Psychother., *9:* 71, 1959.

Kamin, S. H., Llewelleyn, C. J., and Sledge, W. L. Group dynamics in the treatment of epilepsy. J. Pediat., *53:* 410, 1958.

Karush, A., Daniels, G. E., O'Connor, J. F., and Stern, L. O. The response to psychotherapy in chronic ulcerative colitis. I. Pretreatment factors. Psychosom. Med., *30:* 255, 1968.

Karush, A., Daniels, G. E., O'Connor, J. F., and Stern, L. O. The response to psychotherapy in chronic ulcerative colitis. II. Factors arising from the therapeutic situation. Psychosom. Med., *31:* 201, 1969.

Kaufman, M. R., and Heiman, M., editors. *Evolution of Psychosomatic Concepts: Anorexia Nervosa—A Paradigm.* International Universities Press, New York, 1964

Kosofsky, S. An attempt at weight control through group psychotherapy. J. Individ. Psychol., *13:* 68, 1957.

Kurasik, S. Group dynamics in the rehabilitation of hemiplegic patients. J. Amer. Geriat. Soc., *15:* 852, 1967.

Laeder, R., and Francis, W. C. Stuttering workshops: group therapy in a rural high school setting. J. Speech Hearing Dis., *33:* 38, 1968.

Landau, M. E. Group psychotherapy with deaf retardates. Int. J. Group Psychother., *18:* 345, 1968.

Lipowski, Z. J. Review of consultation psychiatry and psychosomatic medicine. III. Theoretical issues. Psychosom. Med., *30:* 395, 1968.

Locke, N. Remarks on the psychology and the group psychotherapy of the hard of hearing. J. Hillside Hosp., *6:* 100, 1957.

Lubin, B., and Slominski, A. A counseling program with adult male cerebral palsied patients. Cereb. Palsy Rev., *21:* 3, 1960.

Ludwig, A. D. Psychotherapy of rheumatoid arthritis. Bull. Amer. Psychoanal. Assoc., *8:* 177, 1952.

Lyons, A. S. An ileostomy club. J. A. M. A., *150:* 812, 1952.

Mees, H. L., and Kenter, C. S. Short term group psychotherapy with obese women. Northwest Med., *66:* 548, 1967.

Milberg, I. Group psychotherapy in the treatment of some neurodermatoses. Int. J. Group Psychother., *6:* 53, 1956.

Mone, L. C. Short-term group psychotherapy with post-cardiac patients. Presented at 27th Annual Conference of American Group Psychotherapy Association, New Orleans, January 1970.

Monteiro, M., and Snyder, L. Social therapy through hospital ward discussions. Ment. Hyg., *11:* 519, 1961.

Murray, N. Malunion of the femur treated by group practice and psychodrama. Southern Med. J., *55:* 921, 1962.

Penick, S. B. Group treatment of obesity in a day hospital. Presented at 27th Annual Conference of American Group Psychotherapy Association, New Orleans, January 1970.

Pion, G., and Caldwell, A. Prenatal care: a group psychotherapeutic approach. Calif. Med., *97:* 281, 1962.

Pratt, J. H. The home sanitorium treatment of consumption. Johns Hopkins Hosp. Bull., *17:* 140, 1906.

Priskor, B. K., and Paleos, S. The group way to banish after-stroke blues. Amer. J. Nurs., *68:* 1500, 1968.

Rainer, J. D., Altshuler, K. Z., Farkas, T., et al. Psychiatric services for deaf patients. I. A comprehensive program in a special unit. Ment. Hosp., *16:* 170, 1965.

Reed, J. Group therapy with asthmatic patients. Geriatrics, *17:* 823, 1962.

Reeder, S. R., and Deck, E. Nurses' participation in a group psychotherapeutic approach to ante-partum management. Nurs. Forum, *2:* 81, 1963.

Rothman, R. Group counseling with parents of visually handicapped children. Int. J. Group Psychother., *6:* 317, 1956.

Sadoff, R. L., and Collins, D. J. Passive dependency in stutterers. Amer. J. Psychiat., *124:* 1126, 1968.

Sadoff, R. L., and Siegel, J. R. Group psychotherapy for stutterers. Int. J. Group Psychother., *15:* 72, 1964.

Sarlin, M. B., and Altshuler, K. Z. Group psychotherapy with deaf adolescents in a school setting. Int. J. Group Psychother., *18:* 337, 1968.

Scarborough, L. Management of convulsive patients with group therapy. Dis. Nerv. Syst., *12:* 233, 1956.

Schneer, H., and Hewlett, I. A family approach to stuttering with group therapy techniques. Int. J. Group Psychother., *8:* 320, 1958.

Shoemaker, R., J., Guy, W. B., and McLaughlin, J. T. Usefulness of group therapy in management of atopic eczema. Penn. Med. J., *58:* 603, 1955.

Slawson, P. F. Group psychotherapy with obese women. Psychosomatics, *6:* 206, 1965.

Sommers, R. K., Schaeffer, M. H., Leiss, R. H., Gerber, A. J., Bray, M. A., Fundrella, D., Olson, J. K., and Tomkins, E. R. The effectiveness of group and individual therapy. J. Speech Hearing Res., *9:* 219, 1966.

Sperling, M. The psychoanalytic treatment of ulcerative colitis. Psychoanal. Quart., *38:* 341, 1957.

Stein, A. Experimental and specific types of group psychotherapy in a general hospital. Int. J. Group Psychother., *2:* 10, 1952.

Stein, A. Psychosomatic disorders. In *The Fields of Group Psychotherapy*, p. 40, S. R. Slavson, editor. International Universities Press, New York, 1956.

Stein, A. Group psychotherapy in a general hospital: principles and practice. Presented at Annual Meeting of American Group Psychotherapy Association, New York, January 1959.

Stein, A. Indications for group psychotherapy and the selection of patients. J. Hillside Hosp., *12:* 145, 1963.

Stein, A., and Lyons, A. S. Group psychotherapy with ileostomy patients: an extension of the ileostomy club. Presented at the Psychosomatic Forum of New York, March 1965.

Stein, A., Steinhardt, R. W., and Cutler, S. I. Group psychotherapy in patients with peptic ulcer. Bull. N. Y. Acad. Med., *31:* 583, 1955.

Sternlieb, S. The development of group psychotherapy for psychosomatic manifestations in various settings. S. Dakota J. Med. Pharm., *16:* 32, 1963.

Stokvis, B. Group psychotherapeutic experiences with asthmatics. Acta Psychother., *7(Suppl.):* 365, 1959.

Suchanek-Frolich, H. Group therapy in psychosomatic medicine. Acta Psychother., *7(Suppl):* 385, 1959.

Teitelbaum, S. H., and Suinn, R. M. A group psychotherapy program with orthopedic patients. Group Psychother., *17:* 49, 1964.

Thomas, G. W. Group psychotherapy: a review of the literature. Psychosom. Med., *15:* 166, 1943.

Titchener, J. L., Sheldon, M. B., and Ross, W. D. Changes in blood pressure of hypertensive patients with and without group psychotherapy. J. Psychosom. Res., *4:* 10, 1959.

Whally, M., and Strehl, C. Evaluation of the three year group therapy program for multiple sclerosis patients. Int. J. Group Psychother., *13:* 328, 1969.

Wittkower, E. D. Treatment of psychosomatic disorders. Canad. Med. Assoc. J., *90:* 1055, 1964.

Wittkower, E. D., and Lipowski, Z. J. Recent developments in psychosomatic medicine. Psychosom. Med., *28:* 722, 1966.

Wohl, T. The role of group psychotherapy for mothers in a rehabilitative approach to juvenile intractable asthma. Ment. Hyg., *47:* 151, 1963.

Wolf, A. Potentialities of group therapy for obesity. Int. Record Med., *171:* 9, 1958.

Wright, K., Brockband, R., Rosenthal, V., Jayne, G., and Sacks, N. Psychiatric aid for the obese. Illinois Med. J., *113:* 15, 1958.

Yaeger, C., Shaskan, D., and Rigney, F. A study of epileptics receiving group psychotherapy. Dis. Nerv. Syst., *21:* 491, 1960.

7

Group Therapy with the Old and Aged

Alvin I. Goldfarb, M.D.

INTRODUCTION

Over the past 20 years, there has been great interest in group therapy of old persons—both those who live in institutions and those who remain at home. Within institutions, the goals have been to increase the discharge rate, decrease disturbing behavior and problems of management, and increase the patient's comfort and well-being by encouraging sociability and social integration. Outside of institutions, the goals have varied. Some groups are organized to alter ways of life by dynamic interaction and therapy based on analytic principles; other groups hope to deal with emotion through ventilation, exposure to the consensus, and the provision of guidance, counsel, and information by group leaders; still other groups are more directly informational and educational.

Group therapy has been used in the treatment of old persons with a wide range of personal and physical characteristics in a variety of settings, and the group leaders have been representatives of many disciplines—psychiatrists, psychologists, social workers, nurses, hospital aides, administrators. Groups have also been led by volunteers with varying backgrounds.

The prevalence of group work with old people is not reflected by the number of reports in the literature. In addition, most reports deal with samples of patients whose characteristics are not clearly described, whose psychiatric problems are not well-defined either descriptively or dynamically, and whose type of treatment is not well-delineated. The results of therapy are usually anecdotally told, and follow-up has been absent or brief. Only rarely have the results been measured against matched untreated controls.

Group therapy of old persons appears to have value both inside and outside of institutions, but its application and efficacy may be misunderstood by persons unfamiliar with old people's special problems, the problems they pose within institutions, and the goals of those who care for them. Because group therapy has been offered to old persons whose psychiatric, physical, and social problems and residential settings cover a wide range and because goals and leadership have varied, the helpfulness of specific methods has not been proved. Different methods may not be efficacious with different populations.

DEFINITIONS

Chronologically old persons, as the term is used here, are persons more than 64 years of age. The aged are chronologically old persons who have suffered a decline in physical or mental functional status to a degree that interferes with the socially acceptable performance of routine activities.

Group therapy is, in Stein's definition, the use of group methods and activities to encourage personal activity, sociability, and social integration of the individual member. The range of group approaches used with old persons goes from motivational through recreational and vocational to physiotherapeutic. Group psychotherapy is the provision of a beneficial, controlled life experience within a group setting by the establishment of relationships with the leader or interaction with group members, or both, together with some clarification of one's motives and those of others in the interaction.

Old-age homes are voluntary, nonprofit institutions, usually under sectarian auspices and selective in admissions. They usually exclude the obviously mentally ill, the severely mentally impaired, and the physically acutely ill. The waiting periods for admission to old-age homes are lengthy—from three months to several years. This waiting period tends to select out those who are in crisis, who have no sustaining family or wealth, or who have poor physical or mental functional status prior to admission.

Nursing homes are proprietary institutions for the long-term care of chronically ill or permanently impaired persons. They vary widely in quality of care. Medicare financing has resulted in a change of many nursing homes to extended-care facilities. These institutions may place emphasis on the admission of short-term convalescent patients, or persons with potential for rehabilitation to the community life.

Social agencies, community centers, day centers, and golden age or senior citizen clubs offer group therapy to the relatively well elderly as a means of enriching the lives of old persons. Many of these noninstitutionalized persons are depressed or feel bored, lonely, or anxious; others resemble institutionalized persons but are ambulatory, capable of using public transportation, and interested in group relationships as a means of getting help.

In state psychiatric hospitals, the old-age population includes a high proportion admitted earlier in life with schizophrenia or other mental illnesses. The preponderant number of patients who are chronologically old when admitted have organic mental syndrome in contrast to those who have aged in the hospital. In the past about 90 per cent of old patients admitted to state hospitals suffered with organic brain syndrome that was either severe and disorganizing of behavior or complicated by association with psychosis. Only 10 per cent of first admissions in old age had a "functional" disorder.

In the past few years state hospitals have defined their psychiatric roles so as to exclude aged persons with brain syndrome unless it is mild or reversible and the patient is not likely to become a permanent resident of the institution. Such selective admission is for the purpose of limiting days in the hospital and emphasizing nonmedical aspects of psychiatric care.

Brain syndrome is the psychiatric reflection of brain damage. It consists of disorientation for time, place, person, and often situation; memory loss, as indicated by a decreased ability to recall events and facts; diminished ability to register, retain, and recall new information; and decreased ability to calculate.

A classification of brain syndrome as mild, moderate, or severe is more useful than a simple statement of its presence or absence. Persons in whom it is mild can be expected to function quite well socially, to be relatively self-sufficient, and to require minimal assistance from family and friends. Persons with moderate brain syndrome are not usually capable of living alone. They cannot shop, cook, or take medicines regularly and properly; if physically impaired, they may need help with dressing, bathing, and grooming. Persons with severe brain syndrome need continuous supervision and assistance with almost every detail of daily living.

Brain syndrome may be acute, that is to say, reversible. The irreversible, persistent forms are known as chronic. Chronic brain syndrome may be uncomplicated: It may occur in persons who are cooperative and agreeable, have insight into their defects, and try to make reasonable adjustments to their deficiencies. On the other hand, chronic brain syndrome may be accompanied by emotional reactions—fear, anger, depression, disorders of thought and perception. The severity of an accompanying disorder of mood or content and the disturbing quality of the emerging behavior are usually unrelated to the severity of the brain syndrome. But where brain syndrome is mild, more resources are available for the patient's reaction to his deficiencies and for the elaboration and expression of psychological and emotional disturbance—in paranoid ways, for example. Thus, the presence of disorder of affect or thought content is indicative of a better outlook for improvement.

Brain syndrome is usually associated with decreased physical functional status for at least three reasons. First, the brain damage that it reflects is a result and reflection of organ impairment or systemic disease—cardiovascular, respiratory, or renal, for example. These diseases are related to disorders that may still be active—such as diabetes, hypertensive cardiovascular disease, and generalized atherosclerosis. Second, brain syndrome interferes with the optional use of the patient's remaining assets. Third, patients with brain syndrome may suffer from self-neglect or accidents.

HISTORY

The pioneer in group therapy, Pratt, was a physician who worked with the physically ill to speed their recovery by instruction, inspiration, and emotional support. His group approach appeared to affect his patients' functional status and physiology favorably. He demonstrated that nature heals and that it is the physician's job to remove obstacles and to place the patient in the most favorable state for reparative processes to occur.

Chronologically old persons, for whose poor physical and mental functional status there were few specific treatments, were offered group therapy in the hope that it would decrease their disability, improve their social functioning, and favorably influence their subjective state. But, despite the use of group therapy with physically ill persons early in the century, its trial with old persons was not reported on until a relatively short time ago.

About 20 years ago, interest in group therapy for the aged rose sharply, paralleling the increased interest in individual psychotherapy with old persons and the improvement in institutional care of the aged. There were many reasons for the rise in interest, the most important of which may have been the increase in the absolute number of old persons in need of comprehensive health care, including psychiatric supervision or treatment.

Silver appears to have been the first to report on group therapy with senile psychotic patients in 1950. A little later, Ginzburg described his experiences in the management of elderly psychotic patients; group meetings were an important part of the program. At the same time, Goldfarb, working in an old-age home, called attention to the need for group orientation programs for new residents of old-age homes. He felt the program should be organized along psychiatric lines to provide information, emotional support, and reassurance to newly admitted patients in their transitional period and to contribute to the growth of their interest in other residents and their healthy dependency on the staff and the institution. He also pointed to the need for staff group meetings to decrease the staff's fear and anger when confronted by the overwhelming problems of the aged.

Linden first described an organized, controlled, continuous, and professionally sophisticated program of group therapy for aged persons in 1953. He also compiled the first comprehensive review of the use of group psychotherapy with aged persons in 1956. Linden, Wolff, Rechtschaffen, Atkinson, and Freeman stimulated others to use and report on group treatment.

THEORETICAL ASPECTS

Group therapy of many kinds has been used with patients with varying characteristics and different psychiatric conditions in a number of inpatient and outpatient settings. In each therapeutic effort the goals, the techniques, and the results have differed. Group therapy, because of its diversity, can do many things for many people but not necessarily the same things for all the people helped. Still, successful therapies may be effective for similar if not identical reasons.

Goals of Therapy

Institutions. Group therapy is used in state hospitals to increase the discharge rate, to decrease problems of patient management, to ameliorate disturbing behavior, to raise staff morale, to improve staff attitudes and conduct toward old and aged patients, to improve patients' adaptation to an institutional environment, to improve interpersonal relationships, and to decrease personal suffering. All of these goals are not always present when group therapy begins. But, when they are not, they tend to become incorporated as the work progresses.

State hospitals have had at least partial success in reaching some of these goals. Other goals, such as continuing a high rate of discharge, have been doomed to failure because of unrealistic expectations. Increased discharge rates appear to be less a direct result of group work than the effect of increased interest and effort by staff and family to find the patient a place outside the hospital.

Old-age homes and nursing homes that care for old persons on a long-term basis have no illusions about rehabilitation for discharge. Some of these institutions, in fact, have been incorrectly regarded in the community and have received patients who were discharged as improved from state hospitals. Most old-age and nursing homes are actually open mental hospitals in their own way. A high proportion of their patients are similar to the less disturbing disorganized, bizarre, and violent patients in institutions formally designated as psychiatric.

In old-age and nursing homes, rehabilitation for sociability and social integration within the congregate living quarters may be the primary goal. Successful treatment carries with it a decrease in personal suffering and interpersonal friction.

Institutionalized patients demonstrate the special problems of therapy with truly aged patients, those who with aging have suffered a decline in their physical or mental functional status or both. Goals of therapy for such patients must necessarily be limited. Persons who have suffered brain damage and have cognitive defects cannot be expected to show true intellectual improvement through group therapy. But group therapy can decrease their fear and anger, improve their behavior, and aid optimal functioning. Even in mentally impaired persons, depression can be lifted, paranoid ideation decreased, and behavior considerably improved. At the same time, other forms of therapy—pharmacological, physical, and individual, must be used as required.

Although group therapy is useful, its limitations must be recognized. Expectations are often excessive. The goals of therapists in various settings are set down in Table 1. By contrast, group therapy's efficacy in meeting these goals in patients with chronic brain syndrome is shown in Table 2.

The likelihood that severely brain-damaged old people will be discharged from a protective institution is slim because even willing and effective families cannot cope with the multiple needs of these patients both day and night. Such patients are severely limited in social interplay and in achieving social integration because of their defects. Even institutional staffs often feel overwhelmed, frightened, or angry. But staff attitudes can be altered by instruction and the morale of personnel can be greatly improved by way of psychiatric supervision, interest, and support. This can be accomplished by modified group therapy with staff under the guise of conferences and also by introducing group treatment for their patients.

Table 1. *Goals in Various Settings**

Goal	State Hospital	Old-Age Home	Social Agency	Outpatient Department
Increase in Discharge Rate	+++	+++	N.A.	N.A.
Decrease in Problems of Management	+++	+++	N.A.	N.A.
Rise in Staff Morale	++	++	+++	0
Improved Staff Attitudes toward the Aged	+	++	+++	+
Improved Interpersonal Relations	+	++	+++	++
Increase in Sociability	+	+	+++	+
Increase in Social Integration	+	+	+++	++
Decrease in Depression	+	+	+++	+++
Decrease in Paranoid Ideation	+	+	+++	+++

* N.A., Not applicable; 0, minimal; +, slight; ++, moderate; +++, considerable.

At first, most therapists working in institutions reported highly encouraging results with group therapy. Wolff, for example, claimed it to be more effective than the dyadic technique. However, aged persons with mental impairment have a limited attention span and tend to lose interest in group meetings; they find little to talk about and do not interact. As Ciompi pointed out, when patients lose all remembrance of the preceding sessions from one session to another, when they do not even recognize the other members of the group and the therapist, as was the case also in experiments by Cosin, Lipsky and Barad, and Villa, group therapy seems to offer little benefit to the individuals. It seems that Linden, Wolff, and others selected—wittingly or not—patients with the greatest potential for behavioral change. Nevertheless, severely brain-damaged patients may carry over a sense of well-being if the sessions are not too widely separated in time and, if sessions are widely separated, a pleasant group experience gives the patients a short time in an oasis in their desert lives.

The intermittent pleasures offered by group treatment appear to have at least a mildly beneficial physiological effect on severely brain-damaged persons. Most important with the brain-damaged, group therapy sessions may demonstrate to the staff how physicians, psychologists, caseworkers, nurses, and other skilled people work with and for old people and serve to show that the efforts of aides, nurses, and all other personnel are valued and appreciated.

Outpatient Departments. In the general hospital outpatient department, traditional psychiatric approaches epitomize the early goals—to change the person by acquainting him with his past ways and their inefficiency or dangers and with his motives and those of others so as to move him toward better understanding of and improvement in interpersonal relations. These approaches have yielded to the discussion of practical problems and the airing of fear and anger. When indicated and possible, accompanying individualized casework gives material assistance.

That old people can take part in and benefit from some of the types of group therapy

Table 2. *Realistic Expectations with Patients Having Different Degrees of Organic Mental Syndrome*

Expectation	Degree of Organic Mental Syndrome*			
	Severe	Moderate	Minimal	None
Increase in Discharge Rate	0	+	+++	+++
Decrease in Problems of Management	0	+	+++	+++
Rise in Staff Morale	+++	+++	+++	+++
Improved Staff Attitudes toward the Aged	+++	+++	+++	+++
Improved Interpersonal Relations	0	+	++	+++
Increase in Sociability	0	+	++	+++
Increase in Social Integration	0	+	++	+++
Decrease in Depression	+	+	+++	+++
Decrease in Paranoid Ideation	+	+	++	+++

* 0, Minimal; +, slight; ++, moderate; +++, considerable.

entered into by younger persons has been dramatically and movingly presented by Mintz in her description of Isbell in the marathon. But old persons like Isbell are only old in years; they are not aged.

Social Agencies. Social agencies reach a somewhat more flexible and adaptable population than is found in institutions. In the community, the opportunities to enrich lives—by encouraging more activity of a personal and social nature, by decreasing family or marital friction, by providing information or aid in the solution of financial, housing, or occupational problems, and by offering opportunities for the ventilation of fear or anger—make group therapy more like that practiced with younger persons. But, in general, old persons show a greater tendency to focus on the leader rather than to interact with the other group members. In day centers and in groups derived from day-center populations, as in institutions, the major effect of group therapy appears to be on the staff. Their morale and attitudes toward the group members make them more effective, more helpful, more accepting, and better problem-solving leaders.

Group therapy has been used to help well persons with preretirement and retirement problems as well as to help those with psychiatric disorders. Spurious questions have been raised about whether activity or disengagement should be considered successful adjustment. Since disengagement is either a special activity or evidence of a depressive reaction, neither activity nor disengagement can be considered a goal of psychotherapy. Similarly, role theory, which considers successful aging the ability to act in ways appropriate to old age, does not, as claimed, seem to provide the most realistic picture of the needs of the aged and the most useful tools for helping them. No special role can be ascribed to chronologically old persons. Variations in retirement practices for various types of work and differences in individual health and in economic and social status are among the factors that make for different roles in old age. The laborer may be retired to leisure when he is relatively young and hale; the professional man may continue to work even when he is ill and, sad to say, mentally incompetent. Old people differ because of their different ways of life, socioeconomic conditions, achievements in youth and middle age; because of their acceptance or refusal of ascribed roles, such as heterosexuality, domestic loyalty, and parental responsibility in younger years; because of changes in society; because of their genetically determined vulnerability to deterioration or disease. Individual differences, therefore, appear to make a Procrustean bed of theories which assume old persons can be dealt with as successful or deviant with respect to fulfilling a socially ascribed role.

Therapy is therefore best considered as having general aims to assist the old person toward having minimal complaints and being minimally complained about; to help him make and keep friends of both sexes and have sexual relationships where interest and capacity for these survive; to help him relieve tensions of biological and cultural origins; and to help him work and play within the limits of his functional status and as determined by his past training, abilities, and self-concept in society.

Ideally, the old person should continue to be or should become a capable self-provider of gratifications and a productive person in terms of social values. These goals are obviously ambitious but, when opportunities and functional status permit, the goals with the aged are the same as the goals with the young. When mental functional status in an old person is good, treatment goals and techniques are similar to those used with young people.

Summary. In general, group therapy supports, directs, and helps old persons with psychiatric problems to understand what their behavior does to them and to others and how these factors have come to be. Several questions arise: How does group therapy support? How does it direct? What in group therapy persuades the old person to do what his life experience and self-observation and the pleas of others have not persuaded him to do?

Techniques

Leadership. Sprague has divided the roles of the therapist into active and passive. Among the passive roles are those of listener and target for the patients' ventilation of emotions. Among the active roles are those of indicator, comforter, explainer, desensitizer, analyzer, lecturer, negotiator, manager, decider, and philosopher.

Stimulating improved social relationships in brain-damaged persons requires staff leadership. Relations are established first with the leader and later, if at all, with peers through the common bond with the leader. For an aged person a relationship is an important factor in the prevention or mitigation of fears and dangers and helps him cope with the disorganizing or personally and interpersonally disturbing effects of fear. The best restraint or corrective for confused, agitated patients is the presence of psychiatrically oriented, alert attendants who recognize that much, if not all, of the seemingly meaningless behavior of aged persons can be handled well if such behavior is regarded as an attempt at problem solving. Also, it is true that many aged institutional residents are more frightened and angry than demented; their behavior is disorganized by emergency emotion. Careful testing for intellectual assets may reveal their presence. Structured, flexible, nondemanding and nonthreatening group programs may reveal the patients' resources in even more gratifying ways—by encouraging and eliciting constructive behavior.

Chronologically old and aged persons, especially those in institutions, have experienced biological and social changes that have strained their adaptive capacities. They have suffered from diseases or accidents, have lost or left jobs, and have lost persons. These losses of resources for adaptation have led to feelings of helplessness, anger, fear—including fear of retaliation and guilty fear. They make restitutive efforts and search for emotional support and aid, but their losses are distressing to them and are symptomatically expressed in ways that may be profoundly disturbing to those around them. Their way of seeking aid may be burdensome and distressing to those around them. In their search for assistance because of their feelings of weakness and vulnerability, aged persons look for and try eagerly to form relationships with persons who appear to have the necessary strengths to help them. Old persons mourn for, long for, search for, and try to win and hold such persons. Their troubled and troubling behavior, which is a continuation of their way of life, can often be successfully channeled toward the group leader, who then becomes a sustaining individual—a friend, confidant, healer—a parent surrogate.

Persons responsible for the care and treatment of the aged with mental disorders, and for the prevention or treatment of such disorders to socially tolerable forms of expression, generally require a program or vehicle for the psychotherapeutic approach; they need a conceptual structure or theory and a "coach" to sustain them. Occupational therapy, vocational therapy, and physiotherapy are examples of such programs or vehicles. One useful conceptual framework is the theory presented above that the behavior of the disturbed or disturbing aged person can be regarded as motivated, goal-seeking, or problem-solving. From this adaptational point of view, the inefficient behavior is seen as a misguided effort to master the environment and to restore feelings of personal control. The coach sustains the staff or therapists by recognizing that their interaction with him and the relationship of student and teacher is similar to the interaction of patient and nurse, or patient and doctor.

Students and nurses, like patients, experience feelings of helplessness when faced by a task that requires the material or informational aid of the teacher, supervisor, or physician. The helping person is automatically thrust into the position of parent surrogate. He must accept the role without playing it; he must do nothing that will destroy the student's or patient's confidence and trust in him. The logical leader of a group, like a teacher, must inspire belief in his knowledge and wisdom. To do this without tricks and without becoming a charlatan, the leader must be well-trained and well-informed. Because aged persons need comprehensive health care, the leader of a group or the coach of those who lead groups should be well-trained in general psychiatry, general medicine, neurology, psychodynamics, and sociology.

For institutions, it is helpful if the supervisor of group leaders is not a member of a staff team. He does best as an "outsider" who brings in interest from the outer world. This therapist helps maintain staff morale and motivates personnel to use themselves effectively to help patients. The therapist helps the staff see that the patients' dependency and exploitative maneuvers are looked upon not as deficits but as resources which can be used for the patients' benefit. The staff members must recognize that a patient's helplessness and angry, ingratiating demands for assistance provide opportunities for the targets of these emotions to be helpful. Otherwise, staff members may feel overwhelmed, irritable, and indignant and may withdraw from, or push away, the aged person who is turning to them for aid. The understanding that they are targets because they are being delegated to aid supports the staff and helps physicians to maintain constructive professional attitudes.

Staff Attitudes. What is done may not be

so important as the fact that something is done, and is done with the intention of helping. This intention helps patients and improves staff morale.

Aides and nurses are probably most effective in reaching and helping the severely brain-damaged since they are constantly present. Their kindly interest helps patients and also has a humanizing influence on other members of the staff with important beneficial ramifications.

Group therapy probably has a more direct effect on staff attitudes than on those of patients. It is the changes in staff attitudes, however, that exert a direct, helpful effect on patients. Once improvements in attitudes of staff have been institutionally assimilated, they form a base for helping more directly with patients in the group.

An institution which is already a good one profits less from the introduction of groups than does a poor one. There may be little need for group therapy where the staff-patient ratio is high, where staff attitudes are therapeutic, where patients are relatively unimpaired mentally, where patients spontaneously develop their own groups, and where facilities for interaction, social integration, and sociability are good. Conversely, the efficacy of group therapy is not great where all patients are severely brain-damaged, where the staff is small or inefficient, where patient-patient and patient-staff interaction is discouraged, and where facilities for social relations are scant.

Thus, group therapy cannot be regarded as a specific isolated technique. Group therapy requires, as well as causes, changes in the total milieu. Success with group therapy efforts may be due less to the actual sessions than to the fact that the staff members become more observant of the patients' needs and more attentive to them at all times. Group therapy inadvertently becomes part of a total push because it requires multiple efforts for its support. Conversely, total-push efforts need group therapy as part of the program. Without group therapy, old persons cannot be continuously engaged socially.

When patients become part of a group, the staff feel encouraged to bathe and dress them with greater care. The staff are indirectly inspired to put their best foot forward because of their new relationships to the patients' therapists, who observe and judge their work. If nothing else, patients are observed who may not have been noticed before. This may lead to the discovery that some patients have improved enough to be discharged.

For a group to function in an institution of ill, aged persons, the efforts require administrative support. For example, patients need to be lifted and transported to group sessions. This is an expensive matter. Also, the scheduling of sessions influences the work of the staff, forces changes in the patients' routines, introduces a new set of goals, and may contribute to seeming restlessness and disorder.

Psychodynamic Processes. Group therapy affects intrapsychic functioning by improving interpersonal relations and increasing self-esteem, self-confidence, sense of purpose, and pleasure; that is, group therapy decreases feelings of helplessness and the fear and anger that usually follow. As in individual psychotherapy, the psychodynamic processes that appear to favor improvement in elderly persons include:

1. The delegation to the therapist of great powers.

2. The patient's belief in the therapist's increasing interest in him.

3. The rise of satisfaction that goes with the belief in the therapist's interest, which is believed to be love.

4. The belief that the therapist's interest guarantees continued care.

5. The rise of satisfaction from having an ally, friend, protector, or parent figure who is more or less constantly present, since the feelings are carried along and incorporated.

6. Gratification from having won over or triumphed over the therapist as proof of one's own strength, wit, or cunning. This gratification is often gained through the receipt of specific practical aid, such as prescriptions for medication, special diets, minor changes in the environment, shifts in room or roommate, and family care.

7. Gratification from feeling favored by the therapist, a victory in sibling rivalry. Gratification from lording it over others.

8. Incidental gratification from true suc-

cess in performances that were motivated by the desire to please the therapist but that have real value. For example, success in occupational therapy—the making of a rug or an ash tray about which the therapist can be told, or that can be given as a gift to the doctor—or success in a sheltered workshop, as evidenced by output and remuneration.

9. Similar gratifications obtained with others about which the therapist may be told or that may be kept as a secret to tell the therapist someday or that are referred to the incorporated parent.

10. Triumphant feelings on the part of the patient from having withheld information of hidden trouble; pride in self-sufficiency, as evidenced by silently endured pain, in relation to the approving incorporated parent.

11. Accentuation of guilty fear (conscience) with some decrease in aggressiveness. Pride, rise in self-esteem on the basis of self-control, and increase in self-confidence on the basis of self-control.

12. Decrease in guilty fear because of permissive or reassuring activities on the part of the group or the leader.

13. The change of disorganizing fear to organizing anger with group members as targets or with the leader as the target and the group as allies.

14. The change of disorganizing anger to organizing fear and the alerting of self to dangers; self-propulsion toward best behavior on the basis of exposure to the consensus, to the leader's comments, and to one's own second thoughts.

CLINICAL ASPECTS

Public Psychiatric Hospitals

Patient Interests. Giving group psychotherapy to senile psychotics in a psychiatric hospital may at first seem futile because of the patients' lack of interest. Silver found that conversation was desultory, the participants commented pathetically on their desire to go home, and they showed no interest in interactional discussion. In intuitive response to their feelings of deprivation, he introduced a party atmosphere by providing milk, cookies, and music. Someone strummed

a guitar and someone else sang. The patients then perked up and became more animated. Semi-weekly meetings of this type tended to improve their social behavior, increase their attention to personal hygiene, and decrease management difficulties.

Silver appears to have been the first to point out, in 1950, that the aged persons' limitations of attention, memory, and understanding make group discussion difficult to initiate, continue, and make interesting. He demonstrated, however, that conversation is not the only way to evoke social improvement. Kastenbaum several years ago and, more recently, Chien advocated the use of mildly alcoholic beverages as a way to induce sociability in the absence of group structure and special leadership. Kastenbaum suggested that ethnic groups might profit from choice of liquor customarily used by them. Chien noted that aged, mentally impaired persons given beer within an area designed to resemble a pub had improved appetite and did show improvement in sociability and self-esteem. Their improvement, however, did not exceed that of a control group who received judicious amounts of thioridazine and no group treatment.

Senility. Senility in the hospitalized aged is not simply a cultural artifact, resulting from social attitudes, as Linden suggested. Self-rejection, insecurity, a fall in self-esteem, fatigue, melancholy, and loss of contact—akin to what Weinberg calls withdrawal syndrome and to what Gruenberg calls the social breakdown syndrome—may lead to reversible impairment of memory and orientation which simulates organic mental syndrome. Spontaneous restitutive efforts may yield spurious improvement but more often results in disturbing behavior. This may, as Linden suggested, be followed by terminal deterioration in which marked emotional dependency, isolation, psychophysiological exhaustion, fantasies, and disorganizing primitive impulses emerge. Linden envisioned group psychotherapy as a way to break into this downward spiral. He wanted leaders to demonstrate their interest and stimulate old persons to marshal their remaining assets within a social context. This was akin to advocating avoidance of permitting a mistaken diagnosis of organic brain disease from becoming a self-fulfilling prophecy.

In his work, however, Linden did not include very recently admitted patients. He initially treated 51 female patients in one large group that was open to any other patients who wished to attend. In this first group, 20 women suffered from organic mental syndrome and 31 had functional disorders of affect or content that had, in some cases, first emerged in old age. Linden chose the patients on the basis of positive criteria: willingness to join the group, appearance of alertness, good personal hygiene, ability to understand English, ambulatory or wheelchair status, at least a minimal range of affect, presenile good social adjustment of some degree, a capacity for evoking positive feeling in the staff, and the presence of sardonic hostility. There were also negative criteria. The patients he chose did not display dementia, advanced physical debility, lifelong paranoid thinking, manic behavior, assaultiveness, persistent incontinence, deafness, hypochondriasis, or unwillingness to participate.

The group met for one hour, twice a week, over a period of two years. Linden was an active leader, an opportunist, calling on persons or lecturing whenever he thought it indicated. He emphasized the universality of patients' problems. He was lighthanded and humorous. He praised participants and at times teased someone in a kindly way to evoke a response from the patient or a defense by the group. And Linden welcomed the accidental emergence of a nurse as cotherapist.

In 43 per cent of the patients, there was considerable improvement; another 16 per cent made moderate gains. Three times the expected number of patients in this group were discharged from the hospital. Active participants did no better than inactive, relatively passive observers. The occasionally incontinent became controlled, gait improved in many, a move toward brisker and more alert behavior was noted in most, and the staff reported a decrease in deafness and an improvement in memory.

In a similar effort, Rechtschaffen, Atkinson, and Freeman used group therapy with 17 old persons in a state psychiatric hospital. The patients were selected because of their good prognosis for discharge. The criteria were good behavioral level and the presence of interest by relatives, which gave evidence that the patients had someplace to go should they improve. The average age of the patients was 72 years, and their average hospital stay was 10 years. About half suffered from senile psychoses; the other half were about equally divided between schizophrenia and effective psychoses.

A psychologist, a social worker, a ward physician, an activities worker, an occupational therapist, nurses, and psychiatric aides formed a treatment team that met frequently for discussions about patients and organization of the program and for staff education. A treatment plan was outlined for each patient. Electroshock, drugs, and special treatments were given as needed. Motivational meetings—occupational therapy, work therapy, current events, discussions—were held. Repeated orientation and informational conversation with the patients were offered. Families were seen regularly to plan for the patients' return home. One-hour group therapy sessions, twice a week, were open to all on a voluntary basis, and about half the patients attended.

Review of the patients revealed many whose recovery had gone unnoticed. As a result, the discharge rate in the first six months of the program was high. In all, 46 of the 171 patients were discharged during the first six months, and only six patients returned. Of the 46 patients discharged, 21 went to live in their own homes, alone or with relatives; the others went to rest homes. The therapists reported:

As a result of the numerous early discharges, the reservoir diminished. As discharges decreased, certain therapeutic aspects of the program showed evidence of improvement and expansion. Staff morale and optimism regarding treatment of the aged increased greatly and proficiency in dealing with elderly patients improved. . . . Patients gained new hope and optimism, and requests for discharge increased.

Thus, what began as an attempt to discharge patients slowly evolved to become a rehabilitation unit for the improvement of permanent residents.

Reporting on the final six months of this program, Atkinson et al. stated that the discharges decreased but stabilized at a rate considerably above that prior to the program, due to the addition of competent, professional personnel to the staff:

Despite the intensive therapeutic effort during the second six months, it would appear that there is no improvement in behavior in the non-discharged patients, whether they reside on the treatment wings or the custodial wings.

In an attempt to reduce persistent senile confusions by a variety of group techniques, Cosin and his co-workers compared a small experimental group with a control group. Group therapy was found to be a suitable way to decrease problems of management and to stimulate patients toward more appropriate social behavior. But maintained improvement of the most severely impaired seemed entirely contingent on continuity of staff efforts. Even the modest gains obtained early in treatment in the less severely impaired declined after six months as the patients' disorders progressed naturally.

Sociability. Group therapy is definitely useful when the emphasis is on increasing sociability and social integration through interpersonal relationships, identification with the group, and encouragement of self-expression, as Wolff reported in 1967:

Repairing the underlying personality conflict is possible and advisable only in limited ways.... Group psychotherapy is more economical of time and provides treatment for a greater number of geriatric patients. Group psychotherapy is also more useful than individual psychotherapy for the geriatric patient by its specific corrective experience in improvement of interpersonal relationships, resocialization in the hospital and motivation to adjust themselves outside the hospital. The degree of initial resistance of the geriatric patient to group psychotherapy is less than to individual psychotherapy. The value of gaining insight into psychodynamics of the geriatric patient is problematic. This is in contrast to the treatment of psychoneurotics and is clearly not always indicated for the geriatric patients.

Wolff attempted to decrease feelings of helplessness by increasing the patients' self-esteem, self-confidence, and purposiveness while making treatment a source of pleasure. He achieved these ends chiefly through the relationship between the patient and the therapist.

Group psychotherapy, although resembling other group activities in encouraging socialization, goes further in relieving the patient's anxiety and improving his adjustment to society. Benaim, like Wolff, thought that a psychiatrist conducting a group might learn more about his patients than he could discover in individual interviews with them.

Staff. Some therapists, such as Gunn, believe that group therapy influences staff members and improves treatment because it leads to more and better observation of the patient. Gunn found that once weekly, hourly sessions with 98 patients—34 men and 64 women—led to an increased use of antidepressants, increased leaves granted to group members, and decreased disturbed behavior on the ward as reported by nurses. These changes, he believes, can be ascribed to an increase in attention paid to patients by the staff because of the group meetings rather than to the direct influence of the sessions, although group meetings might have converted acting out to subjective depression, which ward personnel may regard as less disturbing than other types of mental illness.

Folsom notes that:

the older patient often withdraws into himself, breaks off relationships with others, and in general reduces his awareness and concern for even the simplest things.... Potentially usable parts of the brain soon cease to function.

Folsom attacks the problem in two ways: First, the staff members continually stimulate the patient by tactful, kindly, repetitive orientation. Second, the patient is placed in a group under the leadership of a staff member. There the patient meets and competes with other patients, which forces him out of his isolation and back into his environment.

Folsom claims that the process can reawaken unused neurological pathways and stimulate the patient to develop new ways of functioning to compensate for organic brain damage that resulted from injury, progressive senility, or disuse. However, these unusual and optimistic claims are not well-substantiated by the results. As is the case with other workers, his patients included previously neglected patients with prescribed functional disorders, patients whose recovery had not been noted or had not led to discharge, and patients in whom behavioral aberrations exceeded the degree of brain syndrome present.

His technique involves frequent staff meetings, a high ratio of staff educators, and the use of nurses and aides in important therapeutic roles. It is an effort that tends to heighten staff morale, increase their pride in their work, and increase their interest in and observation of patients. Staff members are also pointed toward humane, supportive care techniques.

Efficacy. Because of the lack of clarity as to what kind of psychiatric hospital patients benefit from group therapy and what these benefits consist of, Wolk and Goldfarb studied the efficacy of group therapy among patients more than 65 years of age in one state hospital. The investigators compared 24 persons with nonorganic mental disorders who had aged in the hospital and 26 persons recently admitted in old age, of whom the preponderant number had brain syndrome with or without associated psychoses. The 50 patients, 27 women and 23 men, were divided randomly into two groups, one for treatment and the other to serve as controls.

The patients were clinically and psychologically tested before and after treatment. Among the psychological tests were the mental-status questionnaire, double simultaneous stimulation (face-hand test), and the chromatic and achromatic house-tree-person test (H.T.P.), from which scores of intensity of depression, anxiety, interpersonal relationships, and degree of chronic brain syndrome were derived.

The patients met for an hour and a half every week for one year in a leader-oriented group in which discussions were elicited, provoked, and controlled, with emphasis on current personal relationships. On occasion, patients were helped to get aid elsewhere—from social service in the hospital, for example.

At the end of the year, both the recent admissions and the long-term patients appeared to have benefited from their experience, but improvement was much greater in those admitted to the hospital before old age (see Table 3). The H.T.P. test as a measure of change agreed with clinical impressions of improvement in interpersonal relationships and in depression. There was also a clinically appreciable decrease in the anxiety level of the patients after treatment.

On initial examination, the group of recent admissions included more persons with chronic brain syndrome, as measured by the mental-status questionnaire and psychiatric examination, than the group of long-term patients. Also, the long-term group showed fewer signs of organicity on the H.T.P. test. After treatment, the H.T.P. signs of organic mental syndrome decreased in number in the long-term group but did not do so in either the controls or any of the recently admitted patients, treated or untreated.

The initial H.T.P. performance of long-term patients may not have been truly indicative of chronic brain syndrome. Their later improved performance could not be explained on the basis of acute reversible brain syndrome, since none of the long-term patients were acutely ill during the year of the study. But the monotonous hospital life of these persons may have contributed to apathy and unresponsiveness, which was reflected in their first figure drawings and incorrectly interpreted as indicative of brain damage. The disappearance of these signs in long-term patients suggests that the drawings do not measure pathology that reflects brain damage. Erroneous diagnostic criteria can lead to mistaken claims of decrease in cognitive defect after treatment.

The H.T.P. signs of organicity in recently admitted patients did not increase in the treated group but did so in their control group. This result is most likely a reflection of the effect of therapy in preventing the development of apathy, withdrawal, and depression—the mental changes that reflected themselves as spurious indicators of organic mental syndrome in the long-term group.

This investigation demonstrates the need

Table 3. *Mean Clinical Ratings of Changes in Surviving Patients after One Year: Over-all Impression by Psychologist* *

Variable	Aged in Hospital		Recent Admissions	
	Experimental (N = 9)	Control (N = 9)	Experimental (N = 9)	Control (N = 8)
Depression	+++	0	+	0
Anxiety	++	0	+	0
Self-Concept	+++	0	+	0
Interpersonal Relationships	+++	0	+	0

* +++, Significant change, positive direction; ++, moderate change; +, mild change; 0, no change.

for comparing mental patients with matched controls, for comparing long-term institutional residents who have no brain syndrome with old persons recently admitted because of brain syndrome, and for using valid measuring devices.

The authors concluded that group psychotherapy appears to be universally helpful but benefits old schizophrenics more than aged persons with chronic brain syndrome, with or without associated disorders, who are first admitted to mental hospitals late in life.

Old-Age Homes

In old-age homes, old persons are expected to live together for the rest of their lives and there is no attempt to rehabilitate them for discharge. Instead, the staff helps the aged persons to make better adjustments to the protective setting and to live more of a social life, despite their defects and deficiencies in their new community, than they could in their own homes.

Sheps organized a group of patients with minimal to moderate evidence of brain syndrome in 1952. The patients were reluctant to talk and tended to skip sessions, pleading illness or periodically increased disability. Their reticence appeared to be based on fear of the psychiatrist as an administrator, on fear of the administration of the home, on fear of each other as potential informers about their discontent with the residence, its staff, and their care. These aged patients made no open attempts to ventilate their resentment or to enlist the psychiatrist as an ally. Unfortunately, in this early trial of group therapy, their appeal for tokens of support were not answered. The group petered out because of nonattendance, lateness, and expressions of unwillingness to participate. Sheps was aware that the patients, because of their backgrounds, were hostile to psychiatry.

A few years later, in 1955, Lipsky and Barad attempted to modify vegetative behavior in a group of aged persons with severe brain syndrome in the same old-age home. They treated 18 women, ranging in age from 74 to 95. All had physical impairments—such as poor vision, deafness, or residual paralysis from cerebral accident—in addition to poor mental functional status.

At the daily group sessions, the patients were placed in a semi-circle and encouraged to talk to the therapist and to each other in answer to simple questions. To reinforce the talk, they held hands, stroked arms, and touched faces. They were encouraged to use simple percussion instruments in accompaniment to music, to sing, and even to dance. Simple occupational activity materials were provided, and the women were helped to use them. Coffee and cake were served after each session. Seven of the women engaged in group conversations. These women expressed concern about their incontinence. There were indications that loss of control was related to feelings of being neglected, to fear, and to resentment. They responded well to retraining programs consisting of scheduling, frequent reminders, and physical help in getting to the facilities. As a result, one patient was recognized as capable of functioning fairly well and was transferred to a better area of the old-age home; ten of the 18 women showed general improvement; four showed fluctuating changes—they did well when they were stimulated and busy, but they subsided into apathy when they were left alone—and three women showed no change. In general, incontinence improved only briefly; it recurred when the saturation of attention was discontinued.

Lipsky and Barad were of the opinion that

a multiple sensory approach—stimulation by voice, touch, sight, and movement—led to social improvement in these completely disoriented persons who had global memory loss and physical disability that greatly exceeded their impairment. They optimistically suggested that, if persons with brain syndrome are flexibly dealt with and if goals are specific but limited, many may respond favorably to such care if it is continuous care. Obviously, this requires a high complement of skilled staff.

The vegetative patients in this study were persons who had drifted down to a level of complete bed-nursing care within a home that was already replete with programs, efforts, and group and individual activities. The staff-patient ratio was high as compared with that in state hospitals. Facilities were plentiful and the relatives of residents were generally alive and interested—frequent visitors who supported the staff and acted to give personal incentives. The 18 women treated were a hard-core group. Also, this experiment was expensive, time-consuming, and disruptive in the home. These factors militated against its continuation.

Rustin and Wolk reported on inpatient group work in an old-age home in 1961. Nine men and three women from 65 to 88 years of age were treated. The weekly sessions lasted 90 minutes. Therapy was active and directive and dealt with immediate problems while recognizing the symbolic impact of these problems. This understanding was used for the patient's benefit without interpretation or construction of a dynamic nature. Anxiety or anger related to the symptoms were relieved as much as possible—often by giving specific aid to the patient. The patient was permitted to feel that he had gained an ally, a friend, and a supporter. In this group, depression decreased, productive activity increased, and interest in recreational activities increased in some patients. Most patients became more sociable.

Severely brain-damaged persons who are ambulatory can be effectively kept busy by a sheltered workshop. At the Hebrew Home for the Aged at Riverdale, New York, patients remained cheerfully occupied during the daily sessions. There was no change in

their cognitive functioning, but the group program appeared to make for greater contentment and tranquility outside of working hours.

Minimally to moderately brain-damaged patients showed considerable improvement in mood and behavior when they were stimulated and motivated. Once offered vocational opportunities with pay, many of the less-severely brain-damaged patients at the Hebrew Home for the Aged went on to seek out nonpaying, diverting occupational or recreational therapy they had previously refused. They were also more receptive to physiotherapy.

The severely brain-damaged patients responded less notably, but they did participate successfully. Cognitive functioning remained unchanged, as did psychoses evidenced by paranoid ideation.

All patients appeared to be less restless, more manageable, and more content in their living areas than they were prior to exposure to the group work. Not only were the work hours important to them, but they obviously enjoyed receiving the remuneration each payday. They appeared to understand the what and why of it, even though many of them could not recall having been paid immediately after the event, and most did not know how to save or spend their new resources.

In the Beth Abraham Home and Hospital of New York, Ferguson set up two types of groups to supplement the home's sheltered workshops and milieu therapy units. The first therapy group met once a week to treat 12 patients with mental disorders. With the exception of the psychiatrist, no staff members were present. The second type of group was open to all ward patients and to all staff. These groups met once a week, with a psychiatrist or a social worker as leader. The role of the staff members was to sit among the patients, help them express their feelings, give factual information on questions that arose, and function as catalysts. They also introduced special topics when patients seemed unable to mention them—for example, a death in the ward. For the most part, however, the patients were expected to select their own topics and were tacitly encouraged to do so. To encourage discussion, the leader would call on individual group members and would attempt to identify and clarify group feelings and opinions. Expressions of anxiety and anger were not discouraged. During critical periods—as when patients were moved to a new building—the leader and staff answered the patients' questions factually to ease the change. An after-group meeting of staff members was an important part of the therapy plan.

Ferguson summarized her observations as follows:

1. For group therapy to succeed in a large, active hospital with many scheduled activities, it must be scheduled to fit into the general framework of the activity program, so that patients are able to attend the group sessions.

2. Staff members may have to help old patients with physical disabilities and lack of mobility to attend meetings. Patients may be able to attend meetings only in or near their own wards. Because of physiological factors, such as the need for frequent micturition and the inability to sit for long periods, meetings should not be too long. Patients must be free to come and go during sessions. Their need for physical assistance at such times may be disruptive and troublesome, especially if staff cooperation is poor.

3. Patients seem to guard themselves against emotional involvement with other people and even against expressing any emotion at all. The ward patients especially use the group mainly to ventilate their complaints.

4. The group permits members to continue or resume activities similar to those they had indulged in before coming to the home. Thus, one patient who had formerly been an active temple officer, sometimes took over leadership of the group and ran it as a formal meeting.

5. The group familiarizes the staff with the patients and enables the psychiatrist to observe not only the interaction between patients but also unsuspected personality difficulties.

6. Many of the patients' complaints are psychologically determined but the patients cannot be expected to change; there must be a modification of the reality situation. Thus,

complaints about food, though essentially based on the patients' feelings of insecurity and deprivation, may be treated by gratifying the request for modification in the mode of serving or type of food and by helping patients feel they have some control over the food situation by permitting them to choose from several dishes.

Ferguson also implies that the relationship with the therapist and with group members could be used to decrease fear and feelings of social deprivation. Occasionally, discussions gave rise to insight, with some behavioral modification. The patients, although for the most part physically disabled, had relatively good mental functional states with no more than moderate brain syndrome.

Outpatient Departments

Stein has described to the author two attempts at group psychotherapy with elderly persons in a general hospital outpatient department. In 1958, a psychiatrist used regular group psychotherapy with 16 patients—ten women and six men. Several patients were in their fifties and sixties. Most of the patients had nondisabling physical illnesses, such as diabetes, hypertension, and arthritis. Several were borderline psychotics, and many had marked character disorders. Depression was an important symptom in most. There were no more than eight patients in the group at any one time and new patients were added when others dropped out. Spontaneous productions were encouraged and these productions formed the basis for the group psychotherapy. The therapist's role was limited to helping the patients participate in the group discussion.

The group was never able to jell and work together in a sustained manner, and the absences and drop-outs were high. Individual members in the group appeared unable to establish relationships with each other. They seemed to regard the therapist as an omnipotent parental figure for whom one must suffer and whom one must please; they expected him to reward them by granting their wishes and removing discomforts. They expressed some disappointment and some angry feelings and they did support each other at times. But, in general, they appeared to be preoccupied with their own needs and to compete with each other for the magic help of the parent-therapist. Only one patient improved markedly, two showed slight improvement, and two others made questionable gains.

As a result of this experience, a more active approach was attempted with a second group, in 1959. Here the aim was specifically to help old persons who felt lonely and isolated and who desired more of a social life. Group work focused on arranging recreational activities; on helping with family, medical, and economic problems; and on guiding individual patients toward increased social participation in community centers or clubs. The group was led by a caseworker who was supervised by a psychiatrist experienced in group psychotherapy. The group of five to seven patients met once a week in the social service department of the hospital. By 1962 some 20 patients, all over the age of 55, had spent some time in the group.

Despite the focus on recreational and practical problems, discussions often extended to such topics as illness, loneliness, family difficulties, and fear of death. As with the first group, all the patients had nondisabling organic illnesses and a variety of moderately severe to severe psychiatric conditions. Early working relationships within the group developed to a greater extent than in the first group. The relationship to the therapist as an omnipotent parental figure with magic powers was obvious but all the patients used the caseworker for practical help, with little disruptive rivalry.

Improvement was measured by the decrease in psychiatric symptoms and by increased sociability and social integration outside the group sessions. Of the 20 patients involved, ten attended less than eight sessions and were considered unimproved. Of the ten who attended fairly regularly, two improved slightly, three improved moderately, and five improved considerably.

Stein was so encouraged by this success that he planned to treat other groups of old persons with this modified group psycho-therapy approach. The approach is modified in the sense that the therapist is actively supportive and may be of material, practical assistance; discussions are not pointed to or focused primarily on psychopathology; rather, they are focused on routine day-to-day problems and current distress.

In another trial of outpatient group therapy, Rustin and Wolk selected a group of elderly patients who had good intelligence, were articulate, showed potential for change, were not psychotic, could travel to the outpatient clinic, and appeared to be able to function in a group setting. The patients were treated in an outpatient department of an old-age home. The goals were to reduce fears and to improve interpersonal relations and the self-concept of the participants. The technique was directive, informative, reassuring, anxiety-decreasing, problem-solving, and materially assisting by facilitating contact with caseworkers or agencies. Group therapy was augmented by individual sessions when indicated. Recreational, social, and dietary facilities of the old-age home were available to patients, many of whom made use of these previously unavailable pleasures. The patients improved in sociability, self-concept, and interpersonal relationships. There was a decrease in preoccupation with somatic complaints and death. Since a preoccupation with death is symptomatic of anxiety, the treatment appears to have been successful in decreasing fear.

Social Agencies

Social workers in many agencies have at various times initiated group therapy for their clients. Many of them have been demonstrations that have come and gone as financial support or charismatic and effective leaders have been available or lost.

The Jewish Family and Community Service of Chicago has described caseworker visits to golden age centers to find out whether persons concerned with realistic problems of aging were interested in becoming involved in discussions about how to achieve greater satisfactions. A number of groups were formed. In all of them, the leader had to suggest topics for discussion and keep the discussions structured. The important therapy goals that emerged were the prevention of crisis and the clarification of the rights and responsibilities of old persons, especially as these tended to counter self-depreciation and contributed to self-esteem.

The most elaborate study of group psychotherapy for old persons in the community was done by Klein, LeShan, and Furman. After pilot experiences in seven New York City day centers for old persons, groups of from 15 to 40 persons, varying in age from 59 to 87 years, met at five centers for five to 13 times. The leaders, social workers, were impressed by the eagerness of the old persons to talk, to share experiences, and to learn from each other and from the leaders. But because of distrust and fear, this eagerness did not show itself at once. Once the initial fear, suspicion, and lack of understanding were overcome, however, individual members demonstrated enthusiastic interest in continued participation. Practical, personal, and philosophical matters were discussed with the aid of mature, stable, warm, and flexible leaders, who tolerated the dependency of the old persons, whether manifested as hostility or its converse. These therapists believed that, to be effective, leaders had to help create a pleasant, constructive climate, encourage discussion, and supply factual information. In addition, economical techniques can help maintain or re-establish mental health. The fact that frightened, angry, aged persons quickly focus on a supportive leader makes it likely that group therapy can bring to the community some of the help it needs and can fill the need for psychiatric work.

Similar work has been done with members of a senior citizen group by Bella Van Bark in New York City. The group is rotating and open; the core consists of 12 women. Under the benevolent eye of the leader, the women, whose social activities have been curtailed, are able once again to pursue their ways with decreased fear. Exposure to the consensus and the opportunity for free expression appear to lead to improvement.

In Washington, D. C., Butler advocates heterogeneity in age distributions of groups. The sick can help the sicker, and the well can help the sick. Butler stresses a non-mystical approach to partial solutions of current problems. Persons with divergent ways of life as well as different ages may interact, and the leader himself is led and changed along with his group.

CONCLUSIONS

Group psychotherapy has been heralded as having great rehabilitative effects. But the goals of such therapy are rarely stated clearly. One goal appears to be discharge from psychiatric hospitals, but discharge is an unreliable measure of therapeutic effectiveness. Accommodation to institutional life is another goal. Rendering patients less troublesome, however, is not always proof of effective psychiatric care.

Nevertheless, group therapy may have several effects. First, when group therapy is instituted, the search for participants, their identification, their physical preparation for therapy, the social processes involved, their transportation to and from the meetings, and the attitudes of the staff and the other patients toward the participants may have a beneficial effect. Second, relatively well but previously neglected persons are discovered. Third, observation of all persons is improved and more treatable conditions are discovered. Patients' complaints are noted, and medications, therapeutic leaves, and correctives for somatic complaints are made available. Fourth, staff morale and their interest in and attention to patients rises. Fifth, staff members are provided with schemes and theories, correct or incorrect, about patients' functioning that help them feel more able and effective. Sixth, staff and patients' attention to personal hygiene rises, and staff members are more inclined to help patients. Seventh, family interest, which is often an incentive to use group therapy, may lead to a trial at home and thus to discharge from the psychiatric hospital. Eighth, for permanent residences and for hospitals with discharge as a goal, group therapy makes the geriatric service more of a community—whether the group therapy is offered in sheltered workshops, activities therapy, physiotherapy, or educational, inspirational, or psychodynamically oriented group meetings—provided the meetings are interesting, attractive, and stimulating. Meetings of any kind with a sociorecreational party atmosphere may be of great value. Ninth, group therapy appears to help or improve behavior in persons with moderately severe brain syndrome and, at least briefly, in persons with severe brain syndrome, although group therapy can be most helpful with some persons who have little or no brain syndrome.

Outside of institutions, group therapy can also do many things. As Maxwell has stated, "groups exist for many different purposes" and arise in many different ways. They may develop spontaneously or be created by an agency in response to patient or community needs—observed or fancied. The goal of those who form the groups may be a desire to decrease suffering or to promote sociability and social integration. The group meetings can be casual or formal, small or large, open or closed, regular or irregular, frequent or seldom. Meetings can be held by arrangement or by accident, and the group's members may be homogeneous or heterogeneous.

Groups provide an opportunity for mutual support and are an aid in the reorganization of behavior in old people who are under the stress of declining resources. Group meetings help them to renew old friendships or to make new ones when there has been a loss of persons by death; the meetings contribute a sense of purpose and of identity. Through alliance with others in the group, the members may feel strengthened and useful. Through group interaction, they may feel of value and importance. Furthermore, group relationships tend to stimulate socially approved hygiene, grooming, and behavior. Group meetings may also be recreational and productive.

For the depressed, group therapy provides targets—the leader and the other members—for their anger. Paranoid patients are exposed to the consensus. Brain-damaged aged patients are helped to remain stimulated, active, oriented, cared-for, and useful; severely brain-damaged patients are given at least a few moments of wakefulness and life in what is otherwise a vacuous existence.

Thus, studies of patients who have been exposed to group therapy in various settings suggest some answers to the question of what kind of care is effective. Care that brings a variety of services to the patient is effective. He responds best to comprehensive health care in a homelike setting within a communitylike social milieu in which there is a wide range of protective, supportive, and reasonably stimulating services and where there are persons with whom he can develop a sustaining, depending relationship. Group therapy aids in and stems from efforts to supply such comprehensive health care.

REFERENCES

Atkinson, S., Fjeld, S. P., and Freeman, J. G. An intensive treatment program for state hospital geriatric patients. Geriatrics, *10:* 111, 1955.

Benaim, S. Group psychotherapy within a psychiatric unit: an experiment. Int. J. Soc. Psychiat., *3:* 123, 1957.

Cosin, L. Z., Mont, M., Post, F., Westrop, C., and Williams, M. Experimental treatment of persistent senile confusion. Int. J. Soc. Psychiat., *4:* 24, 1958.

Delargy, J. Social therapeutics in geriatric medicine. Brit. J. Clin. Pract., *14:* 339, 1960.

Farrar, M., and Ferrari, N. Casework and group work in a home for the aged. Soc. Work, *5:* 58, 1960.

Frenkiel, K. N., Reingold, J., Rusalem, H., and Speiser, A. Establishment of work tolerance limits for participation in a sheltered workshop program in a home for the aged. J. Amer. Geriat. Soc., *13:* 248, 1965.

Ginzberg, R. Geriatric ward psychiatry: techniques in the psychological management of elderly psychotics. Amer. J. Psychiat., *110:* 296, 1953.

Ginzberg, R. Attitude therapy in geriatric ward psychiatry. J. Amer. Geriat. Soc., *3:* 445, 1955.

Goldfarb, A. I. Recommendations for psychiatric care in a home for the aged. J. Geront., *8:* 343, 1953.

Goldfarb, A. I. Psychotherapy of aged persons. I. The orientation of staff in a home for the aged. Ment. Hyg., *37:* 76, 1953.

Goldfarb, A. I. Patient-doctor relationship in the treatment of aged persons. Geriatrics, 18, 1964.

Gruenberg, E. N. The social breakdown syndrome —some origins. Amer. J. Psychiat., *123:* 1481, 1967.

Gunn, J. C. An objective evaluation of geriatric ward meetings. J. Neurol. Neurosurg. Psychiat., *31:* 403, 1968.

Gunn, J. C. An objective evaluation of geriatric ward meetings. J. Neurol. Neurosurg. Psychiat., *19:* 72, 1968.

Hulicka, I. M. Psychologic problems of geriatric patients. J. Amer. Geriat. Soc., *9:* 797, 1961.

Liederman, P. C., Green, R., and Liederman, V. R. An approach to problems of geriatric out patients. Curr. Psychiat. Ther., *7:* 179, 1967.

Liederman, P. C., Green, R., and Liederman, V. R. Out patient group therapy with geriatric patients. Geriatrics, *22:* 148, 1967.

Linden, M. E. Group psychotherapy with institutionalized senile women: study in geriatologic human relations. Int. J. Group Psychother., *3:* 150, 1953.

Linden, M. E. Transference in gerontologic group psychotherapy: studies in gerontologic human relations. Int. J. Group Psychother., *5:* 61, 1955.

Linden, M. E. *Geriatrics in the Field of Group Psychotherapy.* International Universities Press, New York, 1956.

Mintz, E. E. Isbell in the marathon. In *Group Therapy Today*, H. M. Rintenback, editor. Atherton Press, New York, 1969.

Nathanson, A., and Reingold, J. A workshop for mentally impaired aged. Gerontologist, *9:* 293, 1969.

Rechtschaffen, A. Psychotherapy with geriatric patients: a review of the literature. J. Geront., *14:* 73, 1959.

Rechtschaffen, A., Atkinson, S., and Freeman, J. G. An intensive program for state hospital geriatric patients. Geriatrics, *9:* 28, 1953.

Reingold, J. Octogenarians work for a living in three-year health-morale study. Hospitals, *38:* 9, 1964.

Reingold, J. The establishment of a sheltered workshop in a home for the aged: some initial considerations. Jewish Commun. Serv., *42:* 269, 1966.

Ross, M. Recent contributions to gerontologic group psychotherapy. Int. J. Group Psychother., *9:* 442, 1959.

Ross, M. A review of some recent treatment methods for elderly psychiatric patients. Gen. Psychiat., *1:* 578, 1959.

Rubin, R. C. The value of occupational therapy in a home for the aged. Occup. Ther. Rehab., *22:* 38, 1943.

Rustin, S. L., and Wolk, R. L. The use of specialized group psychotherapy techniques in a home for the aged. Group Psychother., *16:* 25, 1963.

Sands, S. L. Discharges from mental hospitals. Amer. J. Psychiat., *115:* 748, 1959.

Silver, A. Group psychotherapy with senile psychiatric patients. Geriatrics, *5:* 147, 1950.

Spaulding, J. C. The therapy of useful work. Geriatrics, *16:* 231, 1961.

Sprague, G. S. The psychiatrist's roles with his patient. Amer. J. Psychiat., *95:* 135, 1938.

Wolff, K. Group psychotherapy with geriatric patients in a mental hospital. J. Amer. Geriat. Soc., *5:* 13, 1957.

Wolff, K. Group psychotherapy with geriatric patients in a state hospital setting: results of a three-year study. Group Psychother., *12:* 218, 1959.

Wolff, K. Group psychotherapy with geriatric patients in a psychiatric hospital: six-year study. J. Amer. Geriat. Soc., *10:* 1077, 1962.

Wolff, K. Comparison of group and individual psychotherapy with geriatric patients. Dis. Nerv. Syst., *28:* 384, 1967.

Wolk, R. L., and Goldfarb, A. I. The response to group psychotherapy of aged recent admissions compared with long-term mental hospital patients. Amer. J. Psychiat., *123:* 10, 1967.

Yalom, I. D., and Terrazas, F. Group therapy for psychotic elderly patients. Amer. J. Nurs., *68:* 1969.

8

An Introduction to Family Group Therapy

E. James Anthony, M.D.

INTRODUCTION

Family therapy can be said to have had a long life but a short history. In unsystematic and unstructured ways, at all times and in all places, people of quite different persuasions have tried to be psychologically helpful to families. Within the past three decades, however, the helpfulness has crystallized into a definite psychotherapeutic form, and a recognized professional group of family therapists has emerged. Today, therefore, one can talk of family therapy with the reasonable assumption that most workers in the clinical field of psychiatry and psychology are cognizant of the topic and that the more sophisticated among them know that the area is as controversial as any in the psychosocial sciences.

They know, for example, that family therapy is a type of group therapy, with which it shares many similarities but from which it also has a few important differences. Like group therapy, it received its main theoretical and technical contributions from psychoanalysis and group dynamics, and, like group therapy, it has been split into the same factions. As a result, the family therapist, like the group therapist, has gravitated in his theory and practice toward the individual, toward the family as a group, or toward both. In his actual work, the family therapist is as unlikely as the group therapist to take a completely one-sided view that relegates either individual or group to the limbo of the therapist's unawareness, but the proclivity to one or other side is definitely there.

As with group therapy, family therapy is apparently confronted with dichotomous choices between the individual and the group, between the intrapsychic and the interpersonal, and between the retrospective and the experiential. The choice of therapeutic approach often seems to be dictated by personal rather than professional reasons and in some cases to be decided by factors of introversion and extroversion.

The early workers in family therapy, especially those who came from group therapy, were inclined to stress the similarities between the two approaches, implying that skills in one could be readily transferred to the other. Middelfort, in 1957, stated very simply that

family therapy is an example of group therapy, and it utilizes the assets in the family group to make real and external, or objective, those activities that satisfy the person's social and cultural needs.

Five years later, Handlon and Parloff were more inclined to discuss differences. There were many of these, they felt, between family and group therapy. The family came to therapy with a long history of mutual adjustment, private understandings, predictable responses, and deep feelings for one another; the termination of treatment did not signify in any way the dissolution of the family. The case of the group was quite different. The group had no childhood, no expectation based on experience that their pressing needs would be gratified, their nebulous thoughts and feelings understood, or their closest secrets already known. Whereas the family members bring their traditions and customs ready-made with them, the members of a stranger group are faced with the task of creating their own group culture and atmosphere from scratch. Furthermore, in group therapy, parental and sibling feelings are gradually transferred to the various members, in contrast again to family therapy, where the original feelings are still deposited with the original members.

It follows that the whole defense system functions differently with respect to both conscious and unconscious resistances. Some of these mechanisms are unique to family therapy and operate in addition to the familiar ones that appear in individual and group therapy. In 1965, Framo tabulated a series of resistances that he apparently regarded as peculiar to family therapy— such as massive resistances at the beginning of treatment, sudden demotivations, long periods of passivity, and stiff opposition to any form of change—but every individual and group therapist is familiar with this repertoire.

The defense system that comes into operation in family therapy does have some idiosyncratic qualities, all of which are deducible from the nature of the therapeutic situation. First of all, there is what could be called a primal resistance, resulting from bringing together the same internal and external objects in the same setting, with the patients attempting to keep deeply incestuous feelings and surface affections as separate as in everyday life. Second, there are resistances that guard against family disloyalty. For children especially, developments in this are can move toward a possibly permanent disruption of the group. Then, there are family secrets to be kept hidden and skeletons in the closet to be kept locked up because the members are too proud to wash their dirty linen in public. Next, there are the twin problems of keeping the two situations, the family at home and the family in treatment, separate without making the situation at home intolerable. Unlike the stranger group, the members of the family group actually live the other 22 hours in close contact with one another. Often, the only way to deal with the overflow of feeling is to dissociate the two situations. It is understandably hard for a family in

treatment to pull down the barriers, confront each other openly and freely, loosen up on inhibitions and prohibitions, and then re-establish the whole conventional framework as soon as they reach home again. In respect to all these idiosyncratic qualities, family therapy constitutes a different therapeutic world and, therefore, demands specialized therapeutic consideration.

In 1970, the Group for the Advancement of Psychiatry Committee on the Family surveyed the field of family therapy and came up with some sobering, if not original, conclusions. They pointed to a striking gap between theory and practice and to the fact that the conceptual approach of the family therapist bore "only a tenuous relationship" to actual treatment. The same is true, of course, for all therapies— whether individual, family, or group. In their experience, therapists often turn to treatment of the family as the result of

a desperate search for *any* effort to bring about change in refractory cases.

If they are successful in this, they gradually begin to extend their practice to less difficult patients. The Committee felt that the most striking characteristic of family therapy at the present time is the tendency of therapists to cluster into two groups, the one viewing the family as a complicating factor in the individual's intrapsychic struggles and the other regarding the family transactions as determining the attitudes and behavior of the individual.

In the same context, Williams has this to say:

We prefer to see it as a vicious circle in which disruptive family relationships cause intrapsychic conflict, but once ingrained these conflicts operate to cause further disruptions.

He adds that there is a real danger in the premature separation of intrapsychic and interpersonal approaches in the future training of therapists, who may become as overspecialized in the conduct of transactional therapy as they are in carrying out psychoanalysis. The answer, according to Williams, is a flexible, comprehensive, and integrative approach that includes the "innerness" of the individual as well as his interpersonal milieu.

The report by Group for the Advancement of Psychiatry echoes this viewpoint. The Committee on the Family felt that the field as a whole would gain if therapists who treat individual patients enlarged their scope of interests to include the family and, conversely, if transactional practitioners assigned to history and past experience some of the importance that analytically oriented therapists have always recognized. Curiously enough, they reserve an opinion that the intermediate position may represent nothing more than an attempt to hold on to the familiar and that the logic of the times may well presuppose a discontinuous shift from the individual to the family. If such a trend were to continue, it could blur the functional boundaries between disciplines, since all members of the traditional teams—psychiatrist, psychologist, and social worker—would perform the same job in the same manner and with the same degree of skill.

Even among family therapists of the interpersonal school, there are technical cleavages. Some are more inclined to focus on subjective experiences and emphasize the goal of improved empathy in family life. Others, especially those who make use of communication theory, perfer to stress the objective, observable, and audible aspects of behavior.

From questionnaire data, the Committee on the Family concluded that the majority of practitioners do not adhere strictly to any single method of family therapy, although they do incline to some form of synthesis of the individual psychodynamic and the family-oriented approaches. This tendency is especially true of psychiatrists and social workers. Psychologists, on the other hand, favor behavioral, learning, and existential approaches to an almost comparable degree. Geography also seems to play a part. Adherence to any particular approach is to some extent governed by the influential figures in family therapy operating in that particular part of the country.

The Committee refrained from passing judgment on whether the family approach will achieve an ultimate value in the therapeutic field, but the members have no doubt that the mental health professions have already been introduced to a wide-ranging wealth of vital and radically new concepts.

One could describe family group therapy at this stage as a method that has learned to run before it can walk or even crawl. The field is loaded with free-floating concepts that seem to have nowhere to go, since they are little better than vivid descriptive terms. What seems to be most required if a scientific future is to be assured is some synthetic endeavor that can bring together the various trends within a total framework. By this is meant not a simple eclecticism but an interrelated, coherent, and internally consistent body of knowledge that can give shape to treatment and direction to research. The concepts must be able to transact within this population of ideas and not proceed on their own autistic courses.

Such a framework would require a solid background of history; a synopsis of relevant anthropological and sociological data on the family; a systematic account of family theory stemming from the intrapsychic, the interpersonal, and the group dynamic approaches; studies devoted to the development of family life over time; operational material from family case histories; living-in experiences with the family; experimental studies of the family; and, above all, protocols from different types of family therapy with follow-up evaluations. The students working in this field should be required not only to familiarize themselves with this knowledge but to have some form of therapeutic experience themselves. This experience is manifestly not possible in family groups but could be carried out in stranger groups. The future family therapist needs a background of psychotherapy not only to assimilate necessary group techniques but also to link the family group therapy to its parent body of group psychotherapy, thus allowing the two therapies to transact together profitably.

FAMILY THEORY AND
PSYCHOANALYSIS

Freud and Family Theory

In 1913, Freud startled the anthropological world by considering two of their well-worn phenomena, totems and taboos, in a fresh psychological perspective. Moreover, he went so far as to postulate that the origins of culture and society meet in the Oedipus complex and that incest drives, incest repressions, and filial ambivalence are constant psychic processes in widespread human institutions. In his 1921 essay on group psychology, he made a second excursion into the anthropological field, enlarging on the Darwinian concept of the primal horde as a prototype of family organization.

His speculations in this area may well have led Freud to develop a dynamic psychology of the family, but his own internal development, monitored by intensive self-analysis, deflected him away from it. However, the three points that he made at the time are still pertinent and fundamental to the elaboration of any family psychology. His first assumption was that there is a family psyche very similar to the individual psyche and using the same kind of psychological processes; second, there is a continuity in emotional life from one generation to the next in the same way that the individual's emotional life continues from one developmental stage to the next; and third, that this surprising continuity is brought about not simply by communication but by some unconscious factor that makes the inner life of one generation accessible to the next. These three basic assumptions indicate that Freud was thinking of the family as a whole and of the ways in which feelings and attitudes are transmitted between the members, but the pressures from within were more influential than the pressures from without, and he turned his creative attention from the interpersonal to the intrapsychic. Psychoanalysts from then on faithfully followed this inward turning until recent developments in ego psychology and child observation brought them resurfacing into the ecosphere.

Manifest and Latent Families

Every person carries his original family inside him and keeps an inner dialogue going with it. The less emancipated his feelings are to members of this first group, the more his current attitudes and behavior are dictated by them. This investment with internal objects makes him less attentive and less responsive to what may be transpiring in his present-day family.

To have family therapy with one's original family is a radically different experience from having it with one's family of procreation. In the first type of situation, the patient is confronted by the external representatives of his internal family. In the second type of situation, the external family may be the recipient of transferred feelings from the internal family. The matter is not quite as clear-cut as stated, since transference, in its psychoanalytic sense, is no respecter of persons, and almost anyone or anything can receive transferred emotions. This means that a person may transfer from his internal objects to the actual latter-day members of his original family. To any particular member of the family, therefore, he may, at one and the same time, experience both transference and interpersonal feelings, adding complexity and confusion to his emotional life.

The psychoanalytically oriented therapist tries to keep clear that it is not the mother or father in the family circle who is central to the patient's illness but rather the patient's distorted introject of that person. The family members themselves may be quite unaware of this unconscious realm of introjected and projected objects belonging to the intrapsychic society. They are unaware, according to Searles in his discussion of individual and family therapy in 1965, of any boundaries between intrapsychic and genuinely interpersonal realms and are unaware that they are not reacting primarily to the other persons in the room as flesh-and-blood persons in outer reality but primarily as the personifications of repressed and projected self-images. They are so unaware that the therapist himself must be alert to these separate, or potentially separate, realms. The clash between internal and external may render the present-day relationship untenable and incongruous.

In 1959, Brodey delineated three different types of relationships that work within the family—the image, the object, and the narcissistic. In the image type of relationship, the inner image of the other person takes precedence, and the effort is to change reality to fit in with the inner expectation rather than the other way around. In the narcissistic type of relationship, two people each make an image relationship and, by so doing, act so as to validate the image-derived expectation of the other. When one adds the object to this picture, any differentiation between internal and external is completely obscured, and the other person's needs may be completely confused with one's own needs projected on him.

Searles has suggested that these unconscious family images may be partly integrated inside the individual as an unconscious family that determines to a large extent what transpires in family treatment or interaction. It is the gray eminence that modulates and manipulates the current situation without occupying a recognized place in the circle. Searles feels that it is

toward the derepression of such "unconscious family" modes of relatedness that one's family therapy efforts must be directed.

The individually oriented family therapist affirms over and over again that the real parent, as a denizen of outer reality, is less central to the patient's neurotic or psychotic functioning than the early image or introject that is projected in transference. Laing, in 1967, carried this basic confusion even further by examining more closely what internalization or introjection could really mean in this context. Being a phenomenologist, he includes as well the phenomenology of the unconscious. Speaking of the room which he is in, for example, Laing says:

My experience of this room is not subjective rather than objective, and not inner rather than outer. My experience of the room is simply the room as I experience it, and the room as I experience it is certainly not inside me, but out there as the room.

This picture, therefore, of the inner or latent or unconscious family is a little different from that of the psychoanalyst. The family inside does not occupy space but has become a factor of the person's experience so that he experiences himself as *in* the family and others as in the *family* along with him. The family exists as an experience that establishes a common inner space and inner time. Laing, accordingly, feels that it is not the family that is internalized as an unconscious family but "patterns of relationship between human presences." Only the study of whole families in vivo can study the internal-external transformations; psychoanalysis cannot do it alone.

The family in fantasy is so far different from the family in fact that a study of transactions and communications can only add a single and shallow dimension, according to this point of view, to a complete understanding of the family. Laing reminds the reader of how Dostoevski depicted Raskolnikov's experience of his family in the interplay of his memories, reveries, dreams, unconscious fantasy, imagination, and actions in relation to actual others. While trying to be what he imagines, Raskolnikov enacts, instead, his fantasy pattern of his family, traceable through his dreams, memories, reveries, and physical experiences from which the he that is doing things in the world is largely dissociated.

The family inside, the family in fantasy, the unconscious family have exercised a powerful hold on the analytic family therapist—so much so that it becomes difficult for him to make the shift from inside to outside, from individual to group, and from then to now. One phenomenon, however, helps him to bridge the gap and, to some extent, brings him into closer relationship with the experiential and transactional. This is the fact of transference, which transformed psychoanalysis from a simplistic hunting for early traumata to a dynamic reactivation of the past in the present. The psychoanalytic therapist, both individual and family, can, therefore, pay more than lip service to the here-and-how, to the actual experiences of the present time, and to the existential crises that take place as a result of projected future impinging crucially on present.

FAMILY THEORY AND INTERMEDIATORS

The integrationists have objected to the individual being regarded as either a collection of drives expressing a culture-free universality or a by-product of group life. Their aim is to find some bridge between the individual and his social functioning that gives reasonable value to both. They are in fairly general agreement that psychoanalysis has done a great deal to further understanding of the individual, but they wonder whether the study of the individual within his family would not bring about an extension of theory or even a revolution in perspective.

As long ago as 1950, Parsons, speaking as an analytically oriented sociologist, expressed the sentiment that

the sociological aspects of the family as a social system have understandably not been explicitly considered by psychoanalysts because they have concentrated on the particular relations of each patient to each of the members of his family in turn. There has been little occasion to consider the total family as a social system although this might well yield insights not derivable from the "atomistic" treatment of each relationship in turn.

Parsons offered, as a bridge-building concept, the internalization of family roles and gave the family the formative developmental task of creating the individual's personality. Clinicians like Spiegel and Pollak later took off from this point and attempted to apply role theory to the diagnosis and treatment of the family. Spiegel made conflict and complementarity central to his conception of role theory, and Pollak has analyzed the role performance

of family members in terms of the reciprocal satisfactions that they offer.

In the realm of therapy, Ackerman—who has worked with individuals, groups, and families—has concluded that the Freudian model of the anonymous analyst reflecting the patient's inner life like a mirror fails to provide "the architecture for a true social experience" (1966). The family therapist needs to develop a complex biopsychosocial model to meet his more complex role in the family—a role concerned with the real and the unreal, the normal and the abnormal, the past as well as the present and future. This continuity of past, present, and future in the patient's behavior adds a new dimension to the phenomenon of transference in the family and becomes connected with social learning. Perhaps Ackerman's most interesting conception is the idea of the family's developing a particular identity over time as it goes its inevitably conflict-ridden way. Not only does the family develop an identity, but the individual members participate in this process, so that the element of family likeness gradually evolves.

The integrationists have, on the whole, a viewpoint not dissimilar from that of the group analytic psychotherapists. It is not simply a question of wanting the best of both worlds, the individual and the group, but of creating workable conceptual models that bridge these worlds and furnish the therapist with a sense of continuity during treatment. With such a sense of continuity, he is not constantly shifting his perspective from individual to group, from individual dynamics to group dynamics, or from one set of theories to another set of theories. His unified viewpoint observes the response of the whole and of its parts to the treatment process.

FAMILY THEORY AND THE TRANSACTIONALISTS

Transactional theory, arising from the communicative-interactive approach, has grown out of the study and treatment of schizophrenic families, and this fact may have had an effect both on the therapeutic approach and on the concepts elaborated. It would have helped to clarify the field if the pioneers of this approach had confined what they had to say to the peculiar and restricted sample of families with a schizophrenic member, but, unfortunately, this type of family has to some extent become prototypical of all families. Family theory and therapy have begun rather than ended in consideration of the grossly abnormal. The same might have happened if Freud had based his metatheory on the Schreber case rather than on the analysis of neurosis.

Schizophrenics and schizophreniclike people may show such resistance to inward-turning procedures that the therapist and theorist are almost bound to end up dealing with the objective, the observable, the audible, and the existential. When, however, the therapist and the theorist turn from the psychotic to the nonpsychotic family and carry their theories and their techniques along with them, the question that arises is whether these theories and techniques are as applicable to the new situation. The transactional approach has thrown a bright new light on the genesis of schizophrenia and, as if this were not enough, has been a major influence in creating the new field of family theory and therapy. But it is time to pause now and consider whether the field is not getting top-heavy with such studies and such articulate formulations of them. If, with Framo, one regards the study of family treatment as still at the stage of hypothesis formation, then all is grist for the mill, but the next generation of transactional family therapists would do well to keep some of their early conceptions between brackets while they study non-psychotic families. Some of the major concepts—for example, double-bind, pseudo-mutuality, three-generation hypothesis, and pathological need complementarity—may be transferable, but this transfer should not be taken for granted.

The idea of family homeostasis, as worked up by Jackson and Weakland, is certainly generalizable and could be incorporated as a central concept in general family theory. Unlike double-bind, homeostasis is a bor-rowed concept, but its application to the field of the family, considered as a closed information system, has been very fruitful. It allows therapists to understand how some persons remain sick and why some become sick when other members of the group get well.

The transactional concepts are concerned with describing and specifying interaction among actual people at a level of directly observable behavior, so that the emphasis is on the real and the current. The present can explain both the development of gross psychopathology within a family and its maintenance. For transactionalists, this emphasis has been both the theory's strength and its weakness in offering a comprehensive explanation. Its neglect of the individual patient has been correlated with the analyst's neglect of the group. Meissner has suggested that the double-bind concept has not explained selective involvement among family members. Nor can the theory be understood without assuming an underlying emotional involvement, which is not dealt with adequately in communicative-interactive theory. The theory also neglects what goes into the making of a conflict, so that the essence of a conflict is not only not understood but perhaps misunderstood.

At its best, the transactional system does illuminate the obscure paradoxes, incompatibilities, and confusions that characterize the everyday life of normal families. At its worst, the approach is too affectless and mechanistic to please the clinician. In the hands of Haley, the physical engineer turned social engineer, the family is a restricted system in which there is

a self-corrective process at work which makes . . . continued association possible even though this self-correction may make continued conflict. If one person goes too far in any direction and exceeds the limits of tolerance of the other family members, they will respond in such a way that the extreme behavior is corrected.

People who work with a mechanical model in mind may develop mechanical techniques for dealing with defects in the system and may end by regarding the human members of the system as defective things. The transformation of patient into thing starts, as Sartre points out, with looking *at* the patient and dominates when the patient is further objectified within a mechanistic model. The family as a machine is the other extreme to the family as a fantasy.

There may be many trials in concept-making before the quintessence of family life is captured. The family as a space-time system, as a homeostatic system, as a communicative system, as a restrictive system, as an unconscious system, as a role-playing system, and so on take the therapist, perhaps, a little on the way that he needs to travel. The danger that all theorists have to bear in mind is that concepts tend to become shibboleths and may outlast their usefulness to a field because they are used to support a cause rather than the advancement of science.

FAMILY THERAPY IN PROCESS

When the Group for the Advancement of Psychiatry considered the contemporary schism in family therapy—between those for whom the central issue in psychopathology is the intrapsychic disequilibrium in the patient, with the family adding an important dimension to this, and those for whom the central issue is the disequilibrium in the family, with the intrapsychic disturbances secondary or even inconsequential —they came to the conclusion that more practitioners fall into the former than into the latter category, although the latter group appears to include a larger number of experienced family therapists. However, the majority of therapists fall between these two extreme positions, so that the over-all distribution resembles a Gaussian curve.

Family therapists seem to make their initial attempts at family therapy as

a desperate search for *any* effort to bring about change in refractory cases.

When this attempt is successful, they gradually extend the procedure to the less serious cases seen in their private offices. Most family therapists do not practice

family therapy exclusively but regard it as one of several possible treatment modes. About 40 per cent of family therapists are social workers, another 40 per cent are psychiatrists and psychologists, and the remaining 20 per cent are marriage counselors, clergymen, nonpsychiatric physicians, sociologists, nurses, and others. This wide range of practitioners is thought to be the result of the theoretical model used, with the underemphasis on the classical medical model.

The route to family therapy is multiple. Some therapists responded to a formal training program, others to a lecture or paper, still others to contact with a family therapist. The majority of family therapists reported having been dissatisfied with the results of individual treatment, and they turned to family therapy out of "general experimental curiosity." It was a striking and almost universal feeling among these practitioners that family therapy was more effective and that results could be obtained more quickly and more clearly. What was also striking, but more surprising, was the opinion that the approach made sense theoretically. Apparently, these practitioners do not feel wracked by the controversies besetting the field.

Types of Family Therapy

Since the method of treatment is still in the experimental stage, many variations have been tried. Single families have been seen by single and multiple therapists, multiple families have been seen by single and multiple therapists, and family couples —marital and parental—have been seen by single and multiple therapists. These trials are all to the good, since they may eventuate in offering a spectrum of approaches to different families with different .family problems or in a single well-defined therapeutic situation that, like its psychoanalytic counterpart, would best meet the needs of a wide variety of cases.

Bringing more than one family together has some diagnostic advantages and offers some economy in time and personnel, but there is understandably a dilution of the therapeutic impact. On the other hand, using more than one therapist for a single family has many advantages that have been exploited in subtle and sophisticated ways by different groups of family therapists. In an interview with Whitaker in 1967, some of the reasons for using a co-therapist with very disturbed families were brought out:

I doubt that it is possible to handle any family with just one therapist. I don't think one therapist alone possesses the amount of power necessary to get in and change the family and get back out again, without getting stuck in the people's salad. . . . I think of it as adding power to myself. The other person gives me a security, a feeling that I am not isolated, that I am not going to be ham-strung by my attachment to one or my antagonism to another. I am able to keep clear of entanglements. . . . There is less chance [of therapy] being interminable or never getting off the ground. . . . I have learned that you can go on holding a family together and staying with it without changing it. I am not willing to do that any more. I wanted to get in with enough power so that I am going to be able to get out. I don't want to stay the rest of my life with my finger stuck in the dike.

Whether this attitude of Whitaker's stems from his own particular needs or whether it is a factor involved in treating severely disturbed families is not easy to decide. One can be fairly certain, however, that the therapeutic team adds its own complex problems to an already complex situation.

On the positive side, the two therapists can alternate in playing administrative or therapeutic roles or can complement each other in the treatment strategies. They help to demonstrate, according to Whitaker, what a confident, direct relationship can be like. On the negative side, as Whitaker describes it, co-therapy is like being

locked in like a husband and wife, so that the two of you can't talk openly. You build up tensions and you have to adapt to them somehow and so you get into a pattern of stalemating and stultifying each other.

When all goes well, however, the two co-therapists can become a new person, yet keep the situations inside and outside

therapy different. Inside therapy, it is like psychodrama, the therapists sometimes insulting and fighting each other; outside, it is a relationship between professionals or an ordinary friendship.

It is difficult to be sure, from the protocols provided, whether the two therapists are relating genuinely and spontaneously to each other or whether they are putting on a show for the benefit of the family. At times, the reading of such accounts inclines one to a remark made by Searles that

some papers on family therapy seem to be written in a spirit largely of childish glee at the writer's having gotten something on the family of the patient.

Multiple-impact therapy includes various team-family contacts. MacGregor et al. describe it as an intensive, family-oriented, brief psychotherapeutic method. The idea is to mobilize self-rehabilitation in the family. Early in treatment, the staff communicate to the family a theory concerning psychopathology and therapy. The team serves as a model of healthy group functioning, with rapport maintained and channels of communication kept open in spite of arguments and disagreements. Its proponents are enthusiastic about it and regard it as the method of choice for initiating therapy when a family crisis exists or for "creating a salutary crisis" when a stalemate exists. But it is difficult not to regard it as a shock treatment that could easily work either way for the family— perhaps increasing its resistances, frightening it off therapy, and making a catastrophe out of a salutary crisis. Like all new approaches, multiple-impact therapy is carried forward triumphantly on the wings of personal gratification, but it may well find a place for itself with recalcitrant types of family situations. At present, the theory offered to sustain the therapist during the arduous few days of encounter is extremely thin and threadbare, and it does not seem to add to one's comprehensive theoretical frame of reference except in terms of empirical data.

Perhaps the most analytically acceptable form of co-therapy is that proffered by

Kadis and Markowitz. The two therapists had known each other as colleagues and collaborators for many years when they came together to treat four married couples. The relationship between them during the development of the group and the group's reaction to their relationship are carefully and honestly considered in the context of the transference. The female therapist introduced the male therapist into her group to counter the lack of male identification in the husbands and the lack of an adequate father model in the wives. Both therapists felt free to assert separateness in their feelings, attitudes, and values. It was felt that this freedom would provide a model for couple interaction. The protocols, however, suggest that the female therapist not only unconsciously thought of herself as the dominant therapist, the all-powerful, magical mother, but was dominant in actual fact. It was she who invited the male therapist into the group, which met in her office; it was she who decided to give him the most comfortable and impressive chair in the room to enhance his significance; and it was she who introduced another couple into the group without first consulting her male colleague. The natural imbalance in this situation was to some extent counterbalanced by the analytic skills and the understanding of the two therapists, but their account points to the implicit dangers of such cooperations unless the male vs. female issue has been completely resolved in both therapists, which it never has been.

Transference and Countertransference

Transference. Transference is an important concern for most family therapists, except those solely dedicated to the communicative-interactive approach. For example, in Satir's *Conjoint Family Therapy*, published in 1964, the word transference has no place in the index.

The phenomenon of transference is different in the three therapies of individual, group, and family. In family therapy, the child is relating to his actual parents, but the intrapsychic images, in part projected onto the real parents and in part onto the therapists, seem altogether more central to his disturbed functioning. In individual psychotherapy, transference is practically everything. In face-to-face group psychotherapy, transference toward the therapist is complicated by simultaneous transference to the other group members, symbolized as siblings. In family therapy, the parental or sibling transference toward the therapist is affected by parental and sibling transferences toward other family members, so that the transference field is more complicated and a transference analysis more difficult to conduct. Furthermore, the group, like the individual therapeutic situation, is a new and fresh one. But in family therapy, the relationships have been operating for many years and are well-systematized and well-defended. In Whitaker's words:

The family comes to a therapeutic situation with greater power than the therapist has.

The therapist has a great deal of catching up to do, and time is certainly not on his side.

The transference distortions of the family members show not only toward the therapist but toward each other, and it is sometimes difficult to distinguish between a real response and an introjective or projective one. In addition, as Framo points out, therapists produce their own transference and countertransference misconstructions. Framo is of the opinion that the transference matrix has been dealt with very little in the literature because it is so intricate. He goes on to suggest that a new kind of transference occurs in family therapy—the transference of the family as a whole, not simply a summation of the individual transferences. According to him, the sicker the family, the more obvious is the family type of transference. Whether Framo's observations can be confirmed by others remains to be seen, but it would be difficult to justify family transference on metatheoretical grounds alone.

Countertransference. Almost every protocol in family therapy throws up countertransference as a huge problem. Families, especially families with psychosis and families with children, are prone to evoke both conscious and unconscious responses in the therapist. At a realistic level, the therapist may be repulsed by a family's appearance, their manner, their style of communication, their organization, and the way they handle their children. On the unconscious or countertransference level, the therapist's reactions may be wholly irrational. Therefore, the therapist's attitudes and behavior at any particular time may be conscious, preconscious, or entirely unconscious. In addition, the stagy setting of family therapy, the drama of multiple interaction, and the tendency of family therapists in general to circumvent defenses leads to exaggerated exhibitionistic and voyeuristic performances on the part of everyone present—including the therapist, whose acting out can make embarrassing reading. Everyone who does family therapy would agree that it makes high emotional demands on the therapist, and they have difficulty in keeping their feelings under control. Framo, among others, has watched therapists from behind the observation mirror while they vented their frustrations childishly on each other, made snide remarks or hostile interpretations about a family, or joked and taunted. It sometimes seems as if consciousness of bad therapeutic behavior gives it a certain amount of sanction.

Whitaker and his co-workers, who have almost specialized in the problem of countertransference, have offered some comments on its appearance and resolution. According to them, family therapy always includes the breaking-up phase, in which old loyalties are undermined, and, if the therapist is to be at all useful to the family, he has to be in it with them deeply and primitively. Countertransference is here made synonymous with involvement, which is not strictly accurate. One can be professionally involved with a family without exhibiting countertransference, but the matter may be different with primitive involvement. Family therapy, even more than individual and group therapy, gives the therapist an opportunity to re-experience his own early family tensions, which he was unable to influence in the way that he now tries to influence—sometimes too strongly. He is rescuing himself from his own predicament. His identification with different members of a family may be too close for comfort, and he may find himself at times in a subgroup, hacking away at his own unresolved problems. In the final phase of treatment, the therapist may find it difficult to disentangle himself from the treatment situation, to give up the family, or to recognize his failure with them.

Whitaker remarks that the most obvious way of dealing with countertransference is by prevention. The therapist should have had adequate treatment himself and should have adequate training and supervision, a secure niche for himself in a professional group, his own satisfying family life outside the office, and a sharing relationship with colleagues. Given all this, he can become a professional rather than an amateur therapist, the latter indicating someone who does psychotherapy simply for the love of it. The world of group psychotherapy is flooded with such amateurs. The professional therapist gradually develops a split within himself, as Whitaker remarks:

> He must be simultaneously involved with the family and separate from it; he must be an entity in himself and at the same time a member of the group, and a primary group at that. He must be able to identify with the child in the family without himself becoming a child. He must be with the parents, yet not a parent.

> If he achieves all this, he can allow himself to admit that the family is more powerful than he is and yet not allow himself to be overwhelmed by its strength.

Indications and Contraindications

In Wynne's paper on indications and contraindications, he says:

> I do not regard family therapy as a psychiatric panacea, but as a valuable addition to our psychiatric repertory.

This can be regarded as a balanced statement, midway between those who feel that family therapy must be limited to simple, superficial, and social conditions and those who have convinced themselves that it is the complete answer to the therapist's prayer.

As indications, Wynne mentions typical adolescent problems (identity crises, rebelliousness, and dependency), conditions involving the trading of dissociations (where the fixed view that someone has of another is unconsciously exchanged for a fixed view of himself by the other, which is an interlocking system), and conditions of collective cognitive chaos (in which transactional-type disorders occur, conditions of amorphous communication and of fixed distances in relationships). These unusual syndromes reflect Wynne's preoccupation with a psychotic population. If he sees such cases responding to family therapy, it would be difficult to anticipate what he would regard as contraindications. In fact, he mentions contraindications only in a small footnote. There he states that, since the patient is the family or, more precisely, the family-therapist unit, it follows that any condition of the family-therapist unit that makes family therapy inadvisable, though it would be otherwise appropriate, constitutes in a broad sense a contraindication to family therapy. This mysterious conclusion not only leaves everyone up in the air but would have little dissuasive effect on rash practitioners.

Ackerman (1963), with much more experience with neurotic family groups, has enumerated almost too many contraindications—where there is evidence of an irreversible trend toward disintegration and breakup of the family; when the barriers to interpersonal communication among family members are so strong that they render intervention with the family therapy method ineffective; when there exists an unyielding cultural or religious prejudice against this type of intervention in private affairs or family life; when organic disease or impairment of a progressive nature precludes the effective participation of family members in family interviews.

In 1966, Ackerman's contraindications were even more specific. They included a malignant, irreversible trend toward the breakup of the family; the concentrated focus of malignant, destructive motivation dominant within the family group; a parent or parents with organized progressive paranoid tendencies, incorrigible psychopathic destructiveness, confirmed criminal or perverted tendencies, or deceitfulness; the existence of a certain kind of family secret or of unyielding cultural, religious, or economic prejudice against family therapy; the presence of extremely rigid defenses that, if broken, might induce a psychosis; psychosomatic states; a chance of physical assault; and, finally, the presence of organic disease or other disablement of a progressive nature. So what is there left to treat? The Group for the Advancement of Psychiatry, after reviewing this list of contraindications, was of the opinion that many family therapists would not subscribe to it.

Other family therapists have felt that treatment is indicated when there is reciprocal pathological interaction between family members but with enough good feeling and mutuality to sustain the period of treatment, when there is a manipulative or controlling adolescent patient, when improvement in a patient results in symptoms among other family members, when there are latency children, when there is a breakdown in communication or lack of trust between the family members, when there is much acting out, and when the central problem is a marital or parental one.

And other family therapists have felt that treatment is contraindicated in families with members who are narcissistic or have an aggressive oral character structure, with partners who cannot agree on common goals or are excessively competitive with each other, and where a major gratification is obtained from the members' supporting each other's destructive defensive maneuvers.

According to the proponents of multiple-impact therapy, as MacGregor et al. report, there are no known contraindications to multiple impact therapy.

CONCLUSION

No one who has observed, participated in, or conducted family therapy could fail to be excited by its potential as a helping procedure. Some, like Searles, have tended to regard it as an escape from the trials of individual therapy. Thus, he remarks,

while this new field is eminently deserving of vigorous exploration, we should not enter into it in a spirit of flight from facing the full depth of the patient's own psychopathology, from facing, for example, the awesome depth of his hostility, his despair, his grief, and his need to give and receive love.

He concludes that therapists may come to view family therapy eventually as a most worthy companion to individual therapy but never as a replacement.

A real family therapist is far less grudging in his appreciation. Whitaker has this to say:

Work with families is the ultimate challenge, the ultimate excitement, the most dangerous and at the same time the most deeply satisfying work that a psychotherapist can attain. It is a real life and death struggle, and the life you save may be your own.

It is from such inward convictions that great developments take place.

REFERENCES

Ackerman, N. In *Encyclopedia of Mental Health*, vol. 2, p. 612. Franklin Watts, New York, 1963.

Ackerman, N. *Treating the Troubled Family*, Basic Books, New York, 1966.

Bateson, G., Jackson, D., Haley, J., and Weakland, J. H. Toward a theory of schizophrenia. Behav. Sci., *1:* 251, 1956.

Bell, J. *Family Group Therapy*. Public Health Monograph No. 64. United States Department of Health, Education and Welfare, Washington, D. C., 1961.

Boszormenyi-Nagy, I., and Framo, J. L., editors. *Intensive Family Therapy: Theoretical and Practical Aspects*. Harper and Row, New York, 1965.

Bowen, M. The use of family theory in clinical practice. Compr. Psychiat., *7:* 345, 1966.

Brodey, W. M. The family as the unit of study and treatment: image, object and narcissistic relationships. Amer. J. Orthopsychiat., *31:* 69, 1961.

Framo, J. L. Rationale and techniques of intensive family therapy. In *Intensive Family Therapy: Theoretical and Practical Aspects*, p. 112, I. Boszormenyi-Nagy and J. L. Framo, editors. Harper and Row, New York, 1965.

Freud, S. *Group Psychology and the Analysis of the Ego*. In *The Standard Edition of the Complete Psychological Works of Sigmund Freud*, vol. 18, p. 67. Hogarth Press, London, 1955.

Freud, S. *Totem and Taboo*. In *The Standard Edition of the Complete Psychological Works of Sigmund Freud*, vol. 13, p. 1. Hogarth Press, London, 1955.

Group for the Advancement of Psychiatry. *The Field of Family Therapy*. Report No. 78. Group for the Advancement of Psychiatry, New York, 1970.

Haley, J., and Hoffman, L. *Techniques of Family Therapy*. Basic Books, New York, 1967.

Jackson, D., editor. *Communication, Family and Marriage*, vol. 1. Science and Behavior Books, Palo Alto, Calif., 1968.

Kadis, A., and Markowitz, M. The therapeutic impact of a co-therapist interaction in a complex group. In *The International Handbook of Group Psychotherapy*, p. 446, J. L. Moreno, editor. Philosophical Library, New York, 1966.

Laing, R. D. Family and individual structure. In *The Predicament of the Family*, p. 107. International Universities Press, New York, 1967.

MacGregor, R., Ritchie, A. M., Serrano, A. C., and Seduster, F. P. *Multiple Impact Therapy with Families*. McGraw-Hill, New York, 1964.

Meissner, W. W. Thinking about the family—psychiatric aspects. Family Process, *3:* 1, 1964.

Middelfort, C. F. *The Family in Psychotherapy*. McGraw-Hill, New York, 1957.

Parsons, T. Psychoanalysis and the social structure. Psychoanal. Quart., *19:* 371, 1950.

Satir, V. *Conjoint Family Therapy*. Science and Behavior Books, Palo Alto, Calif., 1964.

Searles, H. The contributions of family treatment to the psychotherapy of schizophrenia. In *Intensive Family Therapy: Theoretical and Practical Aspects*, p. 463, I. Boszormenyi-Nagy and J. L. Framo, editors. Harper and Row, New York, 1965.

Spiegel, J. P. The resolution of role conflict within the family. In *A Modern Introduction to the Family*, p. 361, N. W. Bell and E. Vogel, editors. Free Press of Glencoe, Glencoe, Ill., 1960.

Stein, J. W. *The Family as a Unit of Study and Treatment*. Region 9 Rehabilitation Research Institute, Monograph 1. University of Washington Press, Seattle, 1969.

Weakland, J. Family therapy as a research arena. Family Process, *1:* 63, 1962.

Whitaker, C. A., Felder, R. E., and Warkentin, J. Countertransference in the family treatment of schizophrenia. In *Intensive Family Therapy: Theoretical and Practical Aspects*, p. 323, I. Boszormenyi-Nagy and J. L. Framo, editors. Harper and Row, New York, 1965.

Wynne, L. Some indications and contraindications for exploratory family therapy. In *Intensive Family Therapy: Theoretical and Practical Aspects*, p. 289, I. Boszormenyi-Nagy and J. L. Framo, editors. Harper and Row, New York, 1965.

9

Family Therapy and Family Group Therapy

Murray Bowen, M.D.

INTRODUCTION

The frequent and confident use of such terms as family therapy, family psychotherapy, and family group therapy implies that they refer to well-defined, standardized procedures. Actually, they are used to refer to such a wide variety of principles, methods, and techniques—all based on such a conglomerate of vague theoretical notions—that the terms are misleading without further clarification. This situation is linked with a similar situation in the more conventional areas of psychiatric theory and practice. Even the oldest and most accepted conventional theories are based on a complex of theoretical assumptions. Theoreticians and early clinicians were aware of the assumptions, but recent generations of clinicians have come to regard the assumptions as fact. When family therapists create new concepts from pieces of pre-existing theory, an interesting theoretical maze results.

The family field is too new to have a body of knowledge about which there is general agreement. Each investigator is so immersed in his own thinking system that it is difficult for any to really hear and know the work of others. A few authors have attempted to survey the field, but each evaluation has been based on the theoretical bias of the author, and others have not agreed with his conclusions.

With the premise that the dilemma will be more quickly resolved if each investigator presents his own thinking as clearly as possible, with the understanding that anything the author says about the work of others will be based on his own theoretical orientation, and with awareness of the inaccuracy entailed in comparing the work of one with another, the author here presents his own theory and method of family psychotherapy in detail and presents some ideas about the work of others that highlight the wide range of theory and practice in the family field.

HISTORY

Antecedents

Family movement refers to the new emphasis on family theory and family therapy that began in the mid-1950's. Some say the family movement is not new, and they refer to family methods used in child guidance clinics and in marriage counseling as early as the 1920's. There is some accuracy to the early claims, but there is probably more accuracy to the thesis that the family movement developed as an evolutionary process, with some early antecedents of family methods discovered in retrospect after the family movement started. A strict historian might validate the thesis that the family movement began when man became literate and recognized the importance of his family in his own life.

On a practical level, the family movement

probably began with the development of psychoanalysis, which has concepts about the ways one life influences another. However, the psychoanalytic focus was on the patient, and the basic concepts were developed from the patient's retroactive memories about his family, as remembered in the transference. The pathogenic family was outside the immediate field of interest. Freud's 1909 paper on the treatment of Little Hans is unique. His work with the father instead of the child is consistent with present family methods in which the designated patient is not a part of the psychotherapy. In 1921 Flugel's book *The Psycho-Analytic Study of the Family* presented individual psychoanalytic formulations about different family members.

The child guidance movement passed very close to present family concepts without seeing them. The focus was on diagnosis and treatment of the sick child. Parents were seen separately to facilitate treatment of the child. Psychiatric social workers came into prominence for casework with parents whose child was in child therapy. By the late 1940's the child guidance model was adopted by adult clinics, with the increasing use of casework for the relatives of adult patients in individual psychotherapy.

Thus, some valid antecedents of the family movement preceded the family movement by some 40 years. However, these developments were not recognized until after the family movement was under way. Not to be ignored is the fact that sociologists and anthropologists were studying the family and contributing to the literature long before the family movement in psychiatry. Also to be remembered is the fact that general systems thinking began in the 1930's, long before there was much recognizable connection between it and psychiatric theory.

Early History

The family movement actually began in the mid-1950's, when the movement surfaced after it had been operating underground in several places for a number of years. There

were too many small roots, each growing independently, for any to say which was first. It was an evolutionary development that suddenly burst into the open when the psychiatric world was ready for it.

Various investigators, each working independently, began to hear about the work of others. Mittelman in 1948 reported on the concurrent analysis of married couples. Middelfort began experimenting with a form of family therapy during his psychiatric training, but did not report on his work for several years. Early work and late reporting was also characteristic of Bell, who in 1951 misheard a comment about individual psychotherapy for family members while visiting a clinic in England. Enroute home, he devised a method that he put into clinical operation. Ackerman, who had been thinking family for several years, began writing in the mid-1950's. Several investigators started family research from previous work with schizophrenia. Among these were Lidz, who started in Baltimore in the early 1950's and continued with his co-workers in New Haven; Jackson and his co-workers in Palo Alto; and Bowen and his co-workers in Bethesda. The formation of the Committee on the Family of the Group for the Advancement of Psychiatry in 1950 was another important event in the early days of the family movement. The Committee was formed at the suggestion of William C. Menninger, who considered the family an important area for study. The Committee worked several years without much knowledge of the field until after the family movement appeared openly. In 1962 two writers visited various family centers, investigating the origin and status of the family movement. Their report, published in *The Saturday Evening Post*, noted that the movement began with several different investigators, including one in Europe—each working without knowledge of the others.

Why did the family movement begin in this way at this time? Most of the originators came from psychoanalytic backgrounds, and the family concepts had been available for years. Why did not the family movement evolve from the child guidance movement a decade or two before? Almost no child psychiatrists have been associated with the family movement.

The family movement seems to be related to the development of psychoanalysis, which gained increasing acceptance in psychiatry during the 1930's, provided concepts for mass use in World War II, and then contributed to the popularity of psychiatry as a specialty after the war. Psychoanalytic theory had explanations for all emotional problems, but treatment techniques had not been developed for the more severe problems. Hundreds of eager psychiatrists began experimenting with modifications of psychoanalytic treatment for the more difficult problems. Those who began family research appear to have been motivated by a search for more effective treatment methods. The strict admonition against contaminating the transference relationship may have accounted for the isolation of the early work and the slowness to report this supposedly unacceptable practice in the literature.

Clinical observations of the entire family together provided a whole new spectrum of clinical patterns never really seen before. Each investigator was on his own in reporting and conceptualizing his observations. Some of the concepts from the early research have remained or have been further developed into the most useful concepts in the field today.

Growth of the Movement

After the family movement was in the open, family sections were held at national professional meetings. The annual meeting of the American Orthopsychiatric Association had a section for family papers in March 1957, and the American Psychiatric Association had a similar section in May 1957. All the papers at both meetings were on research; clinical observation and family psychotherapy were only mentioned. News about family therapy spread rapidly. Beginning in 1958, swarms of therapists crowded the family sections at national meetings. Many therapists soon left the field, but new ones have continued to come in great numbers.

The early workers had arrived at the notion of family therapy as the logical method for the problem as conceptualized by research. The new workers grasped the promise of family therapy without hearing the family orientation on which it was based, which began the widespread empirical use of family therapy as a technique by therapists whose theoretical orientation was in individual theory. Meanwhile, group therapists adapted conventional group therapy to family group therapy.

The rapid increase in therapists was the beginning of a healthy unstructured state of chaos in the family movement. The new therapists, trained in conventional individual theory, stampeded into therapy with a wide spectrum of intuitive feeling techniques based on a conglomerate of discordant partial theories and philosophical principles. Theory was largely ignored, and most therapists operated with the basic assumptions of individual theory, which were quoted as scientific fact. It is difficult to find structure in a field that is exploding with intuitive techniques and when therapists have lost contact with the basic assumptions from which they operate. But this trend had a healthy aspect because conceptual dilemmas come into focus when family members are seen together. The more therapists are exposed to this dilemma, the more some are motivated to find new theoretical concepts and new psychotherapeutic techniques. During the late 1960's, the chaos began to subside as a larger segment of the field became interested in theory and structure and a smaller segment continued the spiral into intuitive techniques.

Current State

In 1970 the Committee on the Family of the Group for the Advancement of Psychiatry completed a report on the family movement. The basis for the study was a long, detailed questionnaire completed by more than 300 family therapists, who represented a cross section of family therapists from all the professional disciplines and with all levels of experience. The questions concerned details of theoretical thinking and clinical practice. The questionnaires, completed in the fall of 1966, covered such a wide range of theory and practice that it was difficult to report the results. Finally, a scheme was devised to designate therapists on a scale from A to Z.

The A therapists are those whose theory and practice is the same as individual psychotherapists. They use family therapy as a technique to supplement individual psychotherapy or as the main technique for a few families. The A therapists are individual therapists who use a little family in their practices. They are usually young or have just started experimenting with family techniques.

The therapists toward the Z end of the scale use theory and techniques that are quite different from individual psychotherapy. They think in terms of systems and emotional fields and relationships. They tend to think family for all emotional problems, and they usually see a number of family members in the treatment of any problem. The Z therapists are the ones who came into the family movement through research or who have been practicing family therapy for a long time.

The overwhelming majority of practicing family therapists are far toward the A end of the scale, with relatively few therapists toward the Z end of the scale. Therapists seem to move from the A end toward the Z end in direct proportion to their experience with family therapy. The A therapist thinks in terms of individual psychopathology and of the therapeutic relationship as the modality for emotional growth; he sees family therapy as a technique to facilitate individual psychotherapy. The Z therapist thinks of symptoms in terms of disordered family relationships and of therapy as a way to help the family restore relationships and achieve better communication or a higher level of differentiation.

The A therapist thinks of several different kinds of family techniques. Designation of the kind of family therapy is determined more by who attends the family sessions than by theory and method. Most family therapists think of individual therapy when

one family member attends the sessions, of couples therapy when both spouses are present, of family therapy or conjoint family therapy for parents and child, and of family group therapy when the entire family is present. Therapists toward the Z end of the scale use terminology determined more by theory than by technique.

THEORETICAL ASPECTS

An Evolution from Individual to Family Theory

Family theory is so different from conventional individual theory that it is difficult to conceptualize and communicate the nuances of difference. Common denominators appear in all systems of family thinking, but to list these misses the clinical rationale for a different approach. In order to present the reasons for a different way of thinking, the author here discusses some of the theoretical nodal points in his experience as he moved from an orientation in psychoanalysis to family theory.

Early Work with Families. The author had considerable early experience with hospitalized patients and a special interest in psychoanalytic psychotherapy with schizophrenic patients. He became interested in the intensity of the emotional attachment between patients and relatives, which could be either an intense, overt overdependence or an equally intense rejection of each by the other.

Hospital treatment and psychotherapy were more orderly when contact between the family and the patient was limited, but the therapist and the hospital staff tended to perceive the patient as the hapless victim of a pathological family, re-integration of the patient into the family was prolonged, and the relatives could remove the patient from treatment just as he appeared to be making progress. With more involvement of the family, therapy went faster, and results appeared to be better, but there were also more emotional upheavals, and some families still terminated treatment prematurely.

A program was started to find better ways to involve the family in the treatment. A special study was made of the intense relationship between parents and young psychotic patients. In addition to providing therapy to the patient, therapists gave the parents a type of supportive information-getting psychotherapy. Progress depended on maintaining a good psychotherapy relationship with the patient and on keeping the parents sufficiently calm so that they did not upset the patient and the patient did not upset them.

At best, even when the patient had one therapist and the parents another, the staff was caught in the intense emotional field between the patient and the parents, trying to manage the parents' relationship with the patient and to protect the patient from parents seen as hurtful. This approach was more, successful than previous approaches, but there were still the unexpected failures, too often blamed on pathological parents. During this period the author did enough psychotherapy with parents to recover somewhat from the hate-the-parents syndrome and to begin concurrent psychotherapy with the parents in addition to the patient, rather than the previous procedure which required one therapist to see the parents and another therapist to see the patient. This experience led to a hypothesis about the mother-patient relationship, which later became the basis for a formal research study started in 1954 at the National Institute of Mental Health in Bethesda, Maryland.

Research Study. As part of the study, mothers lived on the ward with the patients. The original hypothesis excluded fathers, who are usually much less active than mothers in these relationships. After a few months, the hypothesis was extended to include fathers. Within the year, both parents and the normal siblings were included in the live-in study with the patients.

Assumptions. Some important basic assumptions went into the design of the research. In the background was the assumption, derived from psychoanalysis, that emotional growth could take place only in the careful analysis of the patient's relationship with the therapist. An important assumption in the foreground considered the mother's incomplete self to have incorporated the self of the developing fetus and to

have been emotionally unable to give up the child in later years. This one child might fulfill the mother's emotional needs sufficiently so that her other children would not be as incorporated. This emotional stuck-togetherness was considered a primary phenomenon of almost biological proportions. Other phenomena—such as maternal deprivation, hostility, rejection, seductiveness, and castration—were considered to be secondary manifestations of this intense relationship rather than causal factors. The relationship was hypothesized as a locked-in emotional responsiveness that required the complete submission of one for the comfort of the other and that neither one liked or wanted this self-perpetuating enigma in which either could block the other's effort to free himself. The hypothesis further stated that the patient's life-growth force had been blunted in this intense relationship and that the growth force could be freed in a specific therapeutic milieu that toned down the emotional tugging between mother and patient.

This hypothesis was designed to help the therapist understand the mother-patient relationship as a natural phenomenon for which no one is blamed, not even by inference. Systems thinking was not understood at the time, but the hypothesis represented a significant unplanned step into systems thinking. It explained the two-person system as a single unit, and it bypassed large areas of causality formulations necessary in individual theory.

The assumptions implicit in this hypothesis constituted such a departure from the cause-and-effect formulations of individual theory that the implications may not be readily appreciated. Individual theory may assume, with some accuracy, that Event D caused Event E, which followed it. This is a frozen-section assumption that blames D. This assumption could be followed by other assumptions that blame C for causing D or that blame Event E for causing Event F. Systems thinking attempts to conceptualize the total chain of events as a predictable phenomenon, and it obviates the use of the unconscious to postulate a cause.

The clinical operation of the research

study was based on the theoretical assumption that the mother and the patient could resolve the emotional attachment if both were together in a specific supportive milieu in which no one would take sides emotionally or take action for either one against the other in the intense emotional field between the two. It was hypothesized that these two people had lived with each other for years, that each knew the other well, that each had built-in mechanisms to control the other, and that neither had ever seriously hurt the other. The likelihood that either would hurt the other during the clinical research was insignificant enough to take the chance. This one principle remained an unaltered core principle of the research, and it is still a core concept in the family theory developed after the initial research. The concept—a tension system between two people will resolve itself in the presence of a third person who can avoid emotional participation with either while still relating actively to both—is so accurate that it can be predictably repeated in family psychotherapy with less severe emotional problems.

The design in 1954 was to permit the mother to leave the ward at will if tensions between her and her child became too great and to provide each with individual psychotherapy designed to support each without taking sides against the other. The patients and mothers did not begin to grow away from each other, as had been hypothesized. Symptoms subsided rather quickly, but, after the relationship was fairly calm, neither mothers nor patients were motivated to disturb the basic intensity of the interdependence.

Nonparticipation. The staff and therapists found it difficult to acquire more than nominal ability at emotional nonparticipation in family emotions during the early years of the research. Families had many subtle ways to force staff into emotional participation, and personality characteristics in staff members made it automatic for them to feel with the victim or victor. It was commonplace for the staff to maintain a posture of nonparticipation while intimately involved on a deeper feeling level, which families recognized immediately. A cool, aloof, distant posture that feigns nonparticipation and prevents the staff person from relating freely to the family fools no one. Sometimes a family member assumed and acted on the misperception that a staff member was on his side when the staff member was actually neutral.

An incident early in the research study illustrates another facet of the problem. A daughter pushed her mother to the floor. The nurse, acting with a principle of nonparticipation, was in a dilemma. The nurse finally restrained the daughter, after which the nursing staff made a rule of nonparticipation except in situations of physical violence. Thereafter, the families had an automatic mechanism to force the nurses into emotional participation: A family member need only slap or hit another to involve the nurses.

It is difficult to train psychiatrists and psychotherapists to become nonparticipant observers and to regard the family as a phenomenon. Members of the mental health professions, perhaps because of their own early life experiences, are oriented toward understanding and helping the sick and the unfortunate. Individual psychiatric theory, which explains the mechanisms by which the fortunate victimize the oppressed, further fixes the psychiatrist's orientation. Formal training in psychotherapy trains the therapist to hear, to understand, to identify with, to put himself into the patient's situation, and to form a therapeutic alliance with the patient. This alliance is at the core of the therapeutic relationship, the main treatment modality of relationship therapy. The principle of emotional nonparticipation goes against the grain of conventional psychotherapy, but a therapist can be trained to gain this level of functioning if he is willing to work toward that end.

Emotional nonparticipation or staying out of the family emotional system does not mean the therapist is cold, distant, and aloof. Instead, it requires the therapist to recognize his own emotional involvement when it does occur, to gain sufficient control over his emotional system to avoid emotional side-taking with any family member, to observe the family as a phenomenon, and to be able to relate freely to any family member at any time.

Most therapists find it easier to attain a

reasonable level of emotional nonparticipation if they are exposed over and over to the conflicting forces within a family. This exposure helps to force the therapist to a more observational overview of the family in order to maintain his own emotional equilibrium. Psychiatric residents in family psychotherapy training find it easier to attain emotional nonparticipation than do older psychiatrists, for whom the therapeutic relationship has become second nature. But when a resident who is being trained in family and in individual psychotherapy concurrently begins to develop competence at staying out of the emotional system, his supervisors of individual psychotherapy often begin to evaluate him as having a rigid personality with neurotic defensiveness against a warm relationship with his patient.

The author has placed more emphasis on emotional nonparticipation than have other family therapists. But to do successful family therapy, any therapist must gain some control over taking sides with any family faction. Older successful therapists have developed intuitive ways to do what this method attempts to structure and to specify.

One of the important dividends of emotional nonparticipation has to do with more accurate research observations. When the family can function as an emotional unit, the relationship patterns are definite, orderly, and predictable. When an important other person becomes fused into the family emotional system or is removed from the system, the relationship patterns become atypical and important nuances of the relationships are obscured. Family relationship patterns become atypical when a therapist becomes emotionally fused into the family.

The greatest dividend of emotional nonparticipation is in family psychotherapy. Long-term results are far superior, progress is more orderly and consistent, and unresolvable therapeutic impasses are less likely when the therapist can remain relatively outside the system, with freedom to move about and relate to any family member at any time. When the therapist can remain emotionally free while still in contact with any member of the family, the family system becomes calmer and more flexible, and family members become freer within the family. The

therapist can use his knowledge of family systems to guide his effort with the family. When family relationship patterns become atypical, progress shows down, or the family becomes passive and waits for the therapist to solve the problem, the signs indicate that the therapist has become fused into the family emotional system, and he needs to devote attention to his own emotional functioning.

Clinical Experiences. The early research families were not motivated to go beyond symptom relief in individual psychotherapy. Parents neglected to take up significant issues in their psychotherapy, expecting the patient to deal with the issues; and patients neglected issues, expecting the parents to do it. Family psychotherapy was the next logical step.

The theoretical thinking and the research design considered the mother-patient relationship as a unit, and the staff began thinking about psychotherapy for the unit within a few months after the research started. After a year, all families were started in family psychotherapy, the only form of therapy for newly admitted families. The old families continued their already-established individual therapy and began going to family psychotherapy sessions, too. Family therapy for the new families was alive and fast-moving, and progress was more rapid than with any other therapy. The other families were not making progress in either individual or family psychotherapy. In family sessions their attitude was, "I'll take up my problems with *my* therapist." But their individual therapy was also slow, both patients and parents expecting the other to deal with significant issues. After a few months, all individual psychotherapy was discontinued.

In the beginning, family psychotherapy was considered a profitable initial procedure to deal with intense issues until family members were seriously motivated for individual psychotherapy, which was still considered the only modality for significant personality growth. After a relatively brief period with family therapy, therapists saw that this method could do anything that was possible with individual therapy, plus much more. If the goal was to analyze the transference, then every nuance that might come to light in the transference was vividly present in living detail in already-existing family relationships. If the goal was to get at a family member's intrapsychic process through dreams, then one had only to analyze the dreams of that family member—and obtain the added dividend of the thoughts and fantasy reactions of the other family members to the dream.

It was a shaking experience for one long-schooled in psychoanalytic theory to become aware that all he had held to be factual and irrevocable was no more than another theoretical assumption and that psychoanalytic therapy was no longer *the* therapy but simply another method. It was even more shaking when the family investigator reported his findings, expecting that some therapists might hear and become interested, only to have old friends and colleagues listen but continue on in the unshaken belief that psychoanalysis was the one proved theory and that psychoanalytic therapy was the ultimate in therapy. Then the investigator had a choice of going on alone or of giving up the effort.

The type of family psychotherapy started in the research study in 1955 would now be called family group therapy. Any family member could speak at any time and the therapist could ask the silent ones to speak. The method used group therapy techniques, but with a different goal about issues to be defined. There was also multiple-family group therapy, attended by all members of the live-in families (three to five families), and large multiple-group therapy sessions attended by all the members of all the families and the staff. The multiple-family group meetings were useful for communicating feelings and for promoting calmness but not for defining issues in a single family. It was slow plodding for any family member to establish a self in that setting. The large multiple-family groups were discontinued and were not resumed until ten years later, when their principles were incorporated into network therapy.

The patterns seen in the live-in families had always been present between schizo-phrenic patients and their parents. Why had the patterns never really been seen before? The main reason seems to be that the research study had a broad theoretical frame of reference, which opened minds to new data. Other factors facilitating the observations could have been the intensity of the patterns in this live-in project and of the effort to stay outside the family emotional system.

After the patterns were seen in the research families, it was inescapable to see the very same patterns in all degrees of lesser intensity in all other people. Patterns originally thought to be characteristic of schizophrenia were also present in families with less severe problems and even in normal families. To the author this was evidence that schizophrenia and all other forms of emotional illness belong on a continuum, the difference between schizophrenia and the neuroses being one of degree of impairment rather than a qualitative difference. This finding was the beginning of a long effort to classify all levels of human adaptation, from the lowest to the highest possible levels, on a single scale.

The opportunity to observe the same family relationship patterns in all degrees of emotional illness provided an added dimension for the research. Schizophrenia is a relatively fixed state in which change is confined to regression, remission, and changes that evolve over time. The same mechanisms in less severe emotional illness are much more flexible and amenable to significant change in psychotherapy. The same mechanisms in borderline emotional impairment can change slowly, especially under ideal conditions. The opportunity to observe the full spectrum helps to put the human phenomenon in better perspective.

Private Practice. A few months after family group therapy was started for the research study, the method was started with the entire spectrum of emotional problems encountered in a busy private practice, providing an invaluable contrast with the more severe schizophrenic level problems encountered in the research study. The first psychoanalytic patient was changed to family psychotherapy about four months after the method was developed.

This patient was a bright young husband with a phobic reaction in a compulsive personality who was making steady progress after six months of psychoanalysis for four hours a week. The dilemma was discussed with the project consultant, who was a senior psychoanalyst. The therapist said:

This man has a good chance for one of the better psychoanalytic results in three to four years with a total of 600 to 700 hours. There is also a good chance his wife will develop enough problems in about two years to refer her to another analyst for three to four years. About six years from now, after 1,000 or more combined psychoanalytic hours, they should have their lives in reasonable order. How can I in good conscience continue this long and expensive course when I know within me that I can accomplish far more in less time with different approach? On the other hand, how can I in good conscience take a chance and suggest something new and untried when I know the chances are good with the proved psychoanalytic method?

The consultant mused about analysts who hold onto patients too long and wondered how the husband and wife could react to the questions. The issue was discussed with the patient, and one week later his wife accompanied him to her first session. The clinical method used was analysis of the intrapsychic process in one and then the analysis of the corresponding emotional reaction in the other. They continued the family therapy sessions three times a week for 18 months for a total of 203 hours. The result was far better than would ordinarily be expected with 600 hours of psychoanalysis for each. This family has been followed periodically by letter and telephone during the 12 years since the therapy was terminated, and their life course has been ideal.

Hypotheses

The various early family research studies provided a completely new order of observations never previously recognized or reported. Each investigator was observing the same phenomena, but each was using different conceptual models to describe observa-

tions. There were models from psychology, sociology, mythology, biology, physics, mathematics, and chemistry. There were descriptions of see-saws, reciprocities, complementarities, chemical bonds, magnetic fields, rubber fences, and hydraulic and electrical energy systems—all interwoven with concepts from individual theory. Psychoanalytic theory, on which most of the psychotherapies are based, describes a fairly predictable system of dynamisms, but there has never been a solid connection between psychoanalysis and the accepted sciences. Family research had a potential for an eventual new theory of emotional illness. A plan was devised to make the most of new clues.

A hypothesis is necessary for research. Without it, one is confronted with too much data to be sorted or conceptualized, and there is the ever-present problem of losing direction in pursuit of irrelevant interesting details. A specific hypothesis predicts what will be found, but it limits the researcher's ability to see other data that may be important.

Two orders of hypotheses were developed. One was the short-term hypothesis for each substudy in the total research. An effort was made to use similar conceptual models, each consistent with the others and all of them consistent with the other hypothesis—a broad, long-term hypothesis to govern the total study over the years.

The long-term hypothesis had several advantages. It provided a framework for understanding partial concepts already developed, and it provided a source of models for new short-term hypotheses. Most important, it provided predictions for new observations that might otherwise be missed. Most of the observers had been trained in psychoanalysis, and they tended to see only what they had been trained to see. It was hoped that the long-term hypothesis would open thinking to new kinds of observations.

The long-term hypothesis was based on the original concepts about the mother-child relationship, which had proved to be surprisingly accurate in the research study; on observations about the father and other family members, which made them an integral part of the total family system; on observations about the total family system; and on some new hunches and beliefs about the basic nature of emotional illness. There were consistent observations to suggest that emotional illness is a far deeper process than can be explained by emotional trauma in a single generation. The parents of a schizophrenic patient have almost as much basic impairment as the patient. They manage to function at the expense of the patient, who functions poorly. The pattern is one in which children become more impaired than their parents through several generations until the impairment is great enough to make the patient vulnerable to schizophrenia. Symptoms erupt when the emotionally and somatically impaired person is exposed to critical stress. In an opposite process, children can become better integrated than their parents through successive generations. These observations resulted in the concept of the multiple-generation transmission process.

Observations about the difference between feeling and thinking led to concepts central to the theory and to the psychotherapy. Emotionally impaired people do not distinguish between the subjective feeling process and the intellectual thinking process. Their intellectual processes are so flooded with feeling that they are incapable of thinking that is separate from feelings. They routinely say, "I feel that ..." when it would be more accurate to say, "I think" or "I believe" or "It is my opinion." They consider it truthful and honest to speak in terms of feelings and insincere and false to speak of thinking, beliefs, and opinions. They work always for togetherness and agreement in relationship to others and avoid statements that would establish one person as different from another. Better integrated people can distinguish between the feeling and thinking processes, but they usually use, "I feel that ..." when communicating with others. The best integrated people distinguish between the two processes, and they are much more accurate in their use of the terms.

Much study and work with families, from the most impaired to the best inte-grated, went into the effort to clarify feeling-thinking issues. The interplay between feeling and thinking is considered one of the best common denominators for judging levels of emotional integration. The world literature is vague in distinguishing between feelings and emotion, and there is lack of clarity with terms such as philosophies, beliefs, opinions, convictions, and impressions. The literature makes little distinction between the subjectivity of truth and the objectivity of fact. Lacking other than dictionary guidelines, some hypotheses about the terms were made for the purposes of the research.

The long-term hypothesis about the nature of emotional illness considered it to be a disorder of the emotional system, which is an intimate part of man's phylogenetic past, which he shares with lower forms of life, and which is governed by the same laws that govern all other living things. Man's ability to think, his intellectual system, is a function of his newly added cerebral cortex, which was developed last in his evolution and which is the main difference between man and the lower forms of life. The emotional and intellectual systems have different functions, but they are interconnected, each influencing the other. The important connection for this hypothesis is the feeling system, through which certain influences from the upper strata of the emotional system are perceived by the cerebral cortex as feelings.

The literature refers to emotions as much more than states of contentment, agitation, fear, weeping, and laughing. It refers also to states in animals—including contentment after feeding, sleep, and mating and agitation states in fight, flight, and the search for food. One might consider an emotional system present in all forms with an autonomic nervous system, but why exclude states of contentment and agitation in one-cell forms, in which stimuli could be more biochemical in nature? When one considers emotion on this level, it becomes synonymous with instinct which governs the life process of all living things. Emotional illness is viewed as a deep phenomenon that is much more than a disorder of the mind. The term mental illness, connoting a disorder of thinking, has been discontinued in favor of the term emotional illness.

Man's brain is part of his protoplasmic totality, but, through the functioning of his brain, he has been able to do wondrous things. His intellect does best when devoted to subjects outside himself. He has created the sciences, through which he has learned many of the secrets of the universe; he has created technology for modification of his environment; and he has gained control over all lower forms of life. He has even controlled evolution in lower forms within controlled environments. Man has done less well when his intellect is directed at himself. Though related intimately to all living things, he has done far better at defining the ways he is different from lower forms than in defining his kinship with them.

This hypothesis says that the emotional system runs a course as predictable as any natural phenomenon, that emotional illness surfaces in a variety of different ways when the emotional system goes into states of dysfunction, and that the main problem in learning the secrets of emotional illness lies more in the way man denies and rationalizes and thinks about emotional illness than in the nature of emotional illness. Man can do far better than he has done thus far in defining the predictable natural course of emotional illness. Once he knows the secrets, he is in a better position to modify the process.

Family Systems Theory

The Triangle. The theory considers the triangle—a three-person system—as the molecule of any emotional system, whether it exists in a family or in a social system. The term triangle is used instead of the more familiar term triad, which has come to have fixed connotations that do not apply to this concept. The triangle is the smallest stable relationship system. A two-person system is an unstable system that immediately forms a series of interlocking triangles. The triangle has definite relationship patterns that predictably repeat in periods of stress and calm.

In periods of calm, the triangle is made up of a comfortably close twosome and a less comfortable outsider. The twosome works to preserve the togetherness, lest one become uncomfortable and form a better togetherness elsewhere. The outsider seeks to form a togetherness with one of the others, and there are numerous well-known moves to accomplish this. The emotional forces within the triangle are constantly in motion from moment to moment, even in periods of calm. Moderate tension states in the twosome are characteristically felt by one while the other is oblivious. It is the uncomfortable one who initiates a new equilibrium toward more comfortable togetherness for self.

In periods of stress, the outside position is the most comfortable and most desired position. In stress, each works to get the outside position to escape tension in the twosome. When it is not possible to shift forces in the triangle, one of the involved twosome triangles in a fourth person, leaving the former third person aside for re-involvement later. The emotional forces duplicate the exact patterns in the new triangle. Over time, the emotional forces continue to move from one active triangle to another, finally remaining mostly in one triangle as long as the total system is fairly calm.

When tensions are very high in families and available family triangles are exhausted, the family system triangles in people from outside the family, such as police and social agencies. A successful externalization of the tension occurs when outside workers are in conflict about the family while the family is calmer. In emotional systems such as an office staff, the tensions between the two highest administrators can be triangled and retriangled until conflict is acted out between two who are low in the administrative hierarchy. Administrators often settle this conflict by firing or removing one of the conflictual twosome, after which the conflict erupts in another twosome.

A triangle in moderate tension characteristically has two comfortable sides and one side in conflict. As patterns repeat and repeat in a triangle, the people come to have fixed roles in relation to each other. The best example of this is the father-mother-child triangle. Patterns vary, but one of the most common is basic tension between the parents, with the father gaining the outside position—often being called passive, weak, and distant—leaving the conflict between mother and child. The mother—often called aggressive, dominating, and castrating—wins over the child, who moves another step toward chronic functional impairment. This pattern is described as the family projection process. Families replay the same triangular game over and over for years, as though the winner were in doubt, but the final result is always the same. Over the years the child accepts the always-lose outcome more easily, even to volunteering for this position. A variation is the pattern in which the father finally attacks the mother, leaving the child in the outside position. This child then learns the techniques of gaining the outside position by playing the parents off against each other.

Each of the structured patterns in triangles is available for predictable moves and predictable outcomes in families and social systems. A knowledge of triangles provides a far more exact way of understanding the father-mother-child triangle than do the traditional oedipal complex explanations. And triangles provide several times more flexibility in dealing with such problems therapeutically.

Differentiation of Self Scale. This scale is a way of evaluating all people on a single continuum, from the lowest to the highest possible level of human functioning. The scale ranges from 0 to 100. It is comparable to a scale of emotional maturity except that this theory does not use the concept of maturity or immaturity.

At the lowest point on the scale is the lowest possible level of self or the greatest degree of no-self or undifferentiation. At the highest point on the scale is a postulated level of complete differentiation of perfect self, which man has not yet achieved. The level of differentiation is the degree to which one self fuses or merges into another self in a close emotional relationship. The scale eliminates the concept of normal, which has been elusive for psychiatry.

The scale has nothing to do with emotional illness or psychopathology. There are low-scale people who manage to keep their lives in emotional equilibrium without develop-

ing emotional illness, and there are higher-scale people who can develop severe symptoms under great stress. However, lower-scale people are vulnerable to stress and are much more prone to illness, including physical and social illness, and their dysfunction is more likely to become chronic when it does occur. Higher-scale people can recover emotional equilibrium quickly after the stress passes.

Two levels of self have been postulated. One is solid self, made up of firmly held convictions and beliefs. It is formed slowly and can be changed from within self, but it is never changed by coercion or persuasion by others. The other level of self is the pseudoself, made up of knowledge incorporated by the intellect and of principles and beliefs acquired from others. The pseudoself is acquired from others, and it is negotiable in relationship with others. It can be changed by emotional pressure to enhance one's image with others or to oppose the other.

In the average person, the level of solid self is relatively low in comparison with the level of pseudoself. A pseudoself can function well in most relationships; but in an intense emotional relationship, such as marriage, the pseudoself of one merges with the pseudoself of the other. One becomes the functional self and the other a functional no-self. The emotional interplay in fusion states, the undifferentiated family ego mass, is the subject of much of the dynamics in a family emotional system.

Low-scale people live in a feeling world in which they cannot distinguish feeling from fact. So much life energy goes into seeking love or approval or in attacking the other for not providing it that there is no energy for developing a self or for goal-directed activity. The lives of low-scale people are totally relationship-oriented. Major life decisions are based on what feels right. A low-scale person with a life in reasonable asymptomatic adjustment is one who is able to keep the feeling system in equilibrium by giving and receiving love and by the sharing of self with others. Low-scale people do so much borrowing and trading of self and show such wide fluctuations in their functioning levels of self that it is difficult to estimate their basic levels of self except over long periods of time.

As a group, low-scale people have a high incidence of human problems. Relationships are tenuous, and a new problem can arise in an unsuspected area even while they are trying to deal with the previous problem. When the relationship equilibrium fails, the family goes into functional collapse, with illness or other problems. They can be too numb to feel, and there is no longer any energy to seek love and approval. So much energy is devoted to the discomfort of the moment that they live from day to day. At the very lowest point on the scale are those too impaired to live outside an institution.

People in the 25-to-50 segment of the scale also live in a feeling-dominated world, but the fusion of selfs is less intense, and there is increasing capacity to differentiate a self. Major life decisions are based on what feels right rather than on principle, much life energy goes into seeking love and approval, and there is little energy for goal-directed activity.

Those in the 35-to-40 range present some of the best examples of a feeling-oriented life. They are removed from the impairment and life paralysis that characterize the lower-scale people, and the feeling orientation is more clearly seen. They are sensitized to emotional dysharmony, to the opinions of others, and to creating a good impression. They are apt students of facial expressions, gestures, tones of voice, and actions that may mean approval or disapproval. Success in school or at work is determined more by approval from important others than by the basic value of the work. Their spirits can soar with expressions of love and approval or be dashed by the lack of it. These are people with low levels of solid self but reasonable levels of pseudoself, which is obtained from and is negotiable in the relationship system.

People in the upper part of the 25-to-50 segment of the scale have some awareness of intellectual principles, but the system is still so fused with feeling that the budding self is expressed in dogmatic authoritativeness, in the compliance of a disciple, or in the opposition of a rebel. Some of those in this group use intellect in the service of the relationship system. As children, their academic prowess won them approval. They lack their own convictions and beliefs, but they are quick to know the thoughts and feelings of others, and their knowledge provides them with a facile pseudoself. If the relationship system approves, they can be brilliant students and disciples. If their expectations are not met, they assemble a pseudoself in point-by-point opposition to the established order.

People in the 50-to-60 segment of the scale are aware of the difference between feelings and intellectual principle, but they are still so responsive to the relationship system that they hestitate to say what they believe, lest they offend the listener.

People still higher on the scale are operationally clear about the differences between feelings and intellect, and they are free to state beliefs calmly, without attacking the beliefs of others for the enhancement of self and without having to defend themselves against the attacks of others. They are sufficiently free of the control of the feeling system to have a choice between intimate emotional closeness and goal-directed activity, and they can derive satisfaction and pleasure from either. They have a realistic appraisal of self to others, in contrast to lower-scale people, who feel self to be the center of the universe and who either overvalue or devalue self.

The differentiation of self scale is important as a theoretical concept for viewing the total human phenomenon in perspective. It is valuable in estimating the over-all potential of people and in making predictions about the general pattern of their lives. But it is not useful in making month-to-month or even year-to-year evaluations of scale levels. There is so much trading and borrowing and negotiating for pseudoself in the relationship system, especially in the lower half of the scale, and such wide functional shifts in the level of self that it is difficult to estimate scale levels on short-term information.

Most people spend their lives at the same basic level they had when they left their parental families. They consolidate this level in a marriage, after which there are few life experiences that change this basic level. Many life experiences automatically raise or lower the functioning levels of self, but this shift can be as easily lost as gained. There are calculated ways to raise the basic level of self, but doing so is a monumental life task, and it is easy for one to say that the possible gain is not worth the effort. The method of psychotherapy described here is directed at helping families differentiate a few points higher on the scale.

Nuclear Family Emotional System. The term undifferentiated family ego mass was originally used to refer to the emotional system in the nuclear family—father, mother, children. The emotional process has the same basic pattern in extended families and social relationship systems. The original term is still as accurate as ever when applied to the nuclear family, but it is less apt when applied to the extended families, and it is awkward when applied to social systems. Now the terms nuclear family emotional system, extended family emotional system, and social system are used to describe the same emotional process in different areas.

A rough estimate of the spouses' level of differentiation of self conveys an idea about the quantity of undifferentiation potentially present for future trouble in the nuclear family. The greater the undifferentiation, the greater the potential problems. People pick spouses who have equivalent levels of differentiation of self. The life styles of people at one point on the scale are so different from others a few points removed that they consider themselves to be incompatible.

Many spouses experience the closest and most open relationship in their adult lives during courtship. In the commitment of each to the other in the marriage, the two pseudoselfs fuse into a new emotional oneness. The mechanisms they use in dealing with the emotional fusion, which becomes a kind of life style for them, help to determine the kinds of problems they will encounter in the future. Most spouses use some degree of emotional distance from each other to control the symptoms of fusion. The patterns of relationships back to their families

of origin help determine the intensity of nuclear family problems. The more open the relationships to families of origin, the less the tension in the nuclear family.

The undifferentiation in the marriage focuses on three areas. It is as if there is a quantitative amount of undifferentiation to be absorbed, and it may be focused largely in one area or mostly in one area and less in others or distributed evenly in all three areas. If the amount is great enough, it can fill all areas and spill outside to the extended family and social systems. The areas are marital conflict, dysfunction in one spouse, and impairment of one or more children. Families with symptoms in all three areas do best in family psychotherapy. Families with symptoms largely in one area are resistent to change other than symptomatic relief.

Marital Conflict. The basic pattern in conflictual marriages is one in which neither gives in to the other on major issues. These marriages are intense in terms of the amount of emotional energy each invests in the other. The energy may be thinking or action energy, either positive or negative, but the self of each is focused intensely on the self of the other. The relationship cycles through intense closeness, conflict that provides a period of emotional distance, the make-up, and another period of intense closeness. Marital conflict does not in itself harm children unless the parents feel guilt and fear that it will hurt the children. The amount of psychic energy that each invests in the other protects children from emotional overinvolvement. The amount of undifferentiation absorbed by marital conflict reduces the amount to be absorbed elsewhere.

Dysfunction in One Spouse. This is the pattern in which one spouse becomes the adaptive or the submissive one, and the other spouse becomes the dominant one. The pseudoself of the adaptive one merges into the pseudoself of the other, and the dominant one becomes responsible for the twosome. In such a marriage each spouse sees self as adapting to the other, but it is the one who adapts the most who becomes a no-self, dependent on the other to think and act and be for the twosome. The one who remains in the adaptive position is vulnerable to dysfunction, which can be physical illness, emotional illness, or social dysfunction—such as drinking, acting-out behavior, loss of motivation, irresponsible behavior. These illnesses tend to become chronic, and they are hard to reverse. The marriage between one overadequate spouse and a chronically ill spouse is enduring. Chronic illness—such as arthritis, stomach ulcers, or depression—can absorb great quantities of the undifferentiation in a nuclear family and can protect other areas from symptoms.

Impairment of One or More Children. This is the pattern in which parents operate as a "we-ness" to project their undifferentiation to one or more children. This mechanism is so important that in this family theory it has been included as a separate concept, family projection process.

Family Projection Process. This is the basic process by which parental problems are projected to children. It is present in the full range of problems from the mildest to the most severe, such as hard-core schizophrenia and autism. The basic pattern involves a mother whose emotional system is more focused on children than on her husband and a father who is sensitive to his wife's anxiety and who supports her emotional involvement with the children.

The mother has varying degrees of emotional fusion with each child. Most mothers work hard to treat all their children the same, but the average mother has one child with whom the fusion is far more intense. The intensely fused child may be one who has a positive attachment to the mother, one who was considered strange or different from infancy, or one whom the mother repulsed from birth—and vice versa.

Anxiety in the mother is quickly felt in that extension of herself, the most fused child. The mother's sympathetic, over-solicitous, overprotective energy goes into allaying the anxiety in the child instead of in herself, which establishes a self-perpetuating cycle, with the mother infantilizing and the child gradually becoming more impaired. A moderately severe example is one in which the relationship is a positive overattachment in infancy, gradually increasing evidence of behavior problems or internalized problems

as the child approaches adolescence, and a rapid development of severe problems in adolescence, when the relationship with the mother becomes negative. During this period the father either agrees and tries to support the mother or withdraws when he does not agree. The same basic pattern applies to the child who later develops schizophrenia or other severe impairments except that the process is much more intense and additional mechanisms are used to deal with complications of the basic process.

The family projection process is selective in that it typically focuses on one child first. The mother's involvement with this child may so fulfill the deficit in her own self that the other children are relatively uninvolved. The amount of undifferentiation can be so great that it involves more than one child. Among the factors that influence the selection of the child to be fused are sibling position, the mother's preference for boys or girls, and the mother's level of anxiety at the time the child was conceived and born. Among the most vulnerable for the projection process are oldest children, the oldest boy or oldest girl, an only boy or only girl, a child born when anxiety is high, and a child born with a defect.

The family projection process is universal in that it exists in all families to some degree. It alleviates the anxiety of undifferentiation in the present generation at the expense of the next generation. The same process by which the group functions better at the expense of one is present in all emotional systems.

Multigenerational Transmission Process. This concept defines the principle of projection of varying degrees of immaturity (undifferentiation) to different children when the process is repeated over a number of generations. If the process begins with parents with low-level differentiation and the family is one that focuses maximal maturity on one child in several generations, it will eventually produce a child so impaired, both physically and emotionally, that he will collapse into dysfunction, such as schizophrenia, at any effort to survive outside the family.

In any one generation the family projection process involves each child with a different level of intensity. The maximally involved child emerges with a lower level of self than the parents. Minimally involved children may emerge with about the same level as the parents. Children relatively out of the process may emerge with higher levels of self. When each child marries at about the level from which he emerges from the nuclear family, some descendants in the family do better with life than their parents did, and others do less well. The multigenerational process provides a base from which to make predictions in the present generation and gives an overview of what to expect in coming generations.

Personality Profiles of Sibling Positions. Toman's personality profiles of sibling positions are remarkably consistent with the author's own observations except that he does not consider children who are the object of the family projection process. Toman's basic thesis is that important personality characteristics are determined by the family configuration in which the child grows up. With his ten detailed personality profiles of sibling positions, one can determine the profile of all sibling positions. The profiles are so accurate that they can be used to reconstruct the family emotional process of past generations, to understand the emotional process in the present nuclear and extended family, and to make postulations about the future.

Toman studied only normal families, and he made no effort to study the ways a profile can be altered by the family projection process. For instance, if an oldest child is the object of a moderately severe family projection process, he is likely to become helpless and complaining and to marry an equally impaired spouse who overfunctions as the protective mothering one. In this family, the second child in the sibling order is likely to have the characteristics of an oldest child.

Theoretical Trends

The one major theoretical effort since the beginning of the family movement has been to find a way to integrate family concepts with psychoanalytic theory. There have been no major gains in this area, but the effort has resulted in much more detailed definition of the relationship system between family members.

The one most consistent change in family concepts in the past ten years has been toward systems thinking. The relationships between family members constitute a system in the sense that a reaction in one family member is followed by a predictable reaction in another, and that reaction is followed by a predictable reaction in another and then another in a chain-reaction pattern. Jackson and his co-workers were among those who moved far toward systems thinking before his death in 1968. They were originally impressed by distortions in verbal messages and by the breakdown in communication in disturbed families. Their focus was on communication theory and restoration of communication in conjoint family therapy. In their first paper they presented the concept of the double-bind, which has since become one of the most-used terms in the family field. As with any initial concept, it was not sufficiently broad to conceptualize the total phenomenon, and theorists had to add new concepts to enlarge the system. The communication concept was extended to include nonverbal communication, in which the other comes to act and be through modalities and influences. Still later, the theoretical thinking moved into systems thinking with the *quid quo pro*, which conceptualized a chain-reaction phenomenon. In the past several years, a number of family therapists have made an increasing effort to use general systems theory to conceptualize family relationships.

Concepts from outside the family field have also been adopted for understanding family relationships. Games theory provides one of the most flexible ways for describing the constantly moving, predictable, repeating patterns of family relationships. New games can be defined as needed for accurately describing the complexity of the patterns. Some family therapists have tried to help the family recognize the game, as a step toward modifying the pattern. The kinesics research of Birdwhistell and Scheflen has provided new knowledge about un-conscious body action language, which also functions in a systematic chain-reaction pattern between family members. This communication system operates without words—a characteristic of much that is communicated in a family. Some therapists use kinesics concepts in family therapy; the goal is to help make families aware of the kinesics language in the hope that they will modify the pattern. Neither games theory nor knowledge of kinesics lends itself to theoretical concepts, but the use of these concepts is evidence of a search for different kinds of concepts.

Most of the early family investigators were first impressed by the emotional stuck-togetherness of nuclear family members. Later they began to see varying degrees of the same phenomenon in other areas of the family. Ackerman, who had been thinking family before his published papers began in the mid-1950's, was one of the first, with his concept of interlocking psychopathologies, and he has continued to refine and extend his concepts. In the early 1960's, Bos-zormenyi-Nagy developed the concepts of pathological-need complementarity. He and his co-workers are among those who have worked at defining both a relationship system and a personality structure. Their therapeutic system includes family therapy —with co-therapists—for the relationship system and individual psychotherapy for certain family members.

Numerous partial concepts exist more as rationales for family therapy than as theoretical concepts. Sources such as the Group for the Advancement of Psychiatry survey indicate that a majority of family therapists use individual theory for conceptualizing the psychopathology and group therapy methods for working out the problem in group process. The therapy is directed at such issues as lack of communication, perceptual distortions, increasing awareness of feelings in self and others, and the open communication of feelings in family therapy meetings. The therapist serves as a catalyst, directing attention to issues he considers important and facilitating group process.

With the increasing use of family group therapy, therapists tend to use group theory as families go through variations of the same stages characteristic of groups of nonrelated people. And as experience with families has increased, thinking about the nature of emotional problems has gradually shifted. Therapists tend to think less about psychopathology and more about relationships, and they tend to be more aware of a spectrum of patterns not observable in groups of nonrelated people. For instance, a therapist may become aware of passivity as a reciprocal function of activity or aggressiveness in another family member. When he begins to think about passivity-activity as a single pattern, his therapy changes, and the family is less pathology-oriented.

CLINICAL ASPECTS

Background Issues

The process of seeing a number of family members together, with any method or any technique, poses a spectrum of questions and issues not encountered in other forms of psychotherapy. These issues evolve from the premise that the emotional problem involves the entire family, not just the sick patient. One group of issues revolves around the traditional posture of medicine toward disease, which is to examine, diagnose, and treat the sick patient. This medical model is deeply ingrained in society in the form of customs, laws, and social institutions that require medical examination and health reports. Implicit in the doctor-patient relationship is the image of the physician as the healer and of the good patient as one who places himself under the care of the physician and follows instructions. Only when the family therapist attempts to focus on the family does he become aware of the ramifications of the medical orientation he had hardly noticed before.

Another group of issues involves the family projection process, through which the family creates the patient. This powerful emotional force, driven by anxiety, can be very intense when anxiety is high or can be toned down and reasonable when anxiety is low. When anxiety is high, family members can be dogmatic in insisting that it is the patient who is sick and in resisting efforts to involve them in the therapy. When anxiety is low, the family rapidly becomes amenable to a family approach. It is usual for one part of the family or one parent to accept the idea of family therapy and for the other to oppose it. The opposing one may compliantly attend sessions without really participating. Another variation is one in which the family neither accepts nor rejects the family approach. They retain the idea that it is the patient who is sick, and they attend the sessions as co-therapists to help the therapist treat the patient. The goal in therapy with these tenuous situations is to focus on the process that creates the polarized issues rather than to be drawn into debate about the merits of any position.

A third group of issues that govern the situation is the orientation of the therapist. He participated in a family projection process in his own family of origin, and he participates in varying degrees in the family projection process that operates constantly in the setting in which he lives and works. If the therapist is dogmatic, either in diagnosing the patient or in fighting against the forces that would diagnose, he is probably emotionally polarized in his own personal life, and his intellectual beliefs are probably determined more by emotions than by objectivity.

The complex emotional forces in the administrative environment, in the family, and in the therapist's own personal situation all govern the establishment of a setting in which family therapy takes place. In any emotional system, the usual automatic response to an emotional issue is an emotional counterresponse which leads to escalation of the emotional process and to an increase in symptoms in some member of the system. The goal in dealing with an anxious situation is to get the emotional forces as much into neutral as possible. The therapist is the key to the emotional tension when a family first contacts him. He must have a working plan for dealing with operating principles and anxiety in his administrative and professional environment before he can start clinical work in family psycho-

therapy. Once this plan is established, the therapist can begin to deal with anxiety in the family. If he really believes in a family orientation and if he is not emotionally polarized in debates that argue the virtues of one therapy principle against another, the family is amazingly receptive to and even enthusiastic about the notion of family psychotherapy.

The therapist can start family therapy even when the family is in the process of hospitalizing one member; he can so neutralize family anxiety that hospitalization is avoided and the patient is permitted to remain at home with the family. This is the principle in crisis intervention therapy, which is coming into wide use in community mental health centers. The family problem is resolved much more rapidly and the final result is far better if hospitalization is avoided. The act of hospitalization helps to confirm both to the family and to the patient that he is sick. A fluid family projection process can be made more fixed and irreversible by this action. The organization and function of a psychiatric hospital confirm the belief that the patient is the sick one. Verbal statements that deny the family projection process have limited effect when the environment repeatedly takes action to confirm it. There are situations in which hospitalization cannot be avoided. In these cases, the family projection process becomes increasingly difficult to neutralize. Softening the impact of hospitalization on a family requires a knowledge of the family projection process and considerable skill in clinical management.

Once the therapist has established a workable initial family orientation with a family, repeating crises during therapy stir family anxiety and reactivate an intense wave of the family projection process, which focuses on sickness in the patient and absolves the family of responsibility and participation in the therapy. The family stops the effort to work at change within the family and begins to blame the therapist for lack of progress. If the therapy is in a psychiatric center, the family is aware of the difference between family theory and conventional psychiatry. In periods of anxiety, family members complain to the therapist's supervisor or the center administrator, who may agree emotionally with the complaint and take administrative action that defeats the family therapy. If the family members are also involved with school or juvenile court authorities, they may complain there and invoke another kind of outside pressure that agrees with the complaint and impedes or disrupts the family psychotherapy. Even when the therapist is successful in keeping his balance on the tightrope of emotional neutrality in most of these outside emotional forces, other reality issues interfere with maintaining the family premise. The writing of a prescription for a single family member or the diagnosis of a single family member on an insurance form or other medical report acts to confirm sickness in the patient.

Each therapist has to find his own ways to establish and maintain a family orientation. The more successful he is, the more likely the family is to continue the therapy to a favorable result.

The question of diagnosing the patient is an important issue. At one end of the scale are therapists who vigorously oppose the family pressure for an explanation and diagnosis of the patient's illness. There are problems with this approach when the symptomatic one is in a state of collapse that could be accurately diagnosed by the average lay person. At the other end of the scale are therapists who do psychological tests on all family members in order to diagnosis each of them. This approach successfully neutralizes the pressure within the family, but resourceful family members may take the helpless posture of a patient in their effort to change the family. In the middle of the scale are the therapists who attempt to focus on issues that feed into the family projection process. This approach avoids polarized positions and attempts to work out the issues in family therapy.

Therapists also use a variety of ways in dealing with drug prescriptions. Most therapists minimize or avoid the use of drugs. But with nonmedical therapists, families easily assume he would prescribe drugs if he were a physician.

The author attempts to stay as close to the midline as possible in each of these areas. He communicates to families that medical institutions, courts, insurance companies, and social institutions have to operate on policies defined by accepted professional practice. In all matters that have to do with medical reports, he interprets the situation as closely as possible to conventional practice and makes diagnoses and opinions conform to accepted practice. But in dealing with the family, he maintains the family orientation as strictly as possible. Young family therapists usually do not appreciate the structure within which social institutions must operate. Enthusiastic about their results with family therapy, they attempt to explain their family orientation, certain that they will persuade an insurance company, for instance, to make a policy change recognizing their work. Eventually, they become aware that insurance companies change rules in response to the practice of all psychiatrists and not in response to family therapists alone.

Clinical results are several times more effective with a family orientation than with conventional psychotherapy. To facilitate a family orientation, terms that connote a patient-sickness-treatment orientation have been replaced by terms more consistent with a family orientation. In the beginning the new terms seem odd and strange, but, after they are used for a time, the conventional terminology seems odd and out of place. Conventional terminology is retained for communicating with the medical community. In professional writing an effort is made to avoid use of the new words, but conventional terms are used sparingly. Conventional terms are used when it would be awkward to use "symptomatic one" or "impaired one" or the "one in dysfunction" rather than "patient." An effort has been made to discard the term therapy. The therapist can establish himself as a coach in working with families, but the term family *psychotherapy* is retained as the best working compromise between the method and the usual practice in the field. The term designated patient has come into common usage in family clinics to mean the one initially designated as the patient by the family.

Family Group Therapy

This method of family therapy or some extension of it is used by an overwhelming majority of family therapists, and it has led to more technical variations than have other methods. The theory and practice of family group therapy vary from therapist to therapist, but some common denominators apply to the entire field. The basic theoretical formulations are derived largely from conventional individual theory, and the practice is based largely on established principles and techniques from group therapy. The widespread use of the method helps to determine the definition of family therapy more by who attends the sessions than by the method employed. The method is usually called individual psychotherapy when one family member is present, couples therapy or marital therapy when both spouses or both parents attend the sessions, and family therapy only when at least two generations—parents and child—attend the sessions. In the author's method, however, the term is defined by the theory, and the therapy is designed to facilitate change in the family, whether the change is brought about through one or more family members.

Family group therapy is the method of choice for the beginning family therapist. He can use his existing knowledge of individual dynamics and group process to get started. It is difficult to learn about family emotional patterns except in the clinical situation. Once the therapist has started, he has an opportunity to observe the entire family as they relate to each other and to appreciate the fact that family members are not the same in relation to each other as they are in any other setting or as they appear to be from second-hand reports about them. Most psychotherapists with reasonable experience in psychotherapy and group process can do an acceptable professional level of family group therapy without previous experience in family emotional systems.

The greatest advantage of family group therapy is the fact that it can be used as a short-term process. It reaches its highest efficiency when therapist and family have a specific goal in mind, such as improving family communication or understanding the plight of a single family member. A few family group meetings can bring amazing relief in a symptomatic child, in a parent who is feeling frustrated and overburdened, or in a family reacting to a death or some other misfortune.

Family group therapy is effective with all levels of family problems, but it requires much more skill and activity when the family is potentially explosive. Uncontrolled feeling can result in emotional outbursts, disruption of the therapy, and symptomatic repercussions in other family members. Family group therapy can be effective as a long-term method for a certain range of moderately severe problems in which the feeling system is not rigidly controlled or so lacking in control that emotional issues can result in serious acting out.

Family group therapy lends itself well to the use of co-therapists; the second therapist can help if the first therapist becomes emotionally overinvolved. Some of the most experienced family therapists routinely work with co-therapists in a co-ordinated team approach. And some experienced family therapists routinely operate as male-female teams with the theoretical premise that the co-therapy team serves as a father-mother model.

The average family group therapy includes parents and all children who can thoughtfully participate, plus other family members who are available for the sessions. Most therapists want at least one meeting with all family members so that they get to know the total family system. But very young children react to family anxiety, and repeated sessions with them present are not profitable. Most therapists try to include available grandparents for a few sessions.

The therapist serves as chairman of the sessions and as a catalyst to facilitate communication in the family or whatever is his goal. The therapist should have a goal, lest the sessions start nondirected wandering. Some amazing things can happen when the therapist's goal is to re-establish family communication. Therapist and family are fascinated by the astute observations children make about the families, the child is grateful for the opportunity to formulate and express his ideas and for the forum where his thoughts are valued, and the children benefit from hearing the parents' calm expression of viewpoints. The family is so pleased by such a session that they eagerly look forward to more meetings. This processs can reach a point of calm exhilaration, with the parents increasingly aware of the children and the children pleasantly surprised at seeing the human side of parental foibles. The symptoms in family members subside, and the family exhibits more togetherness and understanding.

When this process goes beyond a short-term goal, the parents begin to depend on the more adequate children to assume responsibility for the family problem. The children begin to find repetitive issues boring, and they find reasons to avoid the sessions. If forced to attend, the formerly talkative children became reluctant to speak. The therapist can shield the resourceful child from parental helplessness in the sessions but not at home. The maximal benefit from family group therapy sessions is usually achieved in 12 to 20 sessions, after which the family group diminishes to parents and the most involved child.

Family group therapy for both parents and one symptomatic child presents some formidable therapeutic blocks when used as a long-term method and involves the most intense triangle in the nuclear family. The parents continue to project their problem to the child even in the therapy hours.

The average problem is a moderate-level neurotic or behavior problem in a postadolescent child. The parents' thoughts and feelings are so invested in the child that it is difficult for them to focus on themselves. When the therapist finally focuses on an issue between the parents, the most anxious parent criticizes the child, or the child does something to draw parental attention, and the focus goes back to the child. The average good result comes after about a year—35 to 45 sessions. By that time, the passive father is a little less passive, the nagging mother is calmer, and the child's symptoms are reduced to an acceptable level for the family or for school. The family is usually pleased with the result on termination of therapy, but the therapist may see no basic change in the family pattern.

As a therapy variation, the therapist may schedule separate sessions for the parents together and for the child alone if the child is motivated. The results with this approach have been found to be less satisfactory. The parents tend to go through the motions of therapy without engaging the problem, expecting the therapy with the child to change the problem.

Another technique has been used for more than ten years with only minor changes: The parents begin therapy with the premise that this is a family problem, that the total family can change if the parents change, and that the family therapy will be directed to the parents without involving the child. This approach puts the responsibility for change on the parents, relieves the child of responsibility for change, and permits the child to have an occasional session alone if he is interested. Some of the most striking changes in family psychotherapy have been in families in which the child was never involved in the family therapy. Schools and courts that had recommended psychotherapy for the child were briefly critical when they discovered that the child did not attend the sessions, but this criticism disappeared when the child's symptoms subsided, which usually occurred much sooner than with other approaches.

One of the early techniques of family group therapy encouraged the expression of feeling between family members and offered psychoanalytic interpretations to explain intrapsychic functioning in individual family members. But many families overreacted to feeling expression and suddenly terminated therapy after a few sessions. The interpretations were eagerly awaited by families as authoritative statements of fact, and families were less motivated to seek their own answers.

The plan that finally worked best came after the observation that research families changed more than therapy families. The therapist put himself in the role of a research investigator, asking the families hundreds of questions about the family system and avoiding interpretations. Those were the years when the family theory was being formulated, and there were endless questions. With this technique, the families made faster progress, stayed in therapy longer, and achieved better final results than did previous families studied. Also, they expressed feelings more spontaneously than those who had been encouraged to express feeling.

On a theoretical descriptive level, family group therapy restores emotional harmony in the undifferentiated family ego mass. Open communication and the sharing of feelings seem to spread the family problem more evenly among all family members. Family group therapy works best when the family problem is already fairly evenly distributed between marital conflict, dysfunction in a spouse, and projection to several children. It is far less effective when a major part of the problem is projected to only one area, such as serious impairment of one child. Family group therapy provides an effective short-term method of symptom relief, but it does not provide the structure for a higher level of differentiation of self.

Multiple-Family Group Therapy. In this extension of family group therapy, members of a number of families meet together. The method has come into increased use, especially for hospitalized patients and their families and by community mental health centers. There are many variations in technique, but in the basic method any family can present its problem, and any member of any family can respond to it. Theoretically, the method permits emotional fusion between the families, which prohibits the differentiation of self, but this is essentially impossible with any method. If groups using this method continue indefinitely, permitting families to attend or not attend for long periods, they should do much to provide a wider relationship system, reasonable alleviation of symptoms, and a more comfortable life adjustment. This is a promising method for mass use with severely impaired people.

Network Therapy. This method, devised by Speck in the mid-1960's, is one of the most exciting new extensions of family group therapy in recent years. Many people—relatives and friends of the designated patient—meet in the community to discuss all levels of personal problems. Both

family relationships and friendships are utilized, and the method appears to include many essential elements of small-town relationship systems, in which people share problems and help each other in crisis.

Theoretically, this method probably has the highest potential of the new method in helping the community to help itself and in providing help for the masses. Practically, the method takes much energy to keep the networks motivated, it requires a full evening of the therapist's time, network members tend to go back to their urban isolation, and most therapists tend to permit the networks to dwindle to termination. Still, this method is worthy of careful research and experimentation.

Family Psychotherapy

The author's theory postulates the tri angle as the molecule of any emotional system and the total emotional system as a network of interlocking triangles. The psychotherapy is directed at changing a central triangle, through which all other triangles change automatically. A central concept is the undifferentiated family ego mass. The specific therapy technique is to create a situation through which the central triangle can attain a higher level of differentiation of self. The differentiating force is opposed by emotional forces for togetherness that successfully block any move toward differentiation in any family member.

Responses to Differentiation. When any family member makes a move toward differentiating a self, the family emotional system communicates a three-stage verbal and nonverbal message: (1) You are wrong. (2) Change back. (3) If you do not, these are the consequences. Generally, the messages contain a mixture of subtle sulks, hurt feelings, and angry exchanges, but some communicate all three stages in words. The differentiating one responds in two ways. The first kind of response is within self and can include almost any emotional or psychological symptom or even symptoms of physical illness. The second kind of response is to the family. A high percentage of differentiating ones merge back into the family togetherness within hours. The merger may be to allay one's own distress, or it may come in response to a family accusation of indifference or of not loving. Or the differentiating one may fight back, which is still part of the family reaction-response system. The family emotional system has an automatic response for any emotional stimulus. The differentiating one may react with silence and withdrawal, another emotional reaction to which the family has the balancing response. A family member may run away, never to return—another emotional reaction. Predictably, the member then fuses into another receptive family and duplicates old patterns in the new emotional field. This emotional complex is much deeper than superficial angry retaliation. If one can conceive of the emotional triangle in constant balancing motion, interlocked with a complex of other triangles in the family and with still others in the extended family and social network, with the balances operating within each person and between each one and all the others, it is easier to conceptualize the total system in which each is dependent on the others and the variety of gyroscopic balancing always operates to maintain emotional equilibrium.

This therapeutic system defines an Achilles heel of the emotional system and provides one predictable answer to breaking through the emotional barrier toward differentiation. There is one major secret: An emotional system responds to emotional stimuli. If any member can control his emotional response, it interrupts the chain reaction. The most important factors in successful differentiation are a knowledge of triangles and the ability to observe and predict the chain-reaction events in the family. This knowledge and ability provide some help in controlling one's own responses in the system. The next important factor is an ability to maintain reasonable emotional control in one's responses to the family and within self during the hours or days of the family's attack and rejection—while remaining in constant emotional contact with the family. This last point is important. Silence or withdrawal from the emotional field is a signal of emotional reaction to the others.

In broad terms, a differentiating step requires long and careful deliberation to define a life principle secure enough to become a firm belief that can be stated as such without anger or debate or attack—all of which are emotional stimuli. The life energy that goes into defining a principle for self goes in a self-determined direction, which detracts from the former energy devoted to the system, especially to the important other. When this self-determined position is presented, the system reacts emotionally to win back the differentiating one into the togetherness. The family uses any mechanism to achieve this. There are calm arguments to favor the rightness of togetherness, fervent pleading, accusations, solicitousness, and threats of the consequences in terms of hurt to the family and the family's rejection if this course is continued. A high percentage of differentiating ones, fairly sure of beliefs and principles, can go into a session with the family, be won over by the logical argument of the family, and forget the principles that were carefully thought out before the session. Most people require several attempts to get through the first step.

The therapist can help the differentiating one when family pressure is great. He must do this without being perceived as against the family. At moments when the differentiating one develops such symptoms as stomach distress, the therapist may help with a comment such as:

You may have convinced your head to stand for what you believe, but you have not yet convinced your stomach.

When the differentiating one can finally control self throughout the step without fighting back or withdrawing, the family usually reaches a final showdown session with maximal attack and feelings. If the differentiating one can maintain a calm stand through this, the family anxiety suddenly subsides into a new and different level of closeness, with open appreciation and a higher regard for the differentiating one as a person. This step is usually followed by a calm period, until the other spouse or another family member starts on a similar step of defining self, which repeats the same pattern as the first. The process goes back and forth between the spouses in successive small steps. If one person in a family system can achieve a higher level of functioning and he stays in emotional contact with the others, another family member and another and another will take similar steps. This chain reaction is the basis for the principle that change in a central triangle is followed by automatic change throughout the family system. The change in all the others takes place automatically in the living situations of everyday life. Change is most rapid when the initial triangle involves the most important people in the system.

Togetherness Force. In broad terms, the togetherness force defines family members as being alike in terms of important beliefs, philosophies, life principles, and feelings. It uses the personal pronoun "we" to define what "We feel or think," or it defines the self of another—"My husband thinks that . . ."—or it uses the indefinite "it" to represent common values—"It is wrong" or or "It is the thing to do." In addition, emotional forces overlap and bind together, assigning positive values to thinking about the other before self, being for the other, sacrificing for others, considering others, feeling responsible for the comfort and well-being of others, and showing love and devotion and compassion for others. The togetherness force assumes responsibility for the happiness, comfort, and well-being of others; it feels guilty and asks, "What have I done to cause this?" when the other is unhappy or uncomfortable; and it blames the others for lack of happiness or for failure in self.

Differentiating Force. The differentiating force places the same kind of emphasis on "I" in defining the above characteristics. It has been called the I position, which defines principle and the taking of action in terms such as, "This is what I think or feel or stand for" and "This is what I will do or not do." This is the responsible I, which assumes responsibility for one's own happiness and comfort and well-being. It avoids thinking that tends to blame one's own unhappiness, discomfort, or failure on the other. The responsible I also avoids the posture of the irresponsible or narcissistic I, which makes demands on others with "I want or deserve" or "This is my right or my privilege."

Case History

The husband and wife had a sufficient level of pseudoself to illustrate a fairly intense level of fusion and togetherness early in the marriage, and they also had sufficient solid self to motivate them to go beyond symptom relief in family psychotherapy. Many families with this much initial impairment either stop therapy when the symptoms subside or work at differentiation without the success that was achieved here.

The husband and wife, each 30 years old, had been married at 22, when he began his career in accounting. She was the younger of two daughters. Relationships with her family, living in the same city, had been formal and pleasant. He was the oldest of three, with a younger brother and sister. His family lived 200 miles away. The husband and wife had two children, a son of five and a daughter of three, who were minimally involved in the family problem.

There had been an increasing level of turmoil in the marriage for five years, with moderate dysfunction in the wife. Their selfs were completely invested in each other from the time of marriage until after their first child was born, some three years after the marriage. They had close agreement on most life issues and principles, the agreement achieved by the adaptiveness of the wife, who blindly accepted her husband's operating beliefs and who did not seriously think about such issues. The self of each was highly invested in the happiness, comfort, and well-being of the other. As with most such marital fusions, happiness was stated as their primary goal in life.

More-differentiated spouses state their primary goals in terms of the most important individual life goals. When each is in a satisfying pursuit of individual goals, happiness usually evolves as a dividend. As a result of seeing families with varying levels of differentiation and varying goals, the author believes that happiness as a primary goal is unattainable.

The two spouses in this clinical example achieved a near-perfect state of happiness and nirvanalike marital bliss early in the marriage. Their lives were financially secure, there were no traumatic events in their extended families, and they managed to keep the emotional system between them in almost perfect equilibrium. An excellent sexual adjustment was added evidence of the calm emotional equilibrium.

They paid close attention to expressions of

what the other liked and disliked, and each attempted to provide what the other liked. The husband, for example, would make a mental note about the wife's preference in color and about items she would like, and at the first opportunity he would buy her a present that fitted her wishes. The wife matched the husband's reactions and listened for his comments at dinner to determine his food preferences and dislikes. She spent much time preparing the food he liked. She made note of his comments about women's hair styles and clothing in an effort to wear her hair and dress to please her husband. This pattern of being, acting, and doing for the other included innumerable items in their relationship. The pattern was most pervasive in the wife, who was the most adaptive in acting on what she knew or assumed to be her husband's wishes.

Later, in family psychotherapy, she was asked to estimate her percentage of success in knowing and guessing her husband's wishes. She estimated it to be about 75 per cent. Her husband estimated her percentage of success as no more than half of that figure because he was aware of her effort to please him and he acted pleased in order to please her. She was also asked what percentage of her effort went into being the kind of wife her husband wanted her to be, and what percentage went into being the kind of wife she wanted to be. She quickly responded: "More than 90 per cent! No, it was about 90 per cent to please him and 3 per cent to please me, and the rest was in the middle."

It is amazing how people with this life orientation can quickly assign percentage figures when asked this question.

The idyllic marriage continued until the two-person system became a three-person system, and less of the wife's energy was available for her husband. The harmonious two-person system is unstable, since it does not stand the stress of others in the emotional field.

The marital adjustment was less satisfactory after the birth of the first child and even worse after the second child was born, two years later. The wife became more involved with the children, and the husband devoted more time to his work. As is predictable, the wife, the more adaptive one, began to develop symptoms of dysfunction. She fatigued easily, her mood was depressed, and she spent more time in bed, trying to rest. At first, the husband tried to function for the wife, another predictable characteristic of emotional systems in which one functions for another within the limits of reality. The husband helped with the children in the mornings and evenings, and on weekends he initiated a thorough cleaning of the house. As the husband began to falter in his overfunctioning, the wife's mother became more active in trying to help with the children, and there was increasing conflict between the wife and her mother. The husband gained the outside position in this triangle. He began to work later, and he either fell asleep after dinner or went out with men friends in the evening. On weekends he went to ballgames.

The situation reached a breaking point after eight years of marriage. There was increased conflict between the wife and her mother. The wife was angry with the absent husband, who "demanded everything and gave nothing." The husband was angry with the wife, who was "so demanding no one could please her," and was bothered by her nagging, by her constant complaining, and by the dirty house.

After a series of angry arguments with threats of divorce, they sought the help of a marriage counselor, who considered the problem to be the result of a meddlesome mother-in-law. On his advice, the couple terminated contact with the wife's mother. He diagnosed the marital problem as "failure to recognize and meet the needs of the other." Then the husband and wife each made monumental efforts to be more considerate and loving toward the other, but each effort produced no more than transient relief. The wife felt, that no matter how hard she tried, her husband went back to staying away from home, and the husband felt that no amount of loving would stop the wife's nagging, to which he was very sensitive. The counselor advised more time to talk out the problem, but each effort to talk resulted in long angry outbursts. The couple terminated with the marriage counselor, considering their problem insoluble. The husband moved out to live separately and prepare for a divorce. At this time, the wife heard about family therapy and sought an appointment.

According to family systems theory, and contrary to what the counselor said, the wife's mother had relieved the problem more than she had hurt it. Her additional functioning added something to an already foundering unit and postponed the collapse. Tension within the emotional unit actually decreases when there are open relationships with more family members and friends. Rather than cutting off the relationship with the wife's mother, the spouses were encouraged to enlarge the relationship system. The tension system had increased when the wife's mother was excluded. These two people had already put maximal effort into maintaining emotional harmony within the emotional fusion, and the system had lost flexibility. Rather than encouraging each to work harder at meeting the needs of the other, which would increase the fusion, the effort went to work at being a more contained and responsible self, to meet one's own needs as much as possible and to contain as many more needs as possible, to decrease the demands on each other, to gain control over automatic responsiveness to the demands of the other, and to reduce efforts to communicate at home until they could do so without angry outbursts.

These people continued during three years of twice-a-month appointments to gain a rather good result. The first 15 to 20 sessions went to improving the communication between them. When the conflict disappeared, they had what most would consider to be a happy, normal adjustment. The wife's appearance changed soon after hearing that the husband would really prefer her to choose her own hair style and to dress the way she wished.

A fair percentage of families terminate therapy once emotional harmony is restored. But these spouses were motivated to continue. The differentiation of selfs is a long, slow process made up of many small steps, each accompanied by controlled emotional crises. These crises are different from crises that go with emotional regression, since the involved ones continue to engage each other without threats of action such as divorce.

The husband was the first to take a step. He devoted weeks to thinking through his professional goals and future. His life energy went to individual goals rather than the previous goal of happiness. As his life energy was directed more to the responsible functioning of self, the wife pleaded, accused, attacked, and alternated overinterest in sex and withdrawal of sex—all favoring a return to togetherness. He stayed fairly well on course, with only minor relapses in response to accusations that he was a terrible father, that his children were being harmed by his lack of interest, that he was not capable of a close family relationship or an adequate sexual relationship.

The process reached a breakthrough during a noisy emotional outburst from the wife in which he maintained his calm and was able to stay close. The following day the relationship was calm. The wife said:

"One part of me approved of what you were doing, but somehow I had to do what I did. Even when I was most excited and angry, I was hoping you would not let that change you. I am so glad you did not give in."

There were a few weeks of calm before the wife started on a self-determined course. Then the husband was the petulant, demanding one. It was as though he had lost the gain from his previous effort. Then came another emotional breakthrough and new levels of differentiation for both. This pattern, in which one and then the other changed, continued in several definite cycles over the three years. Meanwhile, each was changing in relationship to families of origin, working through in crises similar to the crises between the spouses. Also, the husband began to find differences in his work situation that were resolved with a new and better job.

In the course of psychotherapy, the couple began to find old friends less attractive. They no longer liked the old social gatherings with gossip, the berating of other people, the intense emotional reactiveness between spouses in the group, and the bias and prejudice in those who crusaded against bias and prejudice. This reaction follows the predictable pattern of people choosing friends from among others with equivalent levels of differentiation. They found new friends with a different orientation to life while maintaining casual, pleasant, infrequent contact with the old friends.

The process of differentiation is never complete. A goal of psychotherapy is that the family members learn the nature of the problem and decide when they are ready to discontinue the formal effort. These two spouses achieved sufficient levels of differentiation for each to stand above the togetherness forces without losing self in fusions. In the marriage relationship they could stand close and function better as a team. The relationship lost the intense nirvanalike emotional ecstasy of the early marriage, but it also lost the conflict and distance of fusion. They described the final relationship this way:

"We are much less close than we were before, but we are also much closer. It is hard to describe."

This is an ideal rather than an average clinical course. The time, the situation, the extended family configuration, and the endowment and motivation of the spouses favored the rapid course. Others with less motivation, more demands, and more pressure from extended families, plus other possible variables, may spend years without developing the emotional stamina to get solidly through the first differentiation step.

Family Psychotherapy with Low-Scale People. Some families are so low on the differentiation scale that a higher level of differentiation is beyond expectation. And some families are so fragmented that there are not enough motivated members to form a single viable triangle. In these situations the various group therapy methods directed at symptom relief and support have much more to offer than does any other kind of psychotherapy. The various group methods are used in any combination that best meets the motivation and needs of the families. A major problem in these families is a lack of motivation for any kind of psychotherapy. The new methods of network therapy and other forms of community therapy have much more potential than does further refinement of most of the present conventional types of psychotherapy.

Clinical Approaches to Differentiation of Self

Three main clinical approaches have been the most effective in family psychotherapy in which the differentiation of self is the goal: psychotherapy with both parents or both spouses, psychotherapy with one family member, and psychotherapy with one spouse in preparation for a long-term effort with both spouses. The choice depends on the family configuration and motivation.

Family Psychotherapy with Both Parents or Both Spouses. This, the most effective of all approaches, accomplishes the most in the least time. It involves the two most important people in the family and the therapist as a potential triangle.

There has been much experience with both parents and one child—one complete triangle from the family. In this therapy situation, the family emotional patterns run their repetitive circuits with little tendency to involve the therapist or to be influenced by him. When the child is removed and the therapist becomes the third side of a potential triangle, the parents attempt to use him as a triangle person for issues between them. If the therapist can remain operationally outside the emotional system between the parents while actively relating to each, the parents begin differentiating selfs from each other. This is part of a central concept about triangles: Conflict between two people will resolve automatically if both remain in

emotional contact with a third person who can relate actively to both without taking sides with either. This reaction is so predictable that it can be used in other areas of the family system and in social systems. The resolution of the problems between the spouses proceeds more rapidly if the therapist has knowledge about triangles, but the concept is so accurate that resolutions between the two would probably proceed with any third person who fulfilled the requirement of emotional contact without taking sides, no matter what the subject matter for discussion, as long as discussion touched emotional issues.

There is another advantage in having both parents or both spouses present. The differentiation of a self does not take place in a vacuum. It involves the definition of self in relation to other selfs about important life issues important to self. The other spouse is one of the best other people for the introduction of important issues.

Since the goal is to modify the most important triangle in any emotional system, this approach is used with all forms of emotional illness in which it is possible to get both parents or both spouses into a working relationship with the therapist. The basic triangular pattern is the same whether symptoms eventually come to focus between the parents, as a dysfunction in one spouse (if both spouses are dysfunctioned, it is a collapsed family), or in a child. There have been spectacular results in which the child is excluded from therapy responsibility and in which the symptomatic child is never seen. In several dozen families, the symptoms have focused in a college student who was never seen by the therapist. The student had no psychiatric help, and the only contact between the parents and the student was the usual contact parents have with college students. The results were characteristically excellent.

Techniques. During the first several years of family therapy, the technique of working with two spouses was changed several times. The present technique, in use more than five years, has been constantly refined and is the most effective approach found thus far. The first format placed strong emphasis on the intrapsychic process in each spouse. There was a focus on dreams and on the emotional reaction in the other spouse. In a later working format, the goal was to reach the point where either spouse could communicate to the other anything that self thought or felt about the other and anything thought or felt about self. This approach focused more on the relationship system. Considerable emphasis was placed on careful discrimination between feelings and thoughts. This was a profitable approach, but the spouses tended to overreact to the communication of feeling. In early approaches there was an emphasis on spouses talking to each other in the sessions, which resulted in emotional reactiveness without either really hearing the other. The present approach involves constant activity by the therapist, who asks questions of one spouse, defocusing feelings, while the other spouse listens. Then the questions shift to the other spouse. With this format, the spouses can hear each other, and the feeling process becomes more spontaneous.

Using the present approach, the therapist maintains the role of an interested clinical investigator with thousands of questions to ask about the details of the problem in the family. In the first interview, he asks each family member how he understands the problem. The responses are usually fumbling generalizations, and the therapist's list of questions grows instead of diminishing. He leaves the impression that, if these questions are to be answered, someone in the family will have to become a better observer. The focus is always on questions. There are no interpretations in the usual sense and only an occasional statement about past experiences with other families that might be considered an interpretation. About a fourth of the comments by the therapist are designed to detriangle the situation when a family member invokes the emotional process in a session. In the background are questions about events since the last session.

One parent usually spends much time thinking about the family problem, and the other has thought little about it. The therapist is always interested in who has been thinking, how much he has thought, what was the pattern of the thoughts, and what kinds of working conclusions came from the thinking. The therapist implies with questions that it is the family's problem to solve. He asks if they have made progress, what is blocking their progress, if they have any ideas about how to get past the block, if they have any plans to speed up progress, and many other questions of this nature.

The opening subject of a session may be left to the family, or the therapist may ask one spouse what he has in mind for this session. Once under way, the working format is to help that spouse express a clear piece of thinking, then to ask the other spouse for a response to what has been said, and back to the first spouse for a response to the second—going back and forth the entire session when possible. A clean session is one in which the therapist says nothing except to direct questions from one spouse to the other. When the first spouse makes minimal comments, the therapist aks him to elaborate and amplify his comment into a word picture to which the other can respond.

Questions range all the way from asking for very intellectual responses to asking for feeling responses, with more than 95 per cent of the questions far to the intellectual end of the scale. For instance, the therapist might ask the wife:

What were you thinking while your husband was talking?

Or the question might move slightly toward feelings:

What is your reaction? What is your impression about this situation?

When the situation is calm and the second spouse appears to have a mild emotional reaction, the question might be:

Can you give a reading on what you were feeling inside yourself the past few minutes?

The over-all plan is to keep the sessions active with clearly expressed thoughts, always keeping questions calm and low-keyed. If a spouse—it is usually the wife—becomes tearful or shows overt feelings, the immediate goal is to get someone to thinking about the feeling rather than expressing it. The question to the wife might be:

Can you tell us the thought that ticked off the feeling?

Or to the husband:

Did you notice your wife's tears? What did you think when you saw them?

Results with this toned-down, intellectual, conceptualizing approach in families have far surpassed results when the emphasis is on the therapeutic externalization of feelings. Family members begin to express feelings more spontaneously and openly and to do so faster than with any other approach. There are frequent exchanges similar to the following after about ten family sessions.

The wife began:
"I can't wait to come to these appointments. They are wonderful!"
The therapist asked what was so wonderful about problems. The wife said:
"I am fascinated by the way my husband thinks."
The therapist asked how she explained living with him for ten years without knowing what he thought. She finally concluded that she could listen to him and really hear what he said when he talked to the therapist, and that had never been possible when he talked directly to her. After a year of rather good progress, the husband was explaining the progress on his learning that went on in his wife. He had been in the dark for 20 years, and it was good to finally know the other side of what had been going on.
Some version of this development occurs in a high percentage of families. One wife watched her husband with intense interest while he talked. When asked what she thought when she looked at him like that, she said:
"I am liking him more every time I hear him talk. I never knew he thought like that."

Most spouses are caught in feeling worlds in which they react and respond to the feeling complex in the other, without ever really knowing the other. Most spouses probably have the most open relationships in their adult lives during the courtship. After marriage, each quickly begins to learn the subjects that make the other anxious. To avoid the discomfort in self when the other is anxious, each avoids anxious issues, and an increasing number of subjects become taboo for discussion in the marriage. This breakdown in communication is present to some degree in most marriages.

Experience with various psychotherapy approaches is consistent with the concept of an intellectual system so interwoven with and submerged in the feeling system that primary attention to expression of feeling increases the fusion and delays or blocks forces toward differentiation. The present psychotherapy approach, which is directed at distinguishing between intellect and feeling, and at verbalization of intellectual ideas and thoughts in the presence of the other spouse, is the most efficient method thus far found for the rapid establishment of communication between spouses. The opening of communication is accompanied by positive reactions of the spouses to each other.

The communication of intellectual thoughts and ideas also sets the stage for beginning differentiation of self. Each spouse begins to know the other and to know self in a way that was not possible before and to become aware of differences in thinking and acting and being. A line of demarcation begins developing between the spouses as they clarify the beliefs and principles that differ one from the other. The point at which one begins to take action stands based on principles and beliefs is the point where they encounter the emotional reactions that go with the steps in differentiation of self. The emotion that accompanies differentiation is contained within the twosome, it is cohesive rather than disruptive, and it is followed by a new level of more mature togetherness.

Special attention goes to defining the details of a system of minor-appearing stimuli that trigger intense emotional responses in the other spouse. Both the stimulus and the response operate more out of awareness than in awareness. There are hundreds and perhaps thousands of these stimuli in any intense emotional interdependence. The responses are more numerous, more intense, and more life-influencing in people with intense emotional fusions and are correspondingly less so in people with better levels of differentiation. The goal is to define the stimulus-response system in a step-by-step sequence to help spouses gain some control over it.

Some responses are unpleasant. Examples are feelings of revulsion in response to habits and mannerisms in the other, reactions in which one's flesh crawls, and jarring emotional responses to sensory stimuli. An equal number of responses range from mildly to hurtfully pleasurable. For example, a wife felt strong sexual attraction at a look of helplessness on her husband's face. The stimuli may involve any of the five senses. There surely must be responses in which one kills in response to the stimulus.

Most of the stimulus-response situations in a marriage are out of conscious intellectual awareness, but they are an intimate part of an automatic relationship system, and they profoundly affect the relationship. The following is an example of a stimulus-response reaction that was out of awareness.

In a conflictual marriage, the husband would slug his wife with his fist in response to a trigger stimulus. Several efforts to discover the stimulus failed. The physical violence usually occurred in a flooded emotional field, and there appeared to be no specific stimulus. Then, in a situation without words, he hit her in response to "that look of hatred in her eyes." That was the last time he hit her. He gained some control by looking away in periods of critical emotional tension, and she gained some control over the looks.

Other common types of stimuli are "that cold icy stare," "that tone of voice," and "that sneer of contempt." The goal in working with spouses is to isolate and define several of the more prominent stimulus-response mechanisms and to teach the spouses to be observers. Knowledge that the mechanism exists gives them some control, the act of observing confers still more control, and any additional conscious control over the reactiveness may add up to enough emotional control to facilitate a step toward differentiation.

Each therapist must define his own way of remaining relatively free of the intense emotional field between the spouses while he helps each spouse in turn to express a piece of thinking for the other spouse. The following is a brief description of the author's way of doing this.

Though the spouses and therapist may be sitting so close that their knees almost touch, as occasionally happens in demonstration and videotaped interviews, the goal is to back up emotionally to the point where the spouses are sufficiently distant to watch the ebb and flow of the emotional process between them while always thinking family systems. The technique is similar to changing from a high-power to a low-power lens while still the same distance from the subject. The therapist's goal is to focus on the chain reaction between the two spouses or on the process or on the flow of events between the spouses and to keep self out of the flow.

The human phenomenon is serious and tragic, but, at the very same time, there is a comical or humorous aspect to most serious situations. If the therapist is too close to the family, he can become entangled in the seriousness. If he is too distant, he is not in effective contact. The right emotional distance for the author is a point between seriousness and humor, where he can shift either way to facilitate the process in the family. This is part of the basic principle: The emotional problem between two people will resolve automatically if they remain in contact with a third person who can remain free of the emotional field between the two while actively relating to each.

The spouses predictably use triangling moves to involve the therapist in the emotional process between the two. Triangling moves are more frequent when tension in the twosome is high. The therapeutic principle is to keep tension low. Tension can build up as one spouse tells a story with emotional overtones. The therapist is extremely vulnerable to becoming part of the triangle when he listens to the content of such a story. Focusing on process rather than on content helps the therapist keep his perspective. If the spouse continues emotional involvement in the story, a reversal or comment that focuses on the opposite side of the issue or that picks up the humorous side of the situation can decompress the mounting tension.

A wife was becoming more and more emotionally involved in describing her nagging, meddlesome mother. There were several valid opposite sides to this image, but the therapist chose a reversal that effectively decompressed the tension. He asked:

How do you account for your lack of appreciation for your mother's life-long effort to make you turn out right?

The spouses laughed, and the tension was lowered.

No one can teach a therapist what to do or say in such situations. If he is sufficiently distant to see the process and to see the humorous side, he will automatically make an effective comment. If the therapist is already emotionally involved, any effort to reverse the emotional process will be heard as sarcastic and mean.

One of the common examples of mounting tension occurs when one spouse interrupts the conversation between the other spouse and the therapist, ignores the therapist, and emotionally rebuts the first spouse directly. If their talk continues for many exchanges, the locked emotional responsiveness between the spouses increases while the silent and involved therapist watches. The therapeutic goal is to maintain the structure of having each spouse talk to the therapist and to increase the calm intellectual questions to a level that excludes the other spouse. The percentage of success with conflictual spouses has been higher with this approach than with any other approach thus far tried.

One of the therapist's other functions in this method of family psychotherapy is to continually demonstrate the taking of the I position. When one member of a family can calmly state his own beliefs and convictions and can take action based on his convictions without criticism of the beliefs of others and without becoming involved in emotional debate, then other family members start the same process of becoming more sure of self and more accepting of the beliefs of others. When the therapist can find occasions to define his own beliefs and principles in the course of the psychotherapy, the spouses begin to do the same in relation to each other.

There are numerous detailed techniques in this method of family psychotherapy with both spouses. Most involve shifting from individual dynamics to systems thinking and avoiding emotional fusion into the family emotional system. When the therapy loses its orderly structure, the problem is usually caused by a lapse back into individual dynamics or by the therapist's becoming fused into the family emotional system. Getting beyond the vestiges of individual dynamics requires long disciplined work by the therapist. When he begins to think in terms of individual dynamics, he is vulnerable to taking sides in the family emotional process.

A good example of the differences between individual theory and systems theory is illustrated by sexual dysharmony. Individual theory has well-defined postulations about impotence in the male and frigidity in the female. Individual psychotherapy has well-defined techniques for examining the dynamics in the context of the transference. Family systems theory sees sexual inadequacy in the male as occurring in the man whose pseudoself fuses into the pseudoself of his wife in close emotional relationships and sees frigidity as occurring in the wife whose self fuses into her husband's self. Systems theory sees the sexual dysharmony as part of the relationship between the spouses. When the therapist continually thinks of sexual dysharmony as a symptom of the relationship, he is much less likely to think in terms of individual dynamics, to become entangled in the family emotional system, and to work toward defining the problem in only one family member. Sexual symptoms resolve much faster when viewed as a relationship problem than when viewed as a crystallized problem in one family member.

The same pattern applies to the entire spectrum of emotional symptoms that tend to become fixed in one family member. For instance, when one spouse has a drinking problem, system thinking focuses on the dysfunction of that spouse in relation to the family rather than on the individual dynamics. Among the most difficult symptoms to view in a family systems context are serious physical illnesses, such as asthma and ulcerative colitis, in which flare-ups of the illness occur in emotional response to the family emotional system. The therapeutic response is more rapid if the physical illness is regarded as another type of dysfunction in the family system, which avoids glib formulations about individual dynamics. It is easy to lose the total family perspective when initial attention goes to dynamics in one family member. The individual dynamics can be considered much later.

Finally, there is a teaching aspect in family psychotherapy. The therapist communicates important principles of systems theory and makes indirect suggestions about directions the family may find profitable in resolving problems. In order to remain outside the family emotional field, the therapist must make sure that these communications are not perceived by the family as telling them what to do or as taking sides in the controversy between the spouses. When there is tension in the family, the spouses routinely hear the therapist's communication differently. They often debate the issue at home and then return to ask the therapist to clarify his statement. At that point the therapist's immediate goal is to detriangle himself from involvement in the family emotional system rather than to clarify his statement, which would only involve him more deeply in the emotional system. Optimally, the teaching communications come when the family tension system is low and they are presented in a way that does not involve the therapist in the family emotional system.

Many comments are made from the I position, in which the therapist presents his views, beliefs, and operating principles in such a way that they can be accepted or rejected by the family. The therapist has much knowledge that can help the family find solutions. The goal is to find a neutral way to present the knowledge. The following framework has been successful in most situations:

I have some experience from work with other families that you may find helpful in planning a course of action. If any of the ideas make sense and if you can incorporate and use them as your own ideas, there is a fair chance your effort will succeed. If the ideas do not make sense, then you are in the position of using someone else's ideas, and the chances of failure are very high.

The suggestions about working out relationships in the extended family are presented in the same way—as detailed as necessary to make a point but with freedom

and deliberation in acceptance of the viewpoint.

Multiple-Family Therapy. The method and techniques of family therapy with a single family—both spouses—were adapted for use with a number of families in the mid-1960's. Early experiences with multiple-family group therapy and later experiences with single families were incorporated into the method.

The goal was to keep each family unit a contained triangle, to work on the emotional process between the spouses, and to avoid emotional communication between families. From past experience, the theorists believed that the emotional exchange between families encouraged a fusion of all the families into a large undifferentiated ego mass, which made it difficult to focus on details within a single family and made the differentiation process difficult in any family. The theorists believed that each family could learn much from the close observation of other families and that the effects of teaching communications might be cumulative and save time.

Families were chosen who did not know each other, and they were asked not to have social contact with each other outside the sessions. The therapist, one side of a potential triangle with each family, approached each family the same as he would if working with only that family while the other families observed. Then the process was repeated with each of the other families. Any family could talk to the therapist about another family but they could not talk directly to the other family.

This method of multiple-family therapy has been so successful in keeping the emotional process contained within each family, in facilitating differentiation in each family, and in bringing profits from observational exposure to other families that the author has converted much of his own practice to this method, and the method has been adopted widely by others. The average family progresses about one and a half times faster than similar families do in single-family therapy. Family members say it is easier to see one's own problem when it is present in another family than when the problem involves self. Families learn from others in their search for solutions to problems.

The optimal number of families is three to five for each multiple-family group. With only two families, the group tends toward emotional fusion between the families, which requires much therapeutic agility to control. Having more than five families in a group reduces the amount of time available for each family. Families become restless and inattentive in sessions of more than two hours. The most effective format is one in which the available time is divided equally between the families at each session. Including families with varying levels of problems in the same group is workable, but families have done best with others who have the same kind of problems. Families in multiple-family therapy have done as well on infrequent appointments as single families have on weekly appointments. The average multiple-family group is seen every two weeks, but some are on monthly schedules, which reduces the number of sessions in the total course of family therapy.

Family Psychotherapy with One Family Member. This is a teaching-supervising method throughout the entire course. The first several sessions are for teaching one motivated family member about the functioning of family systems. The next sessions are devoted to formulations about the part the family member plays in his own family. The family member is encouraged to visit his family as often as possible to observe, to check the accuracy of previous formulations, and to test his own ability to relate within his family. Later appointments are devoted to supervising the family member's effort with his own family. The family member is encouraged to do a multigenerational study of his own family. Supervisory sessions may be as often as every two weeks or as infrequent as every few months, depending on the number of visits with his family and the amount of work done between appointments.

This method involves learning about triangles, keeping an active emotional relationship with important members of the family, and developing an ability to control emotional reactiveness and to stay emotionally outside the triangles in contacts with the family. The goal for the family member is to stay emotionally outside the triangles, just as was described for the therapist in family psychotherapy with both spouses.

The initial sessions with the family member are devoted to didactic teaching about triangles and the functioning of emotional systems. The following sessions are devoted to presenting postulations about the part the family member plays in his own family, instructions about developing the ability to observe his family and himself, and suggestions about ways to stay in emotional contact with the family without taking polarized sides on any issue. Once the effort is under way, the sessions are devoted to supervision of the family member's effort. He reports his experiences with his family and any new observations that may lead to new postulations, and the therapist suggests new techniques that might be tried. The details of the instruction depend on whether it is for a short-term goal or for a long-term definitive effort. The system of triangles is so predictable that any failure to achieve a result can be considered a failure in emotional control rather than an error in the system.

This approach is often used for one motivated spouse when the other spouse is antagonistic to family psychotherapy. Since this is a short-term goal, the instruction is not very detailed. An immediate goal is to reduce the emotional reactiveness to the point where the antagonistic spouse is willing to participate in the family psychotherapy. Understanding the family with systems concept helps to reduce the diagnosing and the blaming of the other. A little knowledge about broad principles of emotional systems can help the motivated one reach a calmer and more contained level of functioning. For instance, family members are dependent on other family members to fulfill certain functions. When the functioning of one fails, the failure impairs the functioning of others. The system tends to blame the one who failed and to exert pressure on that one to resume functioning.

The effort to change the other is best illustrated in a marital interdependency in which the functioning of self depends on the other to meet a variety of needs. When the other's functioning fails, that failure results in distress and impairment in self. The other is often seen as the cause of the problem and is blamed for the problem in self. The effort to change the other can range from a direct assault to subtle efforts, such as giving more love as an inducement to change. In mild states of distress, this effort to change the other can be successful within narrow limits, but in chronic states in which there is no adaptive flexibility in the system, the effort to change the other predictably makes the situation worse. If the motivated one can know intellectually that the effort to change the other is one of the basic forces that creates and intensifies triangles and that this effort is doomed to failure by basic characteristics of emotional systems, the motivated one can then create a formula for reducing the tension. Any effort toward assuming responsibility for one's own distress, toward containing one's own needs a little better, toward blaming the other less, or toward controlling one's emotional responsiveness to the other is a step toward reduction in family tension

Family psychotherapy with one parent is used occasionally to control explosive behavior problems in a teen-age offspring. These are rare situations when control of the acting-out child is sufficiently critical to take precedence over long-term work with both parents. In most situations the symptoms in the child subside when the parents are productively working on their relationship. However, when the primary focus is the child, one parent can gain control much more rapidly than can both parents working together. Parents always disagree on the management of such a child and usually alternate between permissiveness and angry retaliatory punitiveness.

Parents can maintain complete order in their homes by always controlling self and never punishing or controlling the child or doing anything to the child. To act in this way, the motivated parent must carefully define his responsibility for self in his family, the operating rules and principles within the area of his responsibility, and what he will

and will not do in relation to those who go beyond the rules. The rules, like laws, are never made in anger, nor are they personalized to deal with a single situation. Those who live under their jurisdiction have a choice of living within the rule or of risking automatic consequences, which have been previously defined.

The important principle is that the parent calmly defines self and rules and consequences, communicates them when he is sure of them, and is prepared to stand on the consequences of broken rules if need be. Such a system by a calm parent who does not act in anger can bring chaotic behavior problems under control rather quickly, provided the other parent does not interfere. If the family situation is chaotic enough, the other parent will not interfere until after the critical situation is past. Ultimately, the motivated parent has to deal with the disagreements with the other parent, which invokes a triangle between parents and child.

Family psychotherapy with one family member is used frequently with young, single, self-supporting adult children. This approach is best described as coaching the young adult in differentiating a self from his family of origin. The total process continues about the same length of time that would be required for intensive individual psychotherapy, but the total number of appointments is a fraction of the number required for individual psychotherapy, and the results are far-reaching.

Motivation for this kind of effort is highest in oldest sons and daughters and in others who feel a responsibility for family problems and who still maintain reasonable contact with their families. This approach has never been successful with a young adult still financially dependent on his family. They have the aptitude for quickly understanding family emotional systems, but they lack the courage to risk family displeasure in the differentiation process. The effort takes longer in younger children, who are more inclined to expect the environment to change for them and who are slower to grasp the idea that they have the capacity to change family patterns if they so desire.

Primary emphasis goes to differentiating

a self in the triangle of self and both parents, but, because of the interlocking of triangles, it is necessary to include a number of peripheral family members in the effort. If the family member can work toward an open relationship system with every member of his extended family system, the result is highly rewarding. Through such a differentiating process in self, change can occur throughout the entire family system if the family can continue to maintain emotional contact with the various members without taking sides in any of the emotional issues that develop. The process goes better if the family of origin lives a sufficient distance to be outside the immediate emotional field but sufficiently close for frequent visits. The differentiating process may be slowed if parents live in the same town and are in daily contact by telephone or in person. Results have been good with some extended families who live a thousand or more miles away, provided the members make a few personal visits a year and maintain an active emotional interchange through letters and telephone calls.

The basic process for differentiating a self from a family of origin involves establishing a person-to-person relationship with each parent. In the extended family this process is equivalent to establishing personal communication between two spouses. The person-to-person relationship is one in which it is possible to talk about self as a person to the parent as a person. Most people are not capable of more than a few minutes of a person-to-person relationship before one becomes anxious, goes silent or begins to talk about external things, or invokes a triangle and talks about a third person who is absent. Many people have relatively free-talking relationships with one parent and relatively formal and distant relationships with the other parent. Achieving a person-to-person relationship with either parent is a major undertaking, but, if the differentiating person is aware that the result is highly desirable and of great potential benefit to self, he has a long-term assignment at which he can work constantly in his own way. The average young adult who applies self to this effort is able to get a rather good

result in about three years with a total of 50 to 75 psychotherapy hours.

Variations of this approach are possible when one or both parents are dead. But then the young adult needs to make more of an effort to relate to a spectrum of other important extended-family members.

A surprising extension of family therapy with one family member has evolved during the past few years. During the past decade, family psychotherapy for family therapists and their spouses has come to replace psychoanalysis as a method for resolving emotional problems in the therapist. Now there has been an experience with a group of young therapists who devoted their primary energy to defining a self in their families of origin. They had more motivation than average for this effort. Supervision was provided as part of the training program. These young therapists began to develop unusual ability in their clinical work. They were unusually versatile in relating freely to all family members without emotional involvement with the families. After a year or two, they found that they had also changed in relation to their wives and children. They progressed as much in their nuclear families as had other trainees who had been seen in family psychotherapy with their spouses for the same length of time. This development in a number of trainees at the same time was a pleasant surprise. The approach is now the subject of study in other training programs with larger groups of trainees.

This experience suggests that psychotherapy, as it has been known in the past, may one day be considered superfluous for those motivated for the effort in the extended family. The course here suggests that the less intense emotional process in parental families made it easier to observe and define patterns and to take appropriate action stands more quickly than is possible with a spouse, in whom emotional needs are more intimately interwoven. Differentiation of self gains made in peripheral emotional systems may be automatically manifested in the nuclear family.

Family Psychotherapy with One Spouse in Preparation for a Long-Term Effort with Both Spouses. In many families, one spouse is too antagonistic to participate in family psychotherapy. In this situation, the motivated spouse is seen alone until the other spouse is willing to become part of the long-term effort.

This approach is included as a separate method because it provides a technique of family psychotherapy for many people who ordinarily would have no option except individual psychotherapy. Many of these people have already had long periods of individual psychotherapy with little benefit.

The initial phase of the family therapy is similar to that used in family psychotherapy with a single family member. The goal is to teach the family member about the functioning of emotional systems, to discover the part that self plays in the system and especially toward the other spouse, and to modify the system by controlling the part that self plays. If the motivated spouse is successful in toning down emotional reactiveness, the antagonistic spouse often asks to participate in the sessions, after which the method is identical to that already described for both spouses.

Progress with this method depends on the therapist's remaining outside the emotional system when working with one spouse and avoiding the use of sessions for emotional support. This method has been used successfully with a spectrum of difficult disruptive families, including a number in which the spouses have lived separately for long periods. More than half of the antagonistic spouses have entered family therapy within periods of a few months to a year or so.

Clinical Triangle Patterns

The following are clinical examples of predictable change when one motivated family member is finally able to control his emotional responsiveness.

An explosive father developed the persistent pattern of hitting a preadolescent son for poor table manners at dinner. The mother routinely intervened in the child's behalf, after which the conflict would continue between the parents. After months of coaching, the mother was finally able to control her feelings sufficiently to deal adequately with the pattern.

The therapist told them that a child is capable of dealing with a single parent but that he is forced to extreme measures in dealing with both at the same time. The son played his part in this pattern. He knew well the things that would trigger the father's anger and the things that would please the father, and he had some kind of choice about whether or not he angered the father. If the mother really had confidence that the son could manage the father alone, if she communicated this confidence to the son ahead of time, and if she controlled her sympathy for the son, good things would predictably happen. But unless the mother communicated her intention before taking action, the father and son could misinterpret her silence and escalate the conflict to force her to intervene.

One afternoon the mother told the son of her intentions: If he angered the father, he would have to find his own way to deal with the father. The dinner table conflict started earlier than usual that evening. The mother had difficulty in controlling her reactiveness, but she did not take action. One time she left the room briefly to regain her emotional composure. The son handled his own conflict with the father. When she put the son to bed later in the evening, he said, "Thanks, Mom, for what you did tonight." That was the last dinner table conflict between father and son.

Another mother, in frequent verbal and physical conflict with her children, was a strong advocate of the notion that it was the father's responsibility to maintain discipline and punish the children. Through the years he was confronted with repeating conflictual situations between the mother and a child. He followed the predictable triangle pattern of trying to calm the conflictual twosome, but there was no satisfactory solution. The mother could move him toward punishment by saying that he was a poor father or that he was not a man. The pattern became more intense as the children grew larger than the mother, and there were physical fights between the mother and a child when the father was present.

After the therapist talked about triangles and the ability of either parent to manage his relationship with the children, the father decided to stay out of the conflict, but his feelings still participated, and the conflict escalated until he was forced to intervene. As he gained more control, he told the mother that he was going to manage his own relationships with the children and leave her to settle the conflicts she started. In the midst of the next fight, he was able to chuckle slightly at the sequence of events, and he asked the child, "Are you going to let your mother push you around?" The mother ran to the bedroom, slammed the door, and stayed there for an hour. That was the last of the serious conflictual scenes. The father had found a way to stay detached from the mother-child conflict. Thereafter, the mother-child conflicts never went beyond mild words.

Another woman, an only child, was close to her mother and negative and distant with her father. As a child, she and her mother had long confidential talks, in which the mother communicated details about the father's many faults. The woman grew up accepting her mother's views of the family situation. When the woman married and left home, she moved far away, and her return visits were brief and infrequent.

During family therapy the woman found it difficult to develop an open relationship with her father. It became easier when she began to realize that her father was not as terrible as she had believed. Her goal was to detach herself from the emotional dependence on her mother and to foster a situation in which the parents could fulfill the needs of each other.

The breakthrough came when she no longer wished to keep her mother's secrets. In the next meeting with her father she said:

"Daddy, do you know what Mother told me about you? I wonder why she tells me these things instead of telling you?"

A new flexibility developed in the family emotional system. Later, the father attempted to tell the woman some stories about the mother, which she reported to the mother. The woman recovered much self from the fixed parental triangle in which she grew up. The change in her parental family was only a side-dividend of changes in other areas in her life. She developed an open relationship with each parent; visits with her parents were so pleasurable that they visited often, and her parents were closer than they had ever been.

CONCLUSION

The family movement will play an increasingly important role as psychiatry goes into the 1970's. Family psychiatry has changed rapidly in the 15 years since the family movement suddenly evolved as a recognized entity. There is evidence that therapists have hardly scratched the surface of its potential. The movement may eventually have more to offer as a different way of thinking about the human phenomenon than as a therapeutic method.

REFERENCES

Ackerman, N. W. Interlocking pathology in family relationships. In *Changing Concepts in Psychoanalytic Medicine*, S. Rado and G. E. Daniels, editors. Grune & Stratton, New York, 1956.
Ackerman, N. W. *The Psychodynamics of Family Life*. Basic Books, New York, 1958.
Bateson, G., Jackson, D., Haley, J., and Weakland, J. H. Toward a theory of schizophrenia. Behav. Sci., *1:* 251, 1956.
Bell, J. E. *Family Group Therapy*. Public Health Monograph No. 64. United States Department of Health, Education and Welfare, Washington, D. C., 1961.
Birdwhistell, R. *Kinesics and Context*. University of Pennsylvania Press, Philadelphia, 1969.
Boszormenyi-Nagy, I. The concept of schizophrenia from the perspective of family treatment. Family Process, *1:* 103, 1962.
Bowen, M. A family concept of schizophrenia. In *The Etiology of Schizophrenia*, p. 346, D. Jackson, editor. Basic Books, New York, 1960.
Bowen, M. Family psychotherapy. Amer. J. Orthopsychiat., *30:* 40, 1961.
Bowen, M. Family psychotherapy with schizophrenia in the hospital and in private practice. In *Intensive Family Therapy: Theoretical and Practical Aspects*, p. 213, I. Boszormenyi-Nagy and J. L. Framo, editors. Harper and Row, New York, 1965.
Bowen, M. The use of family theory in clinical practice. Compr. Psychiat., *7:* 345, 1966.
Flugel, J. C. *The Psycho-Analytic Study of the Family*. Hogarth Press, London, 1960.
Freud, S. Analysis of a phobia in a five year old boy. In *Collected Papers*, vol. 3, p. 149. Hogarth Press, London, 1949.
Group for the Advancement of Psychiatry. The Field of Family Therapy. Report No. 78. Group for the Advancement of Psychiatry, New York, 1970.
Jackson, D. The marital quid pro quo. In *Family Therapy for Disturbed Families*, G. Zuk and I. Boszormenyi-Nagy, editors. Science and Behavior Books, Palo Alto, Calif., 1966.
Lidz, T., Fleck, S., and Cornelison, A. R. *Schizophrenia and the Family*. International Universities Press, New York, 1965.
Mittelman, B. Concurrent analysis of married couples. Psychoanal. Quart., *17:* 182, 1948.
Scheflen, A. Human communications: behavioral programs and their integration in interaction. Behav. Sci., *13:* 1, 1968.
Speck, R. Psychotherapy of the social network of a schizophrenic family. Family Process, *6:* 208, 1967.
Toman, W. *Family Constellation*. Springer-Verlag, New York, 1969.

10

Group Therapy with Married Couples

Helene Papanek, M.D.

HISTORY

The historical development of psycho-pathology and psychotherapy from the beginning of the century until the present time clearly goes in one direction: Clinical observation, diagnosis, and treatment shift away from the focus on individual psycho-dynamics and toward the understanding of one person's transactions. This trend toward perceiving an individual person as part of a larger whole, a subsystem within a system, has brought much progress to the field of psychiatry and psychotherapy. Understand-ing of a person within his system is more complete and more meaningful; description of behavior is more vivid; behavior is more predictable; and, thereby, therapeutic prog-ress is more effective.

Although it is true that the dyadic thera-peutic transaction can also be viewed as occurring within a system, two people represent a small and special situation, and the opportunity for a variety of observations, experiences, and behavior patterns is defi-nitely limited. In a group, the focus on a network of inter-related behavior patterns not only provides a multiple opportunity for relationships but also changes the viewpoint that personality patterns are the result of what the environment does to a person in the present or did in the past. Instead, there is an understanding that all behavior is mutual, that nothing is done to one person without his doing something to the other. Even the most neutral, passive analyst influences his patients. Even the most

victimized spouse puts himself in the posi-tion of being victimized and affects the victimizer.

Alfred Adler, in 1926, was the first to observe that:

Individual psychology regards and examines the individual as socially embedded. We refuse to recognize and examine an isolated human being.

Many years later, in 1968, Marmor said:

A proper awareness of the transactional opera-tions in the patient's life systems is extremely helpful in enabling the psychoanalytically trained psychiatrist to achieve a more sophisticated understanding of his patient's psychodynamics.

Psychoanalytic theory and practice had established the rule that each spouse had to be treated in separate sessions and by a different therapist. Marmor's statement is a perhaps temporary end point of a develop-ment that started in this country more than 25 years ago, when Mittelman (1944) ques-tioned the psychoanalytic tradition that transference and countertransference remain pure only if analyst and patient confront each other in isolation from any outside influence. Even telephone consultation with a professional who was treating a member of the patient's family was considered con-tamination. Mittelman (1948) focused on the complementary neurotic interaction in mar-riage and pointed out that simultaneous treatment of both mates by the same analyst has many advantages. Ackerman (1954) introduced the concept of spouses parentifying each other and emphasized the importance of family and marriage therapy, especially in social work agencies.

In 1956 Eisenstein collected papers from 25 authors who elaborated on conscious and unconscious interaction in marriage. His paper on group approaches to the treatment of marital problems is of special interest for those who have become convinced of the usefulness of married couples groups. Goller states that groups are considered useful only for the education of pairs of engaged couples or parents. Sherman says that group counseling consists of treating each partner of a disturbed marriage in a separate group, so that in no instance are two individuals from the same family included in the same group. And Hulse describes how therapy groups are used if a patient has an unhappy marriage. Group process then is focused on the psychopathology of the individual with marital difficulties. Hulse presents a case history to show how the untreated spouse and the marriage itself improve when group members become motivated as auxiliary therapists to help their married co-patient. He concludes that theoretical and practical experiences

seem to mediate against *direct* psychotherapeutic group approaches toward marital conflicts.

Hulse's viewpoint was soon modified, first by Ackerman (1958), who described how valuable joint interviews with both spouses are to elucidate neurotic interactions. If necessary, these joint interviews can be combined, with several therapists working as a team and seeing each family member separately. The practice of occasional joint interviews or spouses visiting groups was repeatedly recommended (Jackson and Grotjahn) and, since 1960, many reports of successful marital group psychotherapy have been published (Flint and MacLennan; Kadis and Markowitz; Leichter).

To a therapist who adheres strictly to a psychoanalytic approach and considers the development of fantasies and transferences as the most important therapeutic tool, married couples groups may appear to be based too much on reality conflicts: the couples may try to solve these conflicts by manipulation and retaliation. An excellent

paper by Gottlieb and Pattison summarizes the different viewpoints.

As married couples groups have become generally recognized, more recent papers have dealt with specific techniques, indications, and settings (Grunebaum and Christ; Reckless). All authors seem to agree that the therapist has to be an active participant to turn possible disadvantages into therapeutically useful interventions. As interaction or transaction—the terms are used interchangeably here—between group members is dynamic and emotional, the therapist should not remain distant or neutral.

THEORETICAL ASPECTS

The therapist can observe and infer from people's behavior in a social setting what has happened to them in the past, what is happening in the present, and what they anticipate happening in the future. Lewin said:

Specific experiences may appear, if seen as isolated incidents, almost identical but may have completely different psychological meanings if they occur as parts of a total process, if they are embedded in different contexts of occurrences.

By observing and treating patients in a social setting, the therapist is able to understand the purpose, motivations, and reciprocity of behavioral transactions and their effects on others. From these observations he can draw valid conclusions about the patient's real-life behavior. Only through the therapist's concentrated effort in shifting attention to some of the multiple behavioral items and combining them with other observations can he keep track of specific feelings and communications that go back and forth within his patient or between the patient and the therapist or group members.

Since the therapist obviously cannot focus on everything that is going on, he has to select and check on the relevance of his observations and integrate them into a meaningful whole. The never-ending complexity, unpredictability, and meaningfulness of human behavior can be as stimulating and satisfying for the therapist as creative work is for the artist.

Once the psychiatrist accepts the viewpoint that man can be understood and influenced toward change more effectively in a social setting than in artificial isolation, he automatically becomes interested in his patient's familial environment and in the marital transaction. The spouses together are then considered a small, permanent system of two individuals whose interaction is patterned and whose repetitive dynamics can be observed. The couple also lives within larger social groups, such as their own family, their extended family, their community, and their work group. The effect that each of these groups has on the person and the role that each person plays in these groups influence, in turn, the marital system.

Marital disharmony has existed since the institution of marriage developed, and means of helping to solve such problems are not new but have recently received the attention of psychotherapists. Marital therapy is psychotherapy designed to modify psychologically the interaction of two people who are married and have significant emotional, interactional, marital problems. The goal is to improve their behavior so that their marriage problems may be resolved, allowing for continued growth and development of both members of the marriage. Such therapy may consist of either individual or group techniques.

Individual therapy of each marriage partner may be insufficient, and new therapeutic opportunities open up if the marital pair is perceived by the therapist as a subsystem within a larger group. The therapist's observations on the embeddedness of one spouse in the marriage situation and of the pair in varied other contexts can provide decisive therapeutic leverages.

Various group techniques are used in working therapeutically with married couples. In *group therapy*, the treatment situation consists of a group of one or more married couples with one or two therapists. In *conjoint therapy*, the two marital partners are treated by one or more therapists in joint sessions. In *four-way marital therapy*, each marital partner is seen by his own therapist in individual sessions, and both marital partners and both therapists have regular joint sessions. In *combined individual and group psychotherapy*, marital partners receive both individual therapy and variations of different types of group therapy with one or more therapists.

These group techniques are outgrowths of *individual marital therapy*, where therapy is essentially individual psychotherapy of each of the marriage partners by the same or different therapists, who, if different, may or may not cooperate and communicate with each other. When the partners are in treatment at the same time but with different therapists, the term *concurrent therapy* is used. When the therapists cooperate, the term *collaborative therapy* is used. When all or some of the members in a family unit are treated in a group with one or more therapists, the term *family therapy* is used.

Marital counseling may consist of any of the above variations of marital therapy conducted on a more superficial, supportive basis by a professional—usually by a marriage counselor, a social worker, a general practitioner, or, on occasion, a psychiatrist.

Dyad with Visits from Spouse

The psychotherapist has to recognize the importance of stress or support in the marriage for each patient's psychological problems. It is recognized in good psychiatric practice that, if a child or adolescent needs psychotherapy, the familial transactions have to be taken into consideration; decisions have to be made about whether family members should be treated and, if so, what kind of treatment should be used. Similarly, in individual psychotherapy with married adults, the dyad of patient-therapist should occasionally be opened up to include the spouse. The visiting spouse may provide therapist and patient with new understanding of the patient's pathology and may throw new light on treatment goals and transference-countertransference feelings. This simple procedure of one or two sessions with a visiting spouse should be part of every psychotherapeutic training program.

Triad

If an individual patient or both spouses assume that marital discord is the cause of their unhappiness, they usually ask for marriage therapy or marriage counseling. The technique most widely used is the triangular situation—that is, conjoint therapy of a couple with one professional. Usually the therapist alternates between seeing the pair together and arranging occasional individual sessions.

The Square Interview

In this situation, each spouse has his own therapist, and all four people meet occasionally. This technique is especially fruitful when a married patient is involved in individual therapy. Sooner or later, the patient and his therapist recognize the transactional marriage problems and refer the patient's spouse to another therapist.

Lederer and Jackson enumerate the errors tha may occur in such a situation: (1) A therapist takes sides with his patient—that is, with one spouse. (2) A therapist views his role as a judge and looks for evidence to justify a verdict in favor of one spouse. (3) A therapist considers the spouses mismatched and unconsciously or covertly contributes to destroying the marriage. (4) A therapist feels that one spouse is sicker and delegates to the "well" spouse the role of assistant therapist.

Usually the two therapists try to correct these errors by repeated consultations over the phone or at meetings to discuss their patients. Sometimes these discussions do not clarify much. Another difficulty arises when some results of the consultation should be disclosed to the patient. How should the therapist's new insight be used? A distrusting patient may regard the consultation as a conspiracy.

Case History

At the age of 20, before her marriage to Charles, Greta started therapy. Charles, 24 years old, was referred to another therapist by his friend, a former patient. He would never have accepted a referral by Greta's therapist, whom he did not trust.

The marriage had been a stormy one from the beginning, since neither one of the young people had had adequate mothering, and both were immature and dependent. They had hardly any-

thing in common: Their national and religious backgrounds were different; Charles' tendencies were toward hippie culture and the radical left; Greta espoused middle-class values. They were unprepared for their two small children, whose conceptions were accidental. They fought about everything and made each other continually miserable. They remained together because of the children and because each was afraid of isolation and loneliness. Charles had seen Greta's therapist a few times and was convinced that Greta's doctor was against him, since the doctor reinforced her middle-class values and expected Charles to conform.

The young people fought especially about basic decisions, such as the appearance and location of their apartment, the handling of money, and who should take care of the children. Charles' therapist suggested to Greta's that they meet the couple on their home ground. Greta and Charles had subjective and very different images of their apartment. It was a dirty, depressing hovel for her and an expensive, cheerful place for him. The therapists decided to make their own inspection in order to get a more objective image.

The apartment was partly a hovel and partly bright and pleasant, depending on whether you looked at its rear or front, whether you paid attention to its location in a dismal house and street or focused on the apartment itself and the view over the roofs of New York.

Subjectivity of viewpoints, values, and the hierarchy of what seems to be immediately important became crystal clear. The therapists saw that the differences of opinion between Greta and Charles could be solved easily. Each hid behind the shield of superficial difficulties a deep fear of being swallowed up by the other one and of losing his own identity.

Results. The meeting of both therapists with both patients in their life space and seeing their children and stage of their quarrels not only enabled the two therapists to communicate with each other and to rectify their errors but also helped to demonstrate to the couple the strengths and weaknesses of the marriage. The greatest impact of the visit was an awareness on the part of all four people involved that each person is different from the other but that mutual respect and consideration for each other can prevail. Acceptance of this attitude became the realistic goal for this family, leading to mutual appreciation for each other, therapists included.

Charles' progress in therapy and his development of a more secure and more giving relation with Greta was to a great extent based on the square interview. Both therapists recognized the lack of communication between the spouses, the intensity of their fear to give in and thereby be obliterated by the other. This fear had grown steadily during their therapy; each felt that the "enemy" therapist had strengthened his own patient's attitudes and viewpoints against the spouse. This fear disappeared when the four faced each other and communicated freely.

The therapists understood the mutuality of their patients' neurotic transactions. Each therapist liked and was nice to his own patient but felt a responsibility for the family unit. Therefore, the therapists were firmly committed to help their patients to be less afraid, less stubborn, more helpful, and more accepting of the spouse. It took approximately 20 months for this one interview to bear fruit in the therapeutic process, but all through this time the memory of the common experience influenced all four people.

The square interview illustrates that individual therapy, in spite of its intimate atmosphere, which should be the vehicle for corrective emotional experience, frequently proves insufficient for the achievement of personal change.

Therapy Group with Visits from Spouse

The rationale for this method is similar to the one described before—marital difficulties ascribed by one patient to the other spouse. In the case of the group patient, the four errors mentioned by Lederer and Jackson may be mistaken assumptions by one, several, or all group members.

A married patient repeatedly complains to the group about being mistreated or abused by the spouse. The group member tries to explain why all this happens to him, the innocent victim of this cruelty, but the group cannot find out why the unhappy spouse stays married to such a scoundrel. Frequently, the group feels puzzled or irritated about the absent spouse, who apparently behaves in an irrational or inconsistent way. The member's complaint does not seem to make sense.

The spouse may be invited for one or more visits. The impact of giving group members the opportunity to observe the marital transactions directly is much greater than if the therapist were to explain or make guesses about the marital problems.

Case History

Ann, an attractive, 30-year-old woman, was referred to a therapist for combined individual and group psychotherapy after two years of individual psychotherapy for alcoholism, sexual promiscuity, and depression. Her husband, Arthur, was in treatment with another psychiatrist.

After six months of combined treatment, Ann described one of her drinking bouts, which had been followed by loud, irrational behavior on her part and difficulties with the police. These difficulties endangered her own job and the couple's reputation, which was an important factor for acceptance in their community and in the husband's profession. She also described how Arthur contributed to her alcoholism at home by mixing drinks for her at night.

The group responded with protectiveness toward Ann, was annoyed at the husband, but was also impatient with her repetitive, destructive acting out. They decided to invite Arthur to a group session. This confrontation had tremendous impact on everybody. The marital transaction became very clear to all group members and was followed by working through for many sessions, with stormy and varied emotional participation.

It became clear that Ann and Arthur married because each was searching for a partner who could provide security and companionship in a basically hostile environment. Arthur's present life goal was to gain success in his profession and be respected by his peers in his community for his work. His whole sense of autonomy and identity depended on this.

After a confusing and rejecting childhood, Ann had found only temporary relief from her anxiety and depression in sexual affairs and some short periods of work achievement. Her impatience and selfishness had repeatedly destroyed her hopes for longer-lasting satisfactions, in spite of her intelligence and attractiveness. In her marriage she expected and demanded constant gratification of her insatiable dependency needs. If Arthur did not supply her with endless attention and reassurance, she felt such despair and loneliness that she acted out by drinking, by being promiscuous, and by suicidal gestures.

Arthur explained in the group how impossible it was for him to give her what she wanted. He was tired of her wild behavior and he wanted to get away from her to work for his own life goal—professional success and autonomy. What kept the marriage together was Arthur's guilt about deserting Ann. Her fear of losing whatever support she found in the marriage was another factor, combined with both spouses' hope for a better adjustment through therapy.

When it became clear to Ann that the group members understood the mutuality of the destructive transaction in the marriage, she became extremely upset, angry, and anxious. The confrontation in the group acted as a shock to her. Her feelings of security and acceptance in her own new "family" were shaken by the shared insight of what went on between the spouses. She felt that the group took her husband's side, as he explained that he was well aware that Ann wanted from him only "a warm body next to her" to protect her and that she was neither able to give anything in return nor willing to try. Ann's consecutive treatment in the group and in individual sessions made it possible to use this confrontation constructively.

Results. This method exposes the interlocking marriage neuroses to a group that "belongs" to one spouse. The visit by the other spouse adds a new dimension to a therapy situation that may become symbiotic or to a group where cohesiveness and mutual support hinder progress.

Ann and Arthur were an inward-facing couple, fully occupied with their own misery, which had to be hidden from the world outside. The discussion of their unhappiness with individual therapists and with Ann's group had only strengthened the interlocking marriage neurosis. Confrontation with the spouse had a dramatic impact on opening up the in-fights of the couple and had a lasting effect on the imperviousness of their mutual hatred.

After Ann got over her initial feeling of being betrayed, she, for the first time in her life, developed some sense of social feeling. She realized that acceptance by her peers gave her security and helped her to grow; that mutuality and exchange is essential for acceptance by others; that it is hopeless and self-defeating to be insatiable in one's demands, whether they are directed toward a spouse, a group, or a therapist. Preoccupation with her past life and with the reasons for her neurotically destructive behavior was replaced by a hopeful interest in future possibilities of becoming a person by socially useful behavior.

The episode had a positive effect on all group members. They felt responsible for Ann's upset and for the gradual growth process that followed. The shared experience gave each patient a sense of importance and commitment to each other and to therapeutic work.

Therapy Group with One Married Couple

This method seems especially indicated if fear of intimacy is the focus of the couple's problems. No discord or arguments occur between the spouses, and neither one has infidelity on his mind, but they vacillate between their desire for closeness and their need for privacy. Such indecision can go on for years and may not be solved by interpretation or insight in individual therapy. In the group situation, the partners find corrective emotional experiences and different degrees of closeness and learn that they themselves are able to determine the degree, amount, and times of closeness. They find out that marital intimacy is not an all-or-nothing principle but can be worked on cooperatively if each lets the other one know what he desires and what he fears.

Case History

Sophia started treatment after graduating from college. She was frightened by a lesbian affair with a classmate, especially by her friend's suffocating demands for closeness. Both girls were very intelligent, highly motivated for therapy, and depressed and confused about their involvement. After a joint interview with Sophia and her lesbian friend, the girls decided to break off their friendship, and they started individual therapy with different therapists. Sophia continued with her therapist for about two years, the second year in combined individual and group psychotherapy. After dating several men and after having a short but stormy sexual experience with an aggressive man, she met Joe, a compulsive, bright, and intellectual young man. After a long, drawn-out courtship they got married while both were aware of their conflicts and doubts.

Joe had some months of individual treatment with Sophia's therapist and then, with the therapist's consent, joined Sophia's group. For about 18 months Joe and Sophia were the only couple in a group of eight. In addition to the couple and the therapist, the group consisted of one single man, two married men who were in the group without their wives, one divorced woman, and one widow.

Joe and Sophia's marriage was a typical complementary relationship: Joe had a compulsive personality, with rigid defenses and an intellectualized, cautious approach that protected him from the threat of emotional closeness; Sophia had a hysterical personality, with fluid ego boundaries, shifting identification, and strong dependency needs. Joe detached himself during childhood from a weak, despised father and a complaining, demandingly close mother. Sophia never developed an integrated self-image, since she felt estranged from her cold, ungiving mother and ambivalent toward her inconsistent and at times seductive father.

Both Joe and Sophia wanted closeness but were too frightened to trust and share. Sophia had greatly profited from group psychotherapy. She convinced Joe that their marriage could improve through common experiences in her group.

Results. While the spouses participated as the only pair in the group, they grew much closer by using all opportunities offered for corrective experiences—exposing their individual selves, angers, disappointments, doubts, and affection for each other as far as their anxiety permitted. They got to know each other by communicating, responding, and interacting within the safety of the group.

The group became a new family, providing a milieu with healthier experiences than either spouse had had in the past. As Joe and Sophia found more relatedness to the other members, they discovered more of themselves. Each developed a firmer awareness of his own identity. As each was less anxious about the self, he could go out more completely to the other. On the other hand, the group members perceived and related to them as a pair, although at times one of the spouses was singled out according to the needs of the other members. Independent of the couple's real age, the group assigned them the roles of either advice-giving parents or siblings in need of the group's guidance. Either way, there was much mutual progress.

In the therapy group with one married couple—as in the square interview and the therapy group with visits from a spouse—the therapy situation itself is manipulated and new dimensions are added. This changes not only the neurotic marriage structure but also the homeostasis that has developed between patient and therapist or between patient and group. In the new settings, alternatives of behavior emerge almost automatically. Previous roles do not fit the new therapeutic unit, and, with the

change of the system, the individual people assume new behavior patterns. Then the therapist has the opportunity to encourage patients to communicate, to trust each other. Neurotic anxiety disappears and self-esteem increases if a patient is able to understand and cope with the novel therapeutic situation.

Married Couples Group

One basic conflict characterizes all marriage neuroses: need for closeness and fear of it. People whose fear is greater than their need for closeness do not get married. Those who do not experience closeness as a threat to their identity are able to establish satisfying relationships with their spouses, with mutual respect and understanding of their differences.

The ability to integrate individuation and intimacy is a skill learned in childhood. Adequate satisfaction of dependency needs is an important factor in the child's development. If this growth process occurs, the mature adult is ready for a close, secure, reciprocal relationship. If, however, the parental harmony was never achieved or was interrupted early in a child's life, he will as an adult vacillate between his desire for intimacy and fear of loneliness on the one hand and, on the other hand, his need for separateness and fear of closeness.

Whenever the maturation process is disturbed, the marriage relationship shows disharmony. The married couples group uses all the potentialities that the therapeutic group offers to help each spouse understand what he is missing in their relationship, to loosen the interlocking neurotic pattern, and to promote healthier relationships by strengthening his sense of identity and self-worth and developing his ability for mutuality and cooperation. Marriage bonds are strong and emotional, even if neurotic. Therefore, communications and interactions in the married couples group are at a high pitch. Group process develops by temporarily disrupting an unhealthy, conflict-ridden cohesiveness between the marriage partners. In the beginning, the couple can hardly listen and relate to anybody else except each other.

The other group members are perceived as audience or court of appeal, not as individual people. When attention shifts and group members become individuals, the therapeutic process of insight and correction of neurotic needs, expectations, and fears can begin, and the unfinished maturation process can proceed.

The married couples group usually consists of three to five couples—that is, six to ten patients. The most favorable therapeutic situation seems to be four couples. The therapist does not feel overwhelmed by too large a number and can observe and respond to each group member. At the same time, the group is large enough for varied and shifting interaction between patients.

The married couples group may have either one therapist or two co-therapists (Kadis). If co-therapists are able to express differences, note Gottlieb and Pattison, they provide

a model of two leaders who can work together effectively as individuals, who do not always agree, and yet maintain a respect and personal concern for each other.

It is a well-known fact that marriages can deteriorate, even if each spouse apparently improves in individual therapy. Frequently a patient's resistance to change is so frustrating that the therapist prefers not to recognize a standstill and perceives progress whenever a patient just continues treatment. While therapist and patient work on intrapsychic conflicts, they forget the patient's family. The triadic approach may also prove disappointing, as each spouse tries to pull the therapist to his own side and the therapist's attempt to focus on mutually destructive interaction is ignored by both.

In a married couples group, the therapist learns how to focus on interaction and becomes skilled and secure in confronting couples. Instead of concentrating only on the couple, he perceives their behavior in a broader context. A patient who seems sadistic, stubborn, and rigid in relation to his spouse frequently becomes a helpful, empathic human being with other group members. The couple's distrust and anxiety is lessened if they see that they are not the

only ones who have to appeal as a last resort to the marriage therapist, whom they expect to save them from being failures by telling them who is right or wrong.

Of course, the married couples group is no cure-all, and it has its own difficulties, but it adds a new dimension to treatment. The therapist can try to use the combination of marriage dynamics and group dynamics to exert therapeutic pressure and to overcome resistance. Some patients deny marital dysfunction and want to work on their intrapsychic problems only. Others are committed to work on marital problems only and are unaware that their own anxiety and their own needs may destroy the marriage. For the second group of patients, marital fighting is the final common pathway for all disturbing emotions. Marital discord can be considered a symptom, an expression of intrapersonal and interpersonal maladjustment. In the group, therapist and patients turn the searchlight of attention on the couple, on the individual and his past and present relationships, and also on his transactions in the group. Each patient in turn is lifted from the background of the group to present a well-defined pattern of behavior which is part of his life style and of his family life style.

Case History

From the beginning, the group was a stormy one. The four couples had all been married for more than ten years. Each couple had two children, ranging in age from eight to 15 years. Individual and marital pathology had lasted for many years. All four wives had had previous psychotherapy: Karoline and Roberta for about two years each, Barbara and Sarah on and off for many years before and during marriage. Bill, Barbara's husband, had gone through many prolonged therapeutic attempts, but the other three men had refused any consistent therapy. These three gave in to pressures by their wives and agreed to join the married couples group after one joint interview and occasional individual sessions with the therapist.

The loudest, most outspoken, in-fighting couple were the R's, Robert and Roberta. They exemplified Haley's description of couples who do not agree about rules for living together, about who is to set those rules, and about attempts to enforce rules which are incompatible with each other.

They argued in the group about Robert's double standards. He was jealous if Roberta enjoyed herself at a party, but he wanted to flirt with attractive women. Repeated arguments erupted because Robert was very fond of his parents and visited them every weekend and sometimes after work during the week. Roberta's parents were dead; she did not want closeness with his family and was intensely jealous. Other arguments concerned psychotherapy itself; Robert thought it was a nuisance—nothing was wrong with their marriage or with him. Roberta was "too selfish" and lacking in respect and understanding for him, he said. If she had exaggerated demands, she should continue her therapy and leave him alone. Roberta was never intimidated by his loud, deep voice and his coarse expressions. She talked quickly and emotionally and usually gained the group's sympathy with her sincere wish to improve the marriage, her concern for her teen-age daughters, her unhappiness, and her hopeful trust that therapy would help.

The R's had a tendency to monopolize the group; they always wanted to argue and tried to use the group as a trial court. They were the most immature and outspoken people in the group. They had a symmetrical marriage neurosis; both were dependent, demanding people. The support Robert craved and did not get from Roberta he received from his mother. Roberta felt united with her daughters, but she still felt dissatisfied. She powerfully manipulated Robert into therapy, and she tried to manipulate the therapist to make Robert over so that he would supply what she needed. Roberta frequently complained about Robert, addressing only the therapist and excluding the rest of the group. This behavior, plus the couple's desire to monopolize the group, antagonized others. On the other hand, both were liked because, when they related to their co-patients, they were spontaneous, warm, and empathic.

By contrast, the K's, Karl and Karoline, seemed to get along better while they were in the group. They left when Karoline became secretive and Karl started to distrust her and, consequently, the therapist.

During the period they were in the group, both Karoline and Karl became aware of and verbalized feelings about each other more openly than ever before. But what Satir calls the role discrepancy could not be worked through. Karl could not separate his self from Karoline's, and neither one could accept the needs of the other.

Neither one was able to feel a deep and realistic attachment for the other. Karl had obvious schizoid and paranoid trends and a pervasive anxiety that others, including his wife, would humiliate and exploit him. Only when Karoline was soft, yielding, and pliant could he trust her. Then it was delightful to be close to her. On the other hand, Karoline was very competent, ambitious, critical, and as much on the look-out for the strong man as Karl was for the ideal soft and competent woman. Karoline said that he erected barriers to closeness with his impossible expectations. She had tried before and during the marriage to find the strong man who could vicariously give her the self-esteem she lacked. Her infidelity destroyed Karl's trust in her.

The S's Saul and Sarah, were very bright, striving, and self-searching. Sarah's emotionality frequently broke out in semi-controlled eruptions of anxiety and anger. Her personality pattern certainly could be called hysterical, but it lacked some of the self-dramatization and self-centeredness usually associated with hysteria. Sarah's past history included a childhood of frightening and confusing incidents in war-torn, Nazi-dominated Europe, which explains some of the lack of emotional integration. She married— one would like to say, "of course"—a quiet, withdrawn man, much older than herself. Saul resented being subjected to outside influences. His unwillingness to participate and to get involved was obvious, which became quite a challenge for therapist and group. To this man, who wanted so much to hide and be left alone, the group situation presented a bombardment of external irritations. He could, however, blend into the background in the group, and he found group treatment more tolerable than individual treatment. In fact, he was untreatable in the one-to-one situation because it was too threatening to him.

The B's were both very controlled, intellectual people. Years of therapy had not done much for them. Barbara had repeated attacks of self-doubt and depression, during which Bill took care of her. Bill was a compulsive personality and had his own self-doubts and perfectionistic preoccupations.

Barbara's anger was open; Bill's was hidden. He felt much better when she felt worse. On the other hand, they were similarly damaged people. Rejected as children, they lacked self-acceptance, which made them vulnerable and constantly in need of support by others. They were like babies in need of each other—Bill wanting praise, Barbara desiring an omnipotent father figure. If these needs conflicted, they settled temporarily on disengagement, which, they felt, should solve their own problems and possibly other couples' problems.

Results. The married couples group lasted for about two years. One couple, Karl and Karoline, were divorced a year after terminating therapy. During follow-up sessions with Karoline, she maintained that she was much happier without her husband. No follow-up was possible with Karl; he felt betrayed and angry with therapists in general. The marital relation of the other three couples improved. Robert and Roberta discontinued therapy after two years and considered themselves a happy family, satisfied with their lives and free of symptoms. For Bill and Barbara and for Saul and Sarah, intramarital conflicts and accusations became less frequent and less intense. Their marriages remained stable without major friction. In both cases, sometime after marital therapy had ended, the school authorities advised treatment for the children, and the couples began family counseling at neighborhood agencies.

CLINICAL EXAMPLE

The following excerpts from transcripts of married couples group sessions show how the group moves forward under the therapist's leadership. The members' interaction gives the therapist an opportunity to strengthen the growth potential in every patient, to decrease the need for dependency and the wish to dominate, to increase mutual understanding, and to alleviate the fear of being hurt and dominated by others. Every move in the right direction is encouraged. Attention is focused on specific meanings. Communication is facilitated, and misunderstandings are clarified. Some incidents have a strong emotional impact during the group's development. Within the stream of the group process, spouses stick together as isolated units for better or for worse. They separate and touch as individuals with other individuals. They reunite again as couples in a better integrated and resilient attachment to each other.

First Group Session

Barbara: I get mad when Bill does things like that, you know. And why do I get mad? Because I want him to be different. He's

who he is, and I always want him to be someone else. But when Saul calls Sarah a phony, when she talks about work that means something to her, I don't think this can just be considered as "All right, this is what he is, this is the way he is" and let it go.

Therapist: Yes, something painful happens.

Sarah: Well, with whom am I living? I think it's incredible that I should be living with such a person. Why did I get married to someone like that? If you live with someone, and you cannot have an emotional relationship with someone, I don't see what's the use.

Bill: Well, I don't see the balance of the reaction between you and your husband because in the little bit I've seen between you, you're a very live person, and you're attempting to change something or achieve a goal. But all the time I've seen Saul, he has certainly not been attacking or changing you, he is a very reserved individual, a very closed individual, a very angry individual who can't stand a certain amount of pretense, even in the people here. It's gotten to the point where—I don't *think* I'm that kind of person basically— but I've begun to feel, "Geez, I'd better watch out, or he'll pick me up for something too."

Therapist: You know when I've seen Saul most emotional, when he showed a really tremendous amount of emotion, and he was surprised himself that it came out? It was about the question of Vietnam and peace and these things, and he has his own viewpoint, which conflicts with his friends'. But he really was so unhappy about it, I was terribly surprised.

Roberta: I think Saul tends to get involved with intellectual rather than emotional things, anyway. Saul gets involved, I think, in things that are safe for him—emotionally safe.

Sarah: This isn't safe for him—not this question.

Roberta: What I meant by "safe" was, for him to get this much involved with Sarah is somehow more threatening to him personally. Vietnam is less personal.

Sarah: I have very strong feelings about my work, but I suppress them constantly so I can function as a mother—as a mother and a housewife and whatever goes along with it. But I'm trying very hard to function as this other person.

Barbara: Would you like to paint?

Sarah: It would be marvelous to see what I could do again, after ten years.

Barbara: Well, why not do it?

Karl: Maybe Sarah is a lot like myself now, always crying about not having enough time to do this and that, and, given the time, I don't do it anyway.

Roberta: We have a bit of a problem. About Thanksgiving. This year, I had asked his sister and her family, and I told Robert I would make it. Then I called my brother and my new sister-in-law, Rose, to invite them, and they were most anxious that we come to their house for Thanksgiving dinner. So I said, "All right." And I told Robert we were invited, and he had hysterics. It seemed to be working out just fine with his sister, except that Robert has refused to accept it. He insists that I make Thanksgiving dinner for his family.

Robert: Roberta, I wouldn't like to call you a liar. . . .

Roberta: Call me anything you like—just explain yourself.

Robert: I didn't jump in when you spoke. Now let me speak. It's very rarely that you make a commitment, Roberta. When you make it, I'd like you to fulfill it. The new sister-in-law was just over for dinner this Saturday.

Roberta: She wasn't over for dinner this Saturday.

Robert: All right, it was a party— but dinner was served. What the hell's the difference? All I'm trying to say is she was there this Saturday. All I'm trying to say is there's another group of our relatives that have to come in another month or so. Also, her brother is a fellow that I can't stand. He's a leech. You know what a leech is? It's a guy who has never stood up to his responsibility, a guy who never once shared his responsibility with me. Oh, Roberta, you are disgusting! You have been such a taker through the years. . . .

Roberta: (shouts something at Robert.)

Therapist: Now, look, you can shout at each other all you want at home. It's so nonsensical if you exclude us all. If you really don't think you can get anything out of the group, why do you need us as an audience? It's not the function of the group just to listen to how each raises his voice and repeats things which perhaps don't seem really important to us. I don't know what seems important to the others.

Barbara: Maybe I'm sitting in Saul's chair—I'm feeling like Saul!

(Laughter.)

Sarah: Well, you have an affinity with Saul anyhow!

Barbara: Yeah, now I feel more like him than ever! I couldn't even get what the issue was. I don't know whether I'm dense or I just shut it out.

Bill: I don't like your family; you don't like my family.

Barbara: I want to invite my family to dinner, and he wants to invite his family to dinner.

Bill: I hate this discussion.

Barbara: Well, I guess this is where they get entangled.

Robert: How people can lie—how she can sit there—such garbage.

Therapist: For two years I'm the expert with Roberta and Robert.

Roberta: Not quite.

Therapist: A year and a half. And we don't get anywhere. And this way, you don't know this festers—this thing. And there is something terribly wrong about your way of thinking.

Bill: It seems to me you people ought to decide who you're married to, that's all.

Roberta: Thank you, that's what I've been telling Robert. There are two families—the first family and the second family. I feel the wife and children are the first family; he feels differently.

Barbara: Well, you're really neither of you committed to what you said should be the first family. You're both terribly attached.

Roberta: Well, I'm being very vengeful at this point.

Bill: Well, apparently both of you are.

Barbara: Well, like my family vs. your family— I think everybody has a little bit of that— but with you, it's like your whole life!

Roberta: No, at this point it's me vs. your family. And this is the way it's been for the past few years. It's not my family—it's me.

Robert: You'd better learn one thing, Roberta— there are other people in this world. You've gotta learn that! You're not alone.

Roberta: No, but I'm first.

Robert: You're not alone. Learn that.

Roberta: I answered you. I said I'm not alone, but I'm first.

Robert: You're first?

Roberta: I won't be second, Robert! I'm either first or I'm nothing! And the choice is yours to make!

Robert: Well, you might very well be nothing.

Roberta: Good!

Barbara: Why do you keep competing?

Roberta: Because Robert has put us in opposition.

Karoline: But you're perpetuating it.

Roberta: Yes, I am.

Robert: You know what made me laugh, though? (To Barbara) Last week Roberta somewhat chastised you. Roberta said, "Do you mean, Barbara, to say you're not involved with Bill's needs?" You cater to my needs in some way?

Roberta: Only when you cater to mine.

Sarah: Divorce is the only thing.

Barbara: But where do you go from there? After divorce?

Sarah: You live by yourself.

Bill: Very depressing to most people. We tried it.

Sarah: I haven't tried it.

Bill: We tried it for about six months.

Sarah: It was very hard for you?

Bill: Oh, boy!

Barbara: You find out you torture each other, but there are things you need in each other, I suppose. Although it was harder for me than it was for him, even though *he* moved out, and he had to find a place to live and everything. He seemed to be doing better than I. I kicked him out and then I. . . .

Bill: She kept saying I was a no-good bum, you know. . . .

Barbara: The minute he left—very shortly after he left—he became very attractive to me.

Sarah (to Robert): I was thinking that you were the one who was *so* much against divorce, of all the people in the group.

Robert: There are exceptions, but it's terribly distressing. . . .

Sarah: When I hear this and when I hear all the other horror stories that go on and when I see myself what I go through sometimes. . . .

Barbara: Try separation—don't make it legal.

Sarah: Even separation—it's very difficult with children.

Bill: Everything's difficult. You seem to be very suggestible. You've got to do what's right.

Barbara: All this row about Thanksgiving dinner, and I've totally forgotten what problems we were going to bring up. Maybe that's one advantage of a group.

Sarah: There are people who think, "It's only me." There are millions of groups like ours, Barbara.

Karl: A quiet crisis can often be worse than a stormy, noisy one. I don't quite understand the problem. Karoline's been very depressed lately, and I find it very, very painful—far more painful than our stormy sessions. I have more sympathy for her now.

Second Group Session

Sarah: Saul's brother called us to find out how we are, and I guess he was concerned about Saul, and I promised that we would come as soon as possible, and it so happened that yesterday we could go there, and I was terribly embarrassed because, while we were there, Saul put on the TV for half an hour after not having seen . . . and Saul, he looked at you, you know. Your brother—he was astonished at you, you could do that. He wanted to talk for a half-hour not with the children, with me and with you, and they were looking at that football game. I thought, how you are going to do it after the football game, and you turned the knob and said, "Now let's go," and he looked— you should have seen his look. It was terribly sad. You can't be so inhuman.

Saul: You are completely misinterpreting. . . . Obviously, he was terribly embarrassed by our presence.

Sarah: He was very happy.

Saul: He was very happy and at the same time terribly embarrassed and found it difficult to talk.

Sarah: He always stutters. He has such a severe stutter that he can't, but that it. . . . He wants us to come.

Saul: You asked him a few questions, and he sort of mumbled an answer.

Sarah (raising her voice): The man can talk, Saul, give him a chance, let him stutter, but don't put the TV on and make it even more embarrassing for him and then leave. And aren't you terrible. I can't get over you, really.

Saul: Well, it is difficult to understand.

Sarah (hysterically): No, I understand it perfectly well.

Saul: Understand? The tremendous embarrassment that exists between us always existed between us.

Sarah: But why does he ask us to come?

Saul: He wants to see the children.

Sarah: He wants to see you. Forget about the children.

Karoline: Why is he embarrassed?

Saul: Well, it's this chasm between us, and he is totally paralyzed intellectually and. . . . He works in a factory.

Sarah: Saul, you walked out with your head down because you felt badly.

Saul: No.

Sarah: You want to be completely independent of everyone. It is becoming much worse. Your brother at least says he wants to see you, but you do not say that to anyone.

Therapist: If you torment him much more, he will not want to come here.

Saul: I want to see the friends I want to see. You don't invite them and you don't invite them until I insist. (Loudly) So don't say I don't want to see anybody. There are people I want to see, and I asked you to invite them, and you deliberately insisted on inviting other people. That made me very angry.

Sarah: Very good. You always want only a few people.

Saul: Very well, I have a few good friends I want to see and keep.

Sarah: Very well. I want to see a whole variety of friends. Don't always go to the same ones. . . . Make it a little broader.

Saul: Well, that is not so. Please give an accurate picture of what happened. You asked me whether I wanted a certain couple over for Thanksgiving, and I said I would rather spend the day with somebody I would feel wholly comfortable with. I didn't say it angrily. And you came back with another couple with whom you know I would be more uncomfortable, and that's when I got angry. You accused. . . .

Sarah: I still invited them.

Saul: After I exploded.

Roberta: Doctor, I give up. When we left here, I said to Robert, "if you go to Puerto Rico"—he said he would go to Puerto Rico for four days—I said, "you can't come back." We got in the elevator. He said, "Don't make me hit you." We were right back where we started from. I am not taking any more. I can't. I have not got the stamina.

Robert: I generally threaten to hit you, Roberta, when you start to throw a couple of your fancy adjectives at me.

Barbara: Something occurred to me. Did you have the same feeling while your mother was alive? Did you have the same feeling about Robert and his mother while your mother was alive?

Robert: When your mother was alive, Roberta, your attitude toward my folks was a little different because you would take your mother to the country. You would also take your mother-in-law and father-in-law to the country.

Roberta: I had no choice. The feelings were exactly the same.

Therapist: But your mother was alive.

Roberta: Oh, yes, my mother was only dead it will be two years. . . .

Barbara: She always resented the fact that she no longer has a parent and he has. Somehow she holds this against him. Something has been taken away from her that he still has.

Robert: Maybe I want a little kindness. Roberta, you could say, "No, I would rather you would be here with me tonight." Period. It is as simple as that.

Karl: What would happen?

Robert: I wouldn't go.

Therapist: You, Roberta, really don't believe he cares at all. This is behind all of this.

Roberta: That is not true.

Therapist: You think he cares for you?

Roberta: I think Robert has a very limited capacity for emotion, but as much as he has, I think he cares for me.

Third Group Session

Therapist: Somebody lost her wedding band last time she was here.

Sarah: There's a whole history to my rings. This one I bought for Danny. It became sort of a wedding ring. When Gertie and Danny were babies, I bought them each a ring because I started to believe in jewelry. So now I'm wearing my son's ring, you know, which is also crazy.

Roberta: You got married without a wedding band of any kind?

Sarah: I had a Woolworth's ring—you know, one of those little fake things. I didn't believe in jewelry, but I have a craving for jewelry now. And then, when Gertie and Danny were small, I bought them each a beautiful ring. And the ring that was given to me was no good anymore. So I said, "Well, I'll buy Gertie and Danny one, and I'll wear theirs for a little while because it fitted me." Then in Vermont I found a beautiful ring.

Roberta: I think it's very strange that you buy your children rings when they're small, and you wear them.

Sarah: Yeah, because I want to be a child really —that's what it is. I want to go through that whole thing again. First of all, I buy toys. When I find a toy that I love, there's nothing nicer in the world.

Roberta: That ring that you lost—is that old?

Sarah: That's a very old ring, and I feel terrible that I did not miss it—absolutely terrible.

Robert: But that was Danny's ring, is that it?

Sarah: No, that's the ring that I asked Saul to buy for me this summer. And he said, "Yes," and he bought it for me.

Roberta: When I looked at it, I thought it looked very old.

Robert: Is that the only ring that Saul bought for you?

Sarah: Well, he never gave me a ring that *he* chose. He attaches no meaning to rings either, so he doesn't think it's necessary to give rings, but I find it very beautiful later on that people should have relationships, with jewelry and objects, for sentimental reasons. I'm also wearing my ring that my parents gave me. I had discarded that ring for many years, and I don't dislike my parents so much any more. So now I wear Saul's ring. It has my name in it.

Saul: I'm touched by her attachment to the rings.

Robert: I don't think Saul goes for some of that symbolism.

Bill: You dropped the ring last week?

Sarah: Yeah—and didn't miss it.

Barbara: Well, she's got four of them. All of them she got herself.

Robert: No, this is the only one Saul got for her.

Therapist: Boring, huh, Barbara?

Barbara: If we had something to say. Coming here, I said this to Bill, and he said he thought he wanted to stay, and I said, "Why don't you ever bother to say anything? You're always sitting around, trying to pontificate about other people's. . . ."

Bill: That I don't speak as much as I would like about myself is that I can see in Barbara quite clearly an air of irritation and disgust and short temper whenever I'm involved.

Barbara: Well, it's pretty stupid to sit in the group and not talk because I disapprove, because what are you here for?

Sarah: When you first came into the group and tried to talk a little bit or to participate, it was very forbidding.

Barbara: But if he's going to not talk in a group therapy situation because I'm forbidding, I mean, it seems ludicrous.

Roberta: How do you do in a group when you're by yourself, not with Barbara?

Barbara: It's a good question. Answer it.

Roberta: Is it really Barbara, or is it the way you normally react? Do you tend to hide your own problems?

Bill: I don't think that what Barbara's saying is so valid anyhow. She's just using this as a pretext to avoid what she wants to avoid.

Barbara: Well, it wasn't the reason I wanted to leave. I felt this way, and since you sat here apart from it all and. . . .

Bill: Well, that's the way you categorize it, but is it really an accurate statement?

Barbara: I don't know. You always make points like that—I categorize everything and "accurate statements." Am I supposed to answer that question?

Therapist: You, Barbara, said something like

that—why does he want to come if he doesn't talk? So in a way I think you said his wish doesn't make sense because he doesn't talk enough, which doesn't imply that you are dying to come here. You might have other reasons for not wanting to come here, but perhaps you could agree to Bill's wish if you could see that it makes some sense.

Barbara: You're probably making me much nicer than I am.

Bill: Yeah, I had a very strong impulse to say that one before.

Barbara: It's not only a question of what you want. We're here because it's supposed to do something for the marriage. Does it have to be for you or for me?

Robert: Well, it's not only that she wants you to talk; she wants you to talk in a certain manner. She wants you to talk not up here, she wants you to talk down here.

Sarah: Are you willing to live with this, Barbara? Because if you do, try to understand him. But apparently it has something to do with you, too.

Barbara: I don't know if it's basically to do with me.

Bill: Isn't it amazing? She can sit there so calmly and lie, if you want to use that word. I mean the trouble is that she's a bitch of the worst kind.

Therapist: They're learning fast from the R's.

Roberta: They're learning from us?

Bill: I haven't used that particular phrase, but you know better. Take Sunday morning, take any day you want. How do you react? You spit in my face. You don't get up and do anything. You blame every God-damned, idiotic, stupid thing on me. *I'm* the angry man. It's ridiculous, and you know better. Isn't it true?

Roberta: Undoubtedly, he must contribute somehow—maybe as I contribute by not handling things well. But from the very first day these two came in here—ask Robert—I said over and over, "Why does he take it?" She never opened her mouth to say anything nice or to say it in a nice way when she's dealing with him. And I said this to Karoline and Karl once when I met them coming up here. I come week after week, and I listen very carefully, and I wonder what holds this thing together—and why. I don't see any point unless they can work it out. It seems horrible to me—just horrible—the worst I've ever come across.

Robert: That people are unrelated with each other's needs?

Roberta: He seems to deal with her more feelingly than she deals with him. I don't say that he necessarily does the right thing, but I have a feeling that she spits in his eye, and he turns the other eye.

Therapist: You think he did it tonight?

Roberta: No, I'm talking about the total situation. This is the feeling I keep getting week after week. The only thing about Barbara is that, when she says something really excruciatingly cruel, she says it quietly, so she sort of seems to get by with it. But I don't think that makes any difference.

Robert: But in all fairness, Barbara's not mad at him.

Roberta: She should be mad yet?

Bill: That's not true. She's always mad at me. I play a symbol in her life. All her frustrations and all her bitterness—at her family problems, I suppose—she's always taken out on me, always. She's always angry with me. All right. But what kind of relationship is this where I get up day after day—a symbol—to have to make coffee. I'm not stupid. I know how to make coffee—good, bad, indifferent—I make coffee. She can't make it. I have never sat down at the table that she doesn't give me a long tongue-lashing about "It's too strong." "It's too weak." And about how stupid I am. And she does this not just about coffee but about. . . .

Roberta: But this is very typical. Why do you make the coffee? I'd let her make her own coffee.

Barbara: You mean the impression here is that I don't know how to make coffee?

Bill: The impression is perfectly clear that you've got a big mouth. You talk a lot, you're nasty, and you don't do anything. You let me do it.

Barbara: I really think you're psychotic, Bill.

Sarah: I'll tell you something—we have it the opposite way. In our house I have to wake him. I say, "Saul, time to get up," and I wake the children. And it's a little better now, but there were times when I had to call twice, three times, to come down. Already in the morning I have to yell at people to get up. And it's very annoying. I mean, I should have to say it once, and that's it.

Barbara: What if you didn't wake him?

Sarah: Huh?

Barbara: What if you didn't wake him? He's an adult.

Robert: Or what if he didn't feel like getting up at that time?

Barbara: He's punishing himself. I'm oppressive to you in one way, you're oppressive to me in the other way. I am getting up later and later, so you're out of the house.

Bill: I'm a furious man who imagines all this. I make it up. That's why the children laugh about all this and run away from you.

Barbara: My children run away? I'm very relaxed when Teddy and I are home together. Everything is very nice. You come in, and everything starts to. . . .

Bill: You know everyone knows you're an impossible person to deal with. It's common knowledge in the family.

Therapist (to the R's): You have the same kind of arguments.

Roberta: Not over food.

Therapist: No, not about food but about something else. But it's just as hard to know. I mean, here you have two people who presented an item of five minutes' duration, or 15, on how he makes the coffee. Now, if I understood it correctly, Bill is saying he wouldn't mind getting up earlier and making the coffee if Barbara would appreciate it and not criticize him for it. But she criticizes; therefore, he doesn't make coffee any more. Barbara says it would be very nice if he would get up early and make the coffee, if he would do it right, and he wouldn't expect her to appreciate it.

Roberta: She said something else, too. She said she doesn't like to get up in the morning—she really doesn't like to face him in the morning—and she'd just as soon wait until he gets out of the way.

Robert: Not that she doesn't like to face him. She just doesn't like to get up in the morning.

Roberta: I think this thing in the morning is part of our total relationship. I know that, when Robert and I are getting along, I enjoy having breakfast with him. When we're not getting along, I can't wait until he leaves the house. I can't face him really and start the day that way. I can't look at him. But when we're getting along, I enjoy having breakfast with him and chatting.

Barbara: What a bore to spend your life blaming all your troubles and all your problems on. . . .

Bill: What a bore to be such a nasty individual. Why it is necessary? Who are you to tell me not to play the radio all the time? Do I do that to you?

Therapist (to Saul): You don't like either one? (Laughter.)

Robert: She always puts Saul on the spot! (Laughter.)

Therapist: You like Bill better. (To the S's) You both like Bill better.

Sarah: I like her a little, too.

Therapist: You like Barbara, too? I thought you don't like Barbara.

Barbara: What difference does it make who likes whom? Does it make a difference?

Robert: How someone else sees you, Barbara.

Sarah: That's what it's all about.

Barbara: I don't like people that easily. It takes me a while. I would like to know what the other people think of Bill!

Bill: Speak, speak.

Saul: I like Bill.

Therapist: You like him? Why?

Saul: I don't know. I see in him a lot of what Barbara sees in him.

Therapist: Anger?

Saul: Oh, I see the anger and the tendency to pontificate and generalize. I dislike that in him, but it's not an overwhelming feature in his personality. It's a strong feature.

Bill: I agree with you.

Saul: And that's the only feature you've revealed here today to me, actually. But there's a general cast to your personality which I find attractive and which I like.

Therapist: Can you say what it is?

Saul: Well, I would say there's an openness about him and a directness and a willingness to lend a hand. There's a flexibility in him that I detect.

Therapist: A certain kind of humaneness?

Saul: Yes, for others. So, on the whole, I sort of like Bill. Whereas Barbara, I see sort of a mirror of my least attractive self. She has a lot of the features I detect in myself and don't care for. So that tends to play a very valuable role in this group for me.

Barbara: What are they? Can you be specific?

Saul: Well, I see it as a hostility and an inability to participate—really, fundamentally, that's my sort of paralysis here, too—and a certain arrogance—superiority—toward other people. I mean, it might be misinterpreted as that. I sort of demonstrated those qualities, too. I might even agree with you that you're not arrogant, you're not superior, but there's a certain air about you which might lead people to believe you were.

Therapist: Do you know what he's talking about?

Barbara: Yeah, I know what he's talking about.

Saul: I know these are all sort of unpleasant features.

Bill: I think Saul is a very quiet individual but a keen observer.

Roberta: A tremendous one. I think Barbara's outstanding characteristic is her lack of interest in anybody else or their feelings, where Bill might frequently be on the wrong track, but at least he's somehow involved.

Therapist: I seem to be extremely tolerant of Barbara. I mean, that's my personal bias. I feel always that, like, she is a naughty child —self-centered, annoying.

Bill: Well, I've gone a little beyond that theory by now, as you probably realize. I just think Barbara's problem is that she never grew up in certain....

Therapist: And yet for me she has a certain charm. She has a certain amount of humor, as if she would be aware that it's not quite serious.

Roberta: Well, she's very bright and expresses herself very well, but I think the things that are acceptable in children are surely not acceptable or attractive in adults.

Therapist: If they know they're childish, this is a very winning element. If people are childish and believe they are very grown up, this is much worse.

(Laughter.)

Bill: Well, I've come to the conclusion that many of these irrational things I feel so annoyed at are childish....

Therapist: Well, if you see the childishness, why do you have to make a judge out of her?

Bill: A judge?

Therapist: Why, if a child is in a bad mood in the morning and goes around with a sulky face and lets everyone know about it, why does one have to take it so seriously? I wouldn't mind if you said, if she criticized the coffee, "Oh, please shut up!" But why get angry or hurt about it?

Bill: Oh, I do pass it off. But I don't know if in the basic sense I would be able to adapt that way.

Barbara: You're not so grown up yourself..

Bill: But the interesting thing to me is that the pressure that brought us here—it's about two months or thereabouts—nobody is talking about—neither you nor I. I literally dragged you as gently as I could to some kind of therapy because this was a serious matter for you—you were very disturbed. But no one's talking about this.

Robert: No one knows about it.

Bill: No. I mean, it's irrational to go for six weeks....

Therapist: Without knowing why she was so depressed?

Bill: Not knowing or—it's unrealistic that six weeks ago you couldn't get out of bed, you couldn't talk, you were crying, you were upset, you couldn't work, you couldn't relate to anybody, you couldn't do the simple. . . .

Barbara: You say that with such relish. Boy, oh, boy. And exaggerated. But go on.

Bill: You couldn't perform the simple, humdrum operation known as moving a household. You couldn't even perform a small portion basically. I think the greatest thing you achieved one day was that you brought me a sandwich in the midst of everything. That's why you were dragged here. And six weeks later, "I ain't got any problems," "This thing bores me," etc., etc. This is quite a switch.

Barbara: Fantastic.

Bill: What's fantastic?

Roberta: Well, what did happen, Barbara? You certainly came in very disturbed.

Barbara: Yes, I was, but this complete exaggeration—not, I think, because you want to attack me, but you want to see me as even more helpless than I am when I am helpless.

Bill: What was your major role? You cried; you ran out of the house; you were looking for a hotel; you were running around; you didn't know if you could drive the car; you were screaming; you couldn't pack; you couldn't stand the mess; you were in good shape!

Barbara: But I didn't do anything?

Bill: Basically, no. The major thing you did was attack me furiously for everything I did. I couldn't lift a finger to move before you got hysterical. You don't remember this.

Roberta: What *did* you do, Barbara?

Barbara: Well, it was very distressing, but there were certain things I did—as much as I could—but I couldn't do much.

Bill: You did very little.

Barbara: But tell me something—why is it so important to recapitulate that now? You said this is the most important thing. Why?

Bill: I think this very disturbed behavior and the subsequent way it worked out—where we couldn't relate to one another and couldn't relax, and there was no give-and-take—became a very serious thing.

Roberta: Would you say at this point, now, the marriage is on the level it normally is?

Bill: I have been very tense about this, yes. What do you think the chief source of my feeling tense was? You. It was absolutely impossible to. . . .

Roberta: You asked her what she thought the chief source of your being so tense was, and you didn't let her answer it.

Barbara: Even when I'm not tense, you are—

about every job. And you're very furious about things that are delayed.

Bill: No, that's not true. This is a sort of retaliation. I want to rub your nose in the dirt.

Barbara: I've been going, I've been looking, I've been shopping. I don't feel the pressure. He wants to make it "pressure." Like he said—he never said it before, now I understand—he wants to get even with me.

Bill: That's a view I don't agree with.

Barbara: But I don't think it could be that conscious, really.

Bill: Some of these things are very conscious. In general, I have always bent over backward and borne the brunt of everything that had to be done.

Barbara: This is the whole reason.

Bill: And I always minimized your problems, your failings, your neurosis. But I've gotten pretty God-damned fed up with all your. . . . So I figured it's time to act like other people act and give you the crap you deserve because you're very frightened and you're very inefficient and you don't do things.

Barbara: And you're not for a moment going to let anything settle down peacefully at all.

Bill: The reason things are not settled down is that there's very little interchange between us—there's very little relaxation, sexual or otherwise.

Barbara: But this is an exaggeration. "Only I can do it. She does nothing. She's helpless. She's psychotic."

Therapist: Barbara, nobody's psychotic. I'm sure Bill's not psychotic. So far Bill doesn't convince me you're psychotic either. But the fact is somewhere around four, five, six weeks—you were very disturbed. The non-finished apartment makes you tense. Bill, you said you are tense because you want to do a good job. You are tense in another way than Barbara. If Barbara is tense, she doesn't do anything. You do compulsively. You think about it all the time. You want to do it quickly and as best you can do it. You become very compulsive. Your interest is centered on it. She wants to run away and leave it to George. George is usually you, right? So now she is better—there are still certain things missing. Now you think you can expect her to do her share finally because she's better. And she still doesn't do what you consider her share. So your are still compulsive about it.

Bill: Am I furious?

Barbara: Not outside, but inside.

Robert: You know, I think "Two pats on the head, and you can do it your way"?

Therapist (to Sarah): What do you think about Saul's identification with Barbara and your identification with Bill?

Sarah: What do I think about it? It's correct.

Therapist: Is it?

Sarah: Yes.

Robert: With Bill I get the impression many times of a coiled spring. I don't know why. There's a vast amount of energy there that's looking for release. If he would just relax a little more, I think things would happen.

Roberta: I think, the entire relationship between them is very bad. It's very strained. The normal, daily exchanges aren't there.

Sarah: This couple, our neighbors, with whom we are very friendly—the only people we really like—I completely identify now with him, and I think she is out of this world. I mean, I like her immensely, but I see all the things she does wrong and how impossible she really is. And I like him very much now. And I also think she is a little bit like Saul. Yes, very passive.

Therapist: And he?

Sarah: No, he wants to get things done. The strange thing with me is that, when I think about all the couples in the group, I think they get along very well.

Therapist: You think they get along well?

Sarah: I listen to all of it, and then I leave them, and I think "It must be better than with us. There must be something that's really better."

Barbara: Well, in a way you're right. We bring our problems here. We don't live like this 24 hours a day, seven days a week. Naturally, there are different feeling tones, different times. So you're right.

Sarah: I sort of idealize people very much.

Roberta: Why don't you idealize Saul? Your marriage would be so much better.

Saul: No man is a hero to his wife.

Robert: Roberta says you're probably the easiest guy to get along with in the world—you're kind, you're soft, you're gentle, you've never lashed out at Sarah. . . .

Roberta: He's not cruel; he's never cruel. Robert can be very cruel.

Sarah: He can be very, very, very cruel.

Roberta: It's cruel to her because she finds it hard on her for different reasons. But he never. . . .

Robert: Cruelty is in the eyes of the perceiver.

Sarah: There have been instances of great cruelty. The word "cruelty" is always used when you get a divorce, like "mental cruelty."

Robert (to Bill): I think he should try less to show that she was inadequate, that she was unable to cope.

Robert: Well, does she have to lay out flat? I mean, she tells you, "I can't cope" in many different ways, all right?

Bill: So?

Therapist: Robert would be a good marriage counselor.

Roberta: Yeah, but he can't work out his own problems. (Laughter.) This is very interesting. I was just thinking, as he was talking, the only time in our marriage that I felt Robert was really there—that I could lean on him and count on him—was the time I was completely unable to function. That was right after my mother died. I couldn't do anything. He was wonderful.

Therapist: It's called the "see-saw complex."

Voices: The what?

Therapist: See-saw, see-saw—one is down; the other one is an angel.

(Laughter.)

Robert: Well, Roberta, you've always had to be so powerful. I don't know whether Barbara's this way—with the big muscles. . . .

Therapist: You didn't have to demand then. It all came your way, without demanding.

Roberta: It was offered—willingly. He was there; he was interested.

Therapist (to Roberta): Sometimes I can't listen to you any more. Whether you are right or wrong is completely unimportant for me. And you sit up like a young colt, and you throw your head back, and you are so righteous. "I have to be first!" And you have this movement—I think it's terrible. In a proud colt one likes it.

Roberta: I'm not aware of any of these motions.

Therapist: I think some people might find this attractive. It's not unattractive for an attractive woman to make such a proud movement. But in the context of, "I want to be first!" you know, and with this movement, it expresses to me everything that is called narcissistic. *Me!* You admire me! That kind of thing.

Sarah: You know, when I look at Saul many times, I become upset, just looking at him, because he looks guilty, and he looks withdrawn. I used to baby him when I first married him. When we were first together, I remember what I did, but it didn't work.

Therapist: What did you do?

Sarah: He loves fruit. He eats tremendous quantities of fruit. And I made special fruit salads, and I was always concerned that he should have all that he wanted. I don't do that any more. I buy fruit, but I hide the fruit. It's so completely reversed. I knew all the things he liked, and I did them. I picked him up at work.

Robert: You've done a lot of nice things, but I don't think you've ever really accepted him as he is.

Sarah: As he is? It didn't work out.

Bill: I get the impression you're always trying to do nice things.

Sarah: You think so?

Bill: I certainly do. This is the impression I get.

Robert: No, she's a bit of a nudge. There are times whe she's schlepping him in, he doesn't care to be schlepped in. He says, "Leave me alone." Personally, I don't know how to handle someone who'd like to be on the periphery, and you'd like him in once in a while. You'd have to ask Saul how to deal with this. I can see a measure of her frustration in trying to say, "Come on in." I can understand Saul's point, too: "Look, I'm very content where I am."

Therapist (to Sarah): Do you think if you were less aggressive, less hysterical, less exaggerated, Saul could talk to you in a way which would clarify things? You are so overwhelming in your despair and critical attitude—"It's inhuman. It's wrong." Then you have his withdrawal.

Sarah: I don't see how I can change that personality of mine. I've been working on it for years, you know. I was much worse.

Bill: I don't think you're necessarily bad at all. You may be a victim of your past.

Barbara: He figures she's active, she's the doer, he sits back and lets her do everything. Obviously, Sarah feels she's a victim.

Bill: No, it isn't obvious. As a matter of fact, I think the four lines between us two couples are quite twisted and mixed up. I think Saul is depressed, but in some ways I'm depressed, too. And yet in some ways he's like Barbara. And in some ways I'm like Sarah. I think it's all mixed up. I don't think it's clear at all.

Barbara: Well, obviously, no one's a replica of anyone else.

Bill: You tend to be expressive, and Saul's having difficulty relating on the same level, I think.

Sarah: But he seemed very emotional to me when I met him.

Therapist: The problem is that Saul lacks part of her vivaciousness and emotionality, and, if it becomes overwhelming, it allows him to withdraw more, and then she becomes more angry, and this triggers a vicious circle. She has to have the right dosage of vivaciousness and emotionality—not so much that it's

overwhelming, but just enough so it's stimulating.

(Laughter.)

Saul: What's so difficult, if she works at it?

(Laughter.)

Bill: In little ways, I see Barbara.

Therapist: Come on, go into your childhood—five minutes. (Laughter.) There are many similarities between their childhoods but they are very different in ideology and beliefs.

Sarah: Saul had an Orthodox father.

Bill: Barbara's father is deceased now—a great rabbi.

Sarah: And did you dislike your brothers and sisters?

Bill: She detested them, except.... (Laughter.) Tell the truth, you have no respect for them.

Barbara: I do not detest them! I have great admiration for my brother.

Bill: You do?

Barbara: Well, because he rejected me....

Bill: I'm an atheist. I never go to synagogue or services. Her father was an Orthodox rabbi—looked the role, with a long beard, and didn't speak English easily—and I never had any Hebrew or Yiddish—and yet I was able to stand my ground and respect him and get along with the guy, which was a tremendous thing for me to do.

Sarah: Did you first move out, or did you marry Bill?

Barbara: I had moved out long before.

Sarah: You had moved out, and you were by yourself?

Bill: Well, wait a minute—depends on what you mean by "moved out."

Barbara: I had lived in about ten different places. I found out when my mother died that she had been the power. My father disintegrated. He was a big, strong patriarch, and, after she died, he was nobody. He just never came back to himself. His world was shattered.

Therapist: And you were not close to your mother, either.

Barbara: I was not close to anybody. My mother was very quiet. I think probably I was closer to my father because my father was a more emotional type. And even though he had a great deal of anger in him, he was more emotionally involved with us. Whereas my mother, who was always there and always took care of us—took care of him—didn't express herself very much about anything—very much in the background.

Bill: Well, the fact is that you were very close to your father, and you had a great yearning to be your father's little girl all along.

Barbara: Yes, I had that yearning for his admiration. I could never rate very much, and so, since I couldn't rate, I broke away completely. I had to outdo everybody. I was the most observant at everything. Until a certain age. And then I broke with them. Since I could not make it.

Bill: She happens to be a brilliant person. And do you know what a brilliant woman is in an Orthodox household? I don't know whether you're aware of this. She's shit, to put it bluntly.

Barbara: Oh, Bill, that is so exaggerated—so exaggerated.

Fourth Group Session

Barbara: Weekends become ghastly. I make them ghastly, I think.

Bill: I can remember a time when I used to shake when the weekends came up.

Barbara: It was very bad, and then, after a while, it was all right. It's a matter of being able to live together if you don't live together too much. You know, the disengagement was possible. It was just on the weekends that it was like this. And, you know, I went back to being able to function during the week. It was all right. But I've been trying to figure out why. I've got it all worked out. There's something that makes me absolutely furious—he can make me more furious than anything else. I think I know why, but it's almost too pat an answer. He makes me furious because I seem to want him to make the world work very smoothly—there shouldn't be any problems. He's to take care of things. You know, he's the father, he's the mother. If something goes wrong in my other life, I may get mad or I may not. I act more or less like an adult. If something goes wrong at home or if he does something I don't like, I'm like a child who thinks, "This parent can make things go right—how can you make things go wrong?" It's really crazy. And then, when he reacts—so that, even when I'm not blaming him for the thing that's going wrong, he thinks I'm blaming him. And then I feel, "My God, you know, this is impossible." And it's happened several times this weekend. And yet today is Monday, and I'm fine. I went to work, and I'm an adult. On the weekend I'm a child, or in the evening. And he forgives me—forgives me so much. He's so good. Yesterday I stormed out of the house at about four in the afternoon. He was working, working, working, and there was something he did, and I

didn't like it, and I said so. And he said, "Well, everything, you know, you want me to do, everything's on my back." And he made me sound as if I was attacking him in a way that I wasn't attacking. This was just terrible because I was being criticized unjustly. I'm always criticizing. So I stormed out of the house at four o'clock. We were supposed to go to the ballet in the evening. So I went off by myself to the ballet, and I enjoyed myself. (Astonished.) I felt guilty, but being away from him again, I was an adult. You know, I could drive myself to the ballet, buy a ticket, take a long walk, have a couple of drinks, talk to people, enjoy the ballet (laughs), drive myself home. And at least I felt I shouldn't have done this. I called home. He thought, who knows where I went? I called home to say where I was. I told Teddy, my son. But I was just thinking, you know. I sat in the balcony, in the dark, and I wrote this out. I said, "He makes me furious—I wonder why?" Just what I said. I never can make calm comments about anything when he's around. He thinks I'm attacking, even when I'm not. I'm the complaining type anyway, but my complaints when he's around are—especially if they're crises—become just so exaggerated, so crazy. Frustrations—nothing is right—and he always thinks he's at fault. That's the hardest thing for me to take. Do you think that's going to make anything different? And yet today I felt great. And last night, when I came home, I forgave him, and I wanted him to comfort me, and there was sex, and I went to work this morning, and I was so sure of myself. But the next weekend—too much is not good, you know.

Therapist: If you both become babies when you are with each other. . . .

Barbara: We both become babies?

Therapist: I think so. Because he is so sensitive to your criticism, and he wants your recognition, and he wants Mommy to tell him he's a good boy. . . .

Barbara: And when I complain about *anything*—it can be something out there, the tailor doing something wrong about Teddy's pants or anything—I just blow up and say, "Stupid—why did he do that?" *He* thinks I'm saying it's his fault. Which I don't intend.

Therapist: But you said yourself you want a daddy who takes care of everything, who makes everything fine, and he wants a mommy who should tell him he's all right.

Barbara: Tell him he's doing everything fine.

Because he does things, after all, and he wants to be told he got a gold star. I think it has something to do with unreal expectations that we have about relationships, and, when it gets really close, it's something just tremendous that we expect. It just can't happen.

Karoline: Either that or we're so fearful that we really throw something in the works.

Barbara: We're afraid that it's going to be good, or we're afraid to get close—there's no doubt about that. I know, there's a fear of closeness.

Bill: I don't think I have a fear of closeness.

Barbara: Yes, you do.

Bill: No, wait, wait. Are you talking about in relation to people?

Robert: Well, you weren't referring to people then, were you?

Bill: No, I wasn't, I was thinking of. . . .

Robert: Well, wives are people.

Karl: When we're talking about our wives, we refer to them as our wives. I don't think we have people in mind. And why this fear? I mean, it sounded like a very glib statement— this fear of people. Why should you be so fearful of becoming close with your husband?

Barbara: Well, that's a complicated question.

Karl: No, I have no fear of being close with Karoline.

Bill: On your terms, you mean?

Roberta: I think Karl's fears are rather of not being close with Karoline. He becomes anxious when he feels there's going to be a division rather than a closeness.

Karoline: It doesn't even have to be when I'm being childish. It can be something that's completely nobody's fault, and he gets annoyed and he takes it out. . . .

Karl: I don't see how this applies to, you know, having any fear of being close to Karoline. (Pause.) I might have my tantrums. I find it so delightful to be close with Karoline.

Robert: On your terms.

Karl: Not on my terms. No, she has periods when she's very soft and charming. When I find her yielding, soft, then it's a very delightful state. I mean, I have no fear of being trapped.

Robert: But don't you sense those as your terms? Soft and pliant and the rest?

Barbara: It's always easy to be close. The fear of closeness takes the form of erecting all these barriers—either a temper tantrum or these impossible expectations or being a child who wants somebody to make everything all right.

Karl: I think it's a perfectly delightful state when we're close, and I prefer it to remain that way. I don't think that I erect barriers that are going to suddenly make us both withdraw.

Karoline: Well, I know that I do, and I think that you should certainly examine your actions in more detail and a lot more honestly and openly before you say you don't erect barriers, even though it's been very peaceful for the last ten days or so. I mean, we've had 17 years of barriers, erected very largely by you.

Karl: Well, because of external circumstances.

Karoline: Oh, don't give me that "external" business again—I can't stand it. When the car broke down and he screamed at me when I had nothing to do with the car's breaking down, there was a barrier.

Therapist: The point is, he doesn't feel detached then—he feels angry. Of course, it's true that you, Barbara, really don't feel much detached either. You feel angry, too, don't you?

Barbara: Furious. Furious.

Bill: Barbara for years used to blame me whenever there would be heavy traffic conditions or difficulties.

Barbara: I didn't blame you. If I complain about, "My God, what are we doing here in the midst of this stupid traffic," he thinks I am blaming the traffic on him. That's a perfect example.

Bill: Obviously, it hits me after a while. If you keep ranting, you're ranting at me after a while.

Barbara: The only thing I can do in a case like that is remove myself from the scene. Literally. Why can't I take this? Okay, he's defensive. He thinks I'm attacking him. I tell him I'm not attacking him. Let it go at that. But this is the unjust accusation somehow— when I am innocent, being told I'm guilty.

Therapist: It's like you couldn't forgive it that he's so childish?

Barbara: I am guilty somehow.

Therapist: At whom were you furious as a child? At everybody?

Barbara: The only way, if I were furious, I would cry. I would never get angry at anybody. I complained to whoever was in charge. Whoever could make things better. He wants to feel he's responsible for everything. And so he's to be blamed for everything. Why do you want to be responsible for everything? Why? No. No. That is something that we really have to work on. Believe me, believe me, because this makes me—where do I go from here? If I'm not blaming him, and he still thinks I'm blaming him. . . .

Therapist: Then he wants to be blamed because, otherwise, you deny to him the importance. Obviously, if you say you're only angry at the tailor and not at him, you're ignoring him.

(Laughter.)

Barbara: I'll remember this. If I know he enjoys it, then I won't mind if he thinks he's blamed.

Karoline: I've just been drawing so many comparisons between—of course, it's all mixed up, but I—before we started, I said to Karl, "I see many elements of me in Bill." Bill might not see them, but I do.

Roberta: But, Karoline, does Karl get angry when you do something that doesn't come out just right?

Karoline: He gets hysterical. But, on the other hand, I'm like Barbara in that, if I feel he's unjustly accusing me, I cry.

Saul: The question remains whether, after Barbara clearly says she doesn't blame Bill, whether it isn't really so that some real undercurrent of hostility doesn't exist in her against Bill, which he detects. Now can you answer that honestly?

Barbara: Of course there's hostility—enormous hostility.

Saul: Well, then Bill is not being paranoid in this situation. He's being perfectly sensitive to the real situation. You are not complaining about a situation. You are, in effect, complaining about Bill.

Barbara: I suppose if someone else were sitting there, I wouldn't have gone on at such length.

Therapist: And in a way this is always true. If something goes wrong and one has somebody close by—a husband or a wife—I think you said it—it's like hitting a table. I mean, it's nicer to hit one's spouse than to hit a table, but one would even hit a table. If one feels frustrated, one feels better if in some way one can let out anger against somebody than against an absent person, you know. I think it's more the question whether, in spite of these feelings, she is still rational enough to know that she is wrong.

Robert: I wonder, is she complaining about her lack of ability to do these things, and is there a kind of frustration about your own inability?

Barbara: I didn't feel competent in anything.

Therapist: In school, weren't you a good student?

Barbara: I was a good student, but I never believed I was. I never felt I was as good as the others in the family.

Therapist: And you felt incompetent in other respects, too?

Barbara: I can't remember anything I felt competent at, except to try to do everything perfectly, and I could never do it well enough.

Therapist: You must have married Bill, perhaps, in the hope that he would make you feel more competent.

Barbara: He was going to protect me, and he made me feel—yes—as if I were somebody.

Therapist: So perhaps that's why you expect him to do things perfectly. And he was very insecure himself, and he expects you to praise him for the things he does. And many times he tells me how perfect a piece of furniture he made. There's always something he's done so very, very, very well. And everybody would recognize it. Teddy. All friends. Everybody would know he did it very, very well. But you would come and criticize it.

Barbara: But why? If I recognize his competence and he thinks so highly of me, that opinion should matter more. If he's the only one in the world who thinks highly of me—you know, this is why I married him.

Saul: No, I've been making sort of a parallel between her situation and my own. Whenever I want to find some lost object, my tendency is to take it out on Sarah or the children or whoever is handy, although I might not. If I can't find a hammer, I'm sure to blame Sarah for the missing hammer—totally irrational. So that, in a sense, I understood Barbara's rage, even if she was objectively not complaining about him.

Sarah: Like this weekend. The whole weekend he was very nice to the children and to me, too.

Bill: I gather that you feel very much as I do in this kind of situation, that there are unnamed or unleashed furies against you which you just don't know how to cope with.

Saul: Unleashed furies within me.

Sarah: Well, I have plenty of right to be critical.

Therapist: There was this instance with Danny, when Saul said the whole homework was wrong, and it wasn't wrong. And Saul insists that Danny really wasn't so upset.

Sarah: It was a fantastic episode, you know, where Saul was out of his mind practically in saying it was all wrong, and I said, "Calm down, let's just see, let's see." And then Danny was right, and then Saul apologized. And then a week later, I suddenly hear, "All wrong!" And the voice was just terrible.

Saul: In this case it wasn't your intervention that made me recognize my error.

Sarah: But that thing in your voice that I heard—and I said, "Just a minute!" Then suddenly you calmed down.

Therapist: It's quite possible that at present Danny is less afraid of Saul than you. Because you have said many times that you are really very afraid of Saul when he gets angry.

Bill: I always hear your wife telling about how you react, but how do you feel in this situation? You never say anything. She talks, but you listen.

Saul: Well, on the whole, I think I have a rather good relationship with Danny, but it's true that I'm sort of disappointed in his school-work, and he has incredibly bad handwriting. When he denied he was wrong, he said it quite brightly. He wasn't at all frightened of me. He said, "Dad, I did it correctly," and that was sort of it, you know. And I looked at it again, and, sure enough, it was correct. There was no big, sort of, enduring scene. It blew over very quickly.

Therapist: I think what Sarah means is that Saul sounds angry when the boy doesn't even know why Saul is angry. Saul said he was angry that Danny didn't help in the back yard. And he lets it out like Barbara let it out on Bill. I mean, in a way, then, Danny is the table on whom you let out. You let it out much less on Sarah. You always see Sarah as so vulnerable. You've said you were afraid to hurt her feelings. You're much less afraid to hurt Danny's feelings than any woman's feelings.

Bill: That seems to be true. I've never sat here and heard you really say anything against your wife in terms of grievances.

Roberta: The truth of the matter is that Sarah *is* very vulnerable.

Sarah: That is true. I'm just thinking about it.

Roberta: So he's just realistic about it.

Robert: The truth is she's probably more vulnerable to his silence than to anything he might say. Even his hostility.

Roberta: Do you think Danny is vulnerable, too, or is he less so?

Sarah: Oh, Dan's very vulnerable. He cries very easily.

Roberta: I don't mean in general. I mean to his father in particular.

Sarah: Is he vulnerable to Saul? He's very small and a child, you know. Anyone can hurt him very badly.

Roberta: Yeah, but with Saul he might have a very good balancing relationship. . . .

Sarah: He looks up to Saul. He likes Saul. It's just that it's terribly uneven.

Bill: I must be obtuse, but, as I've sat here, I haven't seen any evidence of your vulnerability. Saul sits quiet so, at least superfi-

cially, I get the picture that, well, you, Sarah, are struggling with problems, maybe, but you're handling them all. You know, you're laying down all the rules.

Barbara: You say that about all women.

Bill: That's not really true, is it?

Barbara: Yes, it is.

Bill: Well, is it objectively what one sees here? At least, that's the way I feel in your case. What you've brought here has not been any evidence of "I goofed this" or "I failed that." Maybe you feel it, but you're not talking about it.

Sarah: When I started out, I did things pretty wrong. Now with Saul, I must have done a few things terribly wrong at the very beginning of the marriage. The whole thing there is about the marriage and how I look at it. I sometimes don't know about myself. The whole thing escapes me—my role. I can't think clearly about it.

Roberta: But suppose Sarah's criticism is justified? Is it still criticism in the same sense?

Sarah: I'm willing more and more to assume all responsibilities, but I cannot replace him as a father.

Bill: That's true, but why are you so anxious to assume all the responsibilities?

Sarah: Because he hates so many things.

Saul: Because she recognizes that I will not assume these responsibilities, and that's a realistic appraisal of the situation.

Bill: I don't know. No, I'm suspicious that you so calmly say, "I don't take my responsibilities."

Saul: I don't take the responsibilities she enumerated. I have my responsibilities in the household—I earn the living, I support the household, I. . . .

Therapist: But you have to take care of your back yard.

Saul: There are a lot of nonessential chores which I don't like to do, and I don't do them.

Karl: As long as you can get away with it.

Roberta: There are a lot of chores that are essential. They're not particularly enjoyable, but they're essential.

Therapist: Even if the standards in an abstract way might be right, let's say, that Saul should be less passive or more active, I think it's easier for Danny to adjust to a father who is less active than to hear that the father is criticized for his lack of activity. That was clear, wasn't it?

Sarah: Yeah.

Bill: Yeah.

Therapist: If Saul doesn't pay any attention at

all to Danny and doesn't enjoy his company and ignores him, then Danny might feel his father doesn't love him. But if he loses his patience and then he can say "I was wrong" I don't think Danny would feel he is not loved by his father.

Roberta: That's myself. I enjoy being treated that way. I enjoy the fact that Robert is more thoughtful. It makes my life much pleasanter in many ways, and, therefore, it makes my relationship with him much pleasanter.

Therapist: Now, if you would say that you just feel he cares more for you—that's really what counts.

Roberta: Well, it goes back to what you said a long time ago. I *was* spoiled. And I am accustomed to people being thoughtful of me, and I am very resentful when they don't treat me nicely.

Therapist: I guess we should get Karoline. What's wrong with you?

Karoline: I just feel like hell, thanks! Oh, I don't know—there's really nothing very specific—just a very general ach-h-h. Nothing's happened. I really had the feeling at this point that maybe I ought to be in a group—a non-married couples group.

Barbara: Well, is that a rule? That you can't bring up anything that has nothing to do. . . .

Therapist: Except she doesn't want Karl to know it.

Karoline: Karl even knows most of these things. Oh, and I'm sort of flirting with somebody now, and I know how absurd this is. And Karl knows about the situation.

Karl: A mild flirtation.

Karoline: A fellow I know in school, a divorced man. He said something about he'd like to drive with me in the country and—I don't know—just general talk back and forth—and I realized it was going further than it ought to go, and I had to figure out a quick way to break it without hurting anybody's feelings. I didn't really want to. And that bothered me because I should know better right now.

Karl: I would encourage an outside flirtation up to a certain point, and I would find myself. . . .

Barbara: He's going to decide what the limitations are going to be.

Karl: We all like to feel that we're still desirable, and if a person is somewhat attractive—and I could understand how this thing could have been carried to this point, and I appreciate the fact that she wants to terminate it and

she's willing to be very frank and open about it and—so what?

Therapist: I guess it's really not so easy to terminate—is that what you said?

Karoline: That's what I'm saying. It's not particularly easy. He's a very nice guy.

Karl: Well, I don't see what's so difficult about the whole situation.

Roberta: Karl, you're hiding your head in the sand.

Robert: You've always spoken quite highly about what you call the minor flirtation. I've heard you speak a number of times about it. Do you still consider it minor? Is it minor?

Karoline: No. When I feel I don't particularly want to stop seeing him for dinner, then it ceases to be minor.

Bill: You know, I've gone to dinner with women —that's one thing—but I don't think you're talking about that, Karoline.

Sarah: The first step—lunch or dinner.

Karl: You know, you never conveyed that you had any strong feeling—you liked the guy, all right, fine. I meet very many women on the outside. I like them very much, too. And when I went to college, I very often had supper with one person or another. I mean, so what?

Karoline: I said I'm not quite sure I want to stop seeing him, and I know very well it's the most absurd thing in the world to continue seeing him. . . .

Karl: Oh, well, you never told me that! The way she's presenting it now is certainly very different than the way she presented it a couple of days ago, I want you to know that.

Roberta: I don't think you made any attempt to read between the lines at all. You took her too much at face value.

Karl: Of course, you like him. There are a lot of girls I like. So what? I guess if the opportunity presented itself, I would even go to bed with them.

Karoline: Karl, that's exactly the point.

Karl: Well, I didn't know it was distressing her to that point.

Therapist: It's good he realizes it. I think you wanted him to realize it.

Robert: That's the whole point.

Fifth Group Session

Karoline: I dreamed I was married to you.

Robert: To me? Oh, you lucky girl!

Karoline: Yeah? Wait till you hear the rest of it. (Laughter.) And it didn't seem to bother you very much, incidentally. You were sort of "around." There was something I wanted to discuss with you, but you didn't want to listen—you just weren't interested, you know. It didn't concern you. And I felt it was very important, and, finally, I became irritated, and I said something to the effect that, "How did I get mixed up with you, you know, you stubborn guy—I would like out of this marriage." And you said to me with—I don't know, maybe hatred—"Ha, what can I expect of someone who seduces men in hotel rooms before they get married?" (Laughter.) So there—that's part of the dream.

Barbara: I think it has little to do with Robert and a lot to do with you.

Karoline: Well, no, I think it has a lot to do with the way I feel about Robert—the fact that he's stubborn, that he doesn't listen, even if it might be a rational argument or discussion—ideas on morality. Well, let's see, now. Right after that in the dream, I was sort of wandering around, looking at hotel rooms, and I left the building after that. I was very frustrated not being able to communicate and have the discussion that I wanted to have with you.

Robert: You don't recall what the discussion was about?

Karoline: No, it wasn't germane to the dream at all.

Roberta: You know, I think one of our biggest problems, really, is what Karoline just brought up—I, too, become terribly frustrated—I can't reach Robert at all.

Barbara: I think your dream is interesting. What about those men in the hotel rooms? You mean you've been seducing them in the hotel rooms?

Karoline: You want to know all about them? I only dreamed about Robert.

Barbara: I want to know why he accused you about that—why he felt you were guilty of that.

Karoline: Well, you heard the discussion when I mentioned that friend of mine in school.

Barbara: I still think it's strange that you dreamed it.

Robert: I represent the outside judgmental world.

Therapist: Yeah, I think you also feel that Karoline has many problems because she had premarital affairs. That's what you said.

Barbara: Well, I've always felt deprived because I didn't. There was something wrong with me. Because of my very strict background.

Karoline: How old were you when you married Bill?

Barbara: Twenty-six.

Sarah: I guess Karoline felt, "What would Robert say if. . .?"

Karoline: I just had a thought about one of the things that really disturbs me about Karl. When I want to go with you to buy clothes which you desperately need, you're always, you know, you're not interested. It bothers me.

Karl: But I think certain kinds of spending and—you know, we go into a restaurant, and if I pay 40 cents for two cups of coffee, I'll go out blazing mad.

Barbara: Oh, really?

Karl: I can't stand being taken, you know?

Barbara: Taken?

Karl: Taken. This disturbs me. If I made a bad purchase, it disturbs me. Like, for example, to spend $1,000 on a hospital bill doesn't bother me.

Karoline: Thanks a lot.

(Laughter.)

Karl: I say there's something very neurotic. . . .

Barbara: You mean, even if it's a very good cup of coffee and you sat there and really enjoyed it. . . .

Karoline: Karl wouldn't enjoy it, you've got to understand.

Barbara: Don't you ever go somewhere where they charge you 50 cents for coffee?

Karl: Never.

Karoline: If he does, I end up wishing I had choked on it.

(Laughter.)

Sarah: It's very hard when you've been poor once and you have. . . .

Karoline: I was poor.

Sarah: I understand it perfectly well. . . .

Saul: It has nothing to do with poverty.

Barbara: This thing of money, though, is a strange thing, because I have a thing about it, too. But it acts—and I've never been able to understand it. I don't think it's money. I think it's this "taken" thing. It's this suspicion. Because I can spend large sums easily, especially if I charge it. If I write checks, it's like it's no money, and it means nothing, and I don't worry about it. But I am always sort of suspicious of someone overcharging me or adding things wrong. I feel—it's this cheated feeling—somebody is cheating me. Then this is the same way when a purchase arrives. It's this thing about these big appliances and everything. Something's going to be wrong with it.

Karl: And, you know, it's realistic, this fear. Because of the things you order, you know that

60 per cent of the time—I'm not exaggerating—it's going to be imperfect.

Barbara: It's not. It's simply that you don't deserve it, that's all. I think it's all these nice things, and there's something about my not deserving it, and so, if I've got it, something must be wrong with it. And until it becomes mine and it's a little bit worn, then it'll be all right. I remember when I got this beautiful piano. I was looking for scratches. Something was wrong with it. Just the fact that it had arrived, and there it was, and everything was wrong with it, and it took a couple of weeks until I settled down to enjoy it. It's being cheated—someone's trying to cheat you.

Karl: It's realistic because. . . .

Barbara: A lot of things are defective, and a lot of things are not.

Karoline: You make shit out of everything!

Barbara: I know, I know exactly what you're doing because I do it, but I know how insane it is, how self-defeating it is, how self-lacerating. It's a self-punishment.

Karoline: Do you realize what you do to the children and to me and to yourself with this?

Karl: Oh, I do, I do.

Karoline: Have a bit of consideration for everybody around you.

Barbara: It's suspicion on the whole world, that everybody is doing things to you—you're being cheated. . . .

Robert: That's right. I got a little radio in the place recently, I got a brand new little radio, and a friend of mine comes in for lunch, and every time he comes in, he says, "Isn't that somewhat warped?" I say, "Gee, I don't know. I never really noticed. I don't think it's warped." He comes in the next day and says, "Isn't that knob a little crooked?" Gee, I didn't notice, but, you know, after a while, I never—I turn it on, and it plays beautifully. It's a good little radio. But if this guy comes in for another week, I'm going to throw the radio at him! He's looking, he's looking. . . .

Saul: Yes. Oh, that's murder, that's murder.

Barbara: I wish we could solve this problem because I have it, too. You know, I used to feel somewhat like. . . .

Saul: First of all, the statistical fact of whether 50 per cent or 60 per cent of the things you buy actually are defective—or 70 per cent—the economy conceivably could not run. I mean, after all, this is not Cuba. I've seen. . . .

Barbara: And look at all those marvelous guarantees. They come and come and come.

Saul: Actually, Karl may have had bad experiences with one out of 15 or 20 sets. I don't know what the point is.

Karl: Oh, I can tell you. In far too many cases. . . .

Saul: If, in fact, the probability of buying something defective is quite small, then the trouble of worrying about it. . . .

Barbara: Concentrating on it. . . .

Saul: Is out of proportion to the probability.

Karoline: You accept that, don't you, Karl?

Karl: Yes, I accept that. It doesn't extend to all purchases.

Karoline: It extends to every area of your living.

Karl: You know, being aware of the problem doesn't necessarily mean it's going to cancel itself out, Karoline.

Karoline: Yes, but you can maybe kind of swallow it a little bit, and it'll go away a little.

Karl: Oh, I can swallow it, but the emotion will still be there. How do I combat that?

Roberta: This is true. If you look carefully enough, there is always something not just perfect. And this was the excuse for not buying it. But as I've become freer with money, I don't even look, and it's much easier to buy. I think it has to do a lot with spending money—parting with it.

Robert: With you there's an enormous latent suspicion, and you've got to hang it somewhere. You started with 60 per cent, and Saul gave you two questions, and it was down to 20 per cent, and I think with a few more it might be down to 5 per cent, and we might put it where it belongs. That's probably where it belongs—a small percentage is damaged. But your need to feel so hostile toward all this out there—I think that's the key. . . .

Barbara: Well, do you feel that most of the damaged stuff is somehow going to reach you? Because that's the irrational feeling I had. It isn't a question of there's so much shoddy merchandise or anything, but, somehow, if I get it, there's going to be something wrong with it. This was this crazy pattern.

Therapist: Barbara, I think, in some way feels that she will get the spoiled stuff and other people will get the good stuff. As you said, you feel you're not worth the good stuff; other people may be. I think Karl really feels helpless. He really feels absolutely at the mercy of those slipshod people.

Karl: Well, you know, we're all at their mercy, actually.

Robert: Well, he sees it that way. How do you unconvince him?

Saul: Karl, you're saying two things. Firstly, you're saying that your feelings are irrational; now you're saying that actually your feelings are based on reality. And you can't say both things. One or the other is incorrect.

Therapist: This is how we spend our individual sessions. Sometimes I feel like I'm chasing my own tail. We start with something, and then he suddenly agrees, and in the next minute we start all over again, and we move around like a crazy weasel or whatever it is in a circle like that—whir-r, whir-r, whir-r, whir-r.

Karl: No, it's not worth it. I mean, it's stupid to live in fear. I mean, one can say there's a reasonable chance that anytime there could be a nuclear disaster, yet to. . . .

Therapist: We don't need a nuclear disaster to make that not important.

Barbara: It's not, "Well, in spite of the fact that all these things are terrible, I'm not going to care." You have to look at the other point. Not all these things are terrible. They are for you.

Robert: Oh, Karl, this pervades every nook.

Therapist: Sure it does.

Robert: Every nook, God!

Barbara: Karoline, you don't look as if you think anything is going. . . .

Karoline: No, I don't think anything is going to come of it. I've been fighting with him for so many years about the same things—the exact same things, year after year.

Karl: Why don't you focus on my virtues, Karoline? Let's talk about that. I feel as if I'd been pushed down to the ground and the dirt has been heaped on top of me.

Therapist: Well, tell us about them.

Karl: No, I want Karoline to tell. She once said a lot of nice things about me, and they're probably still valid today.

Karoline: Well, I certainly think you try harder than you did in terms of seeing into the things that are disturbing between us, and you're not *always* unpleasant. (Laughter.) And when you are relaxed and happy, which I'd like to see more often, you can be very charming. And you do have a nice sense of humor.

Karl: Keep going. I like it.

Karoline: You have a great deal of talent, which is lying dormant—very, very dormant.

Therapist: I don't believe in that talent anymore. I don't believe in it unless I see it.

Karoline: All I can say is I haven't seen it, you know, except what he did before we got married.

Therapist: He says there's nothing. I asked him.

Karoline: That he has no talent?

Therapist: No talent.

Karoline: Excuse me, he's very artistic. He's very skillful with his hands—very quick to pick up planning things, making things from scratch, you know. Very clever. You should see some of the things he's made in the house—the bookcase, the table, the lamp, the hutch. I mean, he made all those things—they're very beautiful. And they're not finished perfectly, incidentally. There are flaws in every one of the things he's made. But so what? They don't bother me.

Robert: It doesn't bother you. Does it bother him?

Karoline: No, it doesn't bother him. Because he did it. He did it the way he wanted to do it. They don't bother him one bit. No, what I'm saying is that the things that you make—and I can appreciate them—are not perfect things. It doesn't mean we enjoy them less. And everything you've made has been under duress—none has been willingly, with a full heart and happiness—everything has been with an argument.

Karl: What, everything?

Karoline: Well, the only thing I didn't fight with you about is the table you had to make in school.

Karl: You can't say "everything."

Karoline: No, I can't say "everything." Okay?

Barbara: Yesterday I got very depressed—suddenly very, very depressed about—and shut in—because once I got back to work today, it was gone. Bill was feeling very sick and very relaxed about it. I've never seen him quite that relaxed about being sick! I didn't resent it as much, his being sick. In the past I thought he had no right to be sick. You know, he takes care of things. I'm supposed to be sick; he's not supposed to be sick.

Karl: Sounds familiar.

Barbara: You feel that way, too? Karoline has no right to be sick?

Karoline: No, as a matter of fact, he was pretty gracious about my last incapacitation. That he was.

Therapist (to Saul): You're never sick? What happens if Sarah is sick?

Saul: Necessary things get done. I don't do it the most pleasant way, I recognize that. I'm not the greatest volunteer! (Laughter.) Sarah is sick very rarely, so I haven't been put to the test. One or two illnesses. . . .

Therapist: She's kind of mellow today, isn't she?

Saul: Yes.

Sarah: Yeah. As a way of not making things, you know, hard, but I don't try to do it in a way that would make me angry. I'm just sort of trying to philosophize about it and, in that way, withdraw.

Saul: Reduce her demands.

Therapist: Yeah?

Saul: It's another way of saying it, I assume.

Therapist: I mean, reduce her demands doesn't have to be to withdraw.

Sarah: Well, I wonder how this. . . .

Therapist: If Roberta, for instance, would be willing to have guests every three weeks, without Robert's helping her, and reduce her demands, she wouldn't withdraw. I don't think so. Perhaps she thinks she would.

Saul: That's because Roberta in that case would be imposing the demands upon herself— that's what you're asking her to do. In this case, Sarah's clearly reducing the demands she's making on me.

Barbara: But that might be an equal strain on her as Roberta's entertaining every three weeks.

Sarah: Well, I take it as long as I can take it.

Barbara: But it is a strain.

Therapist: What effect does it have on Saul if you reduce your demands on him?

Robert: He must flourish.

Sarah: Supposedly, you know.

Therapist: It's good for him?

Sarah: Supposedly. He's supposed to flourish.

Saul: I'm not reacting.

Sarah: No, you certainly are not.

Robert: No. It's very interesting, though, that, whenever Sarah comes in really full-blown and she's in every way draggin' you, you're here quite reluctant. If Sarah sort of leans back kind of morosely, you seem to do much better—infinitely better.

Conclusions

The group reflected in the excerpts above can be considered typical of middle-class people who have tried, more or less unsuccessfully, different kinds of individual therapy and who still feel trapped in their unhappy, conflict-ridden marriages. Haley describes the difficulties of changing a mutually destructive, neurotic marriage:

The first law of human relations: When one individual indicates a change in relation to another, the other will respond in such a way as to diminish the change. Or: a marital couple in difficulty tends to perpetuate their distress by attempting to resolve conflict in such a way that it continues.

Many examples of a couple's attempt to continue their pattern can be found in the tape recordings. As a matter of fact, most of the interchange omitted was purely repetitious of the same opposing statements: "You are a liar!" "No, you are!" Or, "This is a master-slave relation. You want me to be your slave." "Oh, no, you want to be the boss!" It gets very wearing. Sometimes the therapist wishes for a co-therapist, so he can tune out and get a rest instead of listening and trying to be resourceful in breaking up the vicious circle.

All troubled marriages are sadomasochistic in the sense that people continue to hurt each other and get hurt and seem to find satisfaction in it. A colleague, listening to the tapes of one session of the group, was inspired to write this poem:

Who takes shit from whom and why?
Who's angry, who is shy?
Who acts mean and who reacts?
Who lies? Who brings real facts?
Who's the villain, who's the bitch?
Who's the angel, who's the witch?
Who brews, who must drink the brew?
Who stews, and who eats the stew?
Each believes that he is right!
Such a marriage is a blight!

This poem reflects the writer's doubts about whether it is possible to effect a change in these neurotic marriages.

The purpose of married couples groups is to enable the spouses to find a constructive equilibrium instead of maintaining the mutually destructive balance. The system held together by a neurotic balance is rigidly closed off, leaving little room for satisfaction with the outside world of work and friends and even less space for children to grow and develop. Married couples, if neurotically entangled, have their private logic, which separates them from the flow of social events. Established patterns of a neurotic equilibrium have to be destroyed in marriage therapy. Some couples, out of anxiety about facing the world, stay together in spite of mutual, hidden hostility. This fitting together at the expense of differentiation of individual identities has been called pseudo-mutuality by Wynne et al. and Deutsch has described in detail a family life style based on

biased apperception of the outside world and its automatized reactions to or means of coping with this world.

The relationship of the K's exemplifies such an attempt to fit together by denying the intramarital problem. Karl wanted to involve Karoline in his paranoid world picture, vividly described by some of the group members in the fifth session. The fact that others shared Karl's plight is reassuring to him. But even then, he could not see his wife as a separate person. Unwilling to share his distortions, she was pulled into relations with other men, as she hesitatingly confessed in the fourth session.

Then Karoline reported a dream. She had dreamed that she was married to Robert. The group realized that the dream was influenced by the previous week's confession. It reflected Karoline's doubts about her own sexual values and her perception of Robert's judgmental attitude toward women. Karoline focused on her frustration and anger with men; they were "unreachable." This reaction probably pervaded all her experiences with men—her father, her husband, Robert as the prototype in her dream, and, as she revealed later on in her treatment, her lover, whom she had mentioned in the previous session. She did not find genuine self-acceptance or trust in others essential for a relationship with an approachable man. When the K's became aware of how little they really fitted together, they separated. There was never enough destruction in their marriage to enable them to achieve a new level of creativity.

The three other couples had been unable by themselves or in their separate therapies to destroy their old, neurotic marriage patterns and to create something new. When they came for conjoint group psychotherapy, they had battled for many years, but nothing radically new had evolved from it. All three couples were blaming each other and shifting responsibility for necessary change to the partner. The marriages continued through a series of destructions, but no new integration emerged—neither inside the marriage nor in the relation between spouses and outside world. As group members they had to go through a profoundly upsetting experience—first to understand what they hoped to achieve with their fights, then to learn to accept the impossibility of their expectations and each to accept his own share of responsibility for the state of the marriage and, finally, to create new patterns of relatedness.

The steps to be taken during the voyage from destruction to creativity are greatly facilitated by the group. Support and co-operation by peers with similar problems aids in the process. Communication becomes understandable and honest under group pressure. The perception of problems in others helps one to confront his own problems. In the group, patients develop more adult personalities and are less in need of a parent surrogate in the spouse. Loud quarrels, although frightening, sometimes clarify conflicts more than does denial of the realities of hidden anger.

The S's presented problems inherent in a marriage based on two opposite, complementary life styles. In all group sessions, the conflicts between Saul's hypoemotionality and Sarah's hyperemotionality were upsetting to all members. The therapist observed that each was able to have deep emotional responses, even if Saul was too reserved to express himself in a way that Sarah could find acceptable.

Further conflicts were triggered off by the S's perceptual discrepancy in interpreting common experiences—in visiting with Saul's withdrawn, lonely brother or in relation to their little son. Each time, the group raised the possibility that Saul might be, at least partly, more realistic than Sarah, who usually exaggerated.

Saul showed great sensibility to his co-patients. He liked Bill's helpfulness and identified with Barbara, whose arrogance and hostility toward the group process and the group members he shared. He showed warm feelings for Sarah, especially for her pleasure in jewelry and toys. He also encouraged her artistic talents. Roberta saw

Saul as "kind, soft, gentle." Others were impressed by his insight into the fury within him and his awareness of hidden anger in others.

Sarah learned to respect Saul and to accept herself as she developed her artistic creativity. She now finds public recognition as an art teacher and in art exhibits. The spouses communicate better and are able to share their interests and to accept each other.

The poem quoted above refers mostly to the R's and the B's. Roberta and Robert fought consistently and openly. They were most enraged when each insulted the other's family. They desperately wanted the group to take sides, but they received only sarcastic comments, like Bill's summary: "I don't like your family. You don't like my family." Or they were left to their own devices, as when group members agreed that separation or divorce was the only thing. The therapist stopped their arguments if she thought that the R's were wasting the group's time, and she suggested that, if they wanted to trade insults, they did not need an audience.

The session after this outbreak, Barbara helpfully asked whether Roberta had been more hostile toward her mother-in-law since her own mother's death. This seemed to make an impression on the R's. Suddenly they were able to show that they cared for each other. But Roberta kept insisting that Robert had to prove to her that she was first, and Robert blamed his wife for her selfishness. The therapist commented on Roberta's nonverbal communication in her body movements. She had the habit of throwing her head back like a proud colt, expressing: "I have to be first!" This observation induced some change in Roberta's self-centered attitude.

The R's problem with competitiveness—who is to be first, who dominates, and who has to submit—vanished slowly when they observed similar, apparently hopeless fights between the B's. Both couples described and gained understanding of their see-saw complex. When one partner was physically sick or emotionally paralyzed by fears and depression, the other one was most helpful and understanding. When one spouse was all the way down, the other one was high up,

like a helpful angel coming to rescue the helpless one.

Bill and Barbara had a symmetrical marriage. Their mutual criticism and disappointment with each other led to hatred and mutual contempt. Both wanted closeness, but Barbara needed a husband-father, Bill a wife-mother. Barbara usually attacked, and Bill defended himself. It helped Roberta to see Barbara's cruelty toward Bill and his weakness. Both R's felt that their marriage was better.

The therapist defended Barbara and said she acted like a self-centered child. If Bill would recognize her childishness, he would be less vulnerable to her moods. Then their complementary patterns were explained: Bill responded to stress with compulsive activity; Barbara, on the contrary, responded to anxiety by becoming depressed and paralyzed. Sarah identified with Bill's need to take active charge, while Saul and Barbara were the passive ones. Karl felt like Bill; both wanted praise and recognition from their wives. Barbara and to a lesser extent the other female patients wanted complete protection and care from their husbands. The husbands felt blamed and criticized if they did not get recognition. The therapist tried to break the deadlock by commenting on Bill's vengefulness when he was not praised adequately by Barbara. Perhaps his purpose in provoking her was to be criticized rather than ignored, as he at least got negative attention from her.

At this point, a spirit of cooperation and hopefulness prevailed in the group. The therapist suggested that the five minutes left be used for childhood recollections. Bill encouraged Barbara to do so and summarized with great empathy and concern her lonely childhood and her life style of self-doubt, guilt, and anger—a far cry from the B's clawing at each other at the beginning of the session.

One theme united the group more than any other topic: their paranoid distortions toward the outside world. Feelings of helplessness and worthlessness, fears of being taken in and exploited were expressed with intense emotional impact by Karl and Barbara and were, to some extent, shared by all. Karl, especially, held on desperately to his brittle paranoid defenses. The therapist tried, without much success, to help him shift these defenses or replace them with more realistic and less rigid ones. Karl felt more relaxed when he was able to ventilate feelings of distrust and isolation in the supportive atmosphere of the group.

The couples clung together to gain strength against outsiders. Then they were again torn apart and isolated when each spouse did not adequately support the other. Intramarital attacks replaced short-lived harmony. The therapist tried to make the point that the irrationality of hitting anybody or anything when frustrated is universal. One may be aware that the anger one expresses can be more or less destructive, depending on the vulnerability of the family member who is attacked. Robert asked whether vulnerability may be just a pretense used to avoid responsibilities.

The open discussion on basic insecurities and feelings of alienation either within society or within the marriage established a mellow and somewhat hopeful mood in the group. Perhaps it will be possible for the four couples to reduce their demands on each other. It may be a strain in the beginning, but it may help to see each other flourish. But will it be possible for one to see the other flourish without feelings of envy?

SUMMARY

Marriage pathology is the result of individual psychopathology. Two people form a bond in the mistaken expectation of finding security, trust, understanding, and intimacy. They hope that on the basis of such a relation they will be able to develop autonomy, competence, and a feeling of self-worth. If the marriage partners distrust each other and lack understanding, intimacy is replaced by anger and hostility. Each feels undermined by the other. They stick together because neither one knows what went wrong or how to change it. But they try. As long as the therapist is hopeful that he can strengthen the spouses' motivation and can find a way to show them that change is possible, the therapeutic process can move forward.

The first step is diagnosis. That means not only attaching diagnostic labels to a patient—though that, too, may be helpful for prognosis and evaluation of ego strength—but also developing a psychodynamic diagnosis of the marriage. In each group session, the patients try to understand themselves and each other. The therapist frequently clarifies, adds, and summarizes. The patient, unable to understand himself—"I think it's incredible that I should be living with such a person" was said by every one of the eight people when he was most desperate—is helped by the perceptions of the others in the group. Understanding of each person's neurotic transaction emerges. The couple resist confrontation. Each spouse is afraid that realizing his or her own neurotic expectations and distortions will increase vulnerability. The greater the need for closeness, the greater the fear of disrupting any established pattern. Cohesiveness in a neurotic marriage is cohesiveness based on fear.

In the group, patients and therapist see possible alternatives to the spouses' behavior patterns. Sometimes the couple themselves are reminded of their positive feelings for each other if the spouses close ranks against a stranger, who may be the therapist or another group member. At other times, one couple may discover how much understanding they have between themselves if their honest response to another group member shows congruence as far as a situation outside their marriage is concerned.

The most profound change occurs when the couple are confronted with the possibility of divorce or separation. The group then represents a reality setting in which the spouses experience the anxieties of a possible end of their marriage. Each then wants agreement that the other one is at fault and deserves to be removed from the common marital life. Relatives, friends, and sometimes lawyers may support one-sided complaints and ignore neurotic marital transactions. In the group, shifting identifications and projections between individual patients, between couples, and between members of the same sex demonstrate possible solutions. The problem of a neurotic bondage is resolved if fights for control are replaced by the search for constructive alternatives, which are influenced by each spouse's knowledge and evaluation of the situation. Unilateral decisions can be accepted harmoniously if they do not threaten the autonomy and integrity of the other spouse.

Silence is a rare occurrence in the married couples group. Members are upset, angry, anxious. Their interaction is frequently dramatic. The free expression of emotions may temporarily appear to be destructive, especially if intramarital fighting is increased between group sessions. But rash or final decisions rarely occur between married couples group sessions. Being involved in the group process, couples want the confrontation with peers and therapist. They repeatedly realize that, in the heat of furious anger and retaliation, everything becomes distorted and decisions are unreliable.

The therapist's countertransference feelings should never interfere with his genuine interest and attitude of concern for each patient. Group members respond to the therapist's real feelings as sharply as children respond to the unconscious fears and wishes of their parents. The therapist's empathy for the unhappiness and anxiety of each spouse is crucial for the couples' ability to keep lines of communication open. He must be a reality-oriented, impartial adviser and interpreter who is always aware of the mutuality of transactions and who enables the couple to find a constructive equilibrium to replace their mutually destructive balance.

The patient finds new ways of relating to his spouse by going through a process of separation and individuation. As in any other group psychotherapy—though frequently in a more emotional and dramatic way—patients learn to feel secure in their identities. Then the conflict between the need for closeness and the threat of it, which perpetuates neurotic attitudes between the couple and spreads to the next generation, can be resolved.

REFERENCES

Ackerman, N. W. The diagnosis of neurotic marital interaction. Soc. Casework, *35:* 139, 1954.

Ackerman, N. W. *Psychodynamics of Family Life: Diagnosis and Treatment of Family Relationships.* Basic Books, New York, 1958.

Adler, A. *The Individual Psychology of Alfred Adler.* Harper and Row, New York, 1964.

Deutsch, D. Family therapy and family life style, J. Indiv. Psychol., *14:* 218, 1967.

Eisenstein, V. W. *Neurotic Interaction in Marriage.* Basic Books, New York, 1956.

Flint, A. A., and MacLennan, B. W. Some dynamic factors in marital group psychotherapy. Int. J. Group Psychother., *12:* 355, 1962.

Goller, G., Sherman, S. N., and Hulse, W. C. Group approaches to the treatment of marital problems. In *Neurotic Interaction in Marriage,* p. 290, V. W. Eisenstein, editor. Basic Books, New York, 1956.

Gottlieb, A., and Pattison, E. M. Married couples group psychotherapy. Arch. Gen. Psychiat., *14:* 151, 1966.

Greenbaum, H. Discussion of group psychotherapy with married couples. J. Psychoanal. Group, *2:* 43, 1966.

Grunebaum, H., and Christ, J. Interpretation and the task of the therapist with couples. Int. J. Group Psychother., *18:* 495, 1968.

Haley, J. Marriage therapy. Arch. Gen. Psychiat., *8:* 213, 1963.

Jackson, J., and Grotjahn, M. Re-enactment of the marriage neurosis in group psychotherapy. J. Nerv. Ment. Dis., *127:* 503, 1958.

Kadis, A., and Markowitz, M. Short-term analytic treatment of married couples in a group by a therapist-couple. In *New Directions in Mental Health,* Russ, B. F., editor. Grune & Stratton, New York, 1968.

Lederer, W. J., and Jackson, D. D. *Mirages of Marriage.* W. W. Norton, New York, 1968.

Leichter, E. Group psychotherapy with married couples. Int. J. Group Psychother., *12:* 154, 1962.

Lewin, K. *Gesetz und Experiment in der Psychologie.* Wissenschaftliche Buchgesellschaft, Darmstadt, Germany, 1967.

Marmor, J. *Modern Psychoanalysis.* Basic Books, New York, 1968.

Mittelman, B. Complementary neurotic reactions in intimate relationship. Psychoanal. Quart., *13:* 479, 1944.

Mittelman, B. The concomitant analysis of married couples. Psychoanal. Quart., *17:* 182, 1948.

Papanek, H. Group psychotherapy with married couples. In *Current Psychiatric Therapies,* vol. 5, p. 158, J. Masserman, editor. Grune & Stratton, New York, 1965.

Reckless, J. Confrontation technique used with married couples in a group therapy setting. Int. J. Group Psychother., *19:* 203, 1969.

Satir, V. M. *Conjoint Family Thrapy.* Science and Behavior Books, Palo Alto, Calif., 1964.

Wynne, L. C., Ryckoff, I. M., Day, J., and Hirsch, S. I. Pseudomutuality in the family reactions of schizophrenics. Psychiatry, *21:* 205, 1958.

Glossary

Glossary*

Aberration, mental. Pathological deviation from normal thinking. Mental aberration is not related to a person's intelligence. *See also* Mental illness.

Abreaction. A process by which repressed material, particularly a painful experience or a conflict, is brought back to consciousness. In the process of abreacting, the person not only recalls but relives the repressed material, which is accompanied by the appropriate affective response. *See also* Catharsis.

Accelerated interaction. An alternate term for marathon group session that was introduced by one of its co-developers, Frederick Stoller. *See also* Group marathon.

Accountability. The responsibility a member has for his actions within a group and the need to explain to other members the motivations for his behavior.

Acid. Slang for lysergic acid diethylamide (LSD).

Acrophobia. Fear of high places.

Acting out. An action rather than a verbal response to an unconscious instinctual drive or impulse that brings about temporary partial relief of inner tension. Relief is attained by reacting to a present situation as if it were the situation that originally gave rise to the drive or impulse. *See also* Therapeutic crisis.

Actional-deep approach. Group procedure in which communication is effected through various forms of nonverbal behavior as well as or in place of language to produce character change. It is a technique used in psychodrama. *See also* Actional-superficial approach, Activity group therapy, Verbal-deep approach, Verbal-superficial approach.

Actional-superficial approach. Group procedure in which specific activities and verbal communication are used for limited goals. Verbal interchange and patient-to-patient interaction are of relatively minor therapeutic significance, and the groups are usually large. *See also* Actional-deep approach, Verbal-deep approach, Verbal-superficial approach.

Action group (A-group). Group whose purpose is to discuss a problem—community, industrial, or organizational—and to formulate a program of action. Emphasis is put on problem-solving rather than on developing awareness of self and group process. *See also* T-group.

Active therapist. Type of therapist who makes no effort to remain anonymous but is forceful and expresses his personality definitively in the therapy setting. *See also* Passive therapist.

Activity group therapy. A type of group therapy introduced and developed by S. R. Slavson and designed for children and young adolescents, with emphasis on emotional and active interaction in a permissive, nonthreatening atmosphere. The therapist stresses reality-testing, ego-strengthening, and action interpretation. *See also* Actional-deep approach; Activity-interview method; Bender, Lauretta; Play therapy.

Activity-interview method. Screening and diagnostic technique used with children. *See also* Activity group therapy.

Actualization. Process of mobilizing one's potentialities or making them concrete. *See also* Individuation.

---

* Edited by Ernesto A. Amaranto, M.D.

I

Adaptational approach. An approach used in analytic group therapy. Consonant with Sandor Rado's formulations on adaptational psychodynamics, the group focuses on the maladaptive patterns used by patients in the treatment sessions, on how these patterns developed, and on what the patients must do to overcome them and stabilize their functioning at self-reliant, adult levels. New methods of adaptation are practiced by the group members in the therapeutic sessions and later in their regular interpersonal relationships. *See also* Social adaptation.

Adapted Child. In transactional analysis, the primitive ego state that is under the parental influence. The adapted Child is dependent, unexpressive, and constrained. *See also* Natural Child.

Adler, Alfred (1870–1937). Viennese psychiatrist and one of Freud's original followers. Adler broke off from Freud and introduced and developed the concepts of individual psychology, inferiority complex, and overcompensation. A pioneer in group psychotherapy, he believed that the sharing of problems takes precedence over confidentiality. He also made contributions in the understanding of group process. *See also* Individual psychology, Masculine protest.

Adolescence. Period of growth from puberty to maturity. The beginning of adolescence is marked by the appearance of secondary sexual characteristics, usually at about age 12, and the termination is marked by the achievement of sexual maturity at about age 20. *See also* Psychosexual development.

Adult. In transactional analysis, an ego state oriented toward objective, autonomous data-processing and estimating. It is essentially a computer, devoid of feeling. It is also known as neopsychic function.

Affect. Emotional feeling tone attached to an object, idea, or thought. The term includes inner feelings and their external manifestations. *See also* Inappropriate affect, Mood.

Affect, blunted. A disturbance of affect manifested by dullness of externalized feeling tone. Observed in schizophrenia, it is one of that disorder's fundamental symptoms, according to Eugen Bleuler.

Affection phase. Last stage of group treatment. In this phase the members experience reasonable equality with the therapist and dwell on affectionate contact with each other in a give-and-take atmosphere rather than dwelling on dependency or aggression. *See also* Inclusion phase, Power phase.

Affective interaction. Interpersonal experience and exchange that are emotionally charged.

Affectualizing. In transactional analysis, the expression of emotions or feelings in group or individual treatment as part of a pasttime or game. It is distinguished from the expression of authentic feelings, which are characteristic of intimacy.

Afro-American. American Negro of African ancestry. This term has significance for blacks who seek a deeper and more positive sense of identity with their African heritage. *See also* Black separatism.

After-session. Group meeting of patients without the therapist. It is held immediately after a regular therapist-led session. *See also* Alternate session, Premeeting.

Agency. The striving and need to achieve in a person. Agency manifests itself in self-protection, the urge to master, self-expansion, and repression of thought, feeling, and impulse. *See also* Communion.

Aggression. Forceful, goal-directed behavior that may be verbal or physical. It is the motor counterpart of the affects of rage, anger, and hostility.

Aggressive drive. Destructive impulse directed at oneself or another. It is also known as the death instinct. According to contemporary psychoanalytic psychology, it is one of the two basic drives; sexual drive is the other one. Sexual drive operates on the pleasure-pain principle, whereas aggressive drive operates on the repetition-compulsion principle. *See also* Aggression, Libido theory.

Agitation. State of anxiety associated with severe motor restlessness.

Agnosia. Disturbance of perception characterized by inability to recognize a stimulus and interpret the significance of its memory impressions. It is observed in patients with organic brain disease and in certain schizophrenics, hysterics, and depressed patients.

Agoraphobia. Fear of open places. *See also* Claustrophobia.

Agranulocytosis. A rare, serious side effect, occurring with some of the psychotropic drugs. The condition is characterized by sore throat, fever, a sudden sharp decrease in white blood cell count, and a marked reduction in number of granulocytes.

A-group. *See* Action group.

Alcoholics Anonymous (A.A.) An organization of alcoholics formed in 1935. It uses certain group methods, such as inspirational-supportive techniques, to help rehabilitate chronic alcoholics.

Algophobia. Fear of pain.

Allergic jaundice. *See* Jaundice, allergic.

Alliance. *See* Therapeutic alliance, Working alliance.

Allport's group relations theory. Gordon W. Allport's theory that a person's behavior is influenced by his personality and his need to conform to social forces. It illustrates the interrelationship between group therapy and social psychology. For example, dealing with bigotry in a therapy group enhances the opportunity for therapeutic experiences because it challenges the individual patient's need to conform to earlier social determinants or to hold on to familiar but restrictive aspects of his personality.

Alternate session. Scheduled group meeting held without the therapist. Such meetings are held on a regular basis in between therapist-led sessions. Use of this technique was originated by Alexander Wolf. *See also* After-session, Pre-meeting.

Alternating role. Pattern characterized by periodic switching from one type of behavior to another. For example, in a group, alternating role is observed among members who switch from the role of the recipient of help to the giver of help.

Alternating scrutiny. *See* Shifting attention.

Altruism. Regard for and dedication to the welfare of others. The term was originated by Auguste Comte (1798–1857), a French philosopher. In psychiatry the term is closely linked with ethics and morals. Freud recognized altruism as the only basis for the development of community interest; Bleuler equated it with morality.

Ambivalence. Presence of strong and often overwhelming simultaneous contrasting attitudes, ideas, feelings, and drives toward an object, person, or goal. The term was coined by Eugen Bleuler, who differentiated three types: affective, intellectual, and ambivalence of the will.

Amnesia. Disturbance in memory manifested by partial or total inability to recall past experiences.

Amphetamine. A central nervous system stimulant. Its chemical structure and action are closely related to ephedrine and other sympathomimetic amines. *See also* Sympathomimetic drug.

Anal erotism. *See* Anal phase.

Anal phase. The second stage in psychosexual development. It occurs when the child is between the ages of one and three. During this period the infant's activities, interests, and concerns are centered around his anal zone, and the pleasurable experience felt around this area is called anal erotism. *See also* Genital phase, Infantile sexuality, Latency phase, Oral phase, Phallic phase.

Analysis. *See* Psychoanalysis.

Analysis in depth. *See* Psychoanalysis.

Analysis of transference. *See* Psychoanalysis.

Analytic psychodrama. Psychotherapy method in which a hypothesis is tested on a stage to verify its validity. The analyst sits in the audience and observes. Analysis of the material is made immediately after the scene is presented.

Anchor. Point at which the patient settles down to the analytic work involved in the therapeutic experience.

Antianxiety drug. Drug used to reduce pathological anxiety and its related symptoms without influencing cognitive or perceptual disturbance. It is also known as a minor tranquilizer and a psycholeptic drug. Meprobamate derivatives and diazepoxides are typical antianxiety drugs.

Anticholinergic effect. Effect due to a blockade of the cholinergic (parasympathetic and somatic) nerves. It is often seen as a side effect of phenothiazine therapy. Anticholinergic effects include dry mouth and blurred vision. *See also* Paralytic ileus.

Antidepressant drug. Drug used in the treatment of pathological depression. It is also known as a thymoleptic drug and a psychic energizer. The two main classes of antidepressant drugs are the tricyclic drugs and the monoamine oxidase inhibitors. *See also* Hypertensive crisis, Monoamine oxidase inhibitor, Tinnitus, Tricyclic drug.

Antimanic drug. Drug, such as lithium, used to alleviate the symptoms of mania. Lithium is particularly effective in preventing relapses in manic-depressive illness. Other drugs with antimanic effects are haloperidol and chlorpromazine.

Antiparkinsonism drug. Drug used to relieve the symptoms of parkinsonism and the extrapyramidal side effects often induced by antipsychotic drugs. The antiparkinsonism drug acts by diminishing muscle tone and involuntary movements. Antiparkinsonism agents include benztropine, procyclidine, biperiden, and trihexphenidyl. *See also* Cycloplegia, Mydriasis.

Antipsychotic drug. Drug used to treat psychosis, particularly schizophrenia. It is also known as a major tranquilizer and a neuroleptic drug. Phenothiazine derivatives, thioxanthene derivatives, and butyrophenone derivatives are typical antipsychotic drugs. *See also* Autonomic side effect, Dyskinesia, Extrapyramidal effect, Major tranquilizer, Parkinsonismlike effect, Reserpine, Tardive oral dyskinesia.

Antirepression device. Technique used in encounter groups and therapeutic groups to break through the defense of repression. In encounter groups, such techniques are frequently nonverbal and involve physical contact between group members. In therapeutic groups, dream analysis, free association, and role-playing are some antirepression techniques.

Anxiety. Unpleasurable affect consisting of psychophysiological changes in response to an intrapsychic conflict. In contrast to fear, the danger or threat in anxiety is unreal. Physiological changes consist of increased heart rate, disturbed breathing, trembling, sweating, and vasomotor changes. Psychological changes consist of an uncomfortable feeling of impending danger accompanied by overwhelming awareness of being powerless, inability to perceive the unreality of the threat, prolonged feeling of tension, and exhaustive readiness for the expected danger. *See also* Basic anxiety, Fear.

Apathetic withdrawal. *See* Withdrawal.

Apathy. Want of feeling or affect; lack of interest and emotional involvement in one's surroundings. It is observed in certain types of schizophrenia and depression.

Apgar scores. Measurements taken one minute and five minutes after birth to determine physical normality in the neonate. The scores are based on color, respiratory rate, heart beat, reflex action, and muscle tone. Used routinely, they are particularly useful in detecting the effects on the infant of drugs taken by the pregnant mother.

Aphasia. Disturbance in speech due to organic brain disorder. It is characterized by inability to express thoughts verbally. There are several types of aphasia: (1) motor aphasia—inability to speak, although understanding remains; (2) sensory aphasia—inability to comprehend the meaning of words or use of objects; (3) nominal aphasia—difficulty in finding the right name for an object; (4) syntactical aphasia—inability to arrange words in proper sequence.

Apperception. Awareness of the meaning and significance of a particular sensory stimulus as modified by one's own experiences, knowledge, thoughts, and emotions. *See also* Perception.

Archeopsychic function. *See* Child.

Arteriosclerotic cardiovascular disease. A metabolic disturbance characterized by degenerative changes involving the blood vessels of the heart and other arteries, mainly the arterioles. Fatty plaques, deposited within the blood vessels, gradually obstruct the flow of blood. Organic brain syndrome may develop when cerebral arteries are involved in the degenerative process.

Ataractic drug. *See* Major tranquilizer.

Ataxia. Lack of coordination, either physical or mental. In neurology it refers to loss of muscular coordination. In psychiatry the term intrapsychic ataxia refers to lack of coordination between feelings and thoughts; the disturbance is found in schizophrenia.

Atmosphere. *See* Therapeutic atmosphere.

Attention. Concentration; the aspect of consciousness that relates to the amount of effort exerted in focusing on certain aspects of an experience.

Attitude. Preparatory mental posture with which one receives stimuli and reacts to them. Group therapy often involves itself in defining for the group members their attitudes that have unconsciously dominated their reactions.

Auditory hallucination. False auditory sensory perception.

Authenticity. Quality of being authentic, real, and valid. In psychological functioning and personality, it applies to the conscious feelings, perceptions, and thoughts that a person expresses and communicates. It does not apply to the deeper, unconscious layers of the personality. *See also* Honesty.

Authority figure. A real or projected person in a position of power; transferentially, a projected parent.

Authority principle. The idea that each member of an organizational hierarchy tries to comply with the presumed or fantasied wishes of those above him while those below him try to comply with his wishes. *See also* Hierarchical vector, Political therapist, Procedural therapist.

Autism. *See* Autistic thinking.

Autistic thinking. A form of thinking in which the thoughts are largely narcissistic and egocentric, with emphasis on subjectivity rather than objectivity and without regard for reality. The term is used interchangeably with autism and dereism. *See also* Narcissism.

Autoerotism. Sexual arousal of self without the participation of another person. The term, introduced by Havelock Ellis, is at present used interchangeably with masturbation. In psychoanalysis, autoerotism is considered a primitive phase in object-relationship development, preceding the narcissistic stage. In narcissism there is a love object, but there is no love object in autoerotism.

Autonomic side effect. Disturbance of the autonomic nervous system, both central and peripheral. It may be a result of the use of anti-psychotic drugs, particularly the phenothiazine derivatives. The autonomic side effects include hypotension, hypertension, blurred vision, nasal congestion, and dryness of the mouth. *See also* Mydriasis.

Auxiliary ego. In psychodrama, a person, usually a member of the staff, trained to act out different roles during a psychodramatic session to intensify the therapeutic situation. The trained auxiliary ego may represent an important figure in the patient's life. He may express the patient's unconscious wishes and attitudes or portray his unacceptable self. He may represent a delusion, hallucination, symbol, ideal, animal, or object that makes the patient's psychodramatic world real, concrete, and tangible. *See also* Ego model Hallucinatory psychodrama, Mirror, Multiple double.

Auxiliary therapist. Co-therapist. *See also* Co-therapy.

Back-home group. Collection of persons that a patient usually lives with, works with, and socializes with. It does not include the members of his therapy group. *See also* Expanded group.

Bag. Slang for area of classification, interest, or skill. Bringing together members of a group with different bags makes it initially difficult to achieve a feeling of group cohesiveness but later provides the potential for more productive interchange and deeper cohesiveness.

Basic anxiety. As conceptualized by Karen Horney, the mainspring from which neurotic trends get their intensity and pervasiveness. Basic anxiety is characterized by vague feelings of loneliness, helplessness, and fear of a potentially hostile world. *See also* Anxiety, Fear.

Basic skills training. The teaching of leadership functions, communication skills, the use of group processes, and other interpersonal skills. National Training Laboratories' groups include this training as part of the T-group process. *See also* East-Coast-style T-group.

Behavioral group psychotherapy. A type of group therapy that focuses on overt and objectively observable behavior rather than on thoughts and feelings. It aims at symptomatic improvement and the elimination of suffering and maladaptive habits. Various conditioning and anxiety-eliminating techniques derived from learning theory are combined with didactic discussions and techniques adapted from other systems of treatment.

Behind-the-back technique. An encounter group procedure in which a patient talks about himself and then turns his back and listens while the other participants discuss him as if he were physically absent. Later he "returns" to the group to participate in further discussions of his problems.

Bender, Lauretta (1897–). American psychiatrist who has done extensive work in the fields of child psychiatry, neurology, and psychology. She employed group therapy, particularly activity group therapy, with inpatient children in the early 1940's.

Berne, Eric (1910–1970). American psychiatrist. He was the founder of transactional analysis, which is used in both individual and group therapy. *See also* Transactional group psychotherapy.

Bestiality. Sexual deviation in which a person engages in sexual relations with an animal.

Bieber, Irving (1908–). American psychiatrist and psychoanalyst who has done extensive work in the field of homosexuality. He originated the first major scientific study of male homosexuality published as *Homosexuality; A Psychoanalytic Study*.

Bio-energetic group psychotherapy. A type of group therapy developed by Alexander Lowen that directly involves the body and mobilizes energy processes to facilitate the expression of feeling. Verbal interchange and a variety of exercises are designed to improve and coordinate physical functioning with mental functioning.

Bion, Walter R. British psychoanalyst of the Kleinian school. He introduced concepts dealing largely with the group as a whole. He was one of the European workers who demonstrated the use of open wards in mental hospitals and who developed the concept of therapeutic milieu. *See also* Leaderless therapeutic group, Pairing, Therapeutic community.

Bisexuality. Existence of the qualities of both sexes in the same person. Freud postulated that both biologically and psychologically the sexes differentiated from a common core, that differentiation between the two sexes was relative rather than absolute, and that regression to the common core occurs to varying degrees in both normal and abnormal conditions. An adult person who engages in bisexual behavior is one who is sexually attracted to and has contact with members of both sexes. He is also known in lay terms as an AC-DC person. *See also* Heterosexuality, Homosexuality, Latent homosexuality, Overt homosexuality.

Black separatism. Philosophy that blacks, in order to develop a positive identity, must establish cultural, socioeconomic, and political systems that are distinctively black and separate from white systems. *See also* Afro-American.

Blank screen. Neutral backdrop on which the patient projects a gamut of transferential irrationalities. The passivity of the analyst allows him to act as a blank screen.

Blind self. The behavior, feelings, and motivations of a person known to others but not to himself. The blind self is one quadrant of the Johari Window, a diagrammatic concept of human behavior. *See also* Hidden self, Public self, Undeveloped potential.

Blind spot. Area of someone's personality that he is totally unaware of. These unperceived areas are often hidden by repression so that he can avoid painful emotions. In both group and individual therapy, such blind spots often appear obliquely as projected ideas, intentions, and emotions.

Blind walk. A technique used in encounter groups to help a member experience and develop trust. As a group exercise, each member picks a partner; one partner closes his eyes, and the other leads him around, keeping him out of dangerous places. The partners then reverse roles. Later, the group members discuss their reactions to the blind walk.

Blocking. Involuntary cessation of thought processes or speech because of unconscious emotional factors. It is also known as thought deprivation.

Blunted affect. *See* Affect, blunted.

Body-contact-exploration maneuver. Any physical touching of another person for the purpose of becoming more aware of the sensations and emotions aroused by the experience. The technique is used mainly in encounter groups.

Boundary. Physical or psychological factor that separates relevant regions in the group structure. An external boundary separates the group from the external environment. A major internal boundary distinguishes the group leader from the members. A minor internal boundary separates individual members or subgroups from one another.

Brainwashing. Any technique designed to manipulate human thought or action against the desire, will, or knowledge of the person involved. It usually refers to systematic efforts to indoctrinate nonbelievers. *See also* Dog-eat-dog period, Give-up-itis.

Breuer, Josef (1842–1925). Viennese physician with wide scientific and cultural interests. His collaboration with Freud in studies of cathartic therapy were reported in *Studies on Hysteria* (1895). He withdrew as Freud proceeded to introduce psychoanalysis, but he left important imprints on that discipline, such as the concepts of the primary and secondary process.

Brill, A. A. (1874–1948). First American analyst (1908). Freud gave him permission to translate several of his most important works. He was active in the formation of the New York Psychoanalytic Society (1911) and remained in the forefront of propagators of psychoanalysis as a lecturer and writer throughout his life.

Brooding compulsion. *See* Intellectualization.

Bull session. Informal group meeting at which members discuss their opinions, philosophies, and personal feelings about situations and people. Such groups are leaderless, and no attempt is made to perceive group process, but the cathartic value is often great. It is also known as a rap session.

Burned-out anergic schizophrenic. A chronic schizophrenic who is apathetic and withdrawn, with minimal florid psychotic symptoms but with persistent and often severe schizophrenic thought processes.

Burrow, Trigant L. (1875–1951). American student of Freud and Jung who coined the term group analysis and later developed a method called phyloanalysis. Much of Burrow's work was based on his social views and his opinion that individual psychotherapy places the therapist in too authoritarian a role to be therapeutic. He formed groups of patients, students, and colleagues who, living together in a camp, analyzed their interactions.

Catalepsy. *See* Cerea flexibilitas.

Cataphasia. *See* Verbigeration.

Cataplexy. Temporary loss of muscle tone, causing weakness and immobilization. It can be precipitated by a variety of emotional states.

Catecholamine. Monoamine containing a catechol group that has a sympathomimetic property. Norepinephrine, epinephrine, and dopamine are common catecholamines.

Category method. Technique used in structured interactional group psychotherapy. Members are asked to verbally rate one another along a variety of parameters—such as appearance, intelligence, and relatedness.

Catharsis. Release of ideas, thoughts, and repressed materials from the unconscious, accompanied by an affective emotional response and release of tension. Commonly observed in the course of treatment, both individual and group, it can also occur outside therapy. *See also* Abreaction, Bull session, Conversational catharsis.

Cathexis. In psychoanalysis, a conscious or unconscious investment of the psychic energy of a drive in an idea, a concept, or an object.

Cerea flexibilitas. Condition in which a person maintains the body position he is placed into. It is a pathological symptom observed in severe cases of catatonic schizophrenia. It is also known as waxy flexibility or catalepsy.

Chain-reaction phenomenon. Group therapy situation in which information is passed from one group to another, resulting in a loss of confidentiality. This phenomenon is common when members of different groups socialize together.

Chemotherapy. *See* Drug therapy.

Child. In transactional analysis, an ego state that is an archaic relic from an early period of the person's life. It is also known as archeopsychic function. *See also* Adapted Child, Natural Child.

Chlorpromazine. A phenothiazine derivative used primarily as an antipsychotic agent and in the treatment of nausea and vomiting. The drug was synthesized in 1950 and was used in psychiatry for the first time in 1952. At present, chlorpromazine is one of the most widely used drugs in medical practice.

Circumstantiality. Disturbance in the associative thought processes in which the patient digresses into unnecessary details and inappropriate thoughts before communicating the central idea. It is observed in schizophrenia, obsessional disturbances, and certain cases of epileptic dementia. *See also* Tangentiality, Thought process disorder.

Clarification. In transactional analysis, the attainment of Adult control by a patient who understands what he is doing, knows what parts of his personality are involved in what he is doing, and is able to control and decide whether or not to continue his games. Clarification contributes to stability by assuring the patient that his hidden Parent and Child ego states can be monitored by his Adult ego state. *See also* Decontamination, Interpretation.

Class method. Group therapy method that is lecture-centered and designed to enlighten patients as to their condition and provide them with motivations. Joseph Pratt, a Boston physician, first used this method at the turn of the century to help groups of tuberculous patients understand their illness. *See also* Didactic technique, Group bibliotherapy, Mechanical group therapy.

Claustrophobia. Fear of closed places. *See also* Agoraphobia.

Client-centered psychotherapy. A form of psychotherapy, formulated by Carl Rogers, in which the patient or client is believed to possess the ability to improve. The therapist merely helps him clarify his own thinking and feeling. The client-centered approach in both group and individual therapy is democratic, unlike the psychotherapist-centered treatment methods. *See also* Group-centered psychotherapy, Nondirective approach.

Closed group. Treatment group into which no new members are permitted once it has begun the treatment process. *See also* Open group.

Clouding of consciousness. Disturbance of consciousness characterized by unclear sensory perceptions.

Coexistent culture. Alternative system of values, perceptions, and patterns for behavior. The group experience leads to an awareness of other systems as legitimate alternatives to one's own system.

Cognition. Mental process of knowing and becoming aware. One of the ego functions, it is closely associated with judgment. Groups that study their own processes and dynamics use more cognition than do encounter groups, which emphasize emotions. It is also known as thinking.

Cohesion. *See* Group cohesion.

Cold turkey. Abrupt withdrawal from opiates without the benefit of methadone or other drugs. The term was originated by drug addicts to describe their chills and consequent goose flesh. This type of detoxification is generally used by abstinence-oriented therapeutic communities.

Collaborative therapy. A type of marital therapy in which treatment is conducted by two therapists, each of whom sees one spouse. They may confer occasionally or at regular intervals. This form of treatment affords each analyst a double view of his patient—the way in which one patient reports to his analyst and the way in which the patient's mate sees the situation as reported to the analyst's colleague. *See also* Combined therapy, Concurrent therapy, Conjoint therapy, Family therapy, Group marital therapy, Marriage therapy, Quadrangular therapy, Square interview.

Collective experience. The common emotional experiences of a group of people. Identification, mutual support, reduction of ego defenses, sibling transferences, and empathy help integrate the individual member into the group and accelerate the therapeutic process. S. R. Slavson, who coined the phrase, warned against letting the collective experience submerge the individuality of the members or give them an opportunity to escape from their own autonomy and responsibility.

Collective family transference neurosis. A phenomenon observed in a group when a member projects irrational feelings and thoughts onto other members as a result of transferring the family psychopathology from early childhood into the therapeutic group situation. The interpretation and analysis of this phenomenon is one of the cornerstones of psychoanalytic group therapy. *See also* Lateral transference, Multiple transference.

Collective unconscious. Psychic contents outside the realm of awareness that are common to mankind in general, not to one person in particular. Jung, who introduced the term, believed that the collective unconscious is inherited and derived from the collective experience of the species. It transcends cultural differences and explains the analogy between ancient mythological ideas and the primitive archaic projections observed in some patients who have never been exposed to these ideas.

Coma. A profound degree of unconsciousness with minimal or no detectable responsiveness to stimuli. It is seen in conditions involving the brain—such as head injury, cerebral hemorrhage, thrombosis and embolism, and cerebral infection—in such systemic conditions as diabetes, and in drug and alcohol intoxication. In psychiatry, comas may be seen in severe catatonic states.

Coma vigil. A profound degree of unconsciousness in which the patient's eyes remain open but there is minimal or no detectable evidence of responsiveness to stimuli. It is seen in acute brain syndromes secondary to cerebral infection.

Combined therapy. A type of psychotherapy in which the patient is in both individual and group treatment with the same or two different therapists. In marriage therapy, it is the combination of married couples group therapy with either individual sessions with one spouse or conjoint sessions with the marital pair. *See also* Collaborative therapy, Concurrent therapy, Conjoint therapy, Co-therapy, Family therapy, Group marital therapy, Marriage therapy, Quadrangular therapy, Square interview.

Coming on. A colloquial term used in transactional analysis groups to label an emerging ego state. For example, when a patient points his finger and says "should," he is coming on Parent.

Command automation. Condition closely associated with catalepsy in which suggestions are followed automatically.

Command negativism. *See* Negativism.

Common group tension. Common denominator of tension arising out of the dominant unconscious fantasies of all the members in a group.

Each member projects his unconscious fantasy onto the other members and tries to manipulate them accordingly. Interpretation by the group therapist plays a prominent role in bringing about change.

Communion. The union of one living thing with another or the participation of a person in an organization. It is a necessary ingredient in individual and group psychotherapy and in sensitivity training. Both the leader-therapist and the patient-trainee must experience communion for a successful learning experience to occur. *See also* Agency.

Communion-oriented group psychotherapy. A type of group therapy that focuses on developing a spirit of unity and cohesiveness rather than on performing a task.

Community. *See* Therapeutic community.

Community psychiatry. Psychiatry focusing on the detection, prevention, and early treatment of emotional disorders and social deviance as they develop in the community rather than as they are perceived and encountered at large, centralized psychiatric facilities. Particular emphasis is placed on the environmental factors that contribute to mental illness.

Compensation. Conscious or, usually, unconscious defense mechanism by which a person tries to make up for an imagined or real deficiency, physical or psychological or both.

Competition. Struggle for the possession or use of limited goods, concrete or abstract. Gratification for one person largely precludes gratification for another.

Complementarity of interaction. A concept of bipersonal and multipersonal psychology in which behavior is viewed as a response to stimulation and interaction replaces the concept of reaction. Each person in an interactive situation plays both a provocative role and a responsive role.

Complex. A group of inter-related ideas, mainly unconscious, that have a common affective tone. A complex strongly influences the person's attitudes and behavior. *See also* God complex, Inferiority complex, Mother Superior complex, Oedipus complex.

Composition. Make-up of a group according to

sex, age, race, cultural and ethnic background, and psychopathology.

Compulsion. Uncontrollable impulse to perform an act repetitively. It is used as a way to avoid unacceptable ideas and desires. Failure to perform the act leads to anxiety. *See also* Obsession.

Conation. That part of a person's mental life concerned with his strivings, instincts, drives, and wishes as expressed through his behavior.

Concretization of living. As used in psychodrama, the actualization of life in a therapeutic setting, integrating time, space, reality, and cosmos.

Concurrent therapy. A type of family therapy in which one therapist handles two or more members of the same family but sees each member separately. *See also* Collaborative therapy, Combined therapy, Conjoint therapy, Family therapy, Group marital therapy, Marriage therapy, Quadrangular therapy, Square interview.

Conditioning. Procedure designed to alter behavioral potential. There are two main types of conditioning—classical and operant. Classical or Pavlovian conditioning pairs two stimuli—one adequate, such as offering food to a dog to produce salivation, and the other inadequate, such as ringing a bell, which by itself does not have an effect on salivation. After the two stimuli have been paired several times, the dog responds to the inadequate stimulus (ringing of bell) by itself. In operant conditioning, a desired activity is reinforced by giving the subject a reward every time he performs the act. As a result, the activity becomes automatic without the need for further reinforcement.

Confabulation. Unconscious filling of gaps in memory by imagining experiences that have no basis in fact. It is common in organic brain syndromes. *See also* Paramnesia.

Confidentiality. Aspect of medical ethics in which the physician is bound to hold secret all information given him by the patient. Legally, certain states do not recognize confidentiality and can require the physician to divulge such information if needed in a legal proceeding. In group psychotherapy this ethic is adhered to by the members as well as by the therapist.

Confirmation. In transactional analysis, a re-

confrontation that may be undertaken by the patient himself. *See also* Confrontation.

Conflict. Clash of two opposing emotional forces. In a group, the term refers to a clash between group members or between the group members and the leader, a clash that frequently reflects the inner psychic problems of individual members. *See also* Extrapsychic conflict, Intrapsychic conflict.

Conflict-free area. Part of one's personality or ego that is well-integrated and does not cause any conflicts, symptoms, or displeasure. Conflict-free areas are usually not analyzed in individual analysis, but they become obvious in the interaction of an analytic group, where they can then be analyzed.

Confrontation. Act of letting a person know where one stands in relationship to him, what one is experiencing, and how one perceives him. Used in a spirit of deep involvement, this technique is a powerful tool for changing relationships; used as an attempt to destroy another person, it can be harmful. In group and individual therapy, the value of confrontation is likely to be determined by the therapist. *See also* Encounter group, Existential group psychotherapy.

Confusion. Disturbance of consciousness manifested by a disordered orientation in relation to time, place, or person.

Conjoint therapy. A type of marriage therapy in which a therapist sees the partners together in joint sessions. This situation is also called triadic or triangular, since two patients and one therapist work together. *See also* Collaborative therapy, Combined therapy, Concurrent therapy, Family therapy, Group marital therapy, Marriage therapy, Quadrangular therapy, Square interview.

Conscious. One division of Freud's topographical theory of the mind. The content of the conscious is within the realm of awareness at all times. The term is also used to describe a function of organic consciousness. *See also* Preconscious, Unconscious.

Consciousness. *See* Sensorium.

Consensual validation. The continuous comparison of the thoughts and feelings of group members toward one another that tend to modify and correct interpersonal distortions. The term was introduced by Harry Stack Sullivan. Previously, Trigant Burrow referred to consensual observation to describe this process, which results in effective reality-testing.

Contact situation. Encounter between individual persons or groups in which the interaction patterns that develop represent the dynamic interplay of psychological, cultural, and socioeconomic factors.

Contagion. Force that operates in large groups or masses. When the level of psychological functioning has been lowered, some sudden upsurge of anxiety can spread through the group, speeded by a high degree of suggestibility. The anxiety gradually mounts to panic, and the whole group may be simultaneously affected by a primitive emotional upheaval.

Contamination. In transactional analysis, a state in which attitudes, prejudices, and standards that originate in a Parent or Child ego state become part of the Adult ego state's information and are treated as accepted facts. *See also* Clarification, Decontamination.

Contemporaneity. Here-and-now.

Contract. Explicit, bilateral commitment to a well-defined course of action. In group or individual therapy, the therapist-patient contract is to attain the treatment goal.

Conversational catharsis. Release of repressed or suppressed thoughts and feelings in group and individual psychotherapy as a result of verbal interchange.

Conversion. An unconscious defense mechanism by which the anxiety that stems from an intrapsychic conflict is converted and expressed in a symbolic somatic symptom. Seen in a variety of mental disorders, it is particularly common in hysterical neurosis.

Cooperative therapy. *See* Co-therapy.

Co-patients. Members of a treatment group exclusive of the therapist and the recorder or observer. Co-patients are also known as patient peers.

Coprolalia. The use of vulgar, obscene, or dirty words. It is observed in some cases of schizophrenia. The word is derived from the Greek words *kopros* (excrement) and *lalia* (talking). *See also* Gilles de la Tourette's disease.

Corrective emotional experience. Re-exposure, under favorable circumstances, to an emotional situation that the patient could not handle in the past. As advocated by Franz Alexander, the therapist temporarily assumes a particular role to generate the experience and facilitate reality-testing.

Co-therapy. A form of psychotherapy in which more than one therapist treat the individual patient or the group. It is also known as combined therapy, cooperative therapy, dual leadership, multiple therapy, and three-cornered therapy. *See also* Role-divided therapy, Splitting situation.

Counterdependent person. *See* Nontruster.

Countertransference. Conscious or unconscious emotional response of the therapist to the patient. It is determined by the therapist's inner needs rather than by the patient's needs, and it may reinforce the patient's earlier traumatic history if not checked by the therapist.

Co-worker. Professional or paraprofessional who works in the same clinical or institutional setting.

Creativity. Ability to produce something new. Silvano Arieti describes creativity as the tertiary process, a balanced combination of primary and secondary processes, whereby materials from the id are used in the service of the ego.

Crisis-intervention group psychotherapy. Group therapy aimed at decreasing or eliminating an emotional or situational crisis.

Crisis, therapeutic. *See* Therapeutic crisis.

Crystallization. In transactional analysis, a statement of the patient's position from the Adult of the therapist to the Adult of the patient. *See also* Ego state.

Cultural conserve. The finished product of the creative process; anything that preserves the values of a particular culture. Without this repository of the past, man would be forced to create the same forms to meet the same situations day after day. The cultural conserve also entices new creativity.

Cultural deprivation. Restricted participation in the culture of the larger society.

Current material. Data from present interpersonal experiences. *See also* Genetic material.

Cyclazocine. A narcotic antagonist that blocks the effects of heroin but does not relieve heroin craving. It has been used experimentally with a limited number of drug addicts in research programs.

Cycloplegia. Paralysis of the muscles of accommodation in the eye. It is observed at times as an autonomic side effect of phenothiazine and antiparkinsonism drugs.

Dance therapy. Nonverbal communication through rhythmic body movements, used to rehabilitate people with emotional or physical disorders. Pioneered by Marian Chase in 1940, this method is used in both individual and group therapy.

Data. *See* Current material, Genetic material.

Death instinct. *See* Aggressive drive.

Decision. In transactional analysis, a childhood commitment to a certain existential position and life style. *See also* Script analysis.

Decompensation. In medical science, the failure of normal functioning of an organ, as in cardiac decompensation; in psychiatry, the breakdown of the psychological defense mechanisms that maintain the person's optimal psychic functioning. *See also* Depersonalization.

Decontamination. In transactional analysis, a process whereby a person is freed of Parent or Child contaminations. *See also* Clarification.

Defense mechanism. Unconscious intrapsychic process. Protective in nature, it is used to relieve the anxiety and conflict arising from one's impulses and drives. *See also* Compensation, Conversion, Denial, Displacement, Dissociation, Idealization, Identification, Incorporation, Intellectualization, Introjection, Projection, Rationalization, Reaction formation, Regression, Repression, Sublimation, Substitution, Symbolization, Undoing.

Defensive emotion. Strong feeling that serves as a screen for a less acceptable feeling, one that would cause a person to experience anxiety if it

appeared. For example, expressing the emotion of anger is often more acceptable to a group member than expressing the fear that his anger covers up. In this instance, anger is defensive.

Déjà entendu. Illusion of auditory recognition. *See also* Paramnesia.

Déjà vu. Illusion of visual recognition in which a new situation is incorrectly regarded as a repetition of a previous experience. *See also* Paramnesia.

Delirium. A disturbance in the state of consciousness that stems from an acute organic reaction characterized by restlessness, confusion, disorientation, bewilderment, agitation, and affective lability. It is associated with fear, hallucinations, and illusions.

Delusion. A false fixed belief not in accord with one's intelligence and cultural background. Types of delusion include:
Delusion of control. False belief that one is being manipulated by others.
Delusion of grandeur. Exaggerated concept of one's importance.
Delusion of infidelity. False belief that one's lover is unfaithful; it is derived from pathological jealousy.
Delusion of persecution. False belief that one is being harrassed.
Delusion of reference. False belief that the behavior of others refers to oneself; a derivation from ideas of reference in which the patient falsely feels that he is being talked about by others.
Delusion of self-accusation. False feeling of remorse.
Paranoid delusion. Oversuspiciousness leading to false persecutory ideas or beliefs.

Dementia. Organic loss of mental functioning.

Denial. An unconscious defense mechanism in which an aspect of external reality is rejected. At times it is replaced by a more satisfying fantasy or piece of behavior. The term can also refer to the blocking of awareness of internal reality. It is one of the primitive or infantile defenses.

Dependence on therapy. Patient's pathological need for therapy, created out of the belief that he cannot survive without it.

Dependency. A state of reliance on another

for psychological support. It reflects needs for security, love, protection, and mothering.

Dependency phase. *See* Inclusion phase.

Depersonalization. Sensation of unreality concerning oneself, parts of oneself, or one's environment. It is seen in schizophrenics, particularly during the early stages of decompensation. *See also* Decompensation.

Depression. In psychiatry, a morbid state characterized by mood alterations, such as sadness and loneliness; by low self-esteem associated with self-reproach; by psychomotor retardation and, at times, agitation; by withdrawal from interpersonal contact and, at times, a desire to die; and by such vegetative symptoms as insomnia and anorexia. *See also* Grief.

Derailment. *See* Tangentiality.

Derealization. Sensation of distorted spatial relationships. It is seen in certain types of schizophrenia.

Dereism. Mental activity not concordant with logic or experience. This type of thinking is commonly observed in schizophrenic states.

Detoxification. Removal of the toxic effects of a drug. It is also known as detoxication. *See also* Cold turkey, Methadone.

Diagnostic and Statistical Manual of Mental Disorders. A handbook for the classification of mental illnesses. Formulated by the American Psychiatric Association, it was first issued in 1952 (DSM-I). The second edition (DSM-II), issued in 1968, correlates closely with the World Health Organization's *International Classification of Diseases.*

Dialogue. Verbal communication between two or more persons.

Didactic psychodrama. Psychodrama used as a teaching method. It is used with persons involved in the care of psychiatric patients to teach them how to handle typical conflicts.

Didactic technique. Group therapeutic method given prominence by J. M. Klapman that emphasizes the tutorial approach. The group therapist makes use of outlines, texts, and visual aids to teach the group about themselves and

their functioning. *See also* Class method, Group bibliotherapy, Mechanical group therapy.

Differentiation. *See* Individuation.

Dilution of transference. Partial projection of irrational feelings and reactions onto various group members and away from the leader. Some therapists do not believe that dilution of transference occurs. *See also* Multiple transference, Transference.

Dipsomania. Morbid, irrepressible compulsion to drink alcoholic beverages.

Directive-didactic approach. Group therapy approach characterized by guided discussions and active direction by the therapist. Various teaching methods and printed materials are used, and autobiographical material may be presented. Such an approach is common with regressed patients in mental institutions.

Discussion model of group psychotherapy. A type of group therapy in which issues, problems, and facts are deliberated, with the major emphasis on rational understanding.

Disinhibition. Withdrawal of inhibition. Chemical substances such as alcohol can remove inhibitions by interfering with functions of the cerebral cortex. In psychiatry, disinhibition leads to the freedom to act on one's own needs rather than to submit to the demands of others.

Displacement. An unconscious defense mechanism by which the affective component of an unacceptable idea or object is transferred to an acceptable one.

Disposition. Sum total of a person's inclinations as determined by his mood.

Dissociation. An unconscious defense mechanism by which an idea is separated from its accompanying affect, as seen in hysterical dissociative states; an unconscious process by which a group of mental processes are split off from the rest of a person's thinking, resulting in an independent functioning of this group of processes and thus a loss of the usual inter-relationships.

Distortion. Misrepresentation of reality. It is based on historically determined motives.

Distractability. Inability to focus one's attention.

Diversified reality. A condition in a treatment situation that provides various real stimuli with which the patient may interact. In a group, the term refers to the variety of personalities of the co-members, in contrast with the one personality of the analyst in the dyadic relationship.

Doctor-patient relationship. Human interchange that exists between the person who is sick and the person who is selected because of training and experience to heal.

Dog-eat-dog period. Early stage of Communist brainwashing of American prisoners during the Korean War. During this period, as described by former Army psychiatrist William Mayer, the Communists encouraged each prisoner to be selfish and to do only what was best for himself. *See also* Give-up-itis.

Dominant member. The patient in a group who tends to monopolize certain group sessions or situations.

Double. *See* Mirror.

Double-bind. Two conflicting communications from another person. One message is usually nonverbal and the other verbal. For example, parents may tell a child that arguments are to be settled peacefully and yet battle with each other constantly. The concept was formulated by Gregory Bateson.

Double-blind study. A study in which one or more drugs and a placebo are compared in such a way that neither the patient nor the persons directly or indirectly involved in the study know which is being given to the patient. The drugs being investigated and the placebo are coded for identification.

Dream. Mental activity during sleep that is experienced as though it were real. A dream has both a psychological and a biological purpose. It provides an outlet for the release of instinctual impulses and wish fulfillment of archaic needs and fantasies unacceptable in the real world. It permits the partial resolution of conflicts and the healing of traumata too overwhelming to be dealt with in the waking state. And it is the guardian of sleep, which is indispensable for the proper functioning of mind and body during the waking state. *See also* Hypnagogic hallucination, Hypnopompic hallucination, Paramnesia.

Dreamy state. Altered state of consciousness likened to a dream situation. It is accompanied by hallucinations—visual, auditory, and olfactory—and is believed to be associated with temporal lobe lesions. *See also* Marijuana.

Drive. A mental constituent, believed to be genetically determined, that produces a state of tension when it is in operation. This tension or state of psychic excitation motivates the person into action to alleviate the tension. Contemporary psychoanalysts prefer to use the term drive rather than Freud's term, instinct. *See also* Aggressive drive, Instinct, Sexual drive.

Drop-out. Patient who leaves group therapy against the therapist's advice.

Drug therapy. The use of chemical substances in the treatment of illness. It is also known as chemotherapy. *See also* Maintenance drug therapy.

DSM. *See Diagnostic and Statistical Manual of Mental Disorders.*

Dual leadership. *See* Co-therapy.

Dual therapy. *See* Co-therapy.

Dyad. A pair of persons in an interactional situation—such as husband and wife, mother and father, co-therapists, or patient and therapist.

Dyadic session. Psychotherapeutic session involving only two persons, the therapist and the patient.

Dynamic reasoning. Forming all the clinical evidence gained from free-associative anamnesis into a psychological reconstruction of the patient's development. It is a term used by Franz Alexander.

Dyskinesia. Involuntary, stereotyped, rhythmic muscular activity, such as a tic or a spasm. It is sometimes observed as an extrapyramidal side effect of antipsychotic drugs, particularly the phenothiazine derivatives. *See also* Tardive oral dyskinesia.

Dystonia. Extrapyramidal motor disturbance consisting of uncoordinated and spasmodic movements of the body and limbs, such as arching of the back and twisting of the body and neck. It is observed as a side effect of phenothiazine drugs and other major tranquilizers. *See also* Tardive oral dyskinesia.

East-Coast-style T-group. Group that follows the traditional National Training Laboratories orientation by developing awareness of group process. The first T-groups were held in Bethel, Maine. *See also* Basic skills training, West-Coast-style T-group.

Echolalia. Repetition of another person's words or phrases. It is a psychopathological symptom observed in certain cases of schizophrenia, particularly the catatonic types. Some authors consider this behavior to be an attempt by the patient to maintain a continuity of thought processes. *See also* Gilles de la Tourette's disease.

Echopraxia. Imitation of another person's movements. It is a psychopathological symptom observed in some cases of catatonic schizophrenia.

Ecstasy. Affect of intense rapture.

Ego. One of the three components of the psychic apparatus in the Freudian structural framework. The other two components are the id and the superego. Although the ego has some conscious components, many of its operations are automatic. It occupies a position between the primal instincts and the demands of the outer world, and it therefore serves to mediate between the person and external reality. In so doing, it performs the important functions of perceiving the needs of the self, both physical and psychological, and the qualities and attitudes of the environment. It evaluates, coordinates, and integrates these perceptions so that internal demands can be adjusted to external requirements. It is also responsible for certain defensive functions to protect the person against the demands of the id and the superego. It has a host of functions, but adaptation to reality is perhaps the most important one. *See also* Reality-testing.

Ego-coping skill. Adaptive method or capacity developed by a person to deal with or overcome a psychological or social problem.

Ego defense. *See* Defense mechanism.

Ego ideal. Part of the ego during its development that eventually fuses with the superego. It is a social as well as a psychological concept, reflecting the mutual esteem as well as the disillusionment in child-parent and subsequent relationships.

Egomania. Pathological self-preoccupation or self-centeredness. *See also* Narcissism.

Ego model. A person on whom another person patterns his ego. In a group, the therapist or a healthier member acts as an ego model for members with less healthy egos. In psychodrama, the auxiliary ego may act as the ego model.

Ego state. In Eric Berne's structural analysis, a state of mind and its related set of coherent behavior patterns. It includes a system of feelings directly related to a given subject. There are three ego states—Parent, Adult, and Child.

Eitingon, Max (1881–1943). Austrian psychoanalyst. An emissary of the Zurich school, he gained fame as the first person to be analyzed by Freud—in a few sessions in 1907. Later he became the first chief of the Berlin Psychoanalytic Clinic, a founder of the Berlin Psychoanalytic Institute, and a founder of the Palestine Psychoanalytic Society.

Elation. Affect characterized by euphoria, confidence, and enjoyment. It is associated with increased motor activity.

Electrocardiographic effect. Change seen in recordings of the electrical activity of the heart. It is observed as a side effect of phenothiazine derivatives, particularly thioridazine.

Electroconvulsive treatment. *See* Shock treatment.

Emotion. *See* Affect.

Emotional deprivation. Lack of adequate and appropriate interpersonal or environmental experiences or both, usually in the early developmental years. Emotional deprivation is caused by poor mothering or by separation from the mother.

Emotional insight. *See* Insight.

Emotional support. Encouragement, hope, and inspiration given to one person by another. Members of a treatment group often empathize with a patient who needs such support in order to try a new mode of behavior or to face the truth.

Empathy. Ability to put oneself in another person's place, get into his frame of reference, and understand his feelings and behavior objectively. It is one of the major qualities in a successful therapist, facilitator, or helpful group member. *See also* Sympathy.

Encounter group. A form of sensitivity training that emphasizes the experiencing of individual relationships within the group and minimizes intellectual and didactic input. It is a group that focuses on the present rather than concerning itself with the past or outside problems of its members. J. L. Moreno introduced and developed the idea of the encounter group in 1914. *See also* Here-and-now approach, Intervention laboratory, Nonverbal interaction, Task-oriented group.

Encountertapes. Tape recordings designed to provide a group with guidelines for progressive interaction in the absence of a leader. They are copyrighted by the Bell & Howell Company and are available commercially from their Human Development Institute in Atlanta, Georgia.

Epileptic dementia. A form of epilepsy that is accompanied by progressive mental and intellectual impairment. Some believe that the circulatory disturbances during epileptic attacks cause nerve cell degeneration and lead to dementia.

Epinephrine. A sympathomimetic agent. It is the chief hormone secreted by the adrenal medulla. In a state of fear or anxiety, the physiological changes stem from the release of epinephrine. Also known as adrenaline, it is related to norepinephrine, a substance presently linked with mood disturbances in depression.

Eros. *See* Sexual drive.

Erotomania. Pathological preoccupation with sexual activities or fantasies.

Esalen massage. A particular type of massage taught and practiced at the Esalen Institute, a growth center at Big Sur, California. The massage lasts between one and a half and three hours and is intended to be an intimate, loving communion between the participants. A variation is the massage of one person by a group. The massage is given without words.

Ethnocentrism. Conviction that one's own group is superior to other groups. It impairs one's ability to evaluate members of another group realistically or to communicate with them on an open, equal, and person-to-person basis.

Euphoria. An altered state of consciousness characterized by an exaggerated feeling of well-being that is inappropriate to apparent events. It is often associated with opiate, amphetamine, or alcohol abuse.

Evasion. Act of not facing up to or of strategically eluding something. It consists of suppressing an idea that is next in a thought series and replacing it with another idea closely related to it. Evasion is also known as paralogia and perverted logic.

Exaltation. Affect consisting of intense elation and feelings of grandeur.

Exhibitionism. A form of sexual deviation characterized by a compulsive need to expose one's body, particularly the genitals.

Existential group psychotherapy. A type of group therapy that puts the emphasis on confrontation, primarily in the here-and-now interaction, and on feeling experiences rather than on rational thinking. Less attention is put on patient resistances. The therapist is involved on the same level and to the same degree as the patients. *See also* Encounter group.

Expanded group. The friends, immediate family, and interested relatives of a group therapy patient. They are the people with whom he has to relate outside the formal therapy group. *See also* Back-home group.

Experiencing. Feeling emotions and sensations as opposed to thinking; being involved in what is happening rather than standing back at a distance and theorizing. Encounter groups attempt to bring about this personal involvement.

Experiential group. *See* Encounter group.

Experiential stimulator. Anything that stimulates an emotional or sensory response. Several techniques, many of them nonverbal, have been developed for encounter groups to accomplish this stimulation. *See also* Behind-the-back technique, Blind walk.

Extended family therapy. A type of family therapy that involves family members, beyond the nuclear family, who are closely associated with it and affect it. *See also* **Network, Social** network therapy, **Visitor.**

Exteropsychic function. *See* Parent.

Extrapsychic conflict. Conflict that arises between the person and his environment. *See also* Intrapsychic conflict.

Extrapyramidal effect. Bizarre, involuntary motor movement. It is a central nervous system side effect sometimes produced by antipsychotic drugs. *See also* Dyskinesia.

Extratherapeutic contact. Contact between group members outside of a regularly scheduled group session.

Facilitator. Group leader. He may be the therapist or a patient who emerges during the course of an encounter and who channels group interaction. He is also known as the session leader.

Fag hag. Slang, derogatory expression often used by homosexuals to describe a woman who has become part of a homosexual social circle and has assumed a central role as a mother figure.

Family neurosis. Emotional maladaptation in which a person's psychopathology is unconsciously inter-related with that of the other members of his family.

Family therapy. Treatment of a family in conflict. The whole family meets as a group with the therapist and explores its relationships and process. The focus is on the resolution of current reactions to one another rather than on individual members. *See also* Collaborative therapy, Combined therapy, Concurrent therapy, Conjoint therapy, Extended family therapy, Group marital therapy, Marriage therapy, Quadrangular therapy, Square interview.

Fantasy. Day dream; fabricated mental picture or chain of events. A form of thinking dominated by unconscious material and primary processes, it seeks wish-fulfillment and immediate solutions to conflicts. Fantasy may serve as the matrix for creativity or for neurotic distortions of reality.

Father surrogate. Father substitute. In psychoanalysis, the patient projects his father image onto another person and responds to that person unconsciously in an inappropriate and unrealistic manner with the feelings and attitudes he had toward the original father.

Fausse reconnaissance. False recognition. *See* also Paramnesia.

Fear. Unpleasurable affect consisting of psychophysiological changes in response to a realistic threat or danger to one's existence. *See also* Anxiety.

Federn, Paul (1871–1950). Austrian psychoanalyst, one of Freud's earliest followers, and the last survivor of the original Wednesday Evening Society. He made important original contributions to psychoanalysis—such as the concepts of flying dreams and ego feeling—and was instrumental in saving the minutes of the Vienna Psychoanalytic Society for subsequent publication.

Feedback. Expressed response by one person or a group to another person's behavior. *See also* Sociometric feedback, Transaction.

Feeling-driven group. A group in which little or no attention is paid to rational processes, thinking, or cognition and where the expression of all kinds of emotion is rewarded. *See also* Affectualizing, Encounter group, Existential group psychotherapy.

Ferenczi, Sandor (1873–1933). Hungarian psychoanalyst, one of Freud's early followers, and a brilliant contributor to all aspects of psychoanalysis. His temperament was more romantic than Freud's, and he came to favor more active and personal techniques, to the point that his adherence to psychoanalysis during his last years was questioned.

Field theory. Concept postulated by Kurt Lewin that a person is a complex energy field in which all behavior can be conceived of as a change in some state of the field during a given unit of time. Lewin also postulated the presence within the field of psychological tensions—states of readiness or preparation for action. The field theory is concerned essentially with the present field, the here-and-now. The theory has been applied by various group psychotherapists.

Fliess, Wilhelm (1858–1928). Berlin nose and throat specialist. He shared an early interest with Freud in the physiology of sex and entered into a prolonged correspondence that figures importantly in the records of Freud's self-analysis. Freud was influenced by Fliess's concept of bisexuality and his theory of the periodicity of the sex functions.

Focal-conflict theory. Theory elaborated by Thomas French in 1952 that explains the current behavior of a person as an expression of his method of solving currently experienced personality conflicts that originated very early in his life. He constantly resonates to these early-life conflicts.

Focused exercise. Technique used particularly in encounter groups to help participants break through their defensive behavior and express such specific emotional reactions as anger, affection, and joy. A psychodrama, for instance, may focus on a specific problem that a group member is having with his wife. In playing out both his part and her part, he becomes aware of the emotion he has been blocking.

Folie à deux. Emotional illness shared by two persons. If it involves three persons, it is referred to as *folie à trois*, etc.

Forced interaction. Relationship that occurs in a group when the therapist or other members demand that a particular patient respond, react, and be active. *See also* Structured interactional group psychotherapy.

Ford negative personal contacts with Negroes scale. A scale that measures whites' negative social contacts with blacks. *See also* Kelley desegregation scale, Rosander anti-Negro behavior scale, Steckler anti-Negro scale, Steckler anti-white scale.

Ford negative personal contacts with whites scale. A scale that measures blacks' negative personal contacts with whites. It helps assess the extent to which negative social contacts influence prejudiced attitudes, thus contributing to the theoretical basis for the employment of interracial group experiences to reduce prejudice. *See also* Kelley desegregation scale, Rosander anti-Negro behavior scale, Steckler anti-Negro scale, Steckler anti-white scale.

Formal operations. Jean Piaget's label for the complete development of a person's logical thinking capacities.

Foulkes, S. H. (1923–). English psychiatrist and one of the organizers of the group therapy movement in Great Britain. His work combines Moreno's ideas—the here-and-now, the socio-genesis, the social atom, the psychological network—with psypchoanalytic views. He stresses the importance of group-as-a-whole phenomena. *See also* Group analytic psychotherapy, Network.

Free association. Investigative psychoanalytic technique devised by Freud in which the patient seeks to verbalize, without reservation or censor, the passing contents of his mind. The conflicts that emerge while fulfilling this task constitute resistances that are the basis of the analyst's interpretations. *See also* Antirepression device, Conflict.

Free-floating anxiety. Pervasive, unrealistic fear that is not attached to any idea or alleviated by symptom substitution. It is observed particularly in anxiety neurosis, although it may be seen in some cases of latent schizophrenia.

Freud, Sigmund (1856–1939). Austrian psychiatrist and the founder of psychoanalysis. With Josef Breuer, he explored the potentialities of cathartic therapy, then went on to develop the analytic technique and such fundamental concepts of mental phenomena as the unconscious, infantile sexuality, repression, sublimation, superego, ego, and id formation and their applications throughout all spheres of human behavior.

Fulfillment. Satisfaction of needs that may be either real or illusory.

Future projection. Psychodrama technique wherein the patient shows in action how he thinks his future will shape itself. He, sometimes with the assistance of the director, picks the point in time, the place, and the people, if any, he expects to be involved with at that time.

Galactorrhea. Excessive or spontaneous flow of milk from the breast. It may be a result of the endocrine influence of phenothiazine drugs.

Gallows transaction. A transaction in which a person with a self-destructive script smiles while narrating or engaging in a self-destructive act. His smile evokes a smile in the listener, which is in essence an encouragement for self-destruction. *See also* Hamartic script.

Game. Technique that resembles a traditional game in being physical or mental competition conducted according to rules but that is used in the group situation as an experiential learning device. The emphasis is on the process of the game rather than on the objective of the game. A game in Eric Berne's transactional analysis refers to an orderly sequence of social maneuvers with an ulterior motive and resulting in a psychological payoff for the players. *See also* Hit-and-run game, Million-dollar game, Pastime, Survival, Transactional group psychotherapy.

Game analysis. In transactional analysis, the analysis of a person's social interactions that are not honest and straightforward but are contaminated with pretenses for personal gain. *See also* Script analysis, Structural analysis.

Genetic material. Data out of the personal history of the patient that are useful in developing an understanding of the psychodynamics of his present adaptation. *See also* Current material.

Genital phase. The final stage of psychosexual development. It occurs during puberty. In this stage the person's psychosexual development is so organized that he can achieve sexual gratification from genital-to-genital contact and has the capacity for a mature, affectionate relationship with someone of the opposite sex. *See also* Anal phase, Infantile sexuality, Latency phase, Oral phase, Phallic phase.

Gestalt therapy. Type of psychotherapy that emphasizes the treatment of the person as a whole—his biological component parts and their organic functioning, his perceptual configuration, and his inter-relationships with the outside world. Gestalt therapy, developed by Frederic S. Perls, can be used in either an individual or a group therapy setting. It focuses on the sensory awareness of the person's here-and-now experiences rather than on past recollections or future expectations. Gestalt therapy employs role-playing and other techniques to promote the patient's growth process and to develop his full potential. *See also* Nonverbal interaction.

Gilles de la Tourette's disease. A rare illness that has its onset in childhood. The illness, first described by a Paris physician, Gilles de la Tourette, is characterized by involuntary muscular movements and motor incoordination accompanied by echolalia and coprolalia. It is considered by some to be a schizophrenic condition.

Give-up-itis. Syndrome characterized by a giving up of the desire to live. The alienation, isolation, withdrawal, and eventual death associated

with this disease syndrome were experienced by many American prisoners during the Korean War, particularly in the early stages of Communist brainwashing. *See also* Dog-eat-dog period.

Go-around. Technique used in group therapy, particularly in structured interactional group psychotherapy, in which the therapist requires that each member of the group respond to another member, a theme, an association, etc. This procedure encourages participation of all members in the group.

God complex. A belief, sometimes seen in therapists, that one can accomplish more than is humanly possible or that one's word should not be doubted. The God complex of the aging psychoanalyst was first discussed by Ernest Jones, Freud's biographer. *See also* Mother Superior complex.

Gould Academy. Private preparatory school in Bethel, Maine, that has been used during summers as the site of the human relations laboratories run by the National Educational Association.

Grief. Alteration in mood and affect consisting of sadness appropriate to a real loss. *See also* Depression.

Group. *See* Therapeutic group.

Group action technique. Technique used in group work to help the participants achieve skills in interpersonal relations and improve their capacity to perform certain tasks better on the job or at home; technique, often involving physical interaction, aimed at enhancing involvement or communion within a new group.

Group analysand. A person in treatment in a psychoanalytically oriented group.

Group analytic psychotherapy. A type of group therapy in which the group is used as the principal therapeutic agent and all communications and relationships are viewed as part of a total field of interaction. Interventions deal primarily with group forces rather than with individual forces. S. H. Foulkes applied the term to his treatment procedure in 1948. It is also known as therapeutic group analysis. *See also* Phyloanalysis, Psychoanalytic group psychotherapy.

Group apparatus. Those people who preserve order and ensure the survival of a group. The

internal apparatus deals with members' pro-
clivities in order to maintain the structure of the
group and strengthen cohesion. The therapist
usually serves as his own apparatus in a small
therapy group; in a courtroom, a bailiff ensures
internal order. The external apparatus deals with
the environment in order to minimize the threat
of external pressure. The therapist usually acts
as his own external apparatus by setting the time
and place for the meetings and making sure that
outsiders do not interfere; in a war, combat
forces act as the external apparatus.

Group bibliotherapy. A form of group therapy
that focuses on the use of selected readings as
stimulus material. Outside readings and oral
presentations of printed matter by therapist and
patients are designed to encourage verbal interchange in the sessions and to hold the attention
of severely regressed patients. This approach is
used in the treatment of large groups of institutionalized patients. *See also* Class method, Didactic technique, Mechanical group therapy.

Group-centered psychotherapy. A short-
term, nonclinical form of group therapy developed by followers of Carl Rogers and based on
his client-centered method of individual treatment. The therapist maintains a nonjudgmental
attitude, clarifies the feelings expressed in the
sessions, and communicates empathic understanding and respect. The participants are not
diagnosed, and uncovering techniques are not
employed.

Group climate. Atmosphere and emotional
tone of a group therapy session.

Group cohesion. Effect of the mutual bonds
between members of a group as a result of their
concerted effort for a common interest and purpose. Until cohesiveness is achieved, the group
cannot concentrate its full energy on a common
task. *See also* Group growth.

Group dynamics. Phenomena that occur in
groups; the movement of a group from its in-
ception to its termination. Interactions and inter-
relations among members and between the members and the therapist create tension, which
maintains a constantly changing group equilibrium. The interactions and the tension they create are highly influenced by individual members'
psychological make-up, unconscious instinctual
drives, motives, wishes, and fantasies. The understanding and effective use of group dynamics is
essential in group treatment. It is also known as

group process. *See also* Group mobility, Psychodynamics.

Group grope. Belittling reference to procedures
used in certain encounter groups. The procedures
are aimed at providing emotional release through
physical contact.

Group growth. Gradual development of trust
and cohesiveness in a group. It leads to awareness of self and of other group process and to
more effective coping with conflict and intimacy
problems. *See also* Group cohesion.

Group history. Chronology of the experiences
of a group, including group rituals, group traditions, and group themes.

Group inhibition. *See* Group resistance.

Group marathon. Group meeting that usually
lasts from eight to 72 hours, although some sessions last for a week. The session is interrupted
only for eating and sleeping. The leader works
for the development of intimacy and the open
expression of feelings. The time-extended group
experience culminates in intense feelings of excitement and elation. Group marathon was developed by George Bach and Frederick Stoller.
See also Accelerated interaction, Nude marathon,
Too-tired-to-be-polite phenomenon.

Group marital therapy. A type of marriage
therapy that makes use of a group. There are
two basic techniques: (1) Inviting the marital
partner of a group member to a group session.
The other group members are confronted with
the neurotic marriage pattern, which gives them
new insights and awareness. (2) Placing a husband and wife together in a traditional group of
patients. This method seems indicated if the
spouses are unable to achieve meaningful intimacy because they fear the loss of their individual identity at an early phase of the marriage,
before a neurotic equilibrium is established. *See
also* Collaborative therapy, Combined therapy,
Concurrent therapy, Conjoint therapy, Family
therapy, Quadrangular therapy, Square interview.

Group mind. Autonomous and unified mental
life in an assemblage of people bound together by
mutual interests. It is a concept used by group
therapists who focus on the group as a unit
rather than on the individual members.

Group mobility. Spontaneity and movement in

the group brought about by changes in the functions and roles of individual members, relative to their progress. *See also* Group dynamics.

Group-on-group technique. Device used in T-groups wherein one group watches another group in action and then gives feedback to the observed group. Frequently, one group breaks into two sections, each taking turns in observing the other. The technique is intended to sharpen the participants' observation of individual behavior and group process.

Group phenomenon. *See* Group dynamics.

Group pressure. Demand by group members that individual members submit and conform to group standards, values, and behavior.

Group process. *See* Group dynamics.

Group psychotherapy. A type of psychiatric treatment that involves two or more patients participating together in the presence of one or more psychotherapists, who facilitate both emotional and rational cognitive interaction to effect changes in the maladaptive behavior of the members. *See also* Behavioral group psychotherapy, Bio-energetic group psychotherapy, Client-centered psychotherapy, Communion-oriented group psychotherapy, Crisis-intervention group psychotherapy, Existential group psychotherapy, Group analytic psychotherapy, Group bibliotherapy, Group-centered psychotherapy, Individual therapy, Inspirational-supportive group psychotherapy, Psychoanalytic group psychotherapy, Repressive-inspirational group psychotherapy, Social network therapy, Structured interactional group psychotherapy, Traditional group therapy, Transactional group psychotherapy.

Group resistance. Collective natural aversion of the group members toward dealing with unconscious material, emotions, or old patterns of defense.

Group ritual. Tradition or activity that any group establishes to mechanize some of its activities.

Group stimulus. Effect of several group members' communicating together. Each member has a stimulating effect on every other member, and the total stimulation is studied for therapeutic purposes. *See also* Transactions.

Group therapy. *See* Group psychotherapy.

Group tradition. Activity or value established historically by a group. It determines in part the group's manifest behavior.

Group value. Relative worth or standard developed by and agreed on by the members of a group.

Guilt. Affect associated with self-reproach and need for punishment. In psychoanalysis, guilt refers to a neurotic feeling of culpability that stems from a conflict between the ego and the superego. It begins developmentally with parental disapproval and becomes internalized as conscience in the course of superego formation. Guilt has normal psychological and social functions, but special intensity or absence of guilt characterizes many mental disorders, such as depression and antisocial personality. Some psychiatrists distinguish shame as a less internalized form of guilt.

Gustatory hallucination. False sense of taste.

Hallucination. A false sensory perception without a concrete external stimulus. It can be induced by emotional and by organic factors, such as drugs and alcohol. Common hallucinations involve sights or sounds, although any of the senses may be involved. *See also* Auditory hallucination, Gustatory hallucination, Hypnagogic hallucination, Hypnopompic hallucination, Kinesthetic hallucination, Lilliputian hallucination, Tactile hallucination, Visual hallucination.

Hallucinatory psychodrama. A type of psychodrama wherein the patient portrays the voices he hears and the visions he sees. Auxiliary egos are often called on to enact the various phenomena expressed by the patient and to involve him in interaction with them, so as to put them to a reality test. The intended effect on the patient is called psychodramatic shock.

Hallucinogenic drug. *See* Psychotomimetic drug.

Hamartic script. In transactional analysis, a life script that is self-destructive and tragic in character. *See also* Gallows transaction, Script, Script antithesis, Script matrix.

Healthy identification. Modeling of oneself, consciously or unconsciously, on another person who has sound psychic make-up. The identification has constructive purposes. *See also* Imitation.

Herd instinct. Desire to belong to a group and to participate in social activities. Wilfred Trotter used the term to indicate the presence of a hypothetical social instinct in man. In psychoanalysis, herd instinct is viewed as a social phenomenon rather than as an instinct. *See also* Aggressive drive, Sexual drive.

Here-and-now. Contemporaneity. *See also* There-and-then.

Here-and-now approach. A technique that focuses on understanding the interpersonal and intrapersonal responses and reactions as they occur in the on-going treatment session. Little or no emphasis is put on past history and experiences. *See also* Encounter group, Existential group psychotherapy.

Heterogeneous group. A group that consists of patients from both sexes, a wide age range, differing psychopathologies, and divergent socioeconomic, racial, ethnic, and cultural backgrounds. *See also* Homogeneous group.

Heterosexuality. Sexual attraction or contact between opposite-sex persons. The capacity for heterosexual arousal is probably innate, biologically programmed, and triggered in very early life, perhaps by olfactory modalities, as seen in lower animals. *See also* Bisexuality, Homosexuality.

Hidden self. The behavior, feelings, and motivations of a person known to himself but not to others. It is a quadrant of the Johari Window, a diagrammatic concept of human behavior. *See also* Blind self, Public self, Undeveloped potential.

Hierarchical vector. Thrust of relating to the other members of a group or to the therapist in a supraordinate or subordinate way. It is the opposite of relating as peers. It is also known as vertical vector. *See also* Authority principle, Horizontal vector, Political therapist.

Hit-and-run game. Hostile or nonconstructive aggressive activity indiscriminately and irresponsibly carried out against others. *See also* Game, Million dollar game, Survival.

Homogeneous group. A group that consists of patients of the same sex, with similarities in

their psychopathology, and from the same age range and socioeconomic, racial, ethnic, and cultural background. *See also* Heterogeneous group.

Homosexuality. Sexual attraction or contact between same-sex persons. Some authors distinguish two types: overt homosexuality and latent homosexuality. *See also* Bisexuality, Heterosexuality, Inversion, Lesbianism.

Homosexual panic. Sudden, acute onset of severe anxiety, precipitated by the unconscious fear or conflict that one may be a homosexual or act out homosexual impulses. *See also* Homosexuality.

Honesty. Forthrightness of conduct and uprightness of character; truthfulness. In therapy, honesty is a value manifested by the ability to communicate one's immediate experience, including inconsistent, conflicting, or ambivalent feelings and perceptions. *See also* Authenticity.

Hook. In transactional analysis, to switch one's transactions to a new ego state. For example, a patient's Adult ego state is hooked when he goes to the blackboard and draws a diagram.

Horizontal vector. Thrust of relating to the therapist or other members of the group as equals. It is also known as peer vector. *See also* Authority principle, Hierarchical vector, Political therapist.

House encounter. Group meeting of all the persons in a treatment facility. Such a meeting is designed to deal with specific problems within the therapeutic community that affect its functioning, such as poor morale and poor job performances.

Hydrotherapy. External or internal use of water in the treatment of disease. In psychiatry, the use of wet packs to calm an agitated psychotic patient was formerly a popular treatment modality.

Hyperactivity. Increased muscular activity. The term is commonly used to describe a disturbance found in children that is manifested by constant restlessness and movements executed at a rapid rate. The disturbance is believed to be due to brain damage, mental retardation, emotional disturbance, or physiological disturbance. It is also known as hyperkinesis.

Hyperkinesis. *See* Hyperactivity.

Hypermnesia. Exaggerated degree of retention and recall. It is observed in schizophrenia, the manic phase of manic-depressive illness, organic brain syndrome, drug intoxication induced by amphetamines and hallucinogens, hypnosis, and febrile conditions. *See also* Memory.

Hypertensive crisis. Severe rise in blood pressure that can lead to intracranial hemorrhage. It is occasionally seen as a side effect of certain antidepressant drugs.

Hypnagogic hallucination. False sensory perception that occurs just before falling asleep. *See also* Hypnopompic hallucination.

Hypnodrama. Psychodrama under hypnotic trance. The patient is first put into a hypnotic trance. During the trance he is encouraged to act out the various experiences that torment him.

Hypnopompic hallucination. False sensory perception that occurs just before full wakefulness. *See also* Hypnagogic hallucination.

Hypnosis. Artificially induced alteration of consciousness of one person by another. The subject responds with a high degree of suggestibility, both mental and physical, during the trancelike state.

Hypochondriasis. Exaggerated concern with one's physical health. The concern is not based on real organic pathology.

Hypotension, orthostatic. *See* Orthostatic hypotension.

Hysterical anesthesia. Disturbance in sensory perception characterized by absence of sense of feeling in certain areas of the body. It is observed in certain cases of hysterical neurosis, particularly the conversion type, and it is believed to be a defense mechanism.

Id. Part of Freud's concept of the psychic apparatus. According to his structural theory of mental functioning, the id harbors the energy that stems from the instinctual drives and desires of a person. The id is completely in the unconscious realm, unorganized and under the influence of the primary processes. *See also* Conscious, Ego, Preconscious, Primary process, Superego, Unconscious.

Idealization. A defense mechanism in which a

person consciously or, usually, unconsciously overestimates an attribute or an aspect of another person.

Ideas of reference. Misinterpretation of incidents and events in the outside world as having a direct personal reference to oneself. Occasionally observed in normal persons, ideas of reference are frequently seen in paranoid patients. *See also* Projection.

Ideational shield. An intellectual, rational defense against the anxiety a person would feel if he became vulnerable to the criticisms and rejection of others. As a result of his fear of being rejected, he may feel threatened if he criticizes another person—an act that is unacceptable to him. In both group and individual therapy, conditions are set up that allow the participants to lower this ideational shield.

Identification. An unconscious defense mechanism in which a person incorporates into himself the mental picture of an object and then patterns himself after this object; seeing oneself as like the person used as a pattern. It is distinguished from imitation, a conscious process. *See also* Healthy identification, Imitation, Role.

Identification with the aggressor. An unconscious process by which a person incorporates within himself the mental image of a person who represents a source of frustration from the outside world. A primitive defense, it operates in the interest and service of the developing ego. The classical example of this defense occurs toward the end of the oedipal stage, when the male child, whose main source of love and gratification is the mother, identifies with his father. The father represents the source of frustration, being the powerful rival for the mother; the child cannot master or run away from his father, so he is obliged to identify with him. *See also* Psychosexual development.

Idiot. *See* Mental retardation.

I-It. Philosopher Martin Buber's description of damaging interpersonal relationships. If a person treats himself or another person exclusively as an object, he prevents mutuality, trust, and growth. When pervasive in a group, I-It relationships prevent human warmth, destroy cohesiveness, and retard group process. *See also* I-Thou.

Ileus, paralytic. *See* Paralytic ileus.

Illusion. False perception and misinterpretation of an actual sensory stimulus.

Illustration. In transactional analysis, an anecdote, simile, or comparison that reinforces a confrontation or softens its potentially undesirable effects. The illustration may be immediate or remote in time and may refer to the external environment or to the internal situation in the group.

Imbecile. *See* Mental retardation.

Imitation. In psychiatry, a conscious act of mimicking another person's behavior pattern. *See also* Healthy identification, Identification.

Impasse. *See* Therapeutic impasse.

Improvement scale. In transactional analysis, a quantitative specification of a patient's position in terms of improvement in the course of therapy.

Improvisation. In psychodrama, the acting out of problems without prior preparation.

Impulse. Unexpected, instinctive urge motivated by conscious and unconscious feelings over which the person has little or no control. *See also* Drive, Instinct.

Inappropriate affect. Emotional tone that is out of harmony with the idea, object, or thought accompanying it.

Inclusion phase. Early stage of group treatment. In this phase, each group member's concern focuses primarily on belonging and being accepted and recognized, particularly by the therapist. It is also known as the dependency stage. *See also* Affection phase, Power phase.

Incorporation. An unconscious defense mechanism in which an object representation is assimilated into oneself through symbolic oral ingestion. One of the primitive defenses, incorporation is a special form of introjection and is the primary mechanism in identification.

Individual psychology. Holistic theory of personality developed by Alfred Adler. Personality development is explained in terms of adaptation to the social milieu (life style), strivings toward perfection motivated by feelings of inferiority, and the interpersonal nature of the person's problems. Individual psychology is applied in group psychotherapy and counseling by Adlerian practitioners.

Individual therapy. A type of psychotherapy in which a professionally trained psychotherapist treats one patient who either wants relief from disturbing symptoms or improvement in his ability to cope with his problems. This one therapist-one patient relationship, the traditional dyadic therapeutic technique, is opposed to other techniques that deal with more than one patient. *See also* Group psychotherapy, Psychotherapy.

Individuation. Differentiation; the process of molding and developing the individual personality so that it is different from the rest of the group. *See also* Actualization.

Infantile dynamics. Psychodynamic integrations, such as the Oedipus complex, that are organized during childhood and continue to exert unconsciously experienced influences on adult personality.

Infantile sexuality. Freudian concept regarding the erotic life of infants and children. Freud observed that, from birth, infants are capable of erotic activities. Infantile sexuality encompasses the overlapping phases of psychosexual development during the first five years of life and includes the oral phase (birth to 18 months), when erotic activity centers around the mouth; the anal phase (ages one to three), when erotic activity centers around the rectum; and the phallic phase (ages two to six), when erotic activity centers around the genital region. *See also* Psychosexual development.

Inferiority complex. Concept, originated by Alfred Adler, that everyone is born with inferiority or a feeling of inferiority secondary to real or fantasied organic or psychological inadequacies. How this inferiority or feeling of inferiority is handled determines a person's behavior in life. *See also* Masculine protest.

Infra reality. Reduced actuality that is observed in certain therapeutic settings. For example, according to J. L. Moreno, who coined the term, the contact between doctor and patient is not a genuine dialogue but is an interview, research situation, or projective test.

Injunction. In transactional analysis, the instructions given by one ego state to another, usually the Parent ego state to the Child ego state, that become the basis of the person's life script decisions. *See also* Permission, Program, Role, Script analysis.

Inner-directed person. A person who is self-motivated and autonomous and is not easily guided or influenced by the opinions and values of other people. *See also* Other-directed person.

Insight. Conscious awareness and understanding of one's own psychodynamics and symptoms of maladaptive behavior. It is highly important in effecting changes in the personality and behavior of a person. Most therapists distinguish two types: (1) intellectual insight—knowledge and awareness without any change of maladaptive behavior; (2) emotional or visceral insight—awareness, knowledge, and understanding of one's own maladaptive behavior, leading to positive changes in personality and behavior.

Inspirational-supportive group psychotherapy. A type of group therapy that focuses on the positive potential of members and stresses reinforcement for accomplishments or achievements. *See also* Alcoholics Anonymous.

Instinct. A biological, species-specific, genetically determined drive to respond in an automatic, complex, but organized way to a particular stimulus. *See also* Drive, Impulse.

Institute of Industrial Relations. A department of the Graduate School of Business Administration at the University of California at Los Angeles. It has conducted sensitivity training laboratories for business and professional people for nearly 20 years.

Insulin coma therapy. A form of psychiatric treatment originated by Manfred Sakel in which insulin is administered to the patient to produce coma. It is used in certain types of schizophrenia. *See also* Shock treatment.

Intellectual insight. *See* Insight.

Intellectualization. An unconscious defense mechanism in which reasoning or logic is used in an attempt to avoid confrontation with an objectionable impulse or affect. It is also known as brooding or thinking compulsion.

Intelligence. Capacity for understanding, recalling, mobilizing, and integrating constructively what one has learned and for using it to meet new situations.

Intensive group process. Group process designed to evoke a high degree of personal interaction and involvement, often accompanied by the expression of strong or deep feelings.

Interaction. *See* Transaction.

Interpersonal conflict. *See* Extrapsychic conflict.

Interpersonal psychiatry. Dynamic-cultural system of psychoanalytic therapy based on Harry Stack Sullivan's interpersonal theory. Sullivan's formulations were couched in terms of a person's interactions with other people. In group psychotherapy conducted by practitioners of this school, the focus is on the patients' transactions with one another.

Interpersonal skill. Ability of a person in relationship with others to express his feelings appropriately, to be socially responsible, to change and influence, and to work and create. *See also* Socialization.

Interpretation. A psychotherapeutic technique used in psychoanalysis, both individual and group. The therapist conveys to the patient the significance and meaning of his behavior, constructing into a more meaningful form the patient's resistances, defenses, transferences, and symbols (dreams). *See also* Clarification.

Interpretation of Dreams, The. Title of a book by Freud. Published in 1899, this work was a major presentation not only of Freud's discoveries about the meaning of dreams—hitherto regarded as outside scientific interest—but also of his concept of a mental apparatus that is topographically divided into unconscious, preconscious, and conscious areas.

Interracial group. *See* Heterogeneous group.

Intervention laboratory. Human relations laboratory, such as an encounter group or training group, especially designed to intervene and resolve some group conflict or crisis.

Intrapersonal conflict. *See* Intrapsychic conflict.

Intrapsychic ataxia. *See* Ataxia.

Intrapsychic conflict. Conflict that arises from the clash of two opposing forces within oneself.

It is also known as intrapersonal conflict. *See also* Extrapsychic conflict.

Introjection. An unconscious defense mechanism in which a psychic representation of a loved or hated object is taken into one's ego system. In depression, for example, the emotional feelings related to the loss of a loved one are directed toward the introjected mental representation of the loved one. *See also* Identification, Incorporation.

Inversion. Synonym for homosexuality. Inversion was the term used by Freud and his predecessors. There are three types: absolute, amphigenous, and occasional. *See also* Homosexuality, Latent homosexuality, Overt homosexuality.

I-Thou. Philosopher Martin Buber's conception that man's identity develops from true sharing by persons. Basic trust can occur in a living partnership in which each member identifies the particular real personality of the other in his wholeness, unity, and uniqueness. In groups, I-Thou relationships promote warmth, cohesiveness, and constructive group process. *See also* I-It.

Jamais vu. False feeling of unfamiliarity with a real situation one has experienced. *See also* Paramnesia.

Jaundice, allergic. Yellowish staining of the skin and deeper tissues accompanied by bile in the urine secondary to a hypersensitivity reaction. An obstructive type of jaundice, it is occasionally detected during the second to fourth week of phenothiazine therapy.

Johari Window. A schematic diagram used to conceptualize human behavior. It was developed by Joseph (Jo) Luft and Harry (Hari) Ingham at the University of California at Los Angeles in 1955. The diagram is composed of quadrants, each representing some aspect of a person's behavior, feelings, and motivations. *See also* Blind self, Hidden self, Public self, Undeveloped potential.

Jones, Ernest (1879–1958). Welsh psychoanalyst and one of Freud's early followers. He was an organizer of the American Psychoanalytic Association in 1911 and the British Psychoanalytical Society in 1919 and a founder and long-time editor of the journal of the International

Psychoanalytical Association. He was the author of many valuable works, the most important of which is his three-volume biography of Freud.

Judgment. Mental act of comparing or evaluating choices within the framework of a given set of values for the purpose of electing a course of action. Judgment is said to be intact if the course of action chosen is consistent with reality; judgment is said to be impaired if the chosen course of action is not consistent with reality.

Jung, Carl Gustav (1875–1961). Swiss psychiatrist and psychoanalyst. He founded the school of analytic psychology. *See also* Collective unconscious.

Karate-chop experience. A technique used in encounter groups to elicit aggression in timid or inhibited participants in a humorous way. The timid one stands facing a more aggressive member. Both make violent pseudokarate motions at each other, without making physical contact but yelling "Hai!" as loudly as possible at each stroke. After this exercise, the group members discuss the experience.

Kelley desegregation scale. A scale designed to measure the attitudes of whites toward blacks in the area of school integration. The scale provides a rough measure of racial prejudice and may be of help in ascertaining the effects on prejudice of participation in an interracial group. *See also* Ford negative personal contacts with Negroes scale, Ford negative personal contacts with whites scale, Rosander anti-Negro behavior scale, Steckler anti-Negro scale, Steckler anti-white scale.

Kinesthetic hallucination. False perception of muscular movement. An amputee may feel movement in his missing limb; this phenomenon is also known as phantom limb.

Kinesthetic sense. Sensation in the muscles as differentiated from the senses that receive stimulation from outside the body.

Kleptomania. Pathological compulsion to steal. In psychoanalytic theory, it originates in the infantile stage of psychosexual development.

Latency phase. Stage of psychosexual development extending from age five to the beginning of adolescence at age 12. Freud's work on ego psychology showed that the apparent cessation of sexual preoccupation during this period stems from a strong, aggressive blockade of libidinal and sexual impulses in an effort to avoid the dangers of the oedipal relationships. During the latency period, boys and girls are inclined to choose friends and join groups of their own sex. *See also* Identification with the aggressor, Psychosexual development.

Latent homosexuality. Unexpressed conscious or unconscious homoerotic wishes that are held in check. Freud's theory of bisexuality postulated the existence of a constitutionally determined, though experientially influenced, instinctual masculine-feminine duality. Normally, the opposite-sex component is dormant, but a breakdown in the defenses of repression and sublimation may activate latent instincts and result in overt homoeroticism. Many writers have questioned the validity of a universal latent homoeroticism. *See also* Bisexuality, Homosexuality, Overt homosexuality.

Lateral transference. Projection of long-range attitudes, values, and emotions onto the other members of the treatment group rather than onto the therapist. The patient sees other members of the group, co-patients, and peers in terms of his experiences in his original family. *See also* Collective family transference neurosis, Multiple transference.

Leaderless therapeutic group. An extreme form of nondirective group, conducted primarily for research purposes, such as the investigations of intragroup tensions by Walter R. Bion. On occasion, the therapist interacts verbally in a nonauthoritarian manner, but he generally functions as a silent observer—withholding explanations, directions, and support.

Leadership function. *See* Leadership role.

Leadership role. Stance adopted by the therapist in conducting a group. There are three main leadership roles: authoritarian, democratic, and laissez-faire. Any group—social, therapeutic, training, or task-oriented—is primarily influenced by the role practiced by the leader.

Leadership style. *See* Leadership role.

Lesbianism. Female homosexuality. About 600 B.C. on the island of Lesbos in the Aegean Sea, the poetess Sappho encouraged young women to engage in mutual sex practices. Lesbianism is also known as Sapphism. *See also* Bisexuality, Homosexuality, Latent homosexuality, Overt homosexuality.

Lewin, Kurt (1890–1946). German psychologist who emigrated to the United States in 1933. His work on the field theory has been useful in the experimental study of human behavior in a social situation. He was one of the early workers who helped develop the National Training Laboratories.

Libido theory. Freudian theory of sexual instinct, its complex process of development, and its accompanying physical and mental manifestations. Before Freud's introduction and completion of the dual-instinct theory (sexual and aggressive) in 1920, all instinctual manifestations were related to the sexual instinct, making for some confusion at that time. Current psychoanalytic practice assumes the existence of two instincts: sexual (libido) and aggressive (death). *See also* Aggressive drive, Sexual drive.

Life instinct. *See* Sexual drive.

Life lie. A contrary-to-fact conviction around which a person structures his life philosophy and attitudes.

Life line. A group technique in which each member is asked to draw a line representing his life, beginning with birth and ending with death. Comparison and discussion usually reveal that the shape and slope of the lines are based on a variety of personally meaningful parameters, such as maturity and academic achievement.

Lifwynn Foundation. Organization established by Trigant Burrow in 1927 as a social community in which the participants examined their interactions in the daily activities in which they were engaged. Lifwynn is currently under the direction of Hans Syz, M.D., in Westport, Conn.

Lilliputian hallucination. False perception that persons are reduced in size. *See also* Micropsia.

Lobotomy. Neurosurgical procedure in which one or more nerve tracts in a lobe of the cerebrum are severed. Prefrontal lobotomy is the ablation of one or more nerve tracts in the prefrontal area of the brain. It is used in the treatment of certain severe mental disorders that do not respond to other treatments.

Locus. Place of origin.

Logorrhea. Copious, pressured, coherent speech. It is observed in manic-depressive illness, manic type. Logorrhea is also known as tachylogia, verbomania, and volubility.

LSD (lysergic acid diethylamide). A potent psychotogenic drug discovered in 1942. LSD produces psychoticlike symptoms and behavior changes—including hallucinations, delusions, and time-space distortions.

Lysergic acid diethylamide. *See* LSD.

Macropsia. False perception that objects are larger than they really are. *See also* Micropsia.

Maintenance drug therapy. A stage in the course of chemotherapy. After the drug has reached its maximal efficacy, the dosage is reduced and sustained at the minimal therapeutic level that will prevent a relapse or exacerbation.

Major tranquilizer. Drug that has antipsychotic properties. The phenothiazines, thioxanthenes, butyrophenones, and reserpine derivatives are typical major tranquilizers, which are also known as ataractics, neuroleptics, and antipsychotics. *See also* Dystonia, Minor tranquilizer.

Maladaptive way. Poorly adjusted or pathological behavior pattern.

Mannerism. Stereotyped involuntary activity that is peculiar to a person.

MAO inhibitor. *See* Monoamine oxidase inhibitor.

Marathon. *See* Group marathon.

Marijuana. Dried leaves and flowers of *Cannabis sativa* (Indian hemp). It induces somatic and psychic changes in man when smoked or ingested in sufficient quantity. The somatic changes include increased heart rate, rise in blood pressure, dryness of the mouth, increased appetite, and occasional nausea, vomiting, and diarrhea. The psychic changes include dreamy-state level of consciousness, disruptive chain of ideas, perceptual disturbances of time and space, and alterations of mood. In strong doses, marijuana can produce hallucinations and, at times, paranoid ideas and suspiciousness. It is also known as pot, grass, weed, tea, and Mary Jane.

Marital counseling. Process whereby a trained counselor helps married couples resolve problems that arise and trouble them in their relationship. The theory and techniques of this approach were first developed in social agencies as part of family casework. Husband and wife are seen by the same worker in separate and joint counseling sessions, which focus on immediate family problems.

Marital therapy. *See* Marriage therapy.

Marriage therapy. A type of family therapy that involves the husband and the wife and focuses on the marital relationship, which affects the individual psychopathology of the partners. The rationale for this method is the assumption that psychopathological processes within the family structure and in the social matrix of the marriage perpetuate individual pathological personality structures, which find expression in the disturbed marriage and are aggravated by the feedback between partners. *See also* Collaborative therapy, Combined therapy, Concurrent therapy, Conjoint therapy, Family therapy, Group marital therapy, Marital counseling, Quadrangular therapy, Square interview.

Masculine identity. Well-developed sense of gender affiliation with males.

Masculine protest. Adlerian doctrine that depicts a universal human tendency to move from a passive and feminine role to a masculine and active role. This doctrine is an extension of his ideas about organic inferiority. It became the prime motivational force in normal and neurotic behavior in the Adlerian system. *See also* Adler, Alfred; Inferiority complex.

Masculinity-femininity scale. Any scale on a psychological test that assesses the relative masculinity or femininity of the testee. Scales vary and may focus, for example, on basic identification with either sex or preference for a particular sex role.

Masochism. A sexual deviation in which sexual gratification is derived from being maltreated by the partner or oneself. It was first described by an Austrian novelist, Leopold von Sacher-Masoch (1836–1895). *See also* Sadism, Sadomasochistic relationship.

Masturbation. *See* Autoerotism.

Mattress-pounding. A technique used in encounter groups to mobilize repressed or suppressed anger. A group member vents his resentments by beating the mattress with his fists and yelling. Frequently, the mattress becomes in fantasy a hated parent, sibling, or spouse. After this exercise, the group members discuss their reactions. *See also* Pillow-beating.

Maximal expression. Utmost communication. In psychodrama, it is the outcome of an involved sharing by the group of the three portions of the session: the warm-up, the action, and the post-action. During the action period the patient is encouraged to express all action and verbal communication to the limit. To this end, delusions, hallucinations, soliloquies, thoughts, and fantasies are allowed to be part of the production.

Mechanical group therapy. A form of group therapy that makes use of mechanical devices. As applied in the early 1950's, it required neither a group nor a therapist. An example of this form of therapy is the playing of brief recorded messages over the loudspeaker system of a mental hospital; the same statement, bearing on some elementary principle of mental health, is frequently repeated to secure general acceptance. *See also* Class method, Didactic technique, Group bibliotherapy.

Megalomania. Morbid preoccupation with expansive delusions of power and wealth.

Melancholia. Old term for depression that is rarely used at the present time. As used in the term involutional melancholia, it refers to a morbid state of depression and not to a symptom.

Memory. Ability to revive past sensory impressions, experiences, and learned ideas. Memory includes three basic mental processes: registration—the ability to perceive, recognize, and establish information in the central nervous system; retention—the ability to retain registered information; and recall—the ability to retrieve stored information at will. *See also* Amnesia, Hypermnesia, Paramnesia.

Mental aberration. *See* Aberration, mental.

Mental illness. Psychiatric disease included in the list of mental disorders in the *Diagnostic and Statistical Manual of Mental Disorders* published by the American Psychiatric Association and in the *Standard Nomenclature of Diseases*

and Operations approved by the American Medical Association.

Mental retardation. Subnormal general intellectual functioning, which may be evident at birth or may develop during childhood. Learning, social adjustment, and maturation are impaired, and emotional disturbance is often present. The degree of retardation is commonly measured in terms of I.Q.: borderline (68–85), mild (52–67), moderate (36–51), severe (20–35), and profound (under 20). Obsolescent terms that are still used occasionally are idiot (mental age of less than three years), imbecile (mental age of three to seven years), and moron (mental age of eight years).

Methadone. Methadone hydrochloride, a long-acting synthetic narcotic developed in Germany as a substitute for morphine. It is used as an analgesic and in detoxification and maintenance treatment of opiate addicts.

Methadone maintenance treatment. Long-term use of methadone on a daily basis to relieve narcotic craving and avert the effects of narcotic drugs.

Micropsia. False perception that objects are smaller than they really are. *See also* Lilliputian hallucination, Macropsia.

Milieu therapy. Treatment that emphasizes appropriate socioenvironmental manipulation for the benefit of the patient. The setting for milieu therapy is usually the psychiatric hospital.

Million-dollar game. Group game designed to explore the psychological meaning of money and to encourage free, creative thinking. The group is told that it has a million dollars, which is to be used productively in any way, as long as the endeavor actively involves all members of the group. *See also* Game, Hit-and-run game, Survival.

Minnesota Multiphasic Personality Inventory. Questionnaire type of psychological test for ages 16 and over with 550 true-false statements that are coded in 14 scales, ranging from a social scale to a schizophrenia scale. Group and individual forms are available.

Minor tranquilizer. Drug that diminishes tension, restlessness, and pathological anxiety without any antipsychotic effect. Meprobamate and diazepoxides are typical minor tranquilizers, which are also known as psycholeptics. *See also* Major tranquilizer.

Minutes of the Vienna Psychoanalytic Society. Diary of Freud's Wednesday Evening Society (after 1910, the Vienna Psychoanalytic Society) as recorded by Otto Rank, the paid secretary between 1906 and 1915.

Mirror. In psychodrama, the person who represents the patient, copying his behavior and trying to express his feelings in word and movement, showing the patient as if in a mirror how other people experience him. The mirror may exaggerate, employing techniques of deliberate distortion in order to arouse the patient to come forth and change from a passive spectator into an active participant. The mirror is also known as the double. *See also* Auxiliary ego.

Mirroring. A group process by which a person sees himself in the group by the reflections that come back to him in response to the way he presents himself. The image may be true or distorted, depending on the level of truth at which the group is functioning at the time. Mirroring has been used as an exercise in encounter group therapy and as a laboratory procedure in the warming-up period of the psychodrama approach.

Mixed-gender group. *See* Heterogeneous group.

MMPI. *See* Minnesota Multiphasic Personality Inventory.

Mobility. *See* Group mobility.

Monoamine oxidase inhibitor. Agent that inhibits the enzyme monoamine oxidase (MAO), which oxidizes such monoamines as norepinephrine and serotonin. Some of the MAO inhibitors are highly effective as antidepressants. *See also* Tricyclic drug.

Monomania. Morbid mental state characterized by preoccupation with one subject. It is also known as partial insanity.

Mood. Feeling tone that is experienced by a person internally. Mood does not include the external expression of the internal feeling tone. *See also* Affect.

Mood swing. Oscillation of a person's emotional feeling tone between periods of euphoria and depression.

Moron. *See* Mental retardation.

Moses and Monotheism. Title of a book by Freud published in 1939. In this book, Freud undertook a historical but frankly speculative reconstruction of the personality of Moses and examined the concept of monotheism and the abiding effect of the patriarch on the character of the Jews. One of Freud's last works, it bears the imprint of his latter-day outlook and problems.

Mother Superior complex. Tendency of a therapist to play the role of the mother in his relations with his patients. The complex often leads to interference with the therapeutic process. *See also* God complex.

Mother surrogate. Mother substitute. In psychoanalysis, the patient projects his mother image onto another person and responds to that person unconsciously in an inappropriate and unrealistic manner with the feelings and attitudes he had toward the original mother.

Motivation. Force that pushes a person to act to satisfy a need. It implies an incentive or desire that influences the will and causes the person to act.

Mourning. *See* Grief.

Multibody situation. Group situation. The term was originally used in the description of the evolution of social interaction in human beings from narcissism through the dyadic relationship to the three-body constellation of the Oedipus complex to the multibody situation prevailing in groups.

Multiple double. Several representations of the patient, each portraying a part of him—one as he is now, another as he was (for instance, five years ago), another at a crucial moment in his life (for example, when his mother died), a fourth how he may be 20 years hence. The multiple representations of the patient are presented in sequence, each continuing where the last left off. *See also* Auxiliary ego.

Multiple ego states. Many psychological stages, relating to different periods of one's life or to different depths of experience. These states may be of varying degrees of organization and complexity, and they may or may not be capable of being called to awareness consecutively or simultaneously.

Multiple interaction. Group behavior in which many members participate in the transactions, both verbal and nonverbal, at any one moment in the session.

Multiple intragroup transference. *See* Multiple transference.

Multiple reactivity. A phenomenon in which many group members respond in a variety of ways to the provocative role or stimulation afforded by one patient's behavior.

Multiple therapy. *See* Co-therapy.

Multiple transferences. Feelings and attitudes originally held toward members of one's family that become irrationally attached to the therapist and various group members simultaneously. *See also* Collective family transference neurosis, Lateral transference.

Mutism. *See* Stupor.

Mutual support. Expressions of sympathy, understanding, and affection that group members give to one another. *See also* Pairing.

Mydriasis. Dilatation of the pupil. The condition sometimes occurs as an autonomic side effect of phenothiazine and antiparkinsonism drugs.

Nalline test. The use of Nalline, a narcotic antagonist, to determine abstinence from opiates. An injection of Nalline precipitates withdrawal symptoms if opiates have been used recently. The most important use for Nalline, however, is as an antidote in the treatment of opiate overdose.

Narcissism. Self-love. It is linked to autoerotism but is devoid of genitality. The word is derived from Narcissus, a Greek mythology figure who fell in love with his own reflected image. In psychoanalytic theory, it is divided into primary narcissism and secondary narcissism. Primary narcissism refers to the early infantile phase of object relationship development, when the child has not differentiated himself from the outside world. All sources of pleasure are unrealistically recognized as coming from within himself, giving him a false sense of omnipotence.

Secondary narcissism is the type of narcissism that results when the libido once attached to external love objects is redirected back to the self. *See also* Autistic thinking, Autoerotism.

Narcotic hunger. A physiological craving for a drug. It appears in abstinent narcotic addicts.

National Training Laboratories. Organization started in 1947 at Bethel, Maine, to train professionals who work with groups. Interest in personal development eventually led to sensitivity training and encounter groups. The organization is now called the NTL Institute for Applied Behavioral Science. *See also* Basic skills training, East Coast style T-group.

Natural Child. In transactional analysis, the autonomous, expressive, archaic Child ego state that is free from parental influence. *Se also* Adapted Child.

Natural group. Group that tends to evolve spontaneously in human civilization, such as a kinship, tribal, or religious group. In contrast are various contrived groups or aggregates of people who meet for a relatively brief time to achieve some goal.

Negativism. Verbal or nonverbal opposition to outside suggestions and advice. It is also known as command negativism.

Neologism. New word or condensation of several words formed by patient in an effort to express a highly complex idea. It is often seen in schizophrenia.

Neopsychic function. *See* Adult.

Network. The persons in the patient's environment with whom he is most intimately connected. It frequently includes the nuclear family, the extended family, the orbit of relatives and friends, and work and recreational contacts. S. H. Foulkes believes that this dynamically interacting network has a fundamental significance in the production of illness in the patient. *See also* Extended family therapy, Social network therapy, Visitor.

Neuroleptic. *See* Antipsychotic drug, Major tranquilizer.

Neurosis. Mental disorder characterized by anxiety. The anxiety may be experienced and expressed directly, or, through an unconscious psychic process, it may be converted, displaced, or somatized. Although neuroses do not manifest depersonalization or overt distortion of reality, they can be severe enough to impair a person's functioning. The neuroses, also known as psychoneuroses, include the following types: anxiety neurosis, hysterical neurosis, phobic neurosis, obsessive-compulsive neurosis, depressive neurosis, neurasthenic neurosis, depersonalization neurosis, and hypochondriacal neurosis.

Nondirective approach. Technique in which the therapist follows the lead of the patient in the interview rather than introducing his own theories and directing the course of the interview. This method is applied in both individual and group therapy, such as Carl Rogers' client-centered and group-centered therapy. *See also* Passive therapist.

Nontruster. A person who has a strong unfilled need to be nurtured but whose early experience was one of rejection or overprotection. As a defense against repetition of this experience, he develops an overly strong show of independence. Sometimes this independence is manifested in group therapy by a member's constant rejection of support and of attempts by other members to get close to him. *See also* Outsider.

Nonverbal interaction. Technique used without the aid of words in encounter groups to promote communication and intimacy and to bypass verbal defenses. Many exercises of this sort are carried out in complete silence; in others, the participants emit grunts, groans, yells, cries, or sighs. Gestalt therapy pays particular attention to nonverbal expression.

Norepinephrine. A catecholamine that functions as a neurohumoral mediator liberated by postganglionic adrenergic nerves. It is also present in the adrenal medulla and in many areas in the brain, with the highest concentration in the hypothalamus. A disturbance in the metabolism of norepinephrine is considered to be an important factor in the etiology of depression. *See also* Serotonin.

Nuclear family. Immediate members of a family, including the parents and the children. *See also* Extended family therapy, Network, Social network therapy, Visitor.

Nuclear group member. *See* Therapist surrogate.

Nude marathon. Encounter group in which members assemble for an emotional experience of prolonged duration (from a minimum of eight hours to a couple of days), with the added factor of physical nakedness as members go about their activities. The theory is that clothes are themselves defenses against openness, that they connote limiting roles and result in stereotyped responses from others, and that they allow participants to avoid facing conflicts about their own bodies. *See also* Group marathon, Sensory-experiential group.

Nymphomania. Morbid, insatiable need in women for sexual intercourse. *See also* Satyriasis.

Observer. Person who is included but is generally not an active participant in therapy sessions. His observations are later discussed in posttherapy meetings with the staff or supervisor. *See also* Recorder.

Observer therapist. *See* Passive therapist.

Obsession. Persistent idea, thought, or impulse that cannot be eliminated from consciousness by logical effort. *See also* Compulsion.

Oedipus complex. A distinct group of associated ideas, aims, instinctual drives, and fears that are generally observed in children when they are from three to six years of age. During this period, which coincides with the peak of the phallic phase of psychosexual development, the child's sexual interest is attached chiefly to the parent of the opposite sex and is accompanied by aggressive feelings and wishes for the parent of the same sex. One of Freud's most important concepts, the Oedipus complex was discovered in 1897 as a result of his self-analysis. *See also* Totem and Taboo.

Ogre. In structural analysis, the Child ego state in the father that supersedes the nurturing Parent and becomes a pseudo-Parent.

One-gender group. *See* Homogeneous group.

Open group. Treatment group in which new members are continuously added as other members leave. *See also* Closed group.

Oral dyskinesia, tardive. *See* Tardive oral dyskinesia.

Oral phase. The earliest stage in psychosexual development. It lasts through the first 18 months of life. During this period, the oral zone is the center of the infant's needs, expression, and pleasurable erotic experiences. It has a strong influence on the organization and development of the child's psyche. *See also* Anal phase, Genital phase, Infantile sexuality, Latency phase, Phallic phase.

Orientation. State of awareness of one's relationships and surroundings in terms of time, place, and person.

Orthostatic hypotension. Reduction in blood pressure brought about by a shift from a recumbent to an upright position. It is observed as a side effect of several psychotropic drugs.

Other-directed person. A person who is readily influenced and guided by the attitudes and values of other people. *See also* Inner-directed person.

Outsider. In group therapy, a member who feels alienated and isolated from the group. Such a person has usually experienced repetitive rejection in his early life and is wary of trusting people in the present. Often much effort is required by the group and the therapist before the outsider trusts someone. *See also* Nontruster.

Overt homosexuality. Behaviorally expressed homoeroticism as distinct from unconsciously held homosexual wishes or conscious wishes that are held in check. *See also* Homosexuality, Latent homosexuality.

Pairing. Term coined by Walter R. Bion to denote mutual support between two or more group members who wish to avoid the solution of their problems. The term is often used more loosely to denote an attraction between two group members.

Panic. An acute, intense attack of anxiety associated with personality disorganization. Some writers use the term exclusively for psychotic episodes of overwhelming anxiety. *See also* Homosexual panic.

Pantomime. Gesticulation; psychodrama without the use of words.

Paralogia. *See* Evasion.

Paralytic ileus. Intestinal obstruction of the nonmechanical type, secondary to paralysis of the bowel wall, that may lead to fecal retention.

It is a rare anticholinergic side effect of phenothiazine therapy.

Paramnesia. Disturbance of memory in which reality and fantasy are confused. It is observed in dreams and in certain types of schizophrenia and organic brain syndromes. *See also* Confabulation, Déjà entendu, Déjà vu, Fausse reconnaissance, Jamais vu, Retrospective falsification.

Paranoid delusion. *See* Delusion.

Parent. In transactional analysis, an ego state borrowed from a parental figure. It is also known as exteropsychic function.

Parental rejection. Denial of affection and attention to a child by one or both parents. The child in turn develops great affect hunger and hostility, which is directed either outwardly in the form of tantrums, etc., or inwardly toward himself in the form of allergies, etc.

Parkinsonism. Syndrome characterized by rhythmical muscular tremors known as pill rolling accompanied by spasticity and rigidity of movement, propulsive gait, droopy posture, and masklike facies. It is usually seen in later life as a result of arteriosclerotic changes in the basal ganglia.

Parkinsonismlike effect. Symptom that is a frequent side effect of antipsychotic drugs. Typical symptoms are motor retardation, muscular rigidity, alterations of posture, tremor, and autonomic nervous system disturbances. *See also* Phenothiazine derivative.

Partial insanity. *See* Monomania

Passive therapist. Type of therapist who remains inactive but whose presence serves as a stimulus for the patient in the group or individual treatment setting. *See also* Active therapist, Leaderless therapeutic group, Nondirective approach.

Pastime. In transactional analysis, semistereotyped set of transactions dealing with a certain topic. Unlike Berne's term game, a pastime has no ulterior motive and no psychological payoff.

Patient peers. *See* Co-patients.

Patty-cake exercise. An encounter group technique that involves the palm-to-palm contact made by children in the game of patty-cake. This type of contact is familiar and does not usually arouse much anxiety in participants, yet it allows people to bypass verbal defenses in getting to know each other. After this exercise, the group members discuss their reactions. Also called Hand-dance.

Pecking order. Sequence of hierarchy or authority in an organization or social group. *See also* Hierarchical vector.

Peer co-therapist. Therapist who is equal in status to the other therapist treating a group and who relates to him on an equal level.

Peer-group phenomenon. Interaction or reaction of a person with a group of equals. These phenomena include activities he does within the group that he would probably not do individually outside the group.

Peer identification. Unconscious process that occurs in a group when one member incorporates within himself the qualities and attributes of another member. It usually occurs in members with low self-esteem who would like to feel at one with members who have improved.

Peer vector. *See* Horizontal vector.

Perception. Mental process by which data—intellectual, sensory, and emotional—are organized meaningfully. Through perception, a person makes sense out of the many stimuli that bombard him. It is one of the many ego functions. Therapy groups and T-groups aim to expand and alter perception in ways conducive to the development of the potential of each participant. *See also* Agnosia, Apperception, Clouding of consciousness, Ego, Hallucination, Hysterical anesthesia, Memory.

Perceptual expansion. Development of one's ability to recognize and interpret the meaning of sensory stimuli through associations with past experiences with similar stimuli. Perceptual expansion through the relaxation of defenses is one of the goals in both individual and group therapy.

Permission. In transactional analysis, a therapeutic transaction designed to permanently neutralize the parental injunctions.

Personal growth laboratory. A sensitivity training laboratory in which the primary emphasis is on each participant's potentialities for creativity, empathy, and leadership. In such a laboratory the facilitator encourages most modalities of experience and expression—such as art, sensory stimulation, and intellectual, emotional, written, oral, verbal, and nonverbal expression. *See also* National Training Laboratories.

Personality. Habitual configuration of behavior of a person, reflecting his physical and mental activities, attitudes, and interests and corresponding to the sum total of his adjustment to life.

Personality disorder. Mental disorder characterized by maladaptive patterns of adjustment to life. There is no subjective anxiety, as seen in neurosis, and no disturbance in the capacity to recognize reality, as seen in psychosis. The types of personality disorders include passive-aggressive, antisocial, schizoid, hysterical, paranoid, cyclothymic, explosive, obsessive-compulsive, asthenic, and inadequate.

Perversion. Deviation from the expected norm. In psychiatry it commonly signifies sexual perversion. *See also* Sexual deviation.

Perverted logic. *See* Evasion.

Peter Principle. Theory that man tends to advance to his level of incompetence. The idea was popularized in a book of the same name by Laurence J. Peter and Raymond Hull.

Phallic overbearance. Domination of another person by aggressive means. It is generally associated with masculinity in its negative aspects.

Phallic phase. The third stage in psychosexual development. It occurs when the child is from two to six years of age. During this period, the child's interest, curiosity, and pleasurable experiences are centered around the penis in boys and the clitoris in girls. *See also* Anal phase, Genital phase, Infantile sexuality, Latency phase, Oral phase.

Phantasy. *See* Fantasy.

Phantom limb. *See* Kinesthetic hallucination.

Phenothiazine derivative. Compound derived from phenothiazine. It is particularly known for its antipsychotic property. As a class, the phenothiazine derivatives are among the most widely used drugs in medical practice, particularly in psychiatry. Chlorpromazine, triflupromazine, fluphenazine, perphenazine, and thioridazine are some examples of phenothiazine derivatives. *See also* Anticholinergic effect, Autonomic side effect, Electrocardiographic effect, Mydriasis, Paralytic ileus, Parkinsonismlike effect.

Phobia. Pathological fear associated with some specific type of stimulus or situation. *See also* Acrophobia, Agoraphobia, Algophobia, Claustrophobia, Xenophobia, Zoophobia.

Phyloanalysis. A means of investigating disorders of human behavior, both individual and collective, resulting from impaired tensional processes that affected the organism's internal reaction as a whole. Trigant Burrow adopted the word to replace his earlier term, group analysis, which he first used in 1927 to describe the social participation of many persons in their common analysis. Because group analysis was confused with group psychotherapy of the analytic type, Burrow changed his nomenclature to phyloanalysis.

Pillow-beating. A technique used in encounter groups to elicit pent-up rage in a group member who needs to release it in a physical way. The member beats the pillow and yells angry words until he gets tired. The acceptance of his anger by the group is considered therapeutic. After this exercise, the group members discuss their reactions. *See also* Mattress-pounding.

Placebo. Inert substance prepared to resemble the active drug being tested in experimental research. It is sometimes used in clinical practice for a psychotherapeutic effect. The response to the placebo may represent the response due to the psychological effect of taking a pill and not to any pharmacological property.

Play therapy. Type of therapy used with children, usually of preschool and early latency ages. The patient reveals his problems on a fantasy level with dolls, clay, and other toys. The therapist intervenes opportunely with helpful explanations about the patient's responses and behavior in language geared to the child's comprehension. *See also* Activity group therapy.

Political therapist. A therapist who gives strong weight to the personalities of those above him as far as they impinge on his professional activities. He pays particular attention to the personal and historical aspects of authority. *See also* Authority principle, Hierarchical vector, Procedural therapist.

Popular mind. The primitive, fickle, suggestible, impulsive, uncritical type of mind that Le Bon felt was characteristic of the mass. He was referring to the unorganized crowds who lack leadership.

Postsession. *See* After-session.

Power phase. Second stage in group treatment. In this phase members start expressing anger and hostility—usually directed at the leader, sometimes directed at other members—in an attempt to achieve individuation and autonomy. *See also* Affection phase, Inclusion phase.

Pratt, Joseph H. Boston physician born in 1842 generally considered to be the first pioneer in group psychotherapy in America. He is known for his work with tuberculous patients (1900–1906). He formed discussion groups to deal with the physical aspects of tuberculosis. Later, these groups began discussing the emotional problems that stemmed from the illness. *See also* Class method.

Preconscious. In psychoanalysis, one of the three divisions of the psyche according to Freud's topographical psychology. The preconscious includes all ideas, thoughts, past experiences, and other memory impressions that can be consciously recalled with effort. *See also* Conscious, Unconscious.

Prefrontal lobotomy. *See* Lobotomy.

Prejudice. Adverse judgment or opinion formed without factual knowledge. Elements of irrational suspicion or hatred are often involved, as in racial prejudice.

Premeeting. Group meeting of patients without the therapist. It is held immediately before the regular therapist-led session and is also referred to as warming-up session and presession. *See also* After-session, Alternate session.

Preoccupation of thought. *See* Trend of thought.

Pressure cooker. Slang phrase to describe the high degree of group involvement and emotional pitch sought by certain intensive groups, such as marathon groups.

Primal father. Hypothetical head of the tribe. He is depicted by Freud in *Totem and Taboo* as slain by his sons, who subsequently devour him in a cannibalistic rite. Later, he is promoted to a god. The son who murders him is the prototype of the tragic hero, and the memory of the crime is perpetuated in the conscience of the individual and of the culture.

Primal scene. In psychoanalysis, the real or fantasied observation by a child of sexual intercourse, particularly between his parents.

Primary process. In psychoanalysis, the mental process directly related to the functions of the id and characteristic of unconscious mental activity. The primary process is marked by unorganized, illogical thinking and by the tendency to seek immediate discharge and gratification of instinctual demands. *See also* Secondary process.

Probe. An encounter technique designed for a specific purpose—for instance, to determine motivation for admission to treatment. The technique is commonly used in such drug rehabilitation centers as Odyssey House.

Procedural therapist. A therapist who places the most weight on the written word, on formal rules and regulations, and on the hierarchical system. *See also* Authority principle, Political therapist.

Process-centered group. Group whose main purpose is to study the dynamics of the group itself—how it operates and through what stages it progresses. Such groups often ask the question, "What's going on here?" rather than the encounter group question, "What are you experiencing or feeling?" *See also* Group analytic psychotherapy, Group-centered psychotherapy.

Program. In transactional analysis, the teaching by one of the parents of how best to comply with the script injunction.

Projection. Unconscious defense mechanism in which a person attributes to another the ideas, thoughts, feelings, and impulses that are part of his inner perceptions but that are unacceptable to him. Projection protects the person from anxiety arising from an inner conflict. By externalizing whatever is unacceptable, the person deals with it as a situation apart from himself. *See also* Blind spot, Future projection.

Projective method. Group treatment proce-
dure that uses the spontaneous creative work of the patients. For example, group members make and analyze drawings, which are often expressions of their underlying emotional problems.

Protagonist. In psychodrama, the patient who is the focal point of a psychodramatic session. He is asked to be himself, to portray his own private world on the stage.

Pseudoauthenticity. False or copied expression of thoughts and feelings.

Pseudocollusion. Sense of closeness, relationship, or cooperation that is not real but is based on transference.

Psychic determinism. Freudian adaptation of the concept of causality. It states that all phenomena or events have antecedent causes that operate on an unconscious level, beyond the control of the person involved.

Psychoactive drug. Drug that alters thoughts, feelings, or perceptions. Such a drug may help a person in either individual or group therapy overcome depression, anxiety, or rigidity of thought and behavior while he learns new methods of perceiving and responding.

Psychoanalysis. Freud's method of psychic investigation and form of psychotherapy. As a technique for exploring the mental processes, psychoanalysis includes the use of free association and the analysis and interpretation of dreams, resistances, and transferences. As a form of psychotherapy, it uses the investigative technique, guided by Freud's libido and instinct theories and by ego psychology, to gain insight into a person's unconscious motivations, conflicts, and symbols and thus to effect a change in his maladaptive behavior. Several schools of thought are loosely referred to as psychoanalytic at present. Psychoanalysis is also known as analysis in depth.

Psychoanalytically oriented group psychotherapy. *See* Psychoanalytic group psychotherapy.

Psychoanalytic group psychotherapy. A major method of group psychotherapy, pioneered by Alexander Wolf and based on the operational principles of individual psychoanalytic therapy. Analysis and interpretation of a patient's transferences, resistances, and defenses are modified to take place in a group setting. Although strictly designating treatment structured to produce significant character change, the term encompasses the same approach in groups conducted at more superficial levels for lesser goals. *See also* Collective family transference neurosis, Discussion model of group psychotherapy, Verbal-deep approach.

Psychoanalytic treatment. *See* Psychoanalysis.

Psychodrama. Psychotherapy method originated by J. L. Moreno in which personality make-up, interpersonal relationships, conflicts, and emotional problems are explored by means of dramatic methods. The therapeutic dramatization of emotional problems includes: (1) protagonist or patient, the person who presents and acts out his emotional problems with the help of (2) auxiliary egos, persons trained to act and dramatize the different aspects of the patient that are called for in a particular scene in order to help him express his feelings, and (3) director, leader, or therapist, the person who guides those involved in the drama for a fruitful and therapeutic session. *See also* Actional-deep approach, Analytic psychodrama, Concretization of living, Didactic psychodrama, Hallucinatory psychodrama, Hypnodrama, Improvisation, Maximal expression, Mirror, Re-enactment, Regressive-reconstructive approach, Role-playing, Role reversal, Self-realization.

Psychodramatic director. Leader of a psychodrama session. The director has three functions: producer, therapist, and analyst. As producer, he turns every clue the patient offers into dramatic action. As therapist, he attacks and shocks the patient at times, laughs and jokes with him at times, and becomes indirect and passive at times. As analyst, he interprets and elicits responses from the audience.

Psychodramatic shock. *See* Hallucinatory psychodrama.

Psychodynamics. Science of the mind, its mental processes, and affective components that influence human behavior and motivations. *See also* Group dynamics, Infantile dynamics.

Psychological defense system. *See* Defense mechanism.

Psychological procedure. Any technique intended to alter a person's attitude toward and

perception of himself and others. *See also* Group psychotherapy, Psychoanalysis, Psychotherapy.

Psychomotor stimulant. Drug that arouses the patient through its central excitatory and analeptic properties. Amphetamine and methylphenidate are drugs in this class.

Psychopathology. Branch of science that deals with morbidity of the mind.

Psychophysiological disorder. Mental disorder characterized by physical symptoms of psychic origin. It usually involves a single organ system innervated by the autonomic nervous system. The physiological and organic changes stem from a sustained emotional disturbance.

Psychosexual development. Maturation and development of the psychic phase of sexuality from birth to adult life. Its phases are oral, anal, phallic, latency, and genital. *See also* Identification with the aggressor, Infantile sexuality.

Psychosis. Mental disorder in which a person's mental capacity, affective response, and capacity to recognize reality, communicate, and relate to others are impaired enough to interfere with his capacity to deal with the ordinary demands of life. The psychoses are subdivided into two major classifications according to their origin—psychoses associated with organic brain syndromes and functional psychoses.

Psychosomatic illness. *See* Psychophysiological disorder.

Psychosurgery. *See* Lobotomy.

Psychotherapy. Form of treatment for mental illness and behavioral disturbances in which a trained person establishes a professional contract with the patient and through definite therapeutic communication, both verbal and nonverbal, attempts to alleviate the emotional disturbance, reverse or change maladaptive patterns of behavior, and encourage personality growth and development. Psychotherapy is distinguished from such other forms of psychiatric treatment as the use of drugs, surgery, electric shock treatment, and insulin coma treatment. *See also* Growth psychotherapy, Individual therapy, Psychoanalysis.

Psychotomimetic drug. Drug that produces psychic and behavioral changes that resemble psychosis. Unlike other drugs that can produce organic psychosis as a reaction, a psychotomimetic drug does not produce overt memory impairment. It is also known as a hallucinogenic drug. Lysergic acid diethylamide (LSD), tetrahydrocannabinol, and mescaline are examples of psychotomimetic drugs.

Psychotropic drug. Drug that affects psychic function and behavior. Also known as a phrenotropic drug, it may be classified as an antipsychotic drug, antidepressant drug, antimanic drug, antianxiety drug, or hallucinogenic drug. *See also* Agranulocytosis, Orthostatic hypotension.

Public self. The behavior, feelings, and motivations of a person known both to himself and to others. It is a quadrant of the Johari Window, a diagrammatic concept of human behavior. *See also* Blind self, Hidden self, Undeveloped potential.

Quadrangular therapy. A type of marital therapy that involves four people: the married pair and each spouse's therapist. *See also* Collaborative therapy, Combined therapy, Concurrent therapy, Conjoint therapy, Family therapy, Group marital therapy, Marriage therapy, Square interview.

Rank, Otto (1884–1939). Austrian psychoanalyst. He was one of Freud's earliest followers and the long-time secretary and recorder of the minutes of the Vienna Psychoanalytic Society. He wrote such fundamental works as *The Myth of the Birth of the Hero.* He split with Freud on the significance of the birth trauma, which he used as a basis of brief psychotherapy.

Rapport. Conscious, harmonious accord that usually reflects a good relationship between two persons. In a group, rapport is the presence of mutual responsiveness, as evidenced by spontaneous and sympathetic reaction to each other's needs, sentiments, and attitudes. *See also* Countertransference, Transference.

Rap session. *See* Bull session.

Rationalization. An unconscious defense mechanism in which an irrational behavior, motive, or feeling is made to appear reasonable. Ernest Jones introduced the term.

Reaction formation. An unconscious defense mechanism in which a person develops a socialized attitude or interest that is the direct antithesis of some infantile wish or impulse in the unconscious. One of the earliest and most unstable defense mechanisms, it is closely related to repression; both are defenses against impulses or urges that are unacceptable to the ego.

Reality. The totality of objective things and factual events. Reality includes everything that is perceived by a person's special senses and is validated by other people.

Reality-testing. Fundamental ego function that consists of the objective evaluation and judgment of the world outside the self. By interacting with his animate and inanimate environment, a person tests its real nature as well as his own relation to it. How the person evaluates reality and his attitudes toward it are determined by early experiences with the significant persons in his life. *See also* Ego.

Recall. Process of remembering thoughts, words, and actions of a past event in an attempt to recapture what actually happened. It is part of a complex mental function known as memory. *See also* Amnesia, Hypermnesia.

Recathexis. In transactional analysis, the experiencing of different ego states.

Recognition. *See* Memory.

Reconstructive psychotherapy. A form of therapy that seeks not only to alleviate symptoms but to produce alterations in maladaptive character structures and to expedite new adaptive potentials. This aim is achieved by bringing into consciousness an awareness of and insight into conflicts, fears, inhibitions, and their derivatives. *See also* Psychoanalysis.

Recorder. Person who takes notes during the group or individual therapy session. Also referred to as the recorder-observer, he generally does not participate in therapy. *See also* Observer.

Re-enactment. In psychodrama, the acting out of a past experience as if it were happening in the present so that a person can feel, perceive, and act as he did the first time.

Registration. *See* Memory.

Regression. Unconscious defense mechanism in which a person undergoes a partial or total return to earlier patterns of adaptation. Regression is observed in many psychiatric conditions, particularly schizophrenia.

Regressive-reconstructive approach. A psychotherapeutic procedure in which regression is made an integral element of the treatment process. The original traumatic situation is reproduced to gain new insight and to effect significant personality change and emotional maturation. *See also* Psychoanalysis, Reconstructive psychotherapy.

Reik, Theodor (1888–1969). Psychoanalyst and early follower of Freud, who considered him one of his most brilliant pupils. Freud's book, *The Question of Lay Analysis* was written to defend Reik's ability to practice psychoanalysis without medical training. Reik made many valuable contributions to psychoanalysis on the subjects of religion, masochism, and technique. *See also* Third ear.

Relatedness. Sense of sympathy and empathy with regard to others; sense of oneness with others. It is the opposite of isolation and alienation.

Reparenting. A technique evolved in transactional analysis for the treatment of schizophrenia. The patient is first regressed to a Child ego state, and then missing Parent transactions are supplied and contaminations corrected.

Repeater. Group member who has had experience in another group.

Repetitive pattern. Continual attitude or mode of behavior characteristic of a person and performed mechanically or unconsciously.

Repression. An unconscious defense mechanism in which a person removes from consciousness those ideas, impulses, and affects that are unacceptable to him. A term introduced by Freud, it is important in both normal psychological development and in neurotic and psychotic symptom formation. Freud recognized two kinds of repression: (1) repression proper—the repressed material was once in the conscious domain; (2) primal repression—the repressed material was never in the conscious realm. *See also* Suppression.

Repressive-inspirational group psychotherapy. A type of group therapy in which discussion is intended to bolster patients' morale and help them avoid undesired feelings. It is used primarily with large groups of seriously regressed patients in institutional settings.

Reserpine. An alkaloid extracted from the root of the *Rauwolfia serpentina* plant. It is used primarily as an antihypertensive agent. It was formerly used as an antipsychotic agent because of its sedative effect.

Residential treatment facility. A center where the patient lives and receives treatment appropriate for his particular needs. A children's residential treatment facility ideally furnishes both educational and therapeutic experiences for the emotionally disturbed child.

Resistance. A conscious or unconscious opposition to the uncovering of the unconscious. Resistance is linked to underlying psychological defense mechanisms against impulses from the id that are threatening to the ego. *See also* Group resistance.

Resonance. Unconscious response determined by early life experiences. In a group, a member may respond by fantasizing at a particular level of psychosexual development when another member functions regressively at that level. The unconscious sounding board is constructed in the first five years of life. *See also* Focal-conflict theory.

Retardation. Slowness of development or progress. In psychiatry there are two types, mental retardation and psychomotor retardation. Mental retardation refers to slowness or arrest of intellectual maturation. Psychomotor retardation refers to slowness or slackened psychic activity or motor activity or both; it is observed in pathological depression.

Retention. *See* Memory.

Retrospective falsification. Recollection of false memory. *See also* Paramnesia.

Review session. Meeting in which each member reviews with the group his goals and progress in treatment. It is a technique used in structured interactional group psychotherapy.

Ritual. Automatic activity of psychogenic or cultural origin. *See also* Group ritual.

Role. Pattern of behavior that a person takes. It has its roots in childhood and is influenced by significant people with whom the person had primary relationships. When the behavior pattern conforms with the expectations and demands of other people, it is said to be a complementary role. If it does not conform with the demands and expectation of others, it is known as noncomplementary role. *See also* Identification, Injunction, Therapeutic role.

Role-divided therapy. Therapeutic arrangement in a co-therapy situation when each therapist takes on a specific function in treatment. For example, one therapist may take the role of a provocateur, while the other takes the role of a passive observer and interpreter. *See also* Splitting situation.

Role limit. Boundary placed on the therapist or the patient by virtue of his conscious position in the therapy group. The patient plays the patient, and the therapist plays the therapist; there is no reversal of roles.

Role model. In a therapeutic community or methadone program, an ex-addict who, because of his successful adjustment and similarity of experience with the patient population, becomes a source of positive identification and a tangible proof of success. *See also* Ego model.

Role-playing. Psychodrama technique in which a person is trained to function more effectively in his reality roles—such as employer, employee, student, and instructor. In the therapeutic setting of psychodrama, the protagonist is free to try and to fail in his role, for he is given the opportunity to try again until he finally learns new approaches to the situation he fears, approaches that he can then apply outside. *See also* Antirepression device.

Role reversal. Technique used in psychodrama whereby an auxiliary ego plays the role of the patient, and the patient plays the role of the other person. Distortions of interpersonal perception are thereby brought to the surface, explored, and corrected.

Role-training. *See* Role-playing.

Roll and rock. An encounter group technique that is used to develop trust in a participant. A person stands, with eyes closed, in a tight circle of group members and is passed around (rolled) from member to member. Then he is placed on his back on the floor, gently lifted by the group members, and rocked back and forth. He is then put back on the floor. After this exercise, the group members discuss their reactions.

Rosander anti-Negro behavior scale. A scale that measures white attitudes toward blacks by asking respondents what their behavior would be in various hypothetical situations involving black participants. The scale can be of aid in determining the degree of prejudice held by whites toward blacks and the influence of a group experience on such prejudices. *See also* Ford negative personal contacts with Negroes scale, Ford negative personal contacts with whites scale, Kelley desegregation scale, Steckler anti-Negro scale, Steckler anti-white scale.

Rosenberg self-esteem scale. A scale designed to measure a person's opinion of himself. Use of this scale gives the therapist a means of evaluating the effect a group experience has on a member's self-esteem.

Saboteur. One who obstructs progress within a group, either deliberately or unconsciously.

Sadism. A sexual deviation in which sexual gratification is achieved by inflicting pain and humiliation on the partner. Donatien Alphonse François de Sade (1740–1814), a French writer, was the first person to describe this condition. *See also* Masochism, Sadomasochistic relationship.

Sadomasochistic relationship. Relationship in which the enjoyment of suffering by one person and the enjoyment of inflicting pain by the other person are important and complementary attractions in their on-going relationship. *See also* Masochism, Sadism.

Satyriasis. Morbid, insatiable sexual needs or desires in men. It may be caused by organic or psychiatric factors. *See also* Nymphomania.

Schilder, Paul (1886–1940). American neuropsychiatrist. He started the use of group psychotherapy at New York's Bellevue Hospital, combining social and psychoanalytic principles.

Schizophrenia. Mental disorder of psychotic level characterized by disturbances in thinking, mood, and behavior. The thinking disturbance is manifested by a distortion of reality, especially by delusions and hallucinations, accompanied by fragmentation of associations that results in incoherent speech. The mood disturbance is manifested by inappropriate affective responses. The behavior disturbance is manifested by ambivalence, apathetic withdrawal, and bizarre activity. Formerly known as dementia praecox, schizophrenia as a term was introduced by Eugen Bleuler. The causes of schizophrenia remain unknown. The types of schizophrenia include simple type, hebephrenic type, catatonic type, paranoid type, schizo-affective type, childhood type, residual type, latent type, acute schizophrenic episode, and chronic undifferentiated type.

Schreber case. One of Freud's cases. It involved the analysis in 1911 of Daniel Paul Shreber's autobiographical account, *Memoirs of a Neurotic,* published in 1903. Analysis of these memoirs permitted Freud to decipher the fundamental meaning of paranoid processes and ideas, especially the relationship between repressed homosexuality and projective defenses.

Screening. Initial patient evaluation that includes medical and psychiatric history, mental status evaluation, and diagnostic formulation to determine the patient's suitability for a particular treatment modality.

Script. In transactional analysis, a complex set of transactions that are adaptations of infantile responses and experiences. The script is recurrent and operates on an unconscious level. It is the mold on which a person's life adaptation is based. *See also* Hamartic script.

Script analysis. The analysis of a person's life adaption—that is, his injunctions, decisions, and life scripts—and the therapeutic process that helps reverse the maladaptive behavior. It is the last phase in transactional analysis. *See also* Game analysis, Structural analysis.

Script antithesis. In transactional analysis, a therapeutic transaction designed to avert temporarily a tragic event in a script. *See also* Script, Script matrix.

Script matrix. Diagram used in transactional analysis to represent two parents and an offspring. It is useful in representing the genesis of life scripts. *See also* Script, Script antithesis.

Secondary process. In psychoanalysis, the mental process directly related to the functions of the ego and characteristic of conscious and preconscious mental activities. The secondary process is marked by logical thinking and by the tendency to delay gratification by regulation of

discharge of instinctual demands. *See also* Primary process.

Sedative. Drug that produces a calming or relaxing effect through central nervous system depression. Some drugs with sedative properties are barbiturates, chloral hydrate, paraldehyde, and bromide.

Selective inattention. An aspect of attentiveness in which a person blocks out those areas that generate anxiety.

Self-analysis. Investigation of one's own psychic components. It plays a part in all analysis, although to a limited extent, since few are capable of sustaining independent and detached attitudes for it to be therapeutic.

Self-awareness. Sense of knowing what one is experiencing. For example, realizing that one has just responded with anger to another group member as a substitute for the anxiety felt when he attacked a vital part of one's self concept. Self-awareness is a major goal of all therapy, individual and group.

Self-discovery. In psychoanalysis, the freeing of the repressed ego in a person who has been brought up to submit to the wishes of the significant others around him.

Self-presentation. Psychodrama technique in which the patient plays the role of himself and of related persons (father, mother, brother, etc.) as he perceives them in a completely subjective manner.

Self-realization. Psychodrama technique in which the protagonist enacts, with the aid of a few auxiliary egos, the plan of his life, no matter how remote it may be from his present situation. For instance, an accountant who has been taking singing lessons, hoping to try out for a musical comedy part in summer stock, and planning to make the theatre his life's work can explore the effects of success in this venture and of possible failure and return to his old livelihood.

Sensation. Feeling or impression when the sensory nerve endings of any of the six senses—taste, touch, smell, sight, kinesthesia, and sound—are stimulated.

Sensitivity training group. Group in which members seek to develop self-awareness and an understanding of group processes rather than gain relief from an emotional disturbance. *See also* Encounter group, Personal growth laboratory, T-group.

Sensorium. Theoretical sensory center located in the brain that is involved with a person's awareness about his surroundings. In psychiatry, it is often referred to as consciousness.

Sensory-experiential group. An encounter group that is primarily concerned with the emotional and physical interaction of the participants. The experience itself, not the examination of the group process, is considered the *raison d'être* for the group.

Serotonin. A monoamine that is believed to be a neurohumoral transmitter. It is found in the serum and, in high concentrations, in the hypothalamus of the brain. Recent pharmacological investigations link depression to disorders in the metabolism of serotonin and other biogenic amines, such as norepinephrine.

Session leader. *See* Facilitator.

Sexual deviation. Mental disorder characterized by sexual interests and behavior other than what is culturally accepted. Sexual deviation includes sexual interest in objects other than a person of the opposite sex, such as homosexuality or bestiality; bizarre sexual practices, such as necrophilia; and other sexual activities that are not accompanied by copulation. *See also* Bestiality, Exhibitionism, Homosexuality, Masochism, Sadism.

Sexual drive. One of the two primal instincts (the other is the aggressive drive) according to Freud's dual-instinct theory of 1920. It is also known as eros and life instinct. Its main goal is to preserve and maintain life. It operates under the influence of the pleasure-unpleasure principle. *See also* Aggressive drive, Libido theory.

Shifting attention. A characteristic of group therapy in which the focus changes from one patient to another so that no one patient remains continuously in the spotlight. It is also known as alternating scrutiny. *See also* Structured interactional group psychotherapy.

Shock treatment. A form of psychiatric treatment with a chemical substance (ingested, inhaled, or injected) or sufficient electric current to produce a convulsive seizure and unconsciousness. It is used in certain types of schizophrenia

and mood disorders. Shock treatment's mechanism of action is still unknown.

Sibling rivalry. Competition among children for the attention, affection, and esteem of their parents. The children's jealousy is accompanied by hatred and death wishes toward each other. The rivalry need not be limited to actual siblings; it is a factor in both normal and abnormal competitiveness throughout life.

Slavson, S. R. (1890–   ). American theoretician who pioneered in group psychotherapy based on psychoanalytic principles. In his work with children, from which he derived most of his concepts, he introduced and developed activity group therapy. *See also* Collective experience.

Sleep. A temporary physiological state of unconsciousness characterized by a reversible cessation of the person's waking sensorimotor activity. A biological need, sleep recurs periodically to rest the whole body and to regenerate neuromuscular tissue. *See also* Dream.

Social adaptation. Adjustment to the whole complex of interpersonal relationships; the ability to live and express oneself in accordance with society's restrictions and cultural demands. *See also* Adaptational approach.

Social configuration. Arrangement of interpersonal interactions. *See also* Hierarchical vector, Horizontal vector.

Social instinct. *See* Herd instinct.

Socialization. Process of learning interpersonal and interactional skills according to and in conformity with one's society. In a group therapy setting, it includes a member's way of participating both mentally and physically in the group. *See also* Interpersonal skill.

Social network therapy. A type of group therapy in which the therapist assembles all the persons—relatives, friends, social relations, work relations—who have emotional or functional significance in the patient's life. Some or all of the social network may be assembled at any given time. *See also* Extended family therapy, Visitor.

Social psychiatry. Branch of psychiatry interested in ecological, sociological, and cultural variables that engender, intensify, or complicate maladaptive patterns of behavior and their treatment.

Social therapy. A rehabilitative form of therapy with psychiatric patients. The aim is to improve social functioning. Occupational therapy, therapeutic community, recreational therapy, milieu therapy, and attitude therapy are forms of social therapy.

Sociogram. Diagrammatic portrayal of choices, rejections, and indifferences of a number of persons involved in a life situation.

Sociometric distance. The measurable degree of perception one person has for another. It can be hypothesized that the greater the sociometric distance between persons, the more inaccurate will be their social evaluation of their relationship.

Sociometric feedback. Information that people give each other about how much closeness or distance they desire between them. It is a measure of how social one would like to be with another. An example of sociometric feedback would be the answer by a group member to the question, "With what three members of this group would you prefer to spend six months on a desert island?"

Sociometrist. Social investigator engaged in measuring the interpersonal relations and social structures in a community.

Soliloquy. *See* Therapeutic soliloquy.

Somnambulism. Sleepwalking; motor activity during sleep. It is commonly seen in children. In adults, it is observed in persons with schizoid personality disorders and certain types of schizophrenia.

Splitting situation. Condition in a co-therapy group. A patient is often unable to express opposite feelings toward one therapist. The splitting situation allows him to express contrasting feelings—positive-love feeling and negative-hostile feeling—by directing one feeling at one co-therapist and the opposite feeling at the other co-therapist. *See also* Role-divided therapy.

Splitting transference. Breaking of an irrational feeling or attitude into its component parts, which are then assigned to different persons. For example, ambivalence toward a mother may be expressed in a group by reacting to one member as to a good mother and reacting to another member as to a bad mother.

Square interview. Occasional session in marriage therapy in which both spouses and each spouse's therapist are present. The therapists and sometimes the patients are able to observe, experience, and respond to the transactional dynamics among the four of them, thus encouraging a common viewpoint by all four people involved in marital therapy. *See also* Collaborative therapy, Combined therapy, Concurrent therapy, Conjoint therapy, Group marital therapy, Marriage therapy, Quadrangular therapy.

Square situation. *See* Quadrangular therapy, Square interview.

Squeaky wheel. Person who is continually calling attention to himself. Because of his style of interacting, he is likely to get more than his share of a group's effort and energy.

Status value. Worth of a person in terms of such criteria as income, social prestige, intelligence, and education. It is considered an important parameter of one's position in the society.

Steckler anti-Negro scale. A scale designed to measure the attitude of Negroes toward Negroes. It can be of use in ascertaining the degree of prejudice blacks have against their own race and in evaluating the corrective efficacy of group experience. *See also* Ford negative personal contacts with Negroes scale, Ford negative personal contacts with whites scale, Kelley desegregation scale, Rosander anti-Negro behavior scale.

Steckler anti-white scale. A scale designed to measure the attitudes of Negroes toward whites. It can be used to ascertain the amount of prejudice blacks have against whites and to evaluate the influence of a group experience. *See also* Ford negative personal contacts with Negroes scale, Ford negative personal contacts with whites scale, Kelley desegregation scale.

Stegreiftheater. *See* Theatre of Spontaneity.

Stekel, Wilhelm (1868–1940). Viennese psychoanalyst. He suggested the formation of the first Freudian group, the Wednesday Evening Society, which later became the Vienna Psychoanalytic Society. A man given to intuition rather than to systematic research, his insight into dreams proved stimulating and added to the knowledge of symbols. Nevertheless, his superficial wild analysis proved incompatible with the Freudian school. He introduced the word thanatos to signify death wish.

Stereotypy. Continuous repetition of speech or physical activities. It is observed in cases of catatonic schizophrenia.

Stimulant. Drug that affects one or more organ systems to produce an exciting or arousing effect, increase physical activity and vivacity, and promote a sense of well-being. There are, for example, central nervous system stimulants, cardiac stimulants, respiratory stimulants, and psychomotor stimulants.

Stress immunity. Failure to react to emotional stress.

Stroke. In transactional analysis, a unit of human recognition. Early in life, strokes must involve physical contact; later in life, strokes can be symbolic—such as, "Glad to see you!"

Structural analysis. Analysis of the personality into its constituent ego states. The goal of structural analysis is to establish and maintain the predominance of reality-testing ego states, free from contamination. It is considered the first phase of transactional analysis. *See also* Contamination, Ego state, Game analysis, Ogre, Script analysis, Transactional analysis.

Structured interactional group psychotherapy. A type of group psychotherapy, developed by Harold Kaplan and Benjamin Sadock, in which the therapist provides a structural matrix for the group's interactions. The important part of the structure is that a different member of the group is the focus of the interaction in each session. *See also* Forced interaction, Go-around, Up.

Studies on Hysteria. Title of a book by Josef Breuer and Sigmund Freud. Published in 1895, it described the cathartic method of treatment and the beginnings of psychoanalysis. It demonstrated the psychological origins of hysterical symptoms and the possibility of effecting a cure through psychotherapy.

Stupor. Disturbance of consciousness in which the patient is nonreactive to and unaware of his surroundings. Organically, it is synonymous with unconsciousness. In psychiatry, it is referred to as mutism and is commonly found in catatonia and psychotic depression.

Subjectivity. Qualitative appraisal and interpretation of an object or experience as influenced by one's own feelings and thinking.

Subject session. Group technique, used particularly in structured interactional group psychotherapy, in which a topic is introduced by the therapist or a group member and is then explored by the whole group.

Sublimation. An unconscious defense mechanism in which unacceptable instinctual drives are diverted into personally and socially acceptable channels. Unlike other defense mechanisms, sublimation offers some minimal gratification of the instinctual drive or impulse.

Substituting. Providing a nonverbal alternate for something a patient missed in his early life. Crossing the room to sit beside a group member who needs support is an example of substituting.

Substitution. An unconscious defense mechanism in which a person replaces an unacceptable wish, drive, emotion, or goal with one that is more acceptable.

Suggestibility. State of compliant responsiveness to an idea or influence. It is commonly observed among persons with hysterical traits.

Sullivan, Harry Stack (1892–1949). American psychiatrist. He is best known for his interpersonal theory of psychiatry. *See also* Consensual validation.

Summer session. In structured interactional group psychotherapy, regularly scheduled group session during the therapist's vacation.

Superego. One of the three component parts of the psychic apparatus. The other two are the ego and the id. Freud created the theoretical concept of the superego to describe the psychic functions that are expressed in moral attitudes, conscience, and a sense of guilt. The superego results from the internalization of the ethical standards of the society in which the person lives, and it develops by identification with the attitudes of his parents. It is mainly unconscious and is believed to develop as a reaction to the Oedipus complex. It has a protective and rewarding function, referred to as the ego ideal, and a critical and punishing function, which evokes the sense of guilt.

Support. *See* Mutual support.

Suppression. Conscious act of controlling and inhibiting an unacceptable impulse, emotion, or idea. Suppression is differentiated from repression in that the latter is an unconscious process.

Surplus reality. The intangible, invisible dimensions of intrapsychic and extrapsychic life. The term was coined by J. L. Moreno.

Survival. Game used in a professionally homogeneous group. It is designed to create awareness of one another's talents. An imaginary situation is created in which the members are no longer permitted to continue in their particular professions and must, as a group, find some other activity in which to work together meaningfully and profitably. *See also* Game, Hit-and-run game, Million-dollar game.

Symbolization. An unconscious defense mechanism whereby one idea or object comes to stand for another because of some common aspect or quality in both. Symbolization is based on similarity and association. The symbols formed protect the person from the anxiety that may be attached to the original idea or object. *See also* Defense mechanism.

Sympathomimetic drug. Drug that mimics the actions of the sympathetic nervous system. Examples of these drugs are amphetamine and epinephrine.

Sympathy. Sharing of another person's feelings, ideas, and experiences. As opposed to empathy, sympathy is not objective. *See also* Identification, Imitation.

Symptom formation. *See* Symptom substitution.

Symptom substitution. Unconscious psychic process in which a repressed impulse is indirectly released and manifested through a symptom. Such symptoms as obsession, compulsion, phobia, dissociation, anxiety, depression, hallucination, and delusion are examples of symptom substitution. It is also known as symptom formation.

Tachylogia. *See* Logorrhea.

Tactile hallucination. False sense of touch.

Tangentiality. Disturbance in the associative thought processes in which the patient is unable to express his idea. In contrast to circumstantiality, the digression in tangentiality is such that the central idea is not communicated. It is observed in schizophrenia and certain types of or-

ganic brain disorders. Tangentiality is also known as derailment. *See also* Circumstantiality.

Tardive oral dyskinesia. A syndrome characterized by involuntary movements of the lips and jaw and by other bizarre involuntary dystonic movements. It is an extrapyramidal effect occurring late in the course of antipsychotic drug therapy.

Target patient. Group member who is perceptively analyzed by another member. It is a term used in the process of going around in psychoanalytically oriented groups.

Task-oriented group. Group whose main energy is devoted to reaching a goal, finding a solution to a problem, or building a product. Distinguished from this type of group is the experiential group, which is mainly concerned with sharing whatever happens. *See also* Action group.

Tele. In psychodrama, an objective social process that strengthens association and promotes cohesiveness in groups. It is believed to function on the basis of transference and empathy

Tension. An unpleasurable alteration of affect characterized by a strenuous increase in mental and physical activity.

Termination. Orderly conclusion of a group member's therapy or of the whole group's treatment as contrasted with a drop-out that is not advised by the therapist.

T-group (training group). A type of group that emphasizes training in self-awareness and group dynamics. *See also* Action group, Intervention laboratory, National Training Laboratories, Sensitivity training.

Thanatos. Death wish. *See also* Stekel, Wilhelm.

Theatre of Spontaneity (Stegreiftheater). Theatre in Vienna which improvised group processes and which was developed by J. L. Moreno, M.D.

Theoretical orientation. Alignment with a hypothetical point of view already espoused by a person or group.

Therapeutic agent. Anything—people and/or drugs—that causes healing in a maladaptive person. In group therapy, it refers mainly to people who help others.

Therapeutic alliance. Conscious relationship between therapist and patient in which each implicitly agrees that they need to work together by means of insight and control to help the patient with his conflicts. It involves a therapeutic splitting of the patient's ego into observing and experiencing parts. A good therapeutic alliance is especially necessary during phases of strong negative transference in order to keep the treatment going. It is as important in group as in dyadic psychotherapy. *See also* Working alliance.

Therapeutic atmosphere. All therapeutic, maturational, and growth-supporting agents—cultural, social, and medical.

Therapeutic community. Ward or hospital treatment setting that provides an effective environment for behavioral changes in patients through resocialization and rehabilitation.

Therapeutic crisis. Turning point in the treatment process. An example is acting out, which, depending on how it is dealt with, may or may not lead to a therapeutic change in the patient's behavior. *See also* Therapeutic impasse.

Therapeutic group. Group of patients joined together under the leadership of a therapist for the purpose of working together for psychotherapeutic ends—specifically, for the treatment of each patient's emotional disorders.

Therapeutic group analysis. *See* Group analytic psychotherapy.

Therapeutic impasse. Deadlock in the treatment process. Therapy is in a state of imminent failure when there is no further insight or awareness and sessions are reduced to routine meetings of patient and therapist. Unresolved resistances and transference and countertransference conflicts are among the common causes of this phenomenon. *See also* Therapeutic crisis.

Therapeutic role. Position in which one aims to treat, bring about an improvement, or provide alleviation of a distressing condition or state.

Therapeutic soliloquy. Psychodrama technique that involves a patient's portrayal—by side dialogues and side actions—of his hidden thoughts and feelings that parallel his overt thoughts and actions.

Therapeutic transaction. Interplay between therapist and patient or among group members that is intended to improve the patient.

Therapist surrogate. Group member who—by virtue of experience, intuition, or training—is able to be an effective group leader in the absence of or in concert with the group therapist. He is also known as a nuclear group member. *See also* Leaderless therapeutic group.

There-and-then. Past experience rather than immediate experience. *See also* Here-and-now.

Thinking. *See* Cognition.

Thinking compulsion. *See* Intellectualization.

Thinking through. The mental process that occurs in an attempt to understand one's own behavior and gain insight from it.

Third ear. Ability to make use of intuition, sensitivity, and awareness of subliminal cues to interpret clinical observations of individual and group patients. First introduced by the German philosopher Frederic Nietzsche, it was later used in analytic psychotherapy by Theodor Reik.

Thought deprivation. *See* Blocking.

Thought process disorder. A symptom of schizophrenia that involves the intellectual functions. It is manifested by irrelevance and incoherence of the patient's verbal productions. It ranges from simple blocking and mild circumstantiality to total loosening of associations, as in word salad.

Three-cornered therapy. *See* Co-therapy.

Three Essays on the Theory of Sexuality. Title of a book by Freud. Published in 1905, it applied the libido theory to the successive phases of sex instinct maturation in the infant, child, and adolescent. It made possible the integration of a vast diversity of clinical observations and promoted the direct observation of child development.

Tic. Involuntary, spasmodic, repetitive motor movement of a small segment of the body. Mainly psychogenic, it may be seen in certain cases of chronic encephalitis.

Timidity. Inability to assert oneself for fear of some fancied reprisal, even though there is no objective evidence of potential harm. In a therapy group, the timid person may make others fear the destructiveness of their normal aggression.

Tinnitus. Noises in one or both ears, such as ringing and whistling. It is an occasional side effect of some of the antidepressant drugs.

Tolerance. In group therapy, the willingness to put up with disordered behavior by co-patients in the group.

Too-tired-to-be-polite phenomenon. Phenomenon in a marathon group that stems from fatigue and results in the relaxation of the social facades of politeness. Some proponents of marathon groups have stressed the helpfulness of fatigue in breaking through the social games that participants play in the early stages of the group. *See also* Group marathon.

Totem and Taboo. Title of a book by Freud. Published in 1913, it applied his concepts to the data of anthropology. He was able to afford much insight into the meaning of tribal organizations and customs, especially by invoking the Oedipus complex and the characteristics of magical thought as he had discovered them from studies of the unconscious. *See also* Oedipus complex, Primal father.

Toucher. Someone who enjoys touching another person. When the touching is not of the clinging type, such a person in an encounter group usually helps inhibited people lose their anxiety about physical contact and closeness.

Traditional group therapy. Group therapy of a conventional type in which the role of the therapist is clearly delineated and the other participants are understood to be clients or patients who are attending the group meetings to overcome or resolve some definite emotional problems. *See also* Encounter group, Group psychotherapy, Sensitivity training.

Trainer. Professional leader or facilitator of a sensitivity training or T-group; teacher or supervisor of a person learning the science and practice of group therapy.

Training group. *See* T-group.

Tranquilizer. Psychotropic drug that induces tranquility by calming, soothing, quieting, or pacifying without clouding the conscious. The major tranquilizers are antipsychotic drugs, and the minor tranquilizers are antianxiety drugs.

Transaction. Interaction that arises when two or more persons have an encounter. In transactional analysis, it is considered the unit of social interaction. It involves a stimulus and a response. *See also* Complementarity of interaction, Forced interaction, Group stimulus, Structured interactional group psychotherapy, Therapeutic transaction.

Transactional analysis. A system introduced by Eric Berne that centers on the study of interactions going on in the treatment sessions. The system includes four components: (1) structural analysis of intrapsychic phenomena; (2) transactional analysis proper, the determination of the currently dominant ego state (Parent, Child, or Adult) of each participant; (3) game analysis, identification of the games played in their interactions and of the gratifications provided; and (4) script analysis, uncovering of the causes of the patient's emotional problems.

Transactional group psychotherapy. A system of therapy founded by Eric Berne. It is based on the analysis of interactions and on the understanding of patterns of transactions as they occur during treatment sessions. Social control is the main goal of therapy.

Transference. Unconscious phenomenon in which the feelings, attitudes, and wishes originally linked with important figures in one's early life are projected onto others who have come to represent them in current life. *See also* Countertransference, Lateral transference, Multiple transference, Rapport, Transference neurosis.

Transference neurosis. A phenomenon occurring in psychoanalysis in which the patient develops a strong emotional attachment to the therapist as a symbolized nuclear familial figure. The repetition and depth of this misperception or symbolization characterize it as a transference neurosis. In transference analysis, a major therapeutic technique in both individual and group therapy, the therapist uses transference to help the patient understand and gain insight into his behavior. *See also* Collective family transference neurosis, Dilution of transference.

Trend of thought. Thinking that centers on a particular idea associated with an affective tone.

Triad. Father, mother, and child relationship projectively experienced in group therapy. *See also* Nuclear family.

Trichotillomania. Morbid compulsion to pull out one's hair.

Tricyclic drug. Antidepressant drug believed by some to be more effective than monoamine oxidase inhibitors. The tricyclic drugs (imipramine and amitriptyline) are presently the most popular drugs in the treatment of pathological depression.

Tyramine. A sympathomimetic amine that is believed to influence the release of stored norepinephrine. Its degradation is inhibited by monoamine oxidase. The use of monoamine oxidase inhibitors in the treatment of depression prevents the degradation of tyramine. The ingestion of food containing tyramine, such as cheese, may cause a sympathomimetic effect, such as an increase in blood pressure, that could be fatal.

Unconscious. 1. (Noun) Structural division of the mind in which the psychic material—primitive drives, repressed desires, and memories—is not directly accessible to awareness. 2. (Adjective) In a state of insensibility, with absence of orientation and perception. *See also* Conscious, Preconscious.

Underachievement. Failure to reach a biopsychological, age-adequate level.

Underachiever. Person who manifestly does not function up to his capacity. The term usually refers to a bright child whose school test grades fall below expected levels.

Undeveloped potential. The behavior, feelings, and motivations of a person known neither to himself nor to others. It is the unknown quadrant of the Johari Window, a diagrammatic concept of human behavior. *See also* Blind self, Hidden self, Public self.

Undoing. An unconscious defense mechanism by which a person symbolically acts out in reverse something unacceptable that has already been done. A primitive defense mechanism, undoing is a form of magical expiatory action. Repetitive in nature, it is commonly observed in obsessive-compulsive neurosis.

Unisexual group. *See* Homogeneous group.

Universality. Total effect produced when all group members share specific symptoms or problems.

Up. The member who is the focus of discussion in group therapy, particularly in structured interactional group psychotherapy.

Up-tight. Slang term that describes defensive, rigid behavior on the part of a person whose values are threatened or who is afraid of becoming vulnerable and of experiencing painful emotions. Such a person frequently becomes a target for pressure in a therapy group.

Urine-testing. Thin-layer chromatography-testing for the presence of opiates, quinine, barbiturates, and amphetamines. Addict treatment programs use such testing to verify abstinence from illicit drug use.

Vector. An engineering term used to imply a pointed force being felt by the group. *See also* Hierarchical vector, Horizontal vector.

Verbal-deep approach. Procedure used in small groups in which communication is conducted exclusively through verbal means and is oriented to major goals. It is a technique used in analytical group therapy. *See also* Actional-deep approach, Actional-superficial approach, Verbal-superficial approach.

Verbal-superficial approach. Group therapy procedure in which language is the sole medium of communication and the therapeutic process is structured to attain limited objectives. It is a technique traditionally used in the treatment of large groups. *See also* Actional-deep approach, Actional-superficial approach, Verbal-deep approach.

Verbal technique. Any method of group or individual therapy in which words are used. The major part of most psychotherapy is verbal.

Verbigeration. Meaningless repetition of words or phrases. Also known as cataphasia, it is a morbid symptom seen in schizophrenia.

Verbomania. *See* Logorrhea.

Vertical vector. *See* Hierarchical vector.

Vienna Psychoanalytic Society. An outgrowth of the Wednesday Evening Society, an informal group of Freud's earliest followers. The new name was acquired and a reorganization took place in 1910, when the Society became a component of the newly formed International Psychoanalytical Society. Alfred Adler was president from 1910 to 1911, and Freud was president from 1911 until it was disbanded by the Nazis in 1938.

Visceral insight. *See* Insight.

Visitor. Guest who participates in discussions with patients in group therapy. In family therapy, members outside the nuclear family who are invited to the session are considered visitors. *See also* Extended family therapy, Social network therapy.

Visual hallucination. False visual perception.

Volubility. *See* Logorrhea.

Warming-up session. *See* Premeeting.

Waxy flexibility. *See* Cerea flexibilitas.

Wednesday Evening Society. A small group of Freud's followers who in 1902 started meeting with him informally on Wednesday evenings to receive instruction in psychoanalysis. As the society grew in numbers and importance, it evolved in 1910 into the Vienna Psychoanalytic Society.

West-Coast-style T-group. Sensitivity training or encounter group that is oriented toward the experience of union, intimacy, and personal awareness, with relative disregard for the study of group process. It is a style popular in California. *See also* East-Coast-style T-group.

Wild therapy. Group therapy conducted by a leader whose background may not be professional or whose theoretical formulations include widely deviant procedures when compared with conventional techniques.

Withdrawal. Act of retreating or going away from. Observed in schizophrenia and depression, it is characterized by a pathological retreat from interpersonal contact and social involvement, leading to self-preoccupation. In a group setting, this disorder creates a barrier for therapeutic progress.

Wittels, Fritz (1880–1950). Austrian psychoanalyst. One of Freud's early followers, he wrote a biography of him in 1924, during a period of estrangement, when he was under the influence of Wilhelm Stekel. Later, a reconciliation took place, and Freud conceded that some of Wittels' interpretations were probably correct.

Wolf-pack phenomenon. Group process in which a member or the therapist is the scapegoat.

Word salad. An incoherent mixture of words and phrases. This type of speech results from a disturbance in thinking. It is commonly observed in far-advanced states of schizophrenia.

Working alliance. Collaboration between the group as a whole and each patient who is willing to strive for health, growth, and maturation with the help of the therapist. *See also* Therapeutic alliance.

Working out. Stage in the treatment process in which the personal history and psychodynamics of a patient are discovered.

Working through. Process of obtaining more and more insight and personality changes through repeated and varied examination of a conflict or problem. The interactions between free association, resistance, interpretation, and working through constitute the fundamental facets of the analytic process.

Xenophobia. Fear of strangers.

Zoophobia. Fear of animals.

Contributors

Contributors

E. James Anthony, M.D.
Ittleson Professor of Child Psychiatry and Director, Division of Child Psychiatry, Washington University School of Medicine; Physician, Barnes and Allied Hospitals and The Jewish Hospital, St. Louis, Missouri; Training, Teaching and Supervising Psychoanalyst, Chicago Institute for Psychoanalysis; Professorial Lecturer, University of Chicago School of Medicine, Chicago, Illinois

Toby B. Bieber, Ph.D.
Clinical Instructor in Psychiatry, New York Medical College; Lecturer in Psychology, New York University, New York, New York

Murray Bowen, M.D.
Associate Clinical Professor of Psychiatry and Chief of the Family Psychiatric Service, Georgetown University School of Medicine; Chief of Family Psychiatry, Georgetown University Hospital, Washington, D.C.; Clinical Professor and Chairman, Division of Family and Social Psychiatry, Medical College of Virginia, Virginia Commonwealth University, Richmond, Virginia

Max Day, M.D.
Visiting Lecturer in Psychiatry, Boston University School of Medicine; Lecturer in Psychiatry, Harvard Medical School; Attending Psychiatrist, Massachusetts Mental Health Center, Boston, Massachusetts

Alvin I. Goldfarb, M.D.
Associate Professor of Psychiatry, New York School of Psychiatry; Associate Clinical Professor of Psychiatry, New York Medical College; Associate Clinical Professor of Psychiatry, Mount Sinai School of Medicine of the City University of New York; Attending Psychiatrist, Mount Sinai Hospital; Consultant on Psychiatric Services for the Aged, New York State Department of Mental Hygiene, New York, New York

Harold I. Kaplan, M.D.
Professor of Psychiatry and Director of Psychiatric Education and Training, New York Medical College; Attending Psychiatrist, Flower and Fifth Avenue Hospitals; Visiting Psychiatrist, Metropolitan Hospital and Bird S. Coler Memorial Hospital and Home, New York, New York

Helene Papanek, M.D.
Dean and Director, Alfred Adler Institute; Adjunct Psychiatrist, Lenox Hill Hospital; Faculty Member, Postgraduate Center for Mental Health, New York, New York; Adjunct Attending Psychiatrist, Hillside Hospital, Glen Oaks, New York; Consultant, Veterans Administration Hospital, Brooklyn, New York

Benjamin J. Sadock, M.D.
Associate Professor of Psychiatry and Director, Division of Group Process, New York Medical College; Associate Attending Psychiatrist, Flower and Fifth Avenue Hospitals; Associate Visiting Psychiatrist, Metropolitan Hospital; Assistant Attending Psychiatrist, New York State Psychiatric Institute, New York, New York

John Schengber, M.D.
Psychiatric Examiner, Superior Court, San Diego, California

F. Stanley Seifried, M.D.
Fellow in Child Psychiatry, Cincinnati College of Medicine, Cincinnati, Ohio

Elvin Semrad, M.D.
Clinical Professor of Psychiatry, Harvard Medical School; Director of Psychiatry, Massachusetts Mental Health Center; Faculty, Boston Psychoanalytic Institute, Boston, Massachusetts

Aaron Stein, M.D.
Associate Clinical Professor of Psychiatry, Mount Sinai School of Medicine; Associate Attending Psychiatrist and Chief, Adult Group Psychotherapy Division, The Mount Sinai Hospital of the City University of New York; Visiting Psychiatrist and Director, Department of Group Psychotherapy, Hillside Hospital, Glen Oaks, New York; Attending Psychiatrist, Brookdale Hospital Center, Brooklyn, New York

Walter N. Stone, M.D.
Assistant Professor of Psychiatry, University of Cincinnati College of Medicine, Cincinnati, Ohio